M.J. Andrews
Department of Eco...
University of Man...
MANCHESTER M19 9P...

Martyn

UNEMPLOYMENT: AN ECONOMIC ANALYSIS

UNEMPLOYMENT:
An Economic Analysis

K.G. KNIGHT

CROOM HELM
London & Sydney

©1987 K.G. Knight
Croom Helm Ltd, Provident House, Burrell Row,
Beckenham, Kent, BR3 1AT
Croom Helm Australia Pty Ltd, Suite 4, 6th Floor,
64-76 Kippax Street, Surry Hills, NSW 2010, Australia

British Library Cataloguing in Publication Data
Knight, K.G.
    Unemployment: an economic analysis.
    1. Unemployment — Great Britain
    I. Title
    331.13′7941   HD765.A6

    ISBN 0-7099-1510-1
    ISBN 0-7099-1511-X Pbk

Printed and bound in Great Britain by Mackays of Chatham Ltd, Kent

CONTENTS

TABLE OF CONTENTS

ACKNOWLEDGEMENTS

ACKNOWLEDGEMENTS

A great many friends and colleagues have helped me to complete this book. I am especially indebted to Martyn Andrews, David Deaton, Richard Disney, Paul Geroski, Gus O'Donnell, David Peel and Mark Stewart who read part or the whole of the manuscript. They made innumerable improving suggestions for which I am grateful. Needless to say they take no blame for what remains. David Metcalf helped by allowing me to make use of his considerable work (partly with Gavyn Davies) on special employment measures.

Deciphering my handwriting is not an easy task so I am particularly glad of the willing help of Mandy Broom, Shirley Patterson and especially Jenny Johnson and Yvonne Slater in getting the manuscript into a readable form. The diagrams were expertly drawn by Jenny Brown for whose enthusiastic efforts on my behalf I am grateful. Finally I thank Cynthia, Sally and Rosie Knight not for showing me during the preparation of this book any special forebearance for which I would now be ashamed but for actively helping me at many crucial times since the task was begun.

K.G. Knight

Chapter One

UNEMPLOYMENT – COSTS AND MEASUREMENT

Introduction

In the early sixties, academic interest in unemployment from both a theoretical and empirical point of view was at a low ebb. Students were still acquainted with the major theoretical debates of the thirties and forties but the low unemployment levels of the post-war period had convinced much of the economics profession that Keynesian demand management had provided the solution to the problem of unemployment in the industrial economies. In the US where unemployment remained comparatively high, there was a debate about current problems. The issue at stake was whether the unemployment that remained was structural and required specific and partly supply side remedies or cyclical and remediable by a major expansion in aggregate demand. (1) In the UK there remained the vestigial problem of relatively high unemployment in certain regions which generated a rather low key debate on causes and remedies. (2)

Since that time unemployment in most industrial economies has increased significantly. Nowhere has this upward trend been more pronounced than in Britain. Not surprisingly this has led to a major revival of interest in the economics of unemployment. At the theoretical level the reappraisal of Keynesian ideas begun by Clower (1965) and Leijonhufvud (1968) and the re-emergence of interest in classical ideas (3) have led the way. Empirical work and interest in the appropriate policy response to high unemployment has also greatly increased. The gloomy forecasts of continuing and ever worsening high unemployment in the 1980s have reinforced this revival of intellectual interest in the subject.

In later chapters we will review these theoretical developments and consider relevant empirical evidence mostly for Britain but for other economies where relevant. In chapter nine alternative policy approaches to high unemployment will be considered. In this and the next chapter the basic facts of unemployment will be considered with emphasis being given to the labour market aspects of high unemployment.

The Stock of Unemployment - Measurement

From a theoretical point of view the stock of unemployment in an economy at a particular moment in time is most easily defined as

1.1 $\bar{U}_t = L_t - E_t$

where

$\bar{U}_t$ = numbers unemployed
L_t = total labour force
E_t = numbers employed

or in percentage terms by dividing through by L_t.

1.2 $\bar{U}_t/L_t = (1 - E_t/L_t)100 = U_t$

From a practical point of view the measurement of 1.1 or 1.2 presents a great many problems. In Britain the basic method of measurement of $\bar{U}_t$ has traditionally been the monthly count of those registered unemployed at Employment and Careers offices and which appeared in the Department of Employment Gazette.

However since 1982 there has been a change to a count of unemployed on a claimant basis and figures for 1984 are shown in Row 1 of Table 1.1. This involves counting those who claim benefit at Unemployment Benefit offices. There are a number of problems with this measure. Firstly it fails to take account of those who are registered as unemployed but are not eligible or choose not to apply for benefit. The stock of unemployment calculated on the old (registration) basis is a higher total than on the new (claimant) basis. It has been calculated that to compare 1984 figures with those for say, 1980, on a registration basis involves the addition of 287,000 workers. (4) This is done in Table 1.1 in Row 2. Secondly, the new like the old method of counting the unemployed fails to take account of workers out of work and seeking a job and hence economically active but who do not register as unemployed. The most important groups are (a) individuals who leave their

2

job voluntarily or who have been dismissed for industrial misconduct, (b) the self-employed, (c) those who are not eligible for benefit and choose not to register, especially married women who retain the option not to pay the full national insurance contribution, (5) (d) other groups including those regarded as unavailable for work by the Department of Employment. The solution to this problem of the downward bias of the monthly count is to conduct a labour market survey to assess the extent of unregistered unemployment (as in the US) and to base the unemployment count upon this survey. Alternatively use can be made of regular surveys like the Labour Force and General Household Surveys in Britain to provide additional information or of a Census of Population which ask questions about the availability and willingness to work of those currently unemployed. Both of the latter two options are done in Britain and this gives us some idea of the degree of under-estimation of the currently published figures. The surveys give slightly differing answers and the figures used in Table 1.1 employ a weighted average of the evidence from these three sources (LFS, GHS and Census). These show that in 1981 unregistered unemployment was 9.9% of the claimant total for men and much higher (44.9%) for women. Applying these proportions to the total unemployed (on a claimant basis) gives the estimate of unregistered unemployment in Row 3 of Table 1.1. (6) Data published by the Department of Employment (1983) shows that as a proportion of the total unemployed, unregistered unemployment (especially for women) has fallen in the last decade. Mainly this reflects the greater propensity of women to register as unemployed and claim benefits because of changes in national insurance contributions and benefit entitlement which have altered the position of women. However, there are also a growing number of workers (especially women) who are discouraged from entering the labour force because of the depressed labour market conditions of the last decade. (7) Since these individuals are willing to work at current real wages and job conditions but are deterred from doing so by the prospects of unsuccessful job search, they should be added to the total of those unemployed. In a more buoyant labour market this group of workers would be economically active and appear generally in the stock of unregistered unemployed. Metcalf (1984) has recently estimated this group to contain between 240,000 and 281,000 workers. In Table 1.1. (Row 4) the mean of Metcalf's estimates is used to calculate

3

the 1984 total of actual unemployment in Britain.

Table 1.1 Claimant Unemployed and Actual Unemployment (in thousands) 1984

1	Unemployment Claimant Stock	3,125
	plus	
2	Registered Non-Claimants	287
	plus	
3	Unregistered Non-Claimants	629
	plus	
4	Discouraged Workers	261
	minus	
5	Students and those on Special Measures Schemes seeking work	230
	minus	
6	'Unavailable for work' Claimants	188
	Actual Unemployment Stock	3,884

Source: Department of Employment Gazette August 1984, June 1983. D. Metcalf 'On the measurement of employment and unemployment' National Institute Economic Review, August 1984.
Notes: Unemployment is seasonally adjusted (for May 1984) and includes school leavers.

Note that the inclusion of discouraged workers in the unemployment total follows from the emphasis on the willingness to work. Government administrators in Britain have traditionally emphasised availability for work. As a result they ignore unregistered and discouraged workers and also attempt (8) to reduce the true measure of unemployment further by excluding those who are registered and claiming benefit but are discouraged from actively seeking work because of the high probability of failure. In 1983 according to the Labour Force Survey this group consisted of 149,000 unemployed men and 37,000 unemployed women. This attempt to reduce unemployment is unacceptable if we are also concerned with the willingness to work. If we aim to estimate the effects and extent of true labour market slack (excess supply) clearly discouraged workers (not claiming) should be added to the total of claimants and discouraged workers who are claiming benefit should not be deducted.

However, the stock of claimants does include groups of workers who are not available for work and these should be excluded from the total. An important group is of those older (largely male) workers who have retired before the statutory retirement age and signed on at unemployment benefit offices to secure national insurance credits. As a result of a measure in the 1983 Budget this is no longer necessary for men aged over 60. Moreover as a result of a second change in that Budget a man aged 60 or over is eligible for the higher (long term) rate of supplementary benefit if he drops out of the labour force. The number involved is quite large (150,000). However, they are already excluded from the 1984 figure so no adjustment is required in Table 1.1. However, some adjustment would need to be made to Table 1.2 to claimant data before 1983 to ensure compatibility with 1984. The simplest way to do this is to add 150,000 to the time series data shown in Table 1.2 for years 1983 and 1984 (and to Row 1 of Table 1.1 to get the claimant stock on a comparable basis).

There are also some other claimants not available for work who should be excluded. The 1983 Labour Force Survey shows that those who did not want to work for family or other reasons amounted to 6.1% of the claimant total. These are deducted from the total of claimants and non-claimants in Table 1.2. Also deducted are those non-claimant groups who are searching for work but not currently unemployed. They consist mainly of students in full time education and those currently on government training schemes who are seeking work. They are a pretty substantial group (230,000) according to the estimates published by the Department of Employment (1984). They are excluded from the total of unemployed workers because they are not currently unemployed and are equivalent to those in employment who are also looking for a new job.

The exclusion of this group in Table 1.1 is contentious. Some estimates of actual unemployment in Britain include all of those currently in education and those covered by special employment and training measures. This is on the grounds that in the absence of these measures the individuals would be claiming benefit. According to Metcalf (1984) the Department of Employment states that the claimant count is reduced by 440,000 as a consequence of these measures. The major objection to the inclusion of this number in Table 1.1 is that to do so would also justify the inclusion in the total actually unemployed of large numbers of other individuals who would also be without jobs if it were not for public sector spending or fiscal benefits. Since this would be clearly absurd not only are those in work because of special measures not included in Table 1.1 but also those of this group who are searching for future work are also excluded. No attempt has been made to correct for 'unofficial' job holding amongst claimants because there is no firm evidence of its scale.

Once all these corrections are made, it is clear that to a significant extent the claimant count understates the actual unemployment in Britain. Given the inaccuracy of this measure of unemployment an alternative approach might be to calculate unemployment from labour force and employment data. Information about employment is collected monthly from employers. This data has a number of errors partly of recording and partly for other reasons like double job holding by certain individuals. (9) These monthly figures are corrected annually with the aid of a count of national insurance cards or from 1972 until recently, by the annual Census of Employment. Relatively accurate measures are available but with some delay and appear subject to frequent revision. These corrected figures, for example are used by the Department of Employment in its published estimates of equation 1.2.

Calculation of the labour force is generally done by adding together estimates of $\bar{U}$ and E and so, in fact $\bar{U}$ cannot be obtained by the direct subtraction of E from L. Official statistics include a regular series on the working population which is the sum of all employee jobs (excluding domestic service and family workers), employers, the self-employed, HM forces and the unemployed (including the severely disabled plus adult students registered for work). These exclusions plus the omission of the unregistered unemployed <u>and</u> employed make it a somewhat inaccurate measure of L. Others (10) have attempted to calculate the labour force more accurately including most of these excluded groups. These show that although the official measure of L moves in line with the alternative, it is about 400,000 below the true figure. Bearing all this in mind, calculations like those in Table 1.1 are about the best that can be done.

These difficulties in obtaining precise estimates of equation 1.1 and 1.2 have encouraged commentators to exercise considerable latitude in their own calculations. Not surprisingly those horrified at the scale of unemployment in Britain publish estimates much higher than the official figures and much higher than those in Table 1.1, while those more sanguine about the problem inevitably do the opposite.

With these problems in mind we also include in Table 1.2, data on the stock of unemployed for the UK since 1961. This makes clear how over the last 15 years unemployment has risen to an historically high level. Although the percentage rate of unemployment is still significantly below that of the 1930s, the absolute number out of work is now at an all time high. Until the middle of the sixties, post-war unemployment in Britain has been exceptionally low which makes the rate at which it has increased in the seventies, even more dramatic. This increase has been most marked at the end of the seventies and the beginning of the eighties.

Table 1.2 Unemployment in Great Britain 1961-1984 (in thousands on a claimant basis)

1961	329	1979	1,296
1966	349	1980	1,665
1971	751	1981	2,520
1976	1,302	1982	2,917
1977	1,403	1983	3,102
1978	1,383	1984	3,125

Source: National Institute Economic Review 1983, page 39. Department of Employment Gazette 1984
Notes: 1984 data is for the first half only

Data from comparable industrial economies is in Table 1.3 and shows the relative position of the British economy. Since absolute numbers out of work simply reflect the size of the economy and its aggregate labour market, Table 1.3 contains calculations of the percentage rate of unemployment by country, using equation 1.12. The problems of making such inter-country comparisons are quite considerable. The means of measurement differ and the degree of bias in the figures also differs. Attempts have been made in the construction of Table 1.3 to put inter-country statistics on a comparable basis. It is clear that the broad historical pattern of unemployment experience is similar. However, Table 1.3 also shows that the extent of the increase in unemployment in Britain since 1971 is quite exceptional. The result is that in 1985 unemployment is higher in Britain than in any other <u>large</u> industrial economy. In only a handful (11) of smaller

Table 1.3 Unemployment in Major Industrial Countries 1961-1985 (%)

	US	Japan	France	Germany	Italy	Britain	OECD
1971	5.7	1.2	2.9	0.8	3.4	3.7	3.1
1976	7.5	2.0	4.4	3.7	6.6	5.7	5.2
1977	6.9	2.0	4.9	3.6	7.0	6.1	5.3
1978	5.9	2.2	5.2	3.5	7.1	6.0	5.1
1979	5.7	2.1	5.9	3.2	7.5	5.1	5.0
1980	7.0	2.0	6.3	3.0	7.4	6.6	5.7
1981	7.5	2.2	7.3	4.4	8.3	9.9	6.6
1982	9.5	2.4	8.1	6.1	8.9	11.4	8.0
1983	9.5	2.6	8.3	8.0	9.8	12.6	8.6
1984	7.4	2.7	9.7	8.5	10.2	13.0	8.2
1985	7.1	2.6	10.1	8.6	10.5	13.1	8.1

Source: National Institute Economic Review, Statistical Appendix

industrial economies is it greater so that current unemployment in Britain is exceptionally high both on an historical and a cross-country basis.

Employment and Unemployment

When we measure the stock of unemployment we are seeking a measure of the degree of underutilisation of labour in the economy. However it only accurately measures underutilisation if we assume the unemployed are wholly unemployed and the employed are fully utilised. We have already referred to the problem of unofficial job holding by the unemployed but much more serious is the assumption we make about the employed. If the employed are not working at their full capacity should we not regard their underemployment as a form of unemployment. Consider a simple example of 10 workers who are working 90% of the hours they wish to work and are available to work. In terms of measured labour time this is equivalent to one full time unemployed worker.

Bornstein (1978) has drawn attention to this problem when comparing unemployment in Capitalist Market Economies like Britain and Socialist Centrally Planned Economies like the USSR. In the latter, Bornstein emphasises the importance of 'disguised' unemployment which occurs when workers have jobs but are underutilised. There are various forms of underemployment in Socialist economies which result from "the combination of the 'ratchet' principle in planning, tight labour market conditions and restrictions on the dismissal of workers". Such underutilisation of employed labour does not only occur in Socialist economies. Development economists have emphasised its incidence in developing economies but it is an important feature of the labour market in capitalist economies like Britain and it is important to take it into account when we make historical or inter-country comparisons. In order to analyse this problem a simple and useful method is to consider a conventional Cobb-Douglas production function. (12)

$$1.3 \quad Y_t = Ae^{gt}(E_tH_t)^{\alpha}$$

where

H = hours of work
Y = real output

The parameter g captures the growth of output attributable to both growth in the capital stock and technical progress. In order to derive a firm's desired employment level, 1.3 can be inverted and rearranged to give

1.4 $\quad E_t = e^{-gt/\alpha} \cdot Y_t^{1/\alpha} \Big/ A^{1/\alpha} \cdot H_t$

This is the basic employment function developed by Ball and St. Cyr (1966). If we assume that firms minimise costs, we can derive an expression for the desired level of hours of work (H_t). Consider a wage cost (W_{Ht}) relationship of the following form:

1.5 $\quad W_{Ht} = a - bH_t + dH_t^2$

This function implies that wage costs are raised if hours are below the normal level. 'Normal' in this case means the standard working week. The reason for this is that as hours are reduced below the normal level the fixed labour cost per hour <u>actually</u> worked rises. Similarly when hours exceed the normal level wage costs rise because of the payment of overtime premia. In other words, the effective labour cost is minimised if actual hours worked equal the standard working week. We can derive an expression for this by differentiating WH_t with respect to H_t in 1.5 and minimising which gives

1.6 $\quad H_t = b/2d$

and by substitution into 1.4 gives

1.7 $\quad E_t = e^{-gt/\alpha} \cdot Y_t^{1/\alpha} \Big/ A^{1/\alpha} \cdot b/2d$

If we assume the firm adopts the best practice technology with a given capital stock and normal hours are constant we can graphically represent the cost minimising relationship E_t (employment) and Y_t (real output) that firms will seek. The relationship in Figure 1.1 assumes $\alpha < 1$ which is the normal decreasing returns assumption in the Cobb-Douglas function.

We can also derive the profit maximising level of output and employment. Under perfect competition the real wage is set equal to the marginal physical product. Since Figure 1.1 is simply an inverted production function, this is shown graphically as the point of tangency of the real wage line and the production function at $E\pi$ and $Y\pi$. Obviously if the real wage (W/P) falls the point of tangency would lead to higher $E\pi$ and $Y\pi$ and vice versa if W/P rises. The conventional neo-classical labour demand curve

Figure 1.1

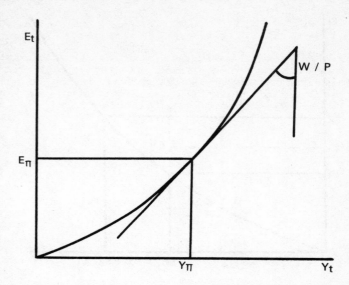

is derived from points of tangency along the cost minimising employment function. If the assumptions of perfect competition that underly the neo-classical demand curve are appropriate then points along the employment function are only observed if the real wage changes. In empirical work, therefore, a neo-classical approach would have no role for exogenous changes in real output. This is an important issue which is pursued further in chapter six.

We are now in a position to analyse underemployment. Consider Figure 1.2.

If the level of output is Y_1, the cost minimising level of employment for firms is E_1, so if the firm produces Y_1 off the employment function, at say, point a, it will employ E_2 workers. (13) There will be underemployment in the sense that if these workers were fully utilised Y_2 could be produced. We can measure the extent of underemployment by noting that labour productivity at a (Y_1/E_2) is less than at b (Y_2/E_2) as

1.8 $U_H = 1 - Y_1/E_2 \Big/ Y_2/E_2 \times 100$

This is the measure of underemployment or labour

11

Figure 1.2

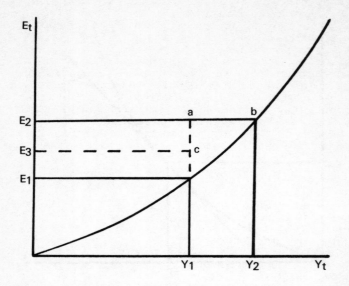

hoarding used by Taylor (1972) (14) who has calculated the extent of underemployment in Britain at different points in time at the industry and aggregate level. There are a multitude of ways in which this underemployment can occur and it is convenient to consider them in two categories. Firstly, workers can simply be required to work fewer hours than they are able or willing to work. Secondly, production per unit of labour time can be lower than is possible given the capital stock available. This could, for example, be the result of workers being overemployed on non-production tasks, or of slower production speeds, or of excessive work breaks or work flow organisation. Any or all of these situations will give rise to underemployment of the employed labour input.

What are the principal causes of the underemployment of the labour input? It is useful to distinguish secular (long run) and cyclical (short run) causes. In the long run firms may produce output at points above the employment function depicted in Figure 1.2. In some cases it may be the result of institutional constraints of the type Bornstein (1978) identifies for the socialist centrally planned economies. In others it may be ignorance of

12

the best practice technique giving rise to what Leibenstein (1966) calls 'X' in efficiency.

Firms may also opt for methods of production which are above the minimum cost possible. Satisficing behaviour on the part of managers in large corporations or the pursuit of non-cost minimising managerial objectives may also be important. (15) Cross-country comparisons, in particular, need to take this into account. If, as is often claimed from studies of international productivity differences that British industry in the sixties and seventies experienced more of this 'overmanning' then comparing unemployment rates understates the relative degree of underemployment in Britain in that period. If it is true that in the eighties overmanning has been reduced to the level of other industrial economies, then there is no such understatement now. In other words, the relatively bad unemployment position of Britain in the last five years and revealed by Table 1.3 may have existed in earlier decades but was concealed because labour in excess of the cost minimising level was being employed.

In the short run underemployment may also result from a fall in the level of output which employers consider to be transitory. Consider a situation in which output is at Y_2 and employment is at E_2 in Figure 1.2. There is a fall in output to Y_1 which firms consider to be transitory as a result of which they decide not to lay off workers. In this extreme case no additional unemployment results from the fall in output. In fact, in practice, firms adopt some intermediate strategy involving a cut in employment to say E_3 in Figure 1.2. Output falls but employment does not fall as much. The result is the procyclical movement in labour productivity which in the US has been called 'Okun's Law'. Taylor's (1972) study shows that underemployment increases when output falls and McKendrick (1975) has shown that the propensity to underemploy (hoard) by industry is positively related to the variability of output through time. In other words firms who are accustomed to big fluctuations in output are more likely to underemploy their employed labour force when output falls since they are more likely to regard such fluctuations as transitory.

Miller (1971) has emphasised the role of inventories of finished goods to the extent to which firms cut both output and employment in the face of a fall in the demand for their product. Where inventory holdings are high, firms are more likely to cut both

13

Y and E which results in more unemployment and underemployment but less of the latter than would prevail if inventory holdings were small. The question still remains as to why firms should behave in this way. Labour economists have given considerable emphasis to the importance of fixed labour costs in explaining this behaviour. Three principal types of cost are significant namely (a) hiring costs; (b) firing costs and (c) training costs. Labour is not costlessly variable and hiring and firing both involve fixed costs. Hiring involves the costs of recruiting suitable workers while firing involves possible trade union resistance, payment of redundancy payments and so on. Of even greater significance are training costs. Firms invest in their labour force and this important fact has been analysed by Oi (1962). Taking these fixed costs into account gives the Marginal Discounted Cost of Labour (MC) as

$$1.9 \quad MC = \sum_{t=0}^{T} W_t (1 + r)^{-t} + HC + KC$$

where

T = prospective date of retirement
W = wage costs
HC = hiring costs
KC = training costs
r = discount rate

The marginal discounted revenue (MR) can be defined as

$$1.10 \quad MR = \sum_{t=0}^{T} (M_t + \Delta M_t) (1 + r)^{-t}$$

where

M_t = marginal product of labour

ΔM_t = the increment to the marginal product as a result of training

If we examine the cost minimising firm that also profit maximises then such a firm will equate the marginal discounted cost (MC) with the marginal

14

discounted revenue (MR). Equating equations 1.9 and 1.10 and re-arranging gives:

$$1.11 \quad HC + KC = \sum_{t=0}^{T} (M_t + \Delta M_t - W_t) (1 + r)^{-t}$$

If we assume M_t, ΔM_t and W_t are constant and single valued, then

$$1.12 \quad \left(HC + KC \middle/ \sum_{t=0}^{T} (1 + r)^{-t} \right) + W^* = M^* + \Delta M^*$$

where

W^*, M^* and ΔM^* are the single values of wages, the marginal product and the training increment to the marginal product. Equation 1.12 embodies the long run equilibrium condition for the firm. The term

$$HC + KC \middle/ \sum_{t=0}^{T} (1 + r)^{-t}$$

is of some importance since it represents the fixed employment cost during each period which is the surplus each marginal worker must earn to amortise the fixed cost the firm has incurred in his or her employment. The greater is the value of this periodic rent the less likely it is that firms will lay off workers as soon as output falls. Unless it can negotiate a special contract (16) with its labour force the firm runs the risk of not amortizing its investment in the worker. Oi argues that this makes labour a quasi-fixed not a freely variable factor of production as elementary textbooks suggest.

The fact that firms invest in their labour force is a powerful reason for the underemployment of workers that characterise slumps in Britain. Differential levels of investment in human capital also help to explain why certain types of workers are more likely to be unemployed and not underemployed. This is discussed further in chapter two. Other fixed costs reinforce the tendency to hoard labour. The firing costs discussed above obviously influence a firm's response to a cut in the output and may persuade it to cut hours of work or adopt some other hoarding device to avoid layoffs.

Legal, technological and other institutional constraints will also have this effect. Indeed

15

recently, Bowers, Deaton and Turk (1982) have argued that hiring, firing and training costs are unimportant in explaining the underemployment of workers in Britain. They note that even in recession the level of voluntary quits is sufficiently high to permit firms to cut employment in line with output without incurring firing or significant rehiring and training costs in any subsequent upturn. The fact that employment is actually cut much less than output in most manufacturing industries results from firms who are constrained by inflexibilities in both their production and organisational technology engaging in 'excess hiring' in recession to ensure optimal long run performance. There are ample reasons to explain the fact that underemployment of workers is significant (especially in recession) in Britain and more significant than in some other countries. (17) Gordon (1982), for example finds employment (E_t) and hence unemployment (U_t) in the post-war period has been more variable in the US than in Britain which in its turn has greater variability than Japan. This is explained by Gordon by differences in the institutional structure of the labour market, but clearly if we are to make sense of the comparisons of Table 2.3 this should be taken into account.

It should also be taken into account when we examine historical patterns of unemployment within an economy. If there is a secular decline in labour hoarding this will be reflected in increasing levels of measured employment. What is the evidence to suggest that this has happened in Britain so that now the unemployment stock is a more accurate measure of underemployment?

Bowers, Deaton and Turk (1982) note a tendency for greater variability in employment to occur in the seventies. In a recent study Wren-Lewis (1984) shows that the sharp decline in employment in the early eighties was the outcome of a downward revision of output expectations. The recession was not thought to be transitory so labour was reduced and hoarding, therefore, did not appear on the scale witnessed in previous recessions in Britain. This view is consistent with analysis of recent British productivity movements in Mendis and Muellbauer (1983). They find the rapid increase in labour productivity in the years 1981 and 1982 was a once and for all movement resulting from 'drastic shedding of plant, labour and management'. The dishoarding was on a sufficiently large scale for the level of unemployment now to be a more accurate indicator of underemployment than in the past. It is probably not unreasonable to conclude that the relative underemployment position of the British economy is now less understated than in the past.

Having outlined some of the problems associated with the meaning and measurement of the unemployed stock at the aggregate level, we now turn to examine the use of this statistic as an indicator of the costs of underemployment.

Costs of Unemployment

Spells of unemployment are costly both for the individual and for the community as a whole. From the community's point of view output is lost and resources are underutilised. Correspondingly for the individual worker income is lost and levels of household consumption are reduced. However, for such an individual this cost of a spell of unemployment is reduced because of (a) the receipt of unemployment compensation; (b) the gain in leisure and (c) the possibility that by using the unemployment spell for search, a job with better pay and/or other conditions of work might be found. As far as the individual is concerned the problem can be analysed using the conventional theory of labour supply and by ignoring (c) above. This gives a utility function of the form

1.13 $\mu = U(Y,1)$

where

Y = real income per year
1 = hours of leisure per year
μ = utility

with $\partial\mu/\partial Y > 0$ $\quad \partial^2\mu/\partial Y^2 < 0$

$\qquad \partial\mu/\partial 1 > 0$ $\quad \partial^2\mu/\partial 1^2 < 0$

This permits us to derive an indifference curve. If we assume that the substitution effect of a wage increase exceeds the income effect we can then derive an individuals' supply curve of hours of work as depicted in Figure 1.3. This tells us the wage rate an individual seeks for a given number of weekly hours and this reflects the compensation he/she requires for giving up an hour of leisure in order to work. The more leisure given up the higher is the compensation required given our assumptions. Points on the supply curve thus represent the individual's valuation of leisure for working weeks of differing

Figure 1.3

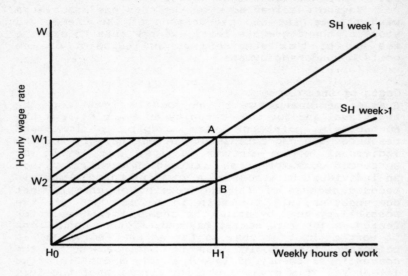

lengths.

Assume the hourly employed wage of an individual is W_1 and he/she works H_1 hours. If the individual is unemployed he/she works H_0 hours and receives zero work income. He/she is, however, partly compensated by the leisure now enjoyed which has a total value described by the triangle AH_0H_1. The total loss of income is depicted by the area of the rectangle $W_1H_0H_1A$ and so the net cost of unemployment is the shaded triangle W_1AH_0. Individuals who place a high value on leisure will have a smaller net cost (steeper supply curve) and vice versa for people who attach a low value to leisure. Whether the individual is actually worse off depends on the level of unemployment compensation and on the prospects of getting a better job as a result of being unemployed. This could exceed W_1AH_0. These are empirical questions to which we return later. It is clear from this analysis, however, that the costs of unemployment increase as the stock of unemployment increases if the net cost of unemployment shown in triangle W_1AH_0 is less than totally offset.

However, the cost to an individual of unemployment is not independent of the duration of a spell of unemployment. Since the marginal utility of

leisure declines in the short run it is not
unreasonable to assume that it declines still further
as a worker experiences successive weeks of
unemployment. The value he attaches to a given number
of hours of leisure will fall, the more complete
weeks of unemployment he has experienced. The result
will be that the supply curve depicted in Figure 1.3
will flatten through the unemployment spell. This
will increase the net cost of a week out of work to
an unemployed individual. In Figure 1.3 the supply
curve shifts to SH week>1 and the net costs of
unemployment increase by the area of the triangle
ABH_0. He will also accept a progressively lower wage
to work a week of length H_1 (W_2 in this case). This
phenomenon has been empirically confirmed by Kasper
(1967) and others (18) who show the acceptance wage
of unemployed workers falls through a spell of
unemployment. Costs borne by individual workers will
also increase with the length of a spell of
unemployment if the probability of receiving a job
offer declines because of the scarring effects of
long unemployment. This is considered in some detail
in chapter two but there is some clear evidence for
this as part of unemployment experience in Britain.

So far we have not explicitly examined the
effects of an unemployment compensation scheme which
reduces the net cost of an unemployment spell (W_1AH_0
in Figure 1.3). In Britain this varies according to
the marital status and number of dependents of the
individual worker. Until recently when the earnings
related supplement was abolished, it also varied with
the length of unemployment spell. Some idea of the
net income loss can be found in the study of Dilnot
and Morris (1983) which contains calculations of the
replacement ratio (out of work income ÷ expected in
work income) in Britain in 1980. This shows the net
income loss of unemployment is greater for single
persons (.34 of expected in work income) than for
those with large families (.18 for married couples
with 3 children). Of course the marginal utility of
leisure may differ for these groups so the difference
in the net costs of unemployment may not be so great
if we assume leisure has greater value to the single
person. If (for simplification) we assume
unemployment compensation is invariant with duration
(19) the net cost to an individual of an unemployment
spell can be derived. This is shown in Figure 1.4.
The actual shape and intercept of the function varies
with the institutional arrangements and re-
employment prospects of the unemployed worker (which
vary across the population and through time) and with

Figure 1.4

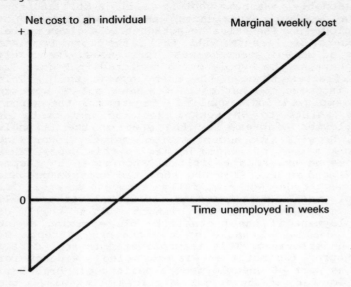

the marginal utility of leisure. In Figure 1.4 we have assumed that at the beginning of a spell of unemployment the net cost of unemployment is actually negative. The value of the extra leisure enjoyed exceeds the net income loss suffered. The positive slope of the marginal cost function shows that both the total and the marginal costs of being out of work will increase with duration and be much higher for the long term unemployed. This is because the declining utility of leisure and the constancy of the net income loss leads to an increase in the net cost of unemployment. Note that had we assumed that the extent of unemployment compensation falls with duration, this effect would be even more pronounced (see note (19)).

So far we have examined the individual costs of unemployment which are clearly proportional to spell duration but what are the costs to the community? When assessing the real costs to community we disregard unemployment compensation since it is a transfer payment. If we assume that the value of real output lost is equal to the real income loss of workers and allow for the value of additional leisure for the unemployed we can simply add together the net cost of unemployment to all individuals. This is the

20

procedure suggested by Layard (1981) and it takes account of the fact that the total cost of unemployment to a community is proportional both to the average duration of uncompleted spells of unemployment and the numbers out of work. Layard performs some calculations which show the total cost of unemployment is twice in the UK its equivalent value in the US for male workers.

Other aspects of the community (social) costs of unemployment are ignored by this procedure. Firstly, it ignores the spin off effects of increasing the stock of unemployed on those currently employed. Simple Keynesian analysis, for example, emphasises the impact of higher unemployment on aggregate demand and hence on the income and job prospects of those currently in work. The total fall in income may thus be greater than the Layard method suggests. Secondly, it fails to take account of the effect of unemployment on the labour productivity of those out of work. If the re-employment chances of the unemployed fall because skills and other attributes necessary for effective employment decline particularly with long periods of unemployment, then the quality of the community's labour force declines with high unemployment and with increases in the average duration. (20) Thirdly, it fails to acknowledge the response of those out of work to their situation and of the costs of intervention of public agencies. Social disruption, sickness and increased crime levels are all correlated with high unemployment. The Report from the Select Committee of the House of Lords on Unemployment (1982) concludes "anecdotal evidence, supported by some research (21) appears to confirm a causal link (between unemployment and crime); and unemployment provides both motive and opportunity for crime" and goes on to say "We believe unemployment to be among the causes of ill-health, mortality, crime or civil disorder."

The work of Rowthorn and Ward (1979) provides evidence in support of this view. They estimate that an increase (sustained over five years) in unemployment in Britain of 1 million, leads to 50,000 more deaths, 60,000 additional cases of mental illness and 140,000 more prison sentences. Further they calculate that this imposes an additional burden on the public services amounting to £560 million over a five year period. Brenner (1979) confirms this adverse effect of unemployment on mortality rates although some of his conclusions have been criticised by Gravelle, Hutchinson and Stern (1981) on the grounds of data reliability. Using an alternative data set they find no relationship of the kind identified by Brenner for 1952-76. They argue that although unemployment may have adverse effects on health and mortality, Brenner's evidence is unconvincing as proof. Despite these reservations, there is some evidence that unemployment and especially long-term unemployment imposes heavy social costs on the community and these need to be taken into account in economic policy making.

We have so far disregarded the exchequer costs of unemployment. In Britain the government itself has calculated that every additional 100,000 unemployed workers cost £340 million in 1981. (22) This only takes account of the unemployment benefit paid and the tax revenue lost not to the whole gamut of social costs referred to above. It also takes no account of the exchequer costs of redundancy payments so it will be biased downwards for this reason as well. Nonetheless in the fiscal year 1981/2 the exchequer costs of unemployment amounted to a staggering £9,792 million which is only slightly smaller than the entire public sector borrowing requirement for that year. Dilnot and Morris (1981) provide some alternative calculations using data from the 1978 Family Expenditure Survey which permits them to take account of indirect tax revenue lost by the exchequer as the result of unemployment. Assuming the structure of unemployment in the fiscal year 1981/2 was unchanged from 1978 they calculate the total exchequer cost to be £12,947 million (6.2% of GDP) which is considerably higher than that obtained from official Treasury calculations.

Clearly the increases in unemployment since 1970 will have added to the exchequer costs and hence to the public sector borrowing requirement. Dilnot and Morris show that between 1977/78 and 1981/2, the exchequer cost went up by 277% at current prices and 155% in real terms. Since 1982 the increase in the numbers of unemployed will have increased these exchequer costs both in money and real terms though government cuts (especially the abolition of ERS) will have offset this to some extent.

It is evident from the analysis of this section that high unemployment is extremely costly. It is also evident that this cost increases with increases in both the duration of spells of unemployment as well as the total number out of work.

Unemployment Duration and Labour Market Dynamics

Much of this chapter has considered the stocks in the

labour market, particularly the stocks of those <u>in</u> and <u>out</u> of work. It is obvious, however, from the analysis of the previous section that this is inadequate because the costs of unemployment depend on its duration as well as the size of the total stock. We need a framework of analysis that permits us also to consider both these aspects of unemployment.

The labour market is in a continuous state of movement even when the stocks of labour, employment and unemployment are unchanging. The principal flows in the labour market are depicted in Figure 1.5. This shows the flows which involve a period unemployed (with a 'u' subscript) and those which involve a direct transition without an intervening spell of unemployment (no subscript). These flows are extremely large. This is shown in Table 1.4 which includes calculations of the annualized size of each flow in Autumn 1976 when the unemployment flows (D_t^u and H_t^u) were equal in size and hence the stock of unemployment was constant. Although there is both cyclical and secular variation in these flows as we will see in the next chapter these data are not a greatly inaccurate picture of other points in time including the 1980s. The annual equivalent inflow to unemployment is over $3\frac{1}{2}$ million (16% of the labour force). The comparable flow rate that measures those who change employment without a spell of unemployment ($\bar{D}_t$) is also high though many labour economists would regard the estimate in Table 1.4 as being on the low side. (23)

The flows described in Table 1.4 indicate the substantial scale of 'normal' turnover in the labour market caused by workers changing jobs either voluntarily or involuntarily, leaving the labour force for reasons of age, sickness or marriage and childbirth, entering the labour force from the educational sector or after child bearing and so on. (24) Much of this turnover involves a spell out of work. This is because some of this movement does not happen instantaneously so that, for example, a discharged worker may find him/herself in the pool of unemployed (registered or unregistered) for a finite period of time. The methods for calculating the length of this period of time which significantly affects the cost of unemployment are discussed more fully in chapter two.

Labour market flows will also be affected if changes occur in the size of the stocks (note: Table 1.4 illustrates a period in which stocks were constant). This can be illustrated by considering the

Table 1.4 Annual Labour Market Flows Britain 1976 (in millions)

Discharges	(a) $\overline{D}_t = 2.391$ (b) $\overline{D}_t^u = 3.579 - \tau_t^u$
Hires from employment	$\overline{H}_t = 2.640$
Hires from unemployment plus retirements from unemployment	$\overline{H}_t^u + \overline{\tau}_t^u = 3.579$
New entrants to employment and unemployment	$\overline{\varepsilon}_t^u + \overline{\varepsilon}_t = 1.079$
Retirements and withdrawals from employment	$\overline{\tau}_t = .891$

Source: $\overline{D}_t^u$, $\overline{H}_t^u$ $\overline{\tau}_t^u$ - Department of Employment Gazette $\overline{\varepsilon}_t^u$, $\overline{\varepsilon}_t$, $\overline{\tau}_t$ - R. Lindley (editor) <u>Britain's Medium Term Prospects</u> pages 11, 12. $\overline{D}_t$, $\overline{H}_t$ - derived from engagement and discharge rates for manufacturing and applied to the whole economy. Department of Employment Gazette.

stock of employed. We have already seen how a firm might determine its desired stock of employment. Suppose for example there is an increase in the level of output that the firm wishes to produce. Suppose also its existing stock of labour is fully utilised. Then Figure 1.2 implies the cost minimising (though not necessarily the profit maximising) firm will increase its labour requirements so that

1.14 $E_t < E_t^*$

where

E_t^* = desired employment
E_t = actual employment

This process will not happen instantaneously so we need to formulate an adjustment process. The simplest formulation to adopt would be

Figure 1.5

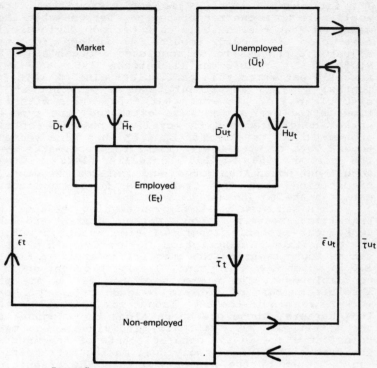

ε = Entrant flows
τ = Retirement (withdrawal flows)
D = Discharge flows (quits plus lay offs)
H = Hiring flows

1.15 $E_t/E_{t-1} = (E_t^*/E_{t-1})^\lambda$

where λ indicates the speed of adjustment and $1/\lambda$ the period of time that complete adjustment would take. If, for example $\lambda = 1/4$ we would know that firms would make up a quarter of the gap between what they want and what they have in each period. Obviously in this case it would require 4 periods for the adjustment process to be completed. Morgan's (1979) study of UK manufacturing between 1963 and 1976 actually estimates this particular value of λ (t = 3 months) so full adjustment takes a year but it is also clear from his work that this varies with the time period over which λ is estimated, the type of worker considered and the cyclical position of the economy (λ is greater for $E_t < E_t^*$ than vice versa). Recent work by Wren-Lewis (1984) that estimates over the period 1964 to 1982 actually finds a lower adjustment speed than Morgan and confirms the general proposition that any transition from one labour market state to another takes time.

This can also be shown by analysing the speed of transition between labour market states and the consequent probable length of time spent in making the transition. A description of this dynamic process can be found by using the transition matrix in Figure 1.6 in which E = employment, U = unemployment and F = non-employment. The elements of the matrix are the absolute numbers of workers in each category. Many workers remain in the same labour market state in the two quarters. These are shown along the diagonal of the matrix (EE, UU, FF). (25) Individuals who make transitions are in the other elements of the matrix. The probability of an individual making a transition can be found by the number who make the transition divided by the number in the original state in the previous time period. If, for example, we wanted to know the probability of an unemployed worker making the transition to unemployment (the inflow probability) we could calculate EU $\div$ E_{t-1}. If, alternatively, we wanted to calculate the inflow probability for the labour force as a whole we could do this by calculation FU + EU $\div$ $(E_{t-1} + U_{t-1})$. This is done in chapter two for a variety of workers at different points in time in Britain. Once we know the probability of a change of state we can calculate the time a typical individual will spend in his current state as the reciprocal of that probability. In the next chapter we will consider the appropriateness of this statistic, its reliability and the alternative methods of calculation which are available.

Figure 1.6

Labour market State in previous quarter	in current quarter E_t	U_t	F_t
E_{t-1}	EE	EU	EF
U_{t-1}	UE	UU	UF
F_{t-1}	FE	FU	FF

More recently economists particularly, but not solely in the US have given attention to the determinants of these transition probabilities. Of particular interest is the probability UE/U_{t-1} since this indicates the chances of re-employment for an unemployed worker and consequently the time he will 'typically' remain unemployed. This research (especially in Britain) will be considered in later chapters since it is obviously crucial in analysing the duration of a spell of unemployment.

Conclusion

In this chapter we have seen how the stock of unemployment has risen in the UK and in most other industrial countries. The meaning and measurement of this stock has also been considered. From a policy point of view, emphasis has been given to the measurement of the cost of unemployment. We have also emphasised the crucial importance of the duration of unemployment to this exercise, and the consequent necessity of taking a dynamic view of the labour market. This is the perspective of subsequent chapters in which we will concentrate on labour market flows that involve a spell of unemployment ($\bar{D}_t$, $\bar{H}^u \bar{\epsilon}_t$ and $\bar{\tau}^u_t$ in Figure 1.5) as well as upon the stock of unemployed workers.

Notes

1. R.G. Lipsey's paper in A.M. Ross (ed.) 1965 provides a flavour of this debate.
2. G. McCrone (1969) provides a useful overview of the issue.
3. Seminal work in this area includes Lucas (1973), Sargent and Wallace (1976) and Barro (1976).
4. This is obtained from Metcalf (1984) and takes account of the greater accuracy of the computerised count of claimants.
5. Women employed before 1975 and still in the same employment before becoming unemployed are the

27

most important.

6. If we add together the previously registered non-claimants and the unregistered we get an estimate of non-claimants. Recent data from the 1983 Labour Force Survey calculates this to be 840,000, compared with 916,000 in Table 1.1.

7. There is extensive evidence of this discouraged worker effect in Britain. The cross-section studies of Greenhalgh (1977) (1980), for example, have shown a 1% increase in local unemployment rates reduces female labour force participation by 0.75% and by 0.23% for men.

8. This is done for example in a special feature in the Department of Employment Gazette 1984, pages 367-370.

9. J. Alden (1978) provides some evidence and analysis of this phenomenon.

10. See for example R.M. Lindley (1980).

11. Holland, Belgium and Eire in 1984.

12. There are several problems with the employment function approach to modelling labour demand. It assumes output is exogenous, the role of real wages in affecting the demand for labour is neglected or ignored in empirical work despite its obvious theoretical importance. It also assumes employers are not constrained by the supply side of the labour market (there is no excess demand for labour). These (and other) matters are discussed more fully in chapter six. However, for the purpose of analysing labour hoarding it has some advantages.

13. If there is a point of tangency of the employment function and the real wage function at E_1 and Y_1 this is also a profit maximising position. If E_2 are employed workers, are being paid in excess of their marginal product, so actual labour demand is above that predicted by profit maximising competitive theory. This could arise for a multitude of reasons. For example firms may pursue non-profit maximising objectives or trade unions may strike bargains with employers that have this effect. This possibility is discussed in chapter five.

14. There are number of other ways in which hoarding can be measured in practice. See J. Bowers and D. Deaton (1980) for a review of the alternatives.

15. Industrial economists like Williamson (1964) have considered the implications for the demand for labour if staff expenditures enter the managerial utility function. The result will be organisational 'slack' which is equivalent to labour hoarding.

16.   A contract which permits a firm to lay off workers and be sure of rehiring them when required.

17.   In chapter two we also will explore these differences between workers within Britain. Some workers are more likely to be hoarded (e.g. non-manual) so there is less cyclical variation (and less turnover) for these groups of workers.

18.   Recent attempts to test and explain the behaviour of the reservation wage include Kiefer and Neumann (1979) and Narendrenathan, Nickell and Stern (1985). The whole issue is considered in greater detail in chapters two and three.

19.   This has not been the case in Britain, especially during the period in which the earnings related supplement (ERS) was paid. Dilnot and Morris (1983) show the proportion of in work income received by the unemployed fell from .66 at 13 weeks to .56 at 53 weeks. The abolition of the ERS will have affected this and will have made the assumption made in the text more appropriate but substantial differences will remain. Recently published data from the 1983 Family Expenditure Survey shows this. The average replacement ratio for those out of work was .59 but for the long-term unemployed was .39.

20.   The evidence for this is considered in chapter two.

21.   Carr-Hill and Stern (1983) and in a recent paper, Junankar (1984) provide econometric evidence for a positive link between unemployment and the incidence of crime.

22.   Economic Progress Report, February 1981.

23.   Estimates based on, for example, the number of changes of P60 (tax) forms suggest the true values of $\bar{D}_t$ and $\bar{H}_t$ could be as high as five million per year.

24.   The data on retirements and entrants included in Table 1.4 is calculated on a net flow basis for flows in and out of the labour force by age. In general this is not a problem since the flows are in one direction. However, particularly in the case of prime age women (25-59) the net flow will underestimate the gross flows.

25.   This transition matrix assumes workers who successfully change jobs makes no change in their labour market state in that they are employed in both quarters. To take account of job to job transitions ($\bar{D}_t$, $\bar{H}_t$ in Figure 1.5) would require a more complex matrix.

Chapter Two

STOCKS, FLOWS, DURATION AND THE INCIDENCE OF UNEMPLOYMENT

Introduction

We have so far analysed the aggregate stock of unemployment and the problems associated with its measurement. How important is this statistic? It certainly conceals as much as it reveals. It provides no clue as to the differential incidence of unemployment amongst different groups of the labour force. Moreover, it tells us nothing about the rate of turnover of the stock. If, however, we are interested in assessing the costs of unemployment and the need for corrective action these are crucial bits of information. For example, in chapter one we explored the relation between the costs of unemployment and its duration. It is clear from that analysis that we should take a different view of, say, a 10% unemployment rate if we know that the stock was made up of a large number of short duration spells (high turnover) than if it consisted of a smaller number of long term spells (low turnover). Equally if the short spells were experienced by a large number of different workers rather than by a small number of individuals experiencing repeated spells of unemployment, we would come to different conclusions about both the cost of total unemployment and the necessity for and the form of the policy action required to correct it. Similarly if all the unemployment is concentrated on, say, a particular region both the need for and the form of corrective action would differ from a situation in which the geographical spread is more even. The degree of concentration of the stock and the turnover within it are, therefore, critical aspects of unemployment that will be explored in this chapter.

Stocks, Flows and Duration of Unemployment

Using the notation employed in Chapter 1 we can initially define the absolute level of unemployment at time t as

2.1 $\bar{U}_t = \bar{U}_{t-1} + (\bar{D}_t^u + \bar{\epsilon}_t^u) - (\bar{H}_t^u + \bar{\tau}_t^u)$

or

2.1a $\Delta\bar{U}_t = (\bar{D}_t^u + \bar{\epsilon}_t^u) - (\bar{H}_t^u + \bar{\tau}_t^u)$

Equation 2.1a simply tells us that the change in the absolute size of the stock of unemployed workers (ΔU_t) equals the difference between the inflow onto the register ($D_t^u + \epsilon_t^u$) minus the outflow ($H_t^u + \tau_t^u$) off it. If we assume the labour force is constant ($L_t = L_{t-1}$) we can rewrite 2.1a as 2.1b with all the flows defined as rates which are standardised on the labour force. These rates are signified by writing 2.1a without bars, namely

2.1b $\Delta U_t = (D_t^u + \epsilon_t^u) - (H_t^u + \tau_t^u)$

where

U_t = the unemployment rate

D_t^u = the rate of entry (discharges) onto the register

H_t^u = the rate of exit (hires) from the register

t = a week

τ_t^u = retirements and withdrawal rate

ϵ_t^u = new entrant rate

It is convenient initially to analyse the aggregate stock, flow and duration relationship by assuming a stationary unemployment register ($\Delta U_t = 0$). Since we make this assumption it follows that the rate of entry to the register is exactly equal to the rate of ouflow.

$(D_t^u + \epsilon_t^u) = (H_t^u + \tau_t^u)$

The relationship between the stock, flows and duration can then be expressed as

2.2 $U_t = (D_t^u + \epsilon_t^u) \, T_t^u$ or as

2.2a $U_t = (H_t^u + \tau_t^u) \, T_t^u$

where

T_t^u = mean expected duration of a completed spell of unemployment (in weeks) beginning in time t.

T_t^u is effectively the average eventual completed duration for a particular inflow cohort that begins its spell of unemployment at time t.

Rearranging 2.2 and 2.2a give expressions for their duration. Namely

2.3 $\quad T_t^u = U_t / (D_t^u + \epsilon_t^u)$ and

2.3a $\quad T_t^u = U_t / (H_t^u + \tau_t^u)$

By using 2.2 the alternative flow/duration compositions of the aggregate stock can be seen. If the weekly inflow rate were 1% of the labour force and the expected duration four weeks the unemployment rate in each week it is measured would be 4%. This high turnover situation results in exactly the same stock as a much lower inflow rate of 0.25% and a much higher expected duration of 16 weeks. However the welfare costs of these identical stocks will differ and the necessity of a policy to reduce the aggregate unemployment rate will also be much less in the high turnover situation. The costs would also depend on the extent to which the same individuals experience these frequent short spells. Knowledge of the duration/flow and spell composition of the stock is not only necessary in the assessment of the need for policy intervention but also its form. In the high turnover case, for example, a policy which increases hiring standards to reduce the proportion of mismatched employments may be desirable. In the low turnover case the opposite policy might need to be pursued. Of course the detailed design of a policy depends on the reasons for differential rates. These are matters we explore in later chapters.

Table 2.1 shows the size of the stock and the flows for all workers in Britain in 1984. Note the substantial size of the flows (the annual inflow exceeds the total stock) which indicates the extent to which normal labour market transitions involve a period on the unemployment register. Also shown is some data on the inflow (α_t) and outflow (θ_t) probabilities. These give an indication of the chances in each week of a worker becoming unemployed (the inflow probability) and of an unemployed worker leaving the register (the outflow probability). These are calculated using data on the inflow and outflow rate itself, i.e. total inflows divided by the labour force. Algebraically

$$2.4 \quad \alpha_t = D_t^u + \varepsilon_t^u$$

This is the method used by the Department of Employment in Britain. One problem is that it provides a biased measure of the unemployment inflow probability for those currently employed. To calculate this we need to divide the absolute number of discharges ($\bar{D}_t^u$) by the number employed (E_t) rather than by the labour force (L_t). Given the large number currently unemployed E_t is significantly less than L_t so that the inflow rate (and probability) shown in Table 2.1 clearly understates the risk of unemployment for those currently employed. The exact extent of this understatement is difficult to gauge because of the presence of the entrant ($\bar{\varepsilon}_t^u$) flow in the inflow data. However given the comparatively small size of this flow (see Table 1.4) it is likely to account for only a little of the bias so that the true weekly inflow probability for employed workers is actually a good deal larger than the 0.3% shown in Table 2.1. Subsequently we shall ignore this bias so that when we use the flow probability interchangeably with that of employed workers this should be borne in mind.

Table 2.1 Total Unemployment: Stocks, Flows and Duration 1984

Unemployment		
(a) % (b) thousands	(a) 12.7 (U_t)	
	(b) 3022.4 (U_t)	
Average Weekly Inflow (thousands)	75.146	
Average Weekly Outflow (thousands)	77.246	
Weekly Inflow (α_t) probability	.003	
Weekly Outflow (θ_t) probability	.026	
Median uncompleted duration (weeks)	36.3	
Mean completed duration (weeks)		
(equation 2.6) from inflow rate	42.33	
(equation 2.6a) from outflow rate	39.13	

Source: Department of Employment Gazette, August 1984
Notes: (1) The unemployment rate and the mean uncompleted duration are for April 1984. All other data are for the time period January-April 1984.
(2) Unemployment is calculated on a claimant basis.

The outflow probability is calculated in an analogous way as the proportion of the unemployed whole are the register in any time period and hence

2.5 $\quad \theta_t = (H^u_t + \tau^u_t)/U_t$

Table 2.1 contains an estimate of θ_t which tells us that unemployed workers had a 2.4% chance of ceasing to be unemployed in any given week in 1984.

Note also the relation of the inflow and outflow probabilities to the calculation of the mean completed duration of a spell of unemployment. Combining equations 2.3 and 2.4 gives

2.6 $\quad T^u_t = U_t/\alpha_t$

Similarly combining 2.3a and 2.5 gives

2.6a $\quad T^u_t = 1/\theta_t$

which is the same relation derived in chapter one as part of the discussion of labour market transitions.

So far we have assumed a stationary register so in this steady state it doesn't matter if we calculate the expected duration of a typical spell of unemployment using the inflow or the outflow rate. The answer will be the same. A great deal of descriptive analysis which we consider later in this chapter, has made use of the stationary register assumption to derive mean completed durations or where this is known to calculate outflow and/or inflow probabilities. There are, however, some problems associated with the use of equation 2.6a which cause some anxiety.

The most important is that outflows record transitions to non-labour market as well as labour market states. If, for example, workers retire from the labour force in greater numbers the outflow rate will rise and the expected duration will fall. This may not be the case for workers not eligible for retirement. The use of 2.6a from aggregate data would in that case overestimate the re-employment probability of an unemployed worker getting a job (transition to a labour market state). This problem should be borne in mind when later we refer to the outflow and re-employment probabilities inter-changeably. For this reason many economists prefer the use of equation 2.6 to estimate the expected duration of unemployment spell lengths. This however also has several problems and a general anxiety associated with its use. In part the source of this

anxiety is the shortness of the estimate of the mean
length of a typical unemployment spell which is
obtained. In the US this is particularly noticeable
where the estimate is, at least for 1972-1977, quite
short. This led to some economists like Hall (1972)
and Perry (1972) suggesting, partially on the basis
of this statistic, that most unemployment was
voluntary and time spent while unemployed was chosen
by workers who were seeking better jobs. Unwilling to
accept this view others have sought alternative
measures to indicate the typical unemployment
duration. The basis of their objection is that the
estimate of the mean duration calculated from
equation 2.6 tells us the expected duration of the
unemployed worker at the moment the spell of
unemployment has begun (the average over the inflow
cohort). However if the register has a heavy
concentration of short spells as a proportion of
total spells there is a high measured inflow
probability and a low estimate of the mean completed
duration. The problem is particularly severe where it
is also the case that the long term unemployed
constitute a high proportion of total unemployment
days. For example, in a study of the US economy,
Clark and Summers (1979) show that although in 1975
the mean duration of a complete spell calculated from
equation 2.6 was 2.22 months, 58% of the unemployed
actually experienced spells of 3 months or more.

Because of these facts Layard (1981) has
suggested that the appropriate measure from a policy
point of view is the traditional published statistic
of the mean uncompleted duration of unemployment.
However this obviously does not tell us the length of
a completed spell since for any individual any
uncompleted spell is clearly shorter than the
completed equivalent. In fact, if the register is
stationary and we randomly select a moment to conduct
an enquiry then the mean uncompleted duration is
exactly half the completed. (1) This has led Main
(1981) to suggest an 'experience weighted' measure of
spell length which is obtained by doubling the
uncompleted spell length (the average over the stock
of unemployed). Table 2.1 shows that this measure in
April 1984 gives a completed spell length of 72.6
weeks compared with the 42 weeks estimate obtained
from the use of equation 2.6. However this
calculation uses the median uncompleted spell rather
than the mean which raises problems. It is likely to
be biased downwards. Because of the heavy incidence
of long spell unemployment the distribution of
uncompleted spells is highly skewed to the right. The

median will therefore, be less than the mean and so
will be the estimate of completed spell length
derived from it. Layard (1981) and Main (1981) both
show the <u>mean</u> uncompleted duration in Britain is
greater than the completed duration calculated from
equation 2.6. As Table 2.1 shows the median
uncompleted duration is less. One of the troubles
with this procedure using the mean or more
arbitrarily the median length is that there are other
reasons for suggesting this method biases upwards.
Since the probability of being observed on the
register depends positively on the length of the
completed spell, long spells are over represented in
the calculation of the mean uncompleted duration.
This is compounded by the exclusion of short spells
that occur within the time period that elapses
between unemployment counts. Taking all of these
problems into account suggests that the 'experience
weighted' measure is no less flawed than the
stationary register method of equation 2.6. Both
statistics provide useful information but it is
important to be aware of their limitations.

A further problem in the use of equation 2.6 is
that because the register may not, in practice, be
stationary it does not generate the same estimate as
that provided in 2.6a. That this is possible can be
seen from inspection of Table 2.1 where the inflow
rate method provides a slightly longer estimate of
the completed duration than the outflow rate
requirement. When the register is non-stationary
there are also problems with the 'experience
weighted' measure. If unemployment is increasing the
inflow exceeds the outflow and there will be a heavy
concentration of short uncompleted spells of
unemployment even for people who will eventually
complete long spells. As a result doubling the mean
uncompleted duration will be biased downward as a
measure of the typical spell duration.

If the unemployment register is falling in size
the bias will be in the opposite direction (upwards)
since the outflow is heavily concentrated with long
spell unemployed people. A further source of
difficulty arises if the outflow is, in fact,
composed largely of workers with short completed
durations. Recently published statistics provide
evidence for believing this to be the case in
Britain. In the three months January to April 1984
when the outflow exceeded the inflow (see Table 2.1)
and unemployment fell, the median completed duration
of those leaving the register was only 14.4 weeks for
males and 13.7 weeks for females. Although, given

36

that the distribution of completed spells is likely
to be highly skewed, the median will be less than the
equivalent mean value it also seems clear that it is
predominantly the short-term unemployed who
dominated the outflow in early 1984. Hence, the
degree of upward bias as in the experience weighted
measure that results, in practice, from a falling
register is bound to be small, likely to be zero and
could even be negative.

Now that we have considered the alternative
measures of inflow probabilities, outflow probabilities and unemployment durations, it is possible to
analyse the composition of the stock of unemployed
workers in greater detail and this is done in the
remainder of this chapter.

Stocks, Flows and Duration by Sex

Table 2.2 provides data on stocks, flows, and the
duration of unemployment in Great Britain and for
males and females separately. The first notable
feature of the table is the lower unemployment rate
for females. We have already seen in chapter one the
problems that arise in measurement of the stock from
the non-registration of certain members of the labour
force and the solutions that can be found. One fact
about registration bias is absolutely clear and that
is that non-registration of unemployment is more
serious amongst female workers. The reason for this
is not hard to find. Women workers spend less time in
market work because of the family responsibilities
they assume in our society. Stewart and Greenhalgh
(1984) show in their study using data for the 1975/6
National Training Survey, that although only 13% of
working women in the age group 45-54 had not
experienced at least one spell of market work the
remainder had only worked for between 55% and 65% of
the total working life available to them. Martin and
Roberts (1984) confirm this and show, using data from
the 1980 Women and Employment Survey that women born
since 1941 have on average spent around 60% of their
lives working. Women are also much more likely than
men to engage in part-time work. In 1981, 41.6% of
women but only 5.9% of men worked part-time. (2)
These facts have a number of effects most notably
that women have less likelihood of entitlement to
unemployment benefit and hence a lower incentive to
register as unemployed.

The extent of non-registration has already been
considered in chapter one. Using data from the 1981
Labour Force Survey the unemployment rates in Table

2.2 can be corrected. This gives 17.1% for males and 13.7% for females. This compares with the correction obtained from the General Household Survey which gives slightly lower rates of unemployment (16.2% and 12.5% for males and females respectively). Estimates of the inflow rate and the inflow probability are similarly affected by the problem of registration bias. Table 2.2 shows the weekly probability of women registering as unemployed is a good deal lower than men. Once we correct for registration bias and calculate the inflow into the unemployed state the numbers are rather different. Using the Labour Force Survey data the comparable probabilities are .0036 for males and at .0039 higher for females. Again slightly lower estimates for both men and women are found if we use General Household Survey data.

Table 2.2 Stocks, Flows and Duration by Sex 1984

	males	females
Unemployment (a) %	15.3	9.0
(b) thousands	2130.9	891.5
Weekly Inflow (thousands)	48.98	26.16
Weekly Outflow (thousands)	50.42	26.82
Weekly Inflow probability	.0033	.0025
Weekly Outflow probability	.024	.030
Median uncompleted duration (weeks)	40.7	29.7
Mean completed duration (weeks)		
(equation 2.6) from inflow rate	46.4	35.3
(equation 2.6a) from outflow rate	41.7	33.2

Source: Department of Employment Gazette, August 1984
Notes: see Table 2.1

This picture of higher turnover amongst women workers is consistent with a variety of other evidence. Data on the employment outflow rate from manufacturing industries is published by the Department of Employment. This consists of workers who enter the unemployment state as well as other labour market states including other jobs. The weekly probability of leaving a job in March 1984 was .0035 for males and .0048 for females which is a more dramatic difference than the unemployment flow statistics reveal. Analysis of the unemployment inflow data by Junankar and Price (1983) confirms this pattern. In a model designed to explain male and

female inflows separately the constant term is a good
deal larger in the females equation indicating the
higher long run level of labour turnover. Further
confirmation of the higher turnover amongst women is
found by examining data on job tenure which are
directly affected by turnover rates. Main (1981) has
shown that women workers have, on average, job
tenures about half that of men. Metcalf (1984) shows
this also to be the general experience of most
western industrial economies.

It is also evident from Table 2.2 that the
higher labour market turnover amongst women is also
reflected in the outflow probability and the duration
of unemployment. The outflow probability is
significantly higher for women workers and as a
result unemployment duration, however measured, is
significantly lower. Women workers are more likely to
leave a job, more likely to become unemployed but are
also much more likely to obtain alternative
employment than are male workers.

In order to explain this pattern of high labour
market turnover we have to look at the role of women
in the labour force. Hakim (1978) has shown the high
degree of occupational segmentation of women workers
in Britain. Martin and Roberts (1984) confirm this
using data from the 1980 Women and Employment Survey
which reveals that 63% of women were in jobs done
only by women. Many of the jobs into which women are
crowded have a low skill content or the skills are of
general use not specific to a particular firm.
Martin and Roberts also show that of the 73% of women
working in non-manual occupations only 9% had
management or professional jobs. The remainder
performed a variety of lower status jobs. Amongst the
27% of women in manual jobs only 18% were in skilled
occupations. Using the same data source, Ballard
(1984) shows 46% of full-time and 69% of part-time
female employees received no training from their
employer. Even when women undergo education and
general training, Greenhalgh and Stewart (1984) show
they attain occupational levels substantially below
those of comparable men. This is particularly the
case with married women who represent a significant
majority of women in work. This has important effects
on employers' behaviour. Female workers, because of
the jobs they do, possess a low degree of quasi-
fixity. Employers have a smaller investment in human
capital tied up in their female labour force. Because
tenures are shorter, 'learning by doing' which
increases productivity will also be less important.

As a result employers are more willing both to

sack and to tolerate the quitting of a female worker as Robinson and Wallace (1984) have shown. This may be reinforced by a collectively negotiated 'last in first out' rule. Other factors also explain the employers' attitude to women workers. The risk of provoking collective resistance to layoffs is much lower amongst women workers. Women are less likely to be union members than are men and as Daniel and Millward (1983) show are unlikely to take an active part in union business. They are also less likely to act collectively. The Department of Employment's Study 'Strikes in Britain' (1978) finds both strike frequency and days lost to be significantly lower with a predominantly female union than it is for predominantly male unions. (3) The heavy concentration of women in part-time occupations also contributes to the high inflow probability. Layoff costs are lower for part-time workers, who in general, receive no redundancy or other severance pay. Not surprisingly, Bowers, Deaton and Turk (1982) found in their study of labour hoarding in Britain that employment varies more when women in general, and part-time workers, in particular, are present. In a similar vein Dex and Perry (1984) provide evidence that part-time employment exhibits much greater cyclical variation than other types of employment. The fact that women are consigned to lower status occupations also adds to their vulnerability to high turnover for reasons that are considered in the next section. In short, for all these reasons, labour turnover amongst women is less costly to employers. A woman worker is generally easier to replace with a similarly productive alternative and if she is sacked the layoff costs arising from collective resistance by workers or from the payment of redundancy or other severance pay are likely to be low.

High inflow rates for women are also, however, the consequence of supply side factors. The character of jobs that women do makes it easier for a female worker to move between firms and industries. Possessing less firm-specific skills aids mobility and promotes turnover. This also helps to explain the higher outflow probability for women and which is shown in Table 2.2. Unemployed women are also more likely to leave the register. In part this reflects the greater ease with which women are discouraged from job search as a result of which they will withdraw (often temporarily) into non-market work. However, as is evident from the hiring rate in manufacturing, it also represents a greater probability of getting a job. Why? Apart from the factors mentioned above the fact that part-time employment is so important to women workers is of crucial importance. Part-time employment responds much more to fluctuations in output as we have seen. New jobs and vacancies appear more frequently even when output is constant and this leads to higher unemployment outflows for women.

The explanation for the importance of part-time employment in Britain also has both a demand and a supply side dimension. On the demand side, part-time employees are cheaper. Ballard (1984), for example presents data that show hourly earnings are lower for part-time workers. Of even greater importance are the low fixed costs of part-time employment. Ballard shows that significantly more part-time women receive no paid holidays, no sick pay and no occupational pension rights than full-timers. As we have already seen, training and firing costs are also lower. In a period in which fixed labour costs as a share of total labour costs reached 17.7% in 1983 this is a significant incentive to the use of lower fixed cost part-time employment. Part-time labour also provides employers with considerable flexibility in matching labour usage with operational requirements especially in unconventional hours. Robinson and Wallace (1984) report from case studies of 21 organisations that employees believe that the productivity of part-time workers was higher than that of full-time labour. (4) They also show in their studies that took place between 1979 and 1982 that there were no reports of shortages of women willing to accept part-time employment. Of course this reflects the depressed market conditions of that period but it also indicates the importance of supply side factors in the growth of part-time employment. Women want to work and many prefer to work part-time.

The family responsibilities borne by women in our society explain these preferences. The 1980 Women and Employment Survey shows that married women are significantly more likely to work part-time than non-married women and the presence of dependent children was the major factor in determining whether women worked full or part-time. The survey confirms that women want to work, accept that working is beneficial and not just for the income derived from work. However, "paid employment was rarely there as a central life interest. It is accommodated to and balanced with domestic demands and for most women takes a secondary role in their lives to family commitment" (Martin and Roberts) (1984). Of course the constraint on womens' labour force behaviour also

41

helps to explain the high turnover amongst women workers who more frequently change jobs to accommodate their family commitments. The result is also a greater readiness to enter non-employment than men. As we have seen, Stewart and Greenhalgh (1984) show the typical woman aged 45-54 has only worked for less than two-thirds of the total possible working life. This is despite the fact that the speed with which these women returned to work after child-birth was at an all time high. (5)

Most of these interruptions result from family exigencies but some do occur after a spell of unemployment. It is not unreasonable to conjecture that in a period of exceptionally high unemployment a greater proportion of interruptions to the working lives of women will result from enforced non-employment. Whatever their cause, Stewart and Greenhalgh also show that these interruptions to women's work experience contribute to the explanation of the fact, observed earlier, that women, given their qualifications and training, attain a lower occupational status than men and this contributes directly to their higher unemployment turnover. In other words, high unemployment flows have effects on job tenures that are self reinforcing. Women who experience current high inflow and outflow probabilities will find this leads to the same experience in future periods.

In summary, family role specialisation (or marital status discrimination (6)) is a critical feature of womens' position in the labour force. It leads to women being consigned to lower status, part-time, higher turnover jobs. Of course, the position of women in work is not only the result of family role specialisation. Sex discrimination per se is also an important feature of women's work experience. (7) Stewart and Greenhalgh for example, show single women earn less and attain a lower occupational status than comparable men. It would not be surprising if their vulnerability to higher turnover and lower job tenure were not also partly explicable in terms of discriminatory behaviour by employers and fellow male workers, despite the terms and conditions of the Sex Discrimination Act which outlawed such behaviour in Britain.

Stocks, Flows and Duration by Occupations

Although the Department of Employment has published (from the monthly count) data on the number unemployed by occupational category, it does not provide unemployment rates. Further the recently published flow data used in the construction of Tables 2.1 and 2.2. do not include information broken down by occupation. Instead we need to rely on calculations performed by Nickell (1980) and Stern (1983). Both use survey data and relate to male workers only although some of the results are relevant to the position of women and which we considered in the last section. It is also possible to construct unemployment rates for males by occupation using the 1982 General Household Survey. This is done in Table 2.3 which shows the enormous disparity in unemployment incidence with a clear inverse association between rates of unemployment and occupational status. One problem with the GHS as a data source is the small size of the sample upon which it is based. The error that arises as a result affects the accuracy of the data in Table 2.3 but is unlikely to affect the ranking by occupation. Nickell (1980) employs a method (8) that attempts to correct for this problem and for the fact that other factors may explain the difference which we observe. In fact Nickell's results using the 1972 GHS reveal the same disparity and the same ranking by occupation as that shown in Table 2.3 for 1982. When he allows for health, qualifications, years of schooling, marital status, number of children, age, wife's labour force participation, region and housing status to calculate a <u>ceteris paribus</u> unemployment rate the disparities narrow but the ranking is unaltered and the differences that do remain are still large.

Information on inflow rates has recently been provided by Stern (1983) for 1978 and by Nickell (1980) for 1972. Table 2.3 contains the data for 1978 which Stern derives from the DHSS Cohort Study of the Unemployed which took place in Autumn 1978. The numerator for the calculation of the inflow rates (α_t) is obtained from that source and divided by data from the GHS and the Family Expenditure Survey (FES). It shows that the difference in unemployment incidence is significantly due to difference in the inflow probability. The calculated inflow probabilities are eleven times as large for unskilled manual workers as they are for senior non-manual. On an annual basis there is approximately a one in two chance that an unskilled manual worker will become unemployed. The only point at which the ranking of unemployment rates and unemployment inflows do not correspond is in the case of skilled manual workers for whom the inflow probability is the same as junior non-manuals yet the unemployment rate is higher. The

43

explanation for this is to be found in the different dates at which this data is available. The proportion of the male unemployed who were skilled rose from 14.7% in March 1978 to 19.4% in 1982. The skilled manual worker was strongly affected by the plant closures and redundancies of 1981/2 and this is reflected in the stock data (and presumably the inflow data if we had it for 1982). Confirmation for this can be found in Nickell's (1980) study for 1972 where there is an exact correspondence in the ranking of unemployment rates and inflow probabilities by occupation. (9)

Table 2.3 Stocks, Flows and Duration by Occupation Males

Occupational category	Unemployment (%)	Weekly Inflow Probability (α_t)	Weekly Outflow Probability (θ_t)	Mean Completed Duration (weeks)
Senior and Intermediate Non-Manual	4.4	.0009	.081	12.3
Junior Non-Manual	7.2	.002	.061	16.3
Skilled Manual	11.7	.002	.065	15.3
Semi-skilled Manual	17.6	.003	.058	17.1
Unskilled Manual	34.8	.010	.056	17.8

Source: General Household Survey 1982. Stern (1983) and Nickell (1980)
Notes: Unemployment Stock is for 1982. The Weekly Inflow probability is for 1978 and the outflow for 1972. Further details are in the text and in notes (8)-(10).

We could calculate the mean completed duration using the stock and the flow data contained in Table 2.3. Since, however, they are for different years and there is a suspicion that the inflow rates for some groups (e.g. the skilled) are too low (lower than 1982) this would produce a rather inaccurate statistic. Instead Table 2.3 contains the outflow probabilities and the mean completed duration derived from them (using equation 2.6a) from Nickell (1980). Although this data relates to 1972 and the values of θ_t are rather large by current standards the ranking by occupation is unlikely to have changed significantly and it is this which is of interest.

Nickell calculates the outflow (re-employment) probability from a sample of 7,492 men over the age of 18 of whom 4.5% were unemployed. He takes account of individual worker characteristics so that it is possible to calculate the outflow (re-employment) probability for an individual in a given week of an unemployment spell, conditional on the particular characteristics of that worker including occupation. This can be done, using the information in the survey which shows the weeks of unemployment of individuals with any particular characteristics, as long as other characteristics are allowed for. (10) Once this re-employment probability is known the expected completed duration for individuals with particular (occupational) characteristics can be calculated. This is also shown in Table 2.3 together with the associated value of the outflow probability (θ_t).

Although the duration figures reveal that the re-employment prospects of unemployed manual workers are generally inferior to their non-manual counterparts (11) the differences are not so pronounced as on the inflow side, which is clearly the dominant source of explanation of the difference in unemployment incidence by occupation. Indeed, the mean duration of unemployment of skilled manuals is less than that of junior non-manuals. How do these differences occur? From the demand side the most obvious explanation is the differential degree of specific training in which firms have invested. We have shown in chapter one how firms seek to amortise their investment in human capital and how as a result certain types of labour are 'quasi-fixed'. It is obvious that firms invest little in their unskilled labour force so their employment is much more likely to be varied by employers. (12) Other explanations rely upon the degree of managerial control of the modern large corporation. This leads to the preservation of jobs for the so-called 'salariat' of white collar workers. Manual workers are far more likely to lose their jobs and be replaced in normal times. Hence their higher turnover. In times of depression, redundancy and layoffs are likely to be even less concentrated on non-manual workers. The stock data for 1982 seems to confirm that view. It is

45

consistent with a major increase in the inflow probability (especially of skilled manual workers) in 1981/2.

On the supply side the nature of unskilled jobs with their low levels of job satisfaction and psychic income are also suggested as explanations of the high degree of turnover amongst the unskilled manual labour force. Radical economists have also pointed to the class system of industrial economies and the position of those who perform manual and especially unskilled work within the wider society. In other words, the pattern of unemployment experience by occupational group reflects in the same way as by sex, the pattern of employment, the structure of the economic system and the wider society.

Stocks, Flows and Duration by Age

The Department of Employment has recently started to publish unemployment rates by age and for males these are shown in Table 2.4. They reveal substantial differences in the rates of unemployment. Comparable flow and duration data is now available and is shown in Table 2.4 for male workers. Again there are marked disparities in the unemployment rates with the oldest (over 50) and the youngest (under 24) experiencing the highest rates. The flow/duration composition of these highest male unemployment age groups are, however, very different. As Table 2.4 reveals, the youngest age groups are characterised by high turnover (high inflows, high outflows and short durations). In fact the shortest spells of unemployment are experienced by the young and the duration of unemployment increases with age. The inflow probability also falls with age until it levels off for the 45 and over age group. In other words the degree of labour turnover falls with age (13) and the high levels of unemployment of the oldest workers is largely the result of a low outflow (re-employment) probability. (14)

The correlation of turnover with age is not difficult to explain. Amongst young workers their low level of specific human capital increases employers' propensity to sack them. Like women, their short job tenures make this a low cost policy for the typical firm. Layoff costs in the form of redundancy payments or collective resistance will be small or even zero. On the supply side, young workers are less constrained by family commitments and responsibilities than prime age and to a lesser extent older (over 50) men. They are freer to sample jobs in an

46

attempt to find employment in a firm that suits them since their high outflow probability indicates a greater willingness of employers to hire them. If they suit the employer has a longer time period over which to recoup any investment he might make and if they don't, layoff is easy and cheap as we have seen.

Amongst older workers the position is different. As workers age the greater is the probability they will have moved up the hierarchy of jobs within their place of employment. Many of these jobs in the internal labour market (15) will not be accessible to outsiders. There will, as a result, be prime age and older workers who, if they changed jobs, would take a cut in pay or in non-pay benefits. Often membership of an occupational pension scheme with non-transferable pension rights or with a minimum number of years of service before entry is permitted will be a significant factor in limiting the mobility of older workers. Family commitments, especially for prime age males will also reduce the propensity to quit. On the demand side, prime age males are more likely to embody a substantial degree of non-amortised specific human capital investment. Learning by doing which enhances productivity is also likely to be at a peak. This will significantly reduce the layoff probability of prime age males which will be reinforced by the higher layoff costs. Redundancy payments which are related to years of service and the possibility of collective resistance will have important effects in this respect. Confirmation for this can also be found in the study by Stern (1983). He shows, using the 1978 DHSS Cohort Study that inflow probabilities are clearly and significantly lower for workers with job tenures greater than one year. Among these workers there is also a less marked but nonetheless clear inverse association between job tenure and inflow probabilities. Since prime age workers are heavily concentrated with individuals with long job tenures, their low inflow probability is unsurprising. However, with the oldest group of male workers there is some change in the pattern as Table 2.4 shows. Their inflow probability is higher (16) than prime age males. Given their outflow probability a high quit rate is an implausible explanation of this. More significant is the heavy concentration of redundancy upon older workers. The study by Mackay (1972) noted in respect of the engineering industry in the Midlands that "those declared redundant tended to be older workers with longer periods of service". Further support comes from the Department of

47

Employment (1978) who conclude that redundancy acts "as a social mechanism to remove from the labour force older people nearing retirement after long service by means of comparatively generous compensation." Nickell (1980) emphasises the desire by employers to get rid of low productivity older workers but others (17) have emphasised the fact that since redundancy payments are most generous (and relatively cheap for employers (18)) to older long service employees the collective resistance of trade unions to any redundancy proposal is undermined.

Table 2.4 Stocks, Flows and Duration by Age. Males 1984

Age Group	Un-employ-ment (%)	Weekly Inflow Probab-ility	Weekly Outflow Probab-ility	Mean Completed Duration (weeks) (from out-flow rate)	Median Un-completed Duration (weeks)
Under 18	20.4	.0098	.039	25.6	19.9
18-19	28.8	.0068	.026	38.5	31.7
20-24	22.3	.0053	.026	38.5	36.0
25-29	16.3	.0037	.025	40.0	41.7
30-34	12.7	.0027	.024	41.7	47.4
35-44	12.4	.0025	.023	43.5	51.1
45-54	11.8	.0020	.018	55.6	59.8
55-59	16.6	.0021	.011	90.9	64.7
60 and over	24.25	.0023	.012	83.3	70.4

Source: Department of Employment Gazette
Notes: Data for the 60 and over age group were corrected by the ratio of this age group and the 55-59 age group in 1983

The outflow probability for males declines with age particularly after 45 and is the most important source of long term unemployment among older workers. (19) The reasons for this are not difficult to find.

The study by Jolly, Mingay and Creigh (1978) reveals that 24% of all vacancies specify an upper age limit of 50. There are simply more jobs from which older workers are barred because many employers believe they are not worth training because of their short prospective working life and greater resistance to change. There is also the belief that productivity declines with old age and so a younger worker is invariably preferred. A survey by the Department of Employment (1974) showed 80% of the unemployed aged over 55 have poor prospects of obtaining long term work. The study of male manual unemployed workers in Scotland by McGregor (1980) confirms this. It reveals that those aged 50 and over have significantly lower re-employment probabilities and consequently longer unemployment durations than prime age (30-49) males. Similarly Knight and Stewart (1982) have shown that in any upturn in the economy, older (over 50) workers are much less likely to be hired so their relative unemployment rate rises. With these factors in mind, it is not difficult to explain the low turnover of the oldest members of the male labour force.

Stocks, Flows and Duration by Personal Characteristic and Income

Nickell (1980) found the unemployment experience of individuals also varies in response to certain demographic factors. Of particular importance is marital status. Married men have a rate of unemployment half that of unmarried (3.8% compared with 7.3%). Although married men are less likely to be unemployed with a weekly inflow rate of .002 compared with .0024 for unmarried (20) the main cause of the difference in unemployment experience is that unmarried men are unemployed for much longer (19.6 weeks compared with 15.3 weeks on average). This is confirmed by McGregor (1980) and Narendrenathan, Nickell and Stern (1985) who show the re-employment probabilities of unemployed married men to be higher, reducing (in the latter study) the expected length of a spell of unemployment by 6.3 weeks. Family responsibilities apparently not only increase the incentive to work on the supply side but also the willingness to employ by employers who believe married men (especially of prime age) to be more reliable and potentially more productive.

However, Nickell's (1980) study also reveals that unemployment rates increase significantly with family size. The unemployment rate is 10.3% for men with 4 children and this high rate results both from a higher rate of flow into unemployment (0.43% per week) than married men as a whole but also a longer period of unemployment (17.8 weeks) on average. (21) One obvious explanation for this is that the unemployment benefit system is relatively more generous to those with large families, but as Nickell says:

the benefit explanation does not hold much water
because the variations in unemployment
incidence with family size are due, in large
part, to variations in the chances of entering
unemployment and not to variations in duration.

These are matters to which we return in chapter
seven. By way of alternative, Nickell notes the
relationship between personal alienation and
fertility from the work of Neal and Groat (1970), and
between alienation and unemployment (Kohn (1976))
but this remains speculative. Stern (1979) concludes
after examining Nickell's work that

> It may be that the unskilled unemployed with
> large families are a group who tend to suffer
> multiple social deprivations, many of which
> were not variables available in his data.

One aspect of these potential social deprivations
which Nickell does consider, is housing. However he
only examines one dimension, namely the form of
tenure. He finds those living in the rented sector
have an unemployment rate significantly higher than
the owner occupier (6.8% compared with 1.9%). Stern
(1983) finds that this arises partly from the greater
inflow probability of tenants while Narendrenathan,
Nickell and Stern (1985) show it also arises from a
lower re-employment probability and higher expected
duration of employment. It is difficult to conclude
much from these results except that insofar as the
form of tenure is likely to be correlated with the
degree of general social deprivation, Stern's view
seems appropriate.

One critical factor that Nickell does not allow
for in his analysis is race. In Britain, government
departments have been remarkably reluctant to
publish relevant data on a racial basis. This
contrasts with the US where the high level of
unemployment amongst blacks has been the subject of
considerable analysis. Some indication of the impact
of racial origin on unemployment experience in
Britain is provided by a recently published study by
the Department of Employment (1984) using data from
the 1981 Labour Force Survey. Unfortunately, only
information relating to the stock of unemployment is
published and this is shown in Table 2.5.

It is clear from Table 2.5 that unemployment is
considerably higher for non-white workers. The
differences are more pronounced in the case of men,
especially those of Caribbean origin. This is a

similar conclusion to that obtained by Barber (1980) using data for 1977-78. The differences for young males are even more dramatic. In the 16-24 age group 18% of whites were out of work in 1981 while the comparable figures for youths of Caribbean origin were 38% and 25% for those of Indian, Pakistani or Bangladeshi origin. (22) The unemployment rates for young women are lower and exhibit less diversity especially in the case of those of Caribbean origin. Unfortunately there is no comparable flow data. (23) As far as inflows are concerned the fact that unemployment of non-whites varies more than among whites, is consistent with a higher inflow probability but there is no direct evidence for this. Lynch (1983), (1984) provides some evidence about outflow probabilities amongst young blacks in London. She finds in Lynch (1984) that the outflow probability for young blacks is significantly lower than comparable whites. This confirms the US evidence of Clark and Summers (1982) who show young white unemployed males are three times as likely to become re-employed as their non-white counterparts. The effects on the expected duration of unemployment are quite dramatic. According to Lynch's calculation, being non-white adds 31.4 weeks to the expected length of a spell of youth unemployment in London.

Table 2.5 Unemployment rates by ethnic origin 1981

	White	West Indian or Guyanese	Indian, Pakistani Bangladeshi	Other	All Ethnic Origins
Male	9.7	20.6	16.9	13.9	9.9
Female	8.7	14.5	17.9	14.7	8.9

Source: Department of Employment Gazette, June 1984

How do we explain these differences? There is little evidence that demonstrates that they arise on the supply side. Indeed there is some evidence that supply side factors understate (via greater registration bias) the extent of the differences especially as far as Asians are concerned. Lynch (1983) shows that non-white young workers are just as likely to accept a job offer as whites and are indeed prepared to accept it at a lower wage. There is no evidence that suggests that adult blacks do not share the same willingness to work despite the low expectations of the return from it.

Some clues may be obtained from looking at the position of non-whites in the labour force. Mayhew and Rosewall (1979) have shown substantial occupational crowding amongst non-white groups. Quoting a study by PEP they show only 8% of West Indians are employed in non-manual occupations compared with 40% of whites. We have already seen the significantly greater liabilities to unemployment of manual workers. Indian and Africans of Asian descent are less concentrated in manual jobs but still do less well than whites. Recent data provided by Brown (1984) shows a growth in the proportion of West Indians in non-manual occupations (15%) but still significantly less than whites (32%) and Asians (26%). Mayhew and Rosewall relate this occupational crowding partly to a generally low level of educational attainment among non-whites, but they also conclude "Job discrimination, as well as supply-side factors contribute to the crowding experienced by social minorities."

There are regrettably few attempts by economists to assess the form and extent of labour market discrimination in Britain although others have documented the facts of the relative economic position of non-whites in Britain with considerable clarity. Of particular importance in this respect is the work of Smith (1976) and Brown (1984) and recent work published in the Department of Employment Gazette (1983, 1984). One recent study that presents quantitative evidence on the extent of job discrimination in Britain is that of Stewart (1983). Using data from the 1975 National Training Survey, Stewart is able to correct for characteristics of black workers other than their ethnic origin and thereby to estimate more accurately the extent of racial discrimination in Britain. This is revealed to be a significant feature of the results. Given their educational and other characteristics, Stewart shows that black male workers earn less (between 9% and 17% less) and receive a much lower return for any further non-statutory education they undertake than whites. Stewart also shows that between 75% and 100% of this differential is due to differences in occupational status. There is clear evidence that although black males move up earnings scales within occupations in the same way as whites, they are much less likely to secure access to higher level occupations. Given the relationship between unemployment experience and occupational status the high unemployment of blacks

Table 2.6 Stocks, Flows and Duration by Region: Males 1984

Region	Unemploy-ment (%)	Weekly Inflow Probab-ility	Weekly Outflow Probab-ility	Mean Completed Duration (weeks) (from out-flow rate)	Mean Un-completed Duration (weeks)
South-East	11.4	.0030	.028	35.7	34.3
Gtr London	11.9	.0030	.025	40.0	36.6
East Anglia	11.9	.0032	.028	35.7	33.0
South-West	13.1	.0034	.028	35.7	32.4
West Midlands	17.7	.0030	.019	52.6	54.0
East Midlands	14.4	.0032	.024	41.7	37.9
Yorkshire & Humberside	16.6	.0034	.022	45.5	41.6
North-West	19.4	.0035	.020	50.0	48.5
North	21.5	.0041	.020	50.0	47.1
Wales	19.2	.0036	.020	50.0	43.1
Scotland	18.1	.0039	.025	40.0	42.3

Source: Department of Employment Gazette, August 1984

is a good deal easier to understand. They are more likely to be consigned to low occupational status, high unemployment prone jobs.

In fact the discrimination against non-white workers may go beyond this. Recent work by the Department of Employment shows black workers are more likely to experience unemployment after correcting for age and occupation. In other words within their generally lower status occupation black workers are more likely to become unemployed and less likely to become re-employed elsewhere in the same occupation. Of course, racial (like sex) discrimination may be understated by these results. If, as many educationists (Coard (1981) and Carby (1982)) argue blacks receive less and lower quality education because of discrimination, this may reduce their occupational status further and hence increase their chances of unemployment. However, even without taking account of this effect it is clear that the high unemployment of blacks in Britain is partly the outcome of discriminatory behaviour.

Stocks, Flows and Duration by Location

A great deal of analysis of the geographical differences in unemployment experience has actually taken place in Britain. In Table 2.6 stocks, flows and duration by region are shown. In general, the high unemployment regions are characterised by high inflow and low outflow rates. The exceptions are Scotland which has a high inflow and outflow probability for males (24) and the West Midlands which has a low value for both. Scotland is now a buoyant labour market characterised by high turnover while the West Midlands is relatively stagnant and characterised by low turnover.

The explanation of these differences in regional unemployment rates has been the subject of considerable research. (25) The central question that has occupied researchers has been whether the high unemployment of certain regions is the outcome of a heavy concentration of declining industries or of particular regional causes that affect employment in all industries of a region. Typical of the conclusions that are generally reached can be found in the study by Cheshire (1973). Cheshire allows for the industrial structure of each region by calculating a standardised unemployment rate

$$2.7 \quad U_r^{s1} = \sum_{i=1}^{j} U_{ir} E_{in}$$

where

U = unemployment rate
E = proportion of employed labour force
r = region
i = industries
n = national

This measure assumes each region has the national industrial structure but its own unemployment rate for the j industries in the region. Cheshire compares this standardised rate with the actual rate and finds the differences to be small. In other words assuming a common industrial structure for each region still leaves major differences in unemployment rates to be explained. Cheshire tests for the impact of regional economic effects by calculating a second standardised unemployment rate.

$$2.8 \qquad U_r^{s2} = \sum_{i=1}^{j} Ui_n \, Ei_r$$

In this case, the standardised rate is calculated by assuming national unemployment rates prevail in all of the industries of a region. The region's own industrial structure is assumed. Cheshire finds that this rate is significantly different from the actual rate for each region and the inter-regional variance in unemployment rates almost disappears. This evidence is therefore quite clear. Since even industries with low unemployment levels nationally have high unemployment in high unemployment regions the differences in unemployment rates by region have far more to do with other characteristics of each region's economy than its industrial structure.

Some research suggests that the composition of the region's labour force is important. Cheshire found that the proportion of the labour force who are unskilled and registered as disabled was higher in the higher unemployment regions. Confirmation for this comes from Metcalf (1975) in a study of differences in urban unemployment in Britain. He finds that high unemployment towns have both a greater percentage of unskilled workers and of older workers. We have already seen the greater unemployment propensity of those groups of workers and of their heavy concentration among the long term unemployed. To some extent this reflects the high level of net emigration of workers from the depressed high unemployment regional economies. Research by

McNabb (1979), for example, has shown migrants are typically skilled and young and so in the depressed regions there is bound to be a higher proportion of unemployment prone workers. However, it is clear that all this is a response to the state of the regional economy. High unemployment regions are characterised both by slow growth in employment and in output. The reasons for this are explored in Dixon and Thirlwall (1976) and in the text by Armstrong and Taylor (1978). We shall return to the question of the role of output and its rate of growth in the explanation of high unemployment in later chapters.

The previous sections of this chapter have indicated the extent to which unemployment is concentrated amongst certain types of worker. Now we consider the degree of concentration of unemployment amongst certain individuals within these unemployment prone categories of worker.

Repeat Spells and Occurrence Dependence

One further difficulty with the use of equation 2.6 and 2.6a to calculate the completed duration of unemployment is that it may well understate the total unemployment experience of unemployed workers and thereby underestimate the full costs of unemployment. It tells us the expected length of a single spell of unemployment but if those individuals who experience unemployment are more likely to experience <u>future</u> unemployment the degree of understatement could be serious. The possibility that an individual who has experienced past unemployment having a greater probability of experiencing current or future unemployment is called occurrence dependence by Heckman and Borjas (1980).

One fact that points towards the importance of occurrence dependence is that repeat spells of unemployment are very likely for those currently unemployed. Using DHSS data Moylan and Davies (1980) show that of males registering for unemployment benefit in late 1978, two-thirds had already experienced at least one previous spell of unemployment in that year. This confirms the results of Disney (1979) who, using DHSS data for 1971-73 examines the unemployment experience of 3 cohorts born in 1928, 1938 and 1948. Disney calculates the mean spell of unemployment to be 1.1 for the 1928 cohort and 1.5 for the 1948 cohort. He also finds further evidence for occurrence dependence by estimating the probability of a second spell of unemployment for those currently unemployed and finds it to be greater than the probability of a first spell for the cohort as a whole, i.e. "unemployment breeds unemployment" (page 111).

Stern (1984) has also provided more recent evidence for the importance of repeat spells in Britain using data from the 1978 DHSS Cohort Study of the Unemployed. He finds 26% of the men whose first spell of unemployment lasted less than 6 months had a repeat spell within 6 months of the end of their first spell and 55% of those whose first spell lasted less than 12 months had at least one more spell within 12 months of the end of their first spell. Stern estimates a logit model of the probability of a repeat spell of unemployment for men with initial spells lasting between 1 and 6 and 1 and 12 months. In both cases having had a spell of registered unemployment in the 12 months previous to the beginning of the current spell had a significant positive impact on the probability of a repeat spell of around .1. In a similar vein Creedy and Disney (1981) find that even individuals who are currently fully employed in a year are more likely to experience unemployment if they have previously been out of work.

These results contrast with those of the US found by Heckman and Borjas (1980). They use a sample of workers for the US and find no evidence for the scarring effect of previous unemployment experience on the job prospects of those currently employed. The difference in results may reflect different labour market behaviour but it may also result from Heckman and Borjas's use of a sample of young workers. High turnover is, as we saw earlier in this chapter, a characteristic of this group. Employers expect greater job instability amongst the young who are less likely to find their job chances unfavourably affected by a spell or even frequent spells of previous employment.

Who are the individuals likely to experience this spell recurrence? Disney (1981) and Stern (1984) provide some evidence. Not surprisingly, individuals possessing characteristics identifying them as members of high inflow probability groups (e.g. young unmarried and manual) are vulnerable. Over and above these factors the lack of educational qualification appears to be important and this is consistent with the general picture that emerges from work by McGregor (1980) who finds in a study of a local labour market in Scotland that workers from a particularly deprived area have a higher incidence of repeat spells of unemployment after correcting for age, occupation and marital status, and he concludes:

> The significance of areas of urban deprivation is that they highlight a more fundamental problem of the uneven incidence of unemployment across different sub-groups of the labour force.

In other words spell recurrence is part of a package of social deprivation that affects certain individuals within particular groups of the labour force. Not surprisingly McGregor shows these individuals have relatively less stable employment histories. This question has also been explored by Main (1981) using the New Earnings Survey information collected by the Department of Employment. He finds that of those currently employed the average male has had his job for 20 years while the comparable figure for females is 12 years. This contrasts with his estimate of previous job tenure for those currently unemployed of $3\frac{1}{2}$ years for males and just over 2 years for females.

It is clear that spell recurrence is a major feature of unemployment in Britain. The calculation of the mean duration of unemployment may, as a result, not only be an underestimate of the total time spent out of work within a year but also over longer periods. Certain individuals experience repeated unemployment over their working lives so that the lifetime distribution of unemployment experience is even more unequal than is suggested by the single period, single spell analysis conducted in this chapter. What remains unclear is whether this is a result of the scarring effects of spell recurrence (occurrence dependence) or the effect of some unobserved characteristic of the individuals concerned. The evidence is consistent with the former but doubts remain because of this unobserved heterogeneity and so the latter remains a competing explanation for the repeat spell phenomenon.

The fact of spell recurrence is important in explaining the heavy concentration of unemployment upon certain (especially younger) individuals in Britain. Disney (1979) shows this for the period 1971-73. Of workers born in 1928, 85% experienced no unemployment over this period. The comparable figure for those born in 1938 and 1948 was 89%. Amongst the older workers this concentration reflects the long duration of spells of unemployment as well as spell recurrence. In the case of younger (born in 1948) workers, Disney finds the heavy concentration of unemployment experience is almost entirely the result of spell recurrence only.

Although unemployment is now a good deal higher and more workers are affected, it remains true that unemployment experience is highly concentrated amongst certain individuals. A not unreasonable conjecture would be that this is, to a greater extent than a decade ago, the result of long durations rather than spell recurrence. Inequality in unemployment experience, however, remains the norm.

Stocks, Flows and Duration – Cyclical Variation

So far in this chapter we have examined cross-section patterns of unemployment. Now we shall consider the variation over time in stocks, flows and duration. In this section we will concentrate on cyclical variation. Unfortunately the data employed in Table 2.1 is available only for the recent past. Instead it is necessary to rely upon estimates using published data on flows and the stock of employed and unemployed workers in each year. Details of the unemployment stocks, flows and duration are contained in Table 2.7. This covers the period 1972 and 1984 but in this section we will concentrate on cyclical variations and in general use 1979 and 1981 as examples of boom and recession years respectively.

Obviously the stock of unemployment is much lower in 1979. Although by post-war standards the boom was modest and recession of 1981 was severe, the differences between the two years are qualitatively typical. As far as males are concerned, unemployment inflows and the duration of employment are both significantly higher in the recession years. However the cyclical movement of the expected duration is much more marked than the inflow rate because of the greater variability of the outflow rate (θ_t). This reflects the fact that the probability of re-employment falls much more rapidly than the probability of becoming unemployed rises in a recession as Table 2.7 shows. In fact in previous recessions the difference is even more pronounced. 1981 was a remarkable year in terms of the rate at which the inflow probability increased. It increased by approximately a third for males compared with an increase of about a fifth between 1973 (boom) and 1975 (slump).

As far as female workers are concerned the general pattern is similar. The problem with Table 2.7 is that because of registration bias it

Table 2.7 Stocks, Flows and Duration by Sex 1972-84 Great Britain

	Unemployment (thousands)		Inflow Probability (α_t)		Outflow Probability (θ_t)		Mean completed Duration (weeks)	
	males	females	males	females	males	females	males	females
1972	686	122	.0037	.0022	.1091	.1509	9.2	6.6
1973	504	96	.0033	.0018	.0995	.1776	10.0	5.6
1974	488	90	.0036	.0018	.1031	.1821	9.7	5.5
1975	716	154	.0039	.0021	.0652	.1134	15.3	8.8
1976	949	254	.0036	.0022	.0542	.0779	18.5	12.8
1977	974	303	.0032	.0021	.0424	.0592	24.6	16.9
1978	943	325	.0031	.0022	.0483	.0631	20.7	15.8
1979	855	322	.0029	.0022	.0513	.066	19.5	15.1
1980	1008	396	.0034	.0026	.0387	.055	25.8	18.1
1981	1725	600	.0038	.0028	.0243	.040	41.1	25.0
1982	1974	696	.0036	.0029	.0235	.038	42.6	26.5
1983	2055	800	.0034	.0024	.0262	.033	38.2	30.0
1984	2042	878	.0032	.0024	.0249	.030	40.2	33.3

Source: Department of Employment Gazette August 1984, January 1983, June 1980
Notes: 1 Unemployment is calculated on a claimant basis and is seasonally adjusted
         2 The mean completed duration is calculated from outflow data using equation 2.6a. The
           trend is almost the same if we calculate equation 2.6 using inflow data

understates the degree of cyclical variation in female unemployment. Comparing 1979 and 1981 also presents problems because of the untypically large scale of male job loss and redundancy in 1981. If we compare 1973 and 1975 it is possible to see more clearly the greater cyclical variation of female employment. The data in Table 2.7 implies this is the result of a greater variability in the outflow rate (unaffected by registration bias) but recall that the inflow probability (α_t) calculated using published statistics is, for women, a severe underestimate of the employment to unemployment flow.

Confirmation of the usual cyclical behaviour of male and female unemployment comes from a recent study of unemployment flows in Britain by Junankar and Price (1983). Using data from 1967 to 1980 they estimate a model of inflows and outflows (26) from which it is possible to measure the response of flows to positive (booms) and negative (slumps) deviations from the trend of GNP. Overall, Junankar and Price show the outflow rate (probability) decreases more in slump than the inflow rate increases. However, when females are considered separately, the response of the outflow rate to slump is actually similar to males but the inflow rate is more than twice as large, i.e. it rises (falls) twice as much as the equivalent male rate in slumps (booms). This reflects the greater probability of job loss and the consequent higher level of turnover amongst female workers, the reasons for which we explored earlier in this chapter.

When we examine the age composition we again see that the high turnover groups in cross section also experience much greater cyclical sensitivity of unemployment (and employment). Cyclical movements in the age composition have been explored in a number of studies. Layard (1982) and the Department of Employment (1978) show that in recession (boom) there is a marked increase (decrease) in the relative unemployment of young workers. A study by Knight and Stewart (1982) shows a low degree of cyclical variation in the unemployment of older (55 and over) workers. Their relative unemployment falls (rises) in slumps (booms) because of the cyclical sensitivity of unemployment amongst the young. From the employment side a study by Hutchinson, Barr and Drobny (1984) estimates an employment function of the general type outlined in the previous chapter and finds that the employment/output elasticity for young workers exceeds unity. In other words, for every one per cent change in output there is a greater than one per cent change in the level of youth employment.

The recently published time series on flows by age is not long enough to provide us with the direct information on the flow/duration composition of unemployment that we require. Some clues can be obtained from the work of Bowers and Harkess (1979) who find the expected duration of unemployment increases for all age groups in recession (the re-employment probability falls). The reduction is greatest for younger workers but the difference is not so great that we can reject the conclusion that both inflow and outflow probabilities are most cyclically variable for younger workers.

Table 2.8 contains data relating to the cyclical movement in the stock of unemployed by occupation in boom and recession. Unfortunately in the absence of relevant data we do not know the flow/duration make-up of these cyclical changes. Once again we can see that the degree of cyclical sensitivity of the stock of unemployed by occupation group is closely related to the extent of turnover observed in cross section. We saw that the high turnover occupational groups were manual. These are precisely the types of workers whose unemployment goes up in the recession more than in proportion to unemployment as a whole. We can see in Table 2.8 the extent to which the relative unemployment rates of manual workers has risen in the recent recession in Britain. Because of the extent of redundancy (permanent job loss) and plant closure which affects all workers, the movement is less marked in this recession. Between 1973 (boom) and 1975 (recession) for example manual worker unemployment rose from 78% to 82.6% of the total. The principal reason for these cyclical patterns in unemployment is the differential propensity of firms to hoard non-manual and manual workers in recession for reasons explored both earlier in this chapter and in chapter one.

Table 2.8: Relative unemployment (as % of total) of manual and non-manual workers, 1979-1981

		1979	1981
Manual Unemployment	males	79.3	81.3
	females	43.6	44.7
Non-Manual Unemployment	males	20.7	22.7
	females	56.4	55.3

Source: Department of Employment Gazette
Notes: These data are for September in each year.

The regional pattern of unemployment also exhibits a high degree of cyclical sensitivity. Thirlwall (1966) showed in the sixties a tendency for the absolute numbers unemployed in the high unemployment regions to rise by more in recession than in the low unemployment regions. In this and subsequent work with Harris (1968) Thirlwall has explored the extent to which this greater degree of cyclical sensitivity is related to a heavier concentration of cyclically sensitive industries. He found this to be a less convincing explanation than that relying upon the different cyclical sensitivity of the regional economies as a whole. This has been further explored by Bell and Hart (1980) who find that the employment elasticity of output estimated from a conventional employment function is significantly higher in both the short and long run in the development areas (high unemployment) of Britain. In other words if output were to fall (rise) by an identical amount in all regions, employment would fall (rise) to the greatest extent in the development areas. Why should this be the case? The most convincing explanation is that the different labour market responses of employers in boom and slump reflect differences in the propensity to hoard labour. As we saw in chapter one, the decision to hoard labour in a recession is directly related to fixed labour costs in general but of importance in this context are the lower costs of hiring and firing in the more depressed regions of Britain. There is less resistance to firing and re-hiring is easier given the secular "looseness" of the regional labour market. The result is that fluctuations in output evoke a stronger response in the labour market of those regions than in the secularly tighter labour market of the south of England.

There are, therefore, clear differences in the cyclical sensitivity of unemployment by both occupation and region in Britain. Data limitations prevent a proper analysis of the inflow/duration patterns but the differences that do exist are closely related to the observed pattern in cross section. Of particular importance in explaining these differences is the variation in the propensity and incentive to hoard labour in recession.

Finally, if we examine cyclical variation in unemployment by race, we note the same tendency for the high unemployment/high turnover groups to do worse in recession. Between 1979 and 1981, for example, unemployed minority group workers in Britain as a proportion of the total, rose from 3.7%

to 4.2%. Now we turn to the examination of long run trends in British unemployment experience.

Stocks, Flows and Duration – Long Term Trends

Table 2.7 shows data on the stocks, flows and duration of unemployment for the years 1972 to 1984. As far as males are concerned the major feature of this table is that despite the marked upward trend in the size of the stock which we noted in chapter one the inflow rates do not show any similar trend. (27) The upward trend of male unemployment in Britain is not the result of a greater tendency to become unemployed but rather a greater tendency to stay unemployed. The duration of unemployment in boom and slump has risen as the re-employment probability of unemployed workers has secularly declined. This is why there is a growing problem of long term unemployment in Britain. In 1984, 43.5% of male unemployed workers had been out of work for more than a year. This compares with 23.5% in 1974 and 16.6% in 1968. The reasons for this trend are explored in later chapters where we will examine both supply and demand side explanations in some detail.

The trend in female unemployment is different from males. Male unemployment started rising in the mid-sixties but until the mid-seventies, unemployment amongst women remained low despite the significant growth in female (especially married female) labour force participation. It is since the mid-seventies that the unemployment position of female workers has deteriorated. Comparison of the boom years of 1973 and 1979 and the slump years of 1972 and 1981 in Table 2.7 make this clear. Part of this deterioration is due to the undoubted increase in registration by women but not all. This deterioration is also reflected in the inflow probability calculation shown in Table 2.7. Comparing the 'boom' years of 1973, 1979 and 1983 and the slump years of 1975 and 1981 there is a clear upward trend in the inflow rate unlike males. In addition and like males, women have experienced a marked secular decline in the outflow (re-employment) probability with the result that the expected duration of unemployment has also gone up. The problem of long term unemployment though is less severe than from males but has also increased over the last decade. In 1974, 12% of unemployed women had been out of work for more than a year. In 1984 the comparable figure is 29.1%. Taking males and females together there were in 1984 1.218 million long term unemployed workers in Britain.

As far as the composition of unemployment is concerned the most remarkable changes for males are in the age pattern of unemployment. There is no data that permits us to calculate an equivalent to Table 2.7 but it is clear that over the past twenty years in which the trend of unemployment has been upwards there has been a significant deterioration in the relative position of older and younger workers. The deterioration began earlier for older workers in the sixties. The work of Bowers and Harkess (1979) documents these events. They show that in both recession and boom years the expected duration of unemployment of men aged 55 and over has deteriorated much more than for males as a whole. The problem of long term unemployment, as a result, has become particularly severe for older workers. In 1984, 47% of those unemployed who were aged 55 and over, were out of work for more than a year compared with 33% for those aged 25 and under. However, it is also the case that in the eighties, the composition of the long term unemployed has shifted towards higher proportions of young people. In 1980 the proportion of older (55 and over) workers who were out of work for more than a year was 46% (almost the same as 1984). Amongst the young (25 and under) the 1980 proportion was only 11%. In other words, since 1980 there has been a three-fold increase in the proportion of the young who are long term unemployed. We have already seen the way in which the statutory redundancy scheme introduced in 1965 has affected the age structure of redundancy. The worsening performance particularly of manufacturing industry has led to increasing levels of redundancies in Britain, and the proportion of those aged 55 and over who are affected is high. The result is that not only are there more older workers in the stock of unemployed but as Bowers and Harkess show, their re-employment chances have fallen to a relatively significant extent.

The position of young workers (male and female) had worsened dramatically since the mid-seventies and this has also occurred in many other industrial economies (28). Bowers and Harkess (1979) show a marked increase (decrease) in the expected unemployment duration (re-employment probability) of younger workers in the recession of 1971 though not in the boom conditions of 1983. Experience from the recessions of 1975 and 1981 suggests the position has further worsened, especially for males although in the latter case special measures mask the full effect

for those under 18. There has been a large increase
in the proportion of the unemployed aged less than 21
as Table 2.9 shows. As we have seen, it is also the
case that the problem of long term unemployment
amongst younger workers has worsened. Each bout of
heavy youth unemployment has left difficult to re-
employ workers. Until recently the Department of
Employment's official view has been that the trend
against young workers reflects the greater and
growing intensity of recession in the British
economy. In 1978 a study of youth unemployment said:

> It is to be expected that youth unemployment,
> like total unemployment is responsive to the
> buoyancy of the economy. However, there are a
> number of reasons why unemployment amongst
> young workers might be relatively worse during a
> recession. Firms will respond to a downturn in
> demand and the need to reduce their labour force
> by ceasing or reducing recruitment ... Cut backs
> in recruitment will particularly affect young
> people who are joining the labour market or who
> have relatively little experience of employ-
> ment. (29)

Table 2.9: Relative unemployment (as % of total) of
young workers

		Under 18		18-19	
		male	female	male	female
Boom Years	1973	3.5	11.5	6.1	15.6
	1979	15.0	25.9	8.0	14.6
	1972	5.1	16.3	4.7	15.7
Slump Years	1975	7.5	19.2	9.9	20.7
	1981	9.8	19.0	7.9	13.7

Source: Department of Employment Gazette

Others have emphasised the increased relative
cost of employing young workers as a significant
factor in explaining their high unemployment. In a
recent Department of Employment working paper, Wells
(1983) has produced evidence in support of this view.
This a matter to which we will return in chapter six.
There is little evidence to suggest that any
major changes have taken place in the occupational
composition of unemployment. The unskilled are, as we

have already seen, especially vulnerable to
unemployment. There is some evidence that the
probability of re-employment has deteriorated
particularly rapidly for the unskilled. In the
recession years of 1971, 1976 and 1981 the proportion
of all vacancies open to the unskilled fell from
11.5% to 5.5% to 3.4%. (30) As a result it is no
surprise that the unskilled are a much larger
proportion of the long term unemployed than of the
unemployed as a whole.

The pattern of regional unemployment has also
exhibited some changes. The studies of Moore and
Rhodes (1973, 1976) indicate that job prospects in
the high unemployment regions of Britain improved in
the 1960s and early 1970s. This evidently had an
impact on relative unemployment rates by region. The
view of Moore and Rhodes (1973) is that these changes
were the result of an active regional policy aiming
to alter the spatial distribution of industry.
Evidence for post-1974 is more sketchy but the
weakening of regional policy will have reduced the
cushioning given to workers in high unemployment
areas by past regional policy. The decline of British
manufacturing industry has also affected the
regional pattern. The West Midlands region has been
particularly affected and its position within the
overall unemployment ranking has deteriorated
significantly in the seventies.

We have seen that during the period in which the
stock of unemployed has risen, major changes in the
composition of the stock have occurred both in terms
of the duration/flow pattern and in the
characteristics of those who are unemployed. The
reason for many of these changes are explored in
later chapters.

Long term unemployment and duration dependence

As the mean completed spell of unemployment and the
proportion of those out of work for more than a year
have gone up, increasing attention has been devoted
to the effects of long spells of unemployment on the
re-employment chances of the affected workers. A
widely held view is that long spells of unemployment
reduce the chances that workers will receive job
offers. The reason is that either long term
unemployment causes a depreciation of skills, a loss
of motivation and generally lowers a worker's
potential productivity or employers believe this to
be the case. Employers may use length of unemployment
as a signal which indicates other employers'

67

attitudes to the worker in question. Those who are long term unemployed have been unable to complete job search successfully and employers may conclude that this is because of previous rejection by other employers who have found the applicant unsuitable, i.e. those who are unemployed for long periods are low productivity, low quality or poorly motivated workers. Long term unemployment may also reduce the willingness to look for work, especially of older workers. The study by White (1983), for example, shows in a survey of the long term unemployed conducted in 1980/81 that about a third of the sample in 1981 defined themselves as being out of the market for jobs. The re-employment chances are, of course, virtually zero for workers who do not search for a job. Amongst men and women, White shows those aged over 45 were much more likely to be in this category. It is important to note that this behaviour does not reflect a reduced willingness to work. White concludes:

> the lack of effort in seeking work was not because of any disinterest or disinclination to work, but because the possibility of employment was not regarded as realistic

White also finds evidence that the number of men and women who actually get jobs declines the longer the individual has been unemployed. This phenomenon which implies that the re-employment probability is a declining function of the length of the current uncompleted spell of unemployed has been documented elsewhere by, for example, the Manpower Services Commission (1981) who show the proportion of those unemployed in 1981 who were unemployed in 1980 increases with the length of unemployment. If this is the direct result of the scarring resulting from long term unemployment it is called by Heckman and Borjas (1980) duration dependence. In their study of young unemployed US workers, they find no evidence once the characteristics of the individuals are allowed for. (31) It is very important to specify a full and comprehensive list of characteristics to eliminate the possibility that duration dependence might be inferred from an analysis of unemployed individuals when the true cause is unobserved heterogeneity (i.e. difference between individuals not allowed for in the analysis). (32)

The method employed in many British studies of this issue is essentially that of Lancaster (1979). The re-employment probability (θi_t) for individual i

at elapsed time t during an unemployment spell is
written as

2.9 $\theta i_t = e^{\tilde{\beta}' X i} \tilde{} at^{a-1}$

where

X_i = a set of characteristics possessed by
individuals in the sample (like age, place of
residence, race and so on)

$\tilde{\beta}$ = the coefficients associated with each of these
characteristics

For our present purposes, the crucial part of 2.9 is
the second term and in particular the value of a. If
a = 1, the re-employment probability is constant (33)
and individual values of θi_t are given by the
characteristics of the individual. If a > 1 the re-
employment probability increases with spell duration
and if a < 1 it will be decreasing. The argument
outlined above suggests a is less than one so the re-
employment chances of an unemployed worker fall the
longer that individual has been unemployed (negative
duration dependence). Some studies (34) in Britain
have found values of a to be less than unity. Typical
is the work of Lynch (1983, 1984) who finds duration
dependency in unemployment with the probability of
re-employment declining with the duration of a spell
of unemployment. On the other hand, the recent study
by Narendrenathan, Nickell and Stern (1985) finds a
value of α which is insignificantly different from
unity so the re-employment probability remains
constant throughout a spell of unemployment. (35)
This is not to say that workers do not get fewer
offers as a spell of unemployment proceeds but that
any such 'scarring' is offset by an enhanced
willingness of workers to accept jobs. The re-
employment probability is determined jointly by
employers' offer behaviour and the acceptance
response of unemployed workers. This is explored
further in the next chapter. One other explanation
for this result is that the Narendrenathan, Nickell
and Stern study is able to specify a fuller set of
characteristics and to minimise the degree of
downward bias in the value of a that might result.
The econometric evidence, therefore, on duration
dependence is mixed though given the assumption that
workers are more willing to accept jobs, it is clear
that some 'scarring' through long spell duration

occurs (36) because employers are less likely <u>ceteris</u> <u>paribus</u> to make offers to workers with long spell duration.

The scar of long term unemployment may occur not only during the current spell but during subsequent spells. This possibility is called by Heckman and Borjas (1980) lagged duration dependence. Stern (1984) finds a significant positive association between the inflow probability for a currently employed individual and the length of a previous unemployment spell. Narendrenathan, Nickell and Stern (1985) show that the length of current spell is greater (lower θi_t) for individuals who have experienced a recent spell of unemployment although the evidence on the adverse effect of a lengthy spell is not conclusive. In contrast, in her study of young workers, Lynch (1984) finds no evidence of lagged duration dependence of this kind.

There is, therefore, for young workers some clear evidence in Britain for duration but not lagged dependence. Young workers are scarred by current long spells of unemployment but if they do get a job the scar does not persist. This suggests any attempt to reduce long term unemployment amongst young workers may require that special measures (training and education) are taken to reduce or undermine their current unacceptability to potential employers. On the other hand, amongst mature adults the scarring effect of long term unemployment has proved more difficult to demonstrate by econometric analysis, although other evidence does suggest it is important. In contrast, lagged duration dependence has been shown to be a feature of adult unemployment in Britain. Unlike adults, young workers are scarred by long periods of unemployment and not so much by frequent spells. One explanation might be that frequent job changing (high turnover) which characterises young workers is regarded by employers as 'normal'. (37) Young workers are less likely to be rejected for frequent spells of unemployment than if they don't change jobs at all and undergo one long period of unemployment. In the case of mature adults, frequent job changing is not regarded as normal and hence those who experience frequent spells or recent lengthy spells of unemployment are likely to be regarded as less satisfactory employees.

One problem with the literature is that most of it concentrates on males. Clearly a test of the importance of 'normal' turnover to the scarring effects of unemployment would involve a comparison between males and females. This has yet to be done and at this moment in time the precise scarring effects of unemployment experience have not been determined. Hopefully future research will plug this gap because from a policy point of view the matter is crucial. This might also reveal whether duration dependence of both forms has become a more important feature of the labour market in the current period of much higher unemployment than that at the times most UK studies have considered (pre-1980).

Conclusion

Unemployment is not a random, isolated event occurring in all individuals' working lives. This chapter has emphasised the heavy concentration of unemployment upon certain types of worker, namely the young, the manual, the old and the unskilled. We have also seen this greater vulnerability to unemployment is heavily concentrated upon certain individuals who possess these characteristics and are likely to experience either long spells of unemployment or repeated spells of unemployment or both. High unemployment, therefore, has the effect of reflecting and magnifying inequalities that already exist both in the labour force and in the wider society.

We have also drawn attention to the duration/flow make-up of the stock of unemployed. Some marked differences in the inflow rates for different groups of workers have been found. However, through time, the inflow rates overall have varied a good deal less than the re-employment rates and hence the duration of unemployment. As unemployment in Britain has risen over the last two decades it is the duration of spells of unemployment that have risen most significantly, especially but not only for male workers. Given the costs of long term unemployment to the individuals concerned and to the wider society this is of considerable practical importance. The reduction of unemployment is a much more urgent priority than it would be if the rise of unemployment in Britain merely reflected increasing levels of labour market turnover.

In subsequent chapters, we will explore the causes and cures for this high unemployment and the reduction in job opportunities and labour market stagnation which is part and parcel of it.

Notes

1.   This is shown in, for example, Layard (1981) footnote 3 on page 74.

2.   This data comes from Robinson and Wallace (1984) which uses information from the Census of Employment. Slightly lower estimates are obtained from the Census of Population (37.1%) and the New Earnings Survey (32.5%) and a slightly higher figure can be obtained from the General Household Survey (43.1%). The data in brackets are for women only.

3.   Page 40.

4.   Robinson and Wallace (1984) argue that this helps the employer to contain wage costs. It helps to explain why female part-time employment has risen so dramatically over the last two decades even though the relatively hourly earnings of women rose over the same period. For a more general discussion of the growth in female employment, see Joshi, Layard and Owen (1983).

5.   Martin and Roberts (1984) show that the median length of time of return to work after the birth of children fell from $7\frac{1}{2}$ years to $3\frac{1}{2}$ years over the period 1950-1976.

6.   These are the terms used by Stewart and Greenhalgh.

7.   There is an extensive literature on sex discrimination in the US and the UK. Useful introductions have been provided by Pike (1984) and Hammermesh and Rees (1984).

8.   Nickell uses a logit model of unemployment incidence. This involves the calculation of the probability that a group of individuals with a given set of characteristics will be unemployed. This permits the calculation of the ceteris paribus unemployment rates. For the details see Nickell (1980) Table 2 footnote (ii) and page 791.

9.   Inflow probabilities are calculated by Nickell using the stationary register assumption. Given an estimated value of the duration of unemployment it is possible to calculate the inflow probability by re-arranging equation 2.6 to $\alpha_t = U_t/Tu_t$. Stern's (1982) study also shows the same relationship between the inflow probability and the level of weekly earnings in work (uncorrected for occupational status).

10.   Brief details of the method are in Nickell (1980) pages 791-2. A fuller account is to be found in Nickell (1979a). Basically the method involves calculating the weekly re-employment (outflow) probability for an individual with a given set of characteristics having reached a given week of a

spell. This enables the calculation of the mean expected duration for such an individual and for groups of individuals possessing a particular characteristic. This is the statistic presented in Nickell's paper and this is used to calculate the outflow probability for each occupational group shown in Table 2.3 using equation 2.6a.

11. The recent study by Narendrenathan, Nickell and Stern (1985) provides further evidence on this. Using methods similar to Nickell (1980) they estimate the re-employment probability of individual males in the 1978 DHSS Cohort of Unemployed Survey. Although they do not include occupational variables they find θ_t to be higher for those with educational qualifications, and training. Since these are correlated with occupational status (see, for example Stewart and Greenhalgh (1984)) this result is consistent with that of Nickell (1980).

12. This is the argument of Oi (1962). However Bowers, Deaton and Turk (1982) find no evidence (see chapter twelve).

13. Data for females shows the same pattern of labour turnover falling with age. Registration bias which is most serious a problem with older women distorts the pattern but correction does not really alter the picture.

14. Narendrenathan, Nickell and Stern (1985) calculate the outflow probability from individual data and find that it declines with age. This produces the same massive difference in the expected duration of unemployment between young and old that we observed in Table 2.4.

15. The internal labour market involves the creation of a hierarchy of jobs and rewards, access to which from outside may be limited to low level, low status 'ports of entry' jobs. For a full account of these influential ideas see Doeringer and Piore (1971). Internal labour markets are particularly important in large firms and plants. Some economists have argued they have evolved as a means of securing worker attachment and discipline in large scale production units. There is some evidence that this also affects the inflow probability which Stern (1983) for example, shows to be inversely correlated with plant size in manufacturing. In large firms employment is more structured and more stable. This has consequences for the macroeconomic analysis of unemployment that takes place in chapters four to six.

16. Nickell (1980) shows a much more marked hump in the inflow probability for the 50 and over

age group than is revealed in Table 2.4.
17. This argument is developed further in Knight (1981).
18. The statutory redundancy scheme has this characteristic. See Foster (1974).
19. Department of Employment data shows the same reduction in the re-employment probability for females aged 45 and over.
20. Stern (1982) shows the inflow probabilities for single men to be much higher than married. However, these are uncorrected for the fact that single men are mostly young and therefore have high inflow probabilities. Nickell's estimates allow for this age effect so the difference is less pronounced.
21. Stern (1982) shows the same positive relationship between the inflow probability and family size with low occupational status.
22. The differences and the totals are even more dramatic for those young (16-19) male workers with no qualifications. In Great Britain the unemployment rate of black males born in the UK was 69.2% (a staggeringly high figure) and 40.1% amongst whites. For females the figures and the black/white difference are not so marked (46.7% and 34.3%).
23. Narendrenathan, Nickell and Stern (1985) do include ethnicity variables in their analysis of re-employment probabilities but they do not match those used in Table 2.5. They do show the re-employment probability of the Irish to be higher than for the 'standard man' who is British and white but shed no light on the position of black workers.
24. Figures for females can be found in the Department of Employment Gazette 1984, page 351. In general they show the same pattern for males shown in Table 2.6.
25. An excellent survey of this work is contained in Armstrong and Taylor (1978).
26. Further discussion of this study occurs in Chapters six, seven and eight.
27. The secular stability in the inflow rate is noted by Nickell (1979) who uses data which goes back into the 1960s to demonstrate this point.
28. This has been documented and discussed in Casson (1979).
29. 'The Young and Out of Work', Department of Employment Gazette, August 1978.
30. This is defined as general labourer's vacancies as a percentage of total vacancies.
31. Other US studies, e.g. Flinn and Heckman (1982) come to different conclusions.
32. A good example of an unobserved

characteristic is individual motivation. Lancaster and Nickell (1980) show that estimates of a are biased downward because of unobserved heterogeneity. Some procedure is therefore necessary to eliminate the possibility that biased estimates of a arise for this reason. Procedures for doing this are pretty ad hoc but they do show the extent of the bias. In Narendrenathan, Nickell and Stern (1985) for example, correcting for unobserved heterogeneity doubles the estimate of a though they say (page 56) "we would not wish to place great weight on our estimate of a which is, upon reflection, absurdly high".

33. Note that if a = 1 the expected duration of unemployment is $1/\theta_t$ as defined in equation 2.6a. In other words, the calculations performed to derive the tables in this chapter assume neither calendar time dependence nor duration dependence in the aggregate, i.e. as the aggregate mean duration increases there is no ensuing change in the re-employment probability.

34. Atkinson, Gomulka, Micklewright and Rau (1984) for example using Family Expenditure data a value of a between .5 and .7.

35. Nickell (1979), Lancaster (1979) and Lancaster and Nickell (1980) find some evidence of negative duration dependence (a < 1) but Lancaster finds a = 1 and Nickell a > 1 once unobserved heterogeneity is allowed for.

36. This follows if we assume a = 1 and the acceptance probability rises through a spell of unemployment. This is discussed further in chapter three.

37. Lynch (1984) in an attempt at reconciling the results obtained from British research places some emphasis upon the nature of the data sets used and, in particular, the use in the Narendrenathan, Nickell and Stern (1985) study of registered unemployment data only and the bias in that survey towards non-urban areas of Britain. Lynch's own data set includes both registered and unregistered unemployed and this may play a part in explaining the difference in the results he obtains for young workers compared with Narendrenathan, Nickell and Stern. Note also that Lynch tests for unobserved heterogeneity as a potential cause of the low value of a she obtains but finds little evidence that this is the case.

Chapter Three

SEARCH, UNEMPLOYMENT AND UNFILLED VACANCIES

Introduction
In the previous chapters considerable emphasis has
been given to the duration of an unemployment spell.
In chapter one we saw its significance in the
measurement of the costs of unemployment. In chapter
two it was clear that the re-employment chances of
the unemployed, which determine the time spent out of
work, are crucial in explaining both cross section
differences in the incidence of unemployment and the
secular increase in unemployment in Britain. Indeed
the duration of a spell of unemployment can be
measured as the reciprocal of the re-employment or
outflow probability (θ_t) for unemployed workers.

   In this and subsequent chapters we consider the
various approaches which can be used to explain not
only the duration but also the rate of inflow to
unemployment using stock statistics as summary
measures. We begin by examining the role of job
search. This permits us to derive a framework within
which the theoretical and empirical analysis of
unemployment can be undertaken.

Job Search and the Outflow from Unemployment
For an individual worker the duration of a spell of
unemployment depends on the probability of re-
employment. This may vary during an unemployment
spell, as we saw in the previous chapter and will
also move procyclically. The basic expression for
this re-employment probability at time t is

3.1 $\theta_t = \kappa_t \, \beta_t \, v_t$

where

θ_t = the probability of re-employment

76

V_t =   the vacancy rate appropriate to the worker

β_t =   the probability that the worker will accept the job (the acceptance probability)

κ_t =   the probability that the worker will be offered the job (the offer probability)

The expression $\kappa_t V_t$ is the rate of arrival of job offers to the individual during the period t. Although $0 \leqslant \kappa_t \leqslant 1$ it normally takes a value between 0 and 1 indicating that the average individual will receive offers from some of the advertised vacancies but he is unlikely to get them from all. β_t indicates the chances of an <u>acceptable</u> job offer being made. What will determine it? This question can be answered with the aid of a model of job search in the labour market.

The starting point for job search models is the recognition that information in the labour market is imperfect and costly to acquire. As far as workers are concerned relevant information relates to alternative job opportunities and knowledge about this is acquired by extensive search. Information about the characteristics of each job opportunity (wages and hours of work, for example) is acquired by intensive search. The comparable search process for employers reveals information about the number of available applicants and their suitability (potential productivity) for the job.

The simplest approach to employee search concentrates on the wage and ignores the non-wage characteristics of the job. It also assumes that each job offer is certain so there is no need for intensive search to reduce uncertainty about each offer. If, in addition, we assume

(a)   the distribution of offers (S) is known to workers before the search actually begins
(b)   the distribution of wage offers is invariant over search time
(c)   workers do not recall rejected offers we can calculate the <u>ex ante</u> benefits of search.

If the distribution of wage offers is normal with a mean $\bar{w}_0$ and variance σ^2 the expected maximum observed offer (W_0) at each job offer independently and randomly sampled can be shown to be (1)

3.2 $W_0 = \bar{w}_0 + \sigma\sqrt{2 \log S}$

If a worker looks at 1 job offer (S = 1) he can expect to receive the mean wage ($\overline{w}_0$), (log S = 0 in this case). As S increases higher offers will be experienced but 3.2 implies the marginal wage benefit of this search will decline (the improvement in the offers obtained will fall). Also the greater is the variance of the distribution the greater, not surprisingly, are the benefits observed. This kind of analysis permits us to derive a total search benefit schedule as depicted in Figure 3.1.

Figure 3.1

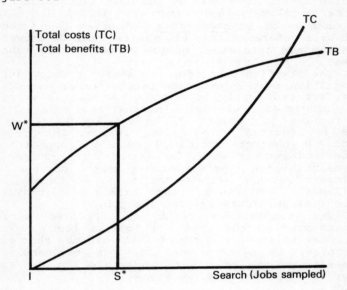

If we assume that both total and marginal costs of search increase with search activity we can superimpose a total cost of search schedule as shown in Figure 3.1. Search involves an input of both time and commodities (newspapers, transport etc.) and both these are costly. One important reason for believing the marginal costs of job search will increase is geographical. Generally, progressive sampling of the distribution of job offers will involve greater distance of search travel which will increase both the time and commodity costs of search at the margin.

An optimising employee will seek to maximise the

total net benefits (TB - TC) of search where the marginal costs and benefits are also equated. This implies a wage offer that will be received (W* in Figure 3.1) as a result of this search. This wage offer is the 'reservation wage' and this simple search model results in the simple decision rule.

3.3 If $W_0 \geqslant W*$ accept the offer

$W_0 < W*$ reject the offer

The acceptance probability β_t at any moment of time is

3.4 $\beta_t = P_r \mid W_0 > W* \mid$

Having defined the optimal number of job offers (S*u Figure 3.1) the searching worker might sample, it is a simple matter to calculate the optimal search time. If we define μ as the number of offers sampled in each time period (t_s) of search, then

3.5 $t_s = \dfrac{S}{\mu}$ and

3.5a $t_s^* = \dfrac{S*}{\mu}$

where t_s^* = optimal search time

If we assume μ is also known to workers <u>ex ante</u> it is possible to derive the optimal duration of search for a worker (t^* in 3.5a).

One of^s the problems with this simple 'optimal sample size' model is that there exists a positive probability that a wage in excess of or equal to the reservation wage will be found before t^* has elapsed. If workers insist on searching for t_s^* periods they will, in general, search more than ^{s}they need to obtain W*. An alternative and more satisfactory approach is to be found in the sequential search model. Here it is the reservation wage that is actively determined and this alone guides the search process.

The basic ideas are relatively simple. The benefit from search is the value of the expected wage if the search is successful plus the return from further search if it is unsuccessful. Successful in this context means that the wage offered exceeds or is equal to the reservation wage. In other words the decision rule is the same as before (see equation

3.3). If we assume the distribution of offers is continuous, defined as f(w) and is known <u>ex ante</u> then the expected value of the wage if search is successful is

3.6 $\int_{W^*}^{\infty}$ W f(w) dW

where f(w) is the frequency of each wage in the distribution of offers in excess of W*. The return from further search is

3.7 V(W*) F(W*)

where F(W*) is the cumulative frequency i.e. the chances of getting another offer less than W* and V(W*) is the return to that search. If the costs (including time costs) of searching for W* are C per firm searched then the net benefits (V(W*), are

3.8 V(W*) = $\int_{W^*}^{\infty}$ W f(w) dW + V(W*) F(W*) - C

and therefore

3.8a V(W*) = $\dfrac{\int_{W^*}^{\infty} W\ f(w)\ dW}{1 - F(W^*)}$ - $\dfrac{C}{1 - F(W^*)}$

The greater is the reservation wage, the lower is the probability of success. The probability of success is 1 - F(W*). Hence we can see from 3.8a that both total benefits and total costs will increase as the acceptable (reservation) wage increases. As before if the distribution is normal the expected gain (i.e. the increase in the expected wage) from raising the acceptable wage will decline. In other words the <u>marginal</u> benefit of choosing a higher reservation wage will decline. For reasons considered above, marginal costs will rise. The outcome of this kind of search process is shown in Figure 3.2.

Workers choose a minimum acceptable wage knowing the actual wage may be higher. How much higher is unknown but what is certain is that the improvement in that expected wage will decline as the reservation wage chosen rises. If a worker optimises by equating the marginal costs with the marginal

Figure 3.2

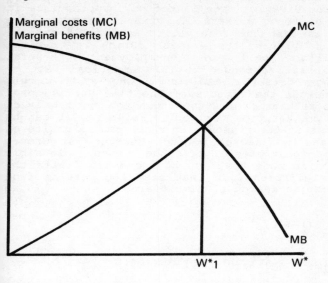

benefits of search then W_1^* will be chosen in Figure 3.2 with the decision rule.

3.3a Accept if $W^0 > W_1^*$, Reject if $W^0 < W_1^*$

The time taken to search is determined solely by W^*. (2) The higher is the reservation wage the longer it will take. This is, of course, taken account of in the cost function used in this model.

The sequential decision model gives us a simple and straightforward way of determining the acceptance probability (β) but it has a number of major limitations. One of the most serious problems is the implication that the reservation wage is determined <u>ex ante</u> and is constant throughout the period of search. However, Kasper (1966) has shown in his study of job search of unemployed in Minnesota in 1961 that the acceptance wage fell by 3% per month of search. This has been confirmed more recently by, for example, Barnes (1975) who finds the rate of fall of the acceptance wage increases as the period of search lengthens and by Kiefer and Neumann (1979).

In the UK, confirmation of this result has recently been provided by Narendrenathan, Nickell and Stern (1985). They consider the experience of male workers of all ages. In contrast, Lynch (1983) has shown that the assumption of a constant or nearly constant reservation wage is not so inappropriate in the case of young workers. In general, however, the evidence is that the reservation wage falls and the acceptance probability rises during a typical individual's spell of unemployment. Several theorists have responded to this empirical fact by developing models that explain it. One way to do this is to consider the effects of the time horizon over which the returns from accepting a job are received. If we assume the time horizon is infinite, it can be shown (3) that the reservation wage remains unaltered through the job search period. However, as Gronau (1971) demonstrates, if the more plausible assumption is made that job horizons are finite the result is different. In that case the returns from successful job search at time t are

$$3.9 \quad \sum_{t=0}^{T} W_t \, (1 + r)^{-t}$$

and at time t + 1 are

$$3.9a \quad \sum_{t=1}^{T} W_{t+1} \, (1 + r)^{-t}$$

where

r = the rate at which the individual worker discounts future earnings

T = the expected length of the job tenure

W_t = the expected wage from the distribution f(w) assuming it is greater than or equal to the reservation wage (W*)

Since as the search period increases, e.g. to t + 1 the time (T - t) over which job returns can be earned is necessarily shortened, there will be a decline in the returns from successful job search. Only in part does the improvement $(W_{t+1} - W_t)$ in the job offer obtained offset this decline. As a result Gronau demonstrates the reservation wage will fall. The trouble with this kind of model is that it overlooks the possibility (by assuming a constant T) that by continuing search, workers may also obtain a job with greater job security (a longer T). In this case the result obtained by Gronau may not hold.

    An alternative approach has been suggested

amongst others, by McCall (1970). He argues that workers do not know the distribution of wage offers and search is a process through which the distribution becomes known. Search is thus adaptive and is a method of verifying an initial guess of the distribution of wages and adjusting both the view of the distribution itself and of the acceptance wage appropriate to each view. Salop (1974), on the other hand, assumes that workers not only know the distribution of offers but can distinguish firms at each point of the distribution. They systematically search for vacancies in the high paying firms first and then sample an increasingly truncated sample of lower paying firms. If a vacancy is not found then workers revise their acceptance wage downwards because the maximum expected wage from a truncated distribution is less than from the total distribution with the kind of search procedure assumed by Salop. In many respects this model seems closer to the realities of job search than the alternatives and it does predict the decline in the reservation wage.

The process of job search generates an explanation of the acceptance probability emphasising the role of wage offers. Of course, other features of a job will be important in practice including hours of work, fringe benefits, work conditions and so on. Workers who search in labour markets collect information on these matters as well. We could construct a search model with workers having target levels of each of these non-wage issues and implying an analogous decision rule to that employed in respect of wages. Since the procedure would be the same, little is gained by pursuing this. The only additional (and highly complex) question would be the modelling of the mix of objectives that the worker actually uses. This is not a matter we shall pursue except to note that a job offer may be refused even if the wage is acceptable to the searching worker because some other aspect of the job offer is not.

Employer Search

The probability of re-employment not only depends on the acceptance probability but also on the arrival rate of job offers. Many theorists and much empirical work assumes a constant arrival rate of job offers during an individual's unemployment spell. Often offers are assumed to arrive in a purely random stream. If, on the other hand, we want to explain the job offer rate, it is necessary to consider the stock of potential and effective vacancies actually available to an unemployed individual. To explain the latter requires some consideration of the offer probability (κ_t). In order to explain this, it is necessary to consider labour market search by employers.

Employer search involves costs in the same way as for employees. Extensive research to identify potential applicants involves advertising and other similar costs. The selection by intensive search is likely to a firm to be even more costly. It requires interview or an alternative procedure to permit firms to assess the potential productivity of an applicant. In big firms this filtering task is performed by a whole department of people. For the firm therefore, job search involves both fixed and variable direct costs.

There is a further component of the costs of search by the employer. Time taken to fill a vacancy means that output and sales are foregone. The value of these lost sales needs to be taken into account and is likely to be particularly important in explaining cyclical variations in employer search behaviour. In slump the cost of foregone output is small, even zero, while in boom, time spent on search can prove expensive. The implications of this we will explore later. At this point we shall assume a cost function as depicted in Figure 3.3. Note that as search (applicants) proceeds, costs increase both in total and at the margin. Again, the geographical arrangement of potential employees would be sufficient to justify this assumption.

What are the benefits of search to the employer? If the labour market were homogeneous and all workers were identical as elementary textbooks assume, the only gain to the employer would be if he could obtain workers with a lower acceptance wage as a result of search. Petersen (1971) has argued this kind of search would not occur because compensation rates are fixed by collective agreement or administrative decisions. If this were true and labour was homogeneous, there would be no gain from search – the rational employer would not bother to search. The assumption implicit in much theorising, that search is only undertaken by the employee would be justified. However, as an empirical fact, workers are not identical and it is the construction of models to explain the consequences of this heterogeneity that is an important concern of modern labour economics. Some of the differences arise from differences in education and training, but not all. Different aptitudes, motivation and experience lead to

Figure 3.3

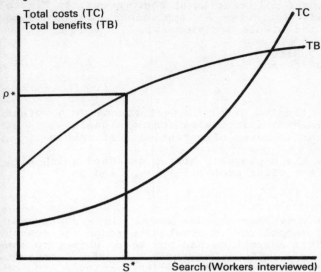

differences in performance of workers equally formally trained to do a given task. The gain from employer's search is the possibility of obtaining more productive and higher quality workers. Of considerable importance in assessing potential performance are reliable signals and indices. Spence (1973) has described the hiring of workers as a form of investment under uncertainty. As a result, employers look for reliable indicators of potential performance. The crude forms of signals (like years of education) which Spence emphasises are often supplemented by selection tests, like that used to guide recruitment to the British Civil Service.

We shall assume that the greater the number of applicants sampled, the better will be the worker hired, but the marginal increment to the marginal product will itself decline. If we assume the potential performance of applicants is normally distributed with mean ρ and variance σ_ρ^2 the maximum level of performance from applicants at each sample will be

3.10 $\rho = \bar{\rho} + \sigma_\rho \sqrt{2\log S}$

The benefits from employer search are known in Figure 3.3. If we assume that the employer seeks to maximise

85

the net benefits of search he will equate the
marginal costs and benefits of the process. In Figure
3.3 he will interview S* applicants. We can also
arrive at the simple decision rule

3.11 $\rho \geqslant \rho*$ hire
      $\rho < \rho*$ reject

where

ρ = the estimated level of performance of a worker
      obtained from interview (using signals)
$\rho*$ = the target level of potential performance

Thus it is the employer's hiring standard which will
determine the offer probability (κ_t) and so

3.12 $\kappa_t = P_r |\rho \geqslant \rho*|$

In this optimal sample size model (like employees)
the offer probability is constant through the search
process. This assumption has not been subject to the
same kind of empirical scrutiny as the 'constant
reservation wage' assumption on the employee side of
the market, but it does seem a good deal more
reasonable. Because of this we shall assume that
although the hiring standard can change it remains
constant through the search time chosen as optimal in
filling any given vacancy by the employer.
    In an analogous fashion to that used for
employee job search we can also derive the optimal
duration of (in this case) a vacancy. If

3.13 $S = \delta_s t_s$

where

$\delta_s = S/t_s$

(employer's search productivity = applicants
interviewed per time period). Then the optimal
duration of a vacancy is

3.14 $t_s^* = S*/\delta_s$

    The problem with this approach is the same as in
the case of workers. There is a positive probability
that an acceptable worker will be found before t* has
elapsed. The solution to this ambiguity is the same.
The adoption of a sequential search approach will
deal with this difficulty and produce the same

86

decision rule as in 3.11.

Labour market search models have provided a fruitful framework within which offer and acceptance probabilities can be analysed and now we apply these ideas to unemployment flows. However, it is worth emphasising that the treatment so far has implied that these two probabilities are determined independently but this is unlikely to be the case. Employers, for example, may respond to a high refusal rate by workers (lower β_t) by lowering their hiring standard (raising κ_t). Similarly workers may respond to changes in the arrival rate of job offers.

Figure 3.2a

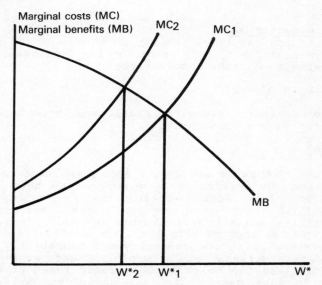

One obvious reason for this interdependence is that by altering for workers the arrival rate of offers or the acceptance rate for employers the <u>costs</u> of search are changed. If search time becomes less productive for both parties then total and marginal costs of search will increase. Consider Figures 3.1, 3.2 and 3.3. In all cases an increase in costs of this type will reduce both the optimal sample size and the reservation wage if the search strategy is sequential. This is shown below for Figure 3.2a. For workers a reduction in the arrival rate of offers will shift the costs of search to MC_2 reducing the reservation wage to W_2^* and therefore increasing the acceptance probability. This is essentially the effect shown by Mortensen (1970). Some evidence for this in the study of young workers in London has been found by Lynch (1983). Of course this may not be sufficient to increase the re-employment probability. This effect merely offsets the direct effect of a fall in κ_t V_t on θ_t. Although Mortensen argues it will more than offset the direct effect, Lynch shows the opposite. Despite the decrease in reservation wages, a decrease in the job offer rate lowers the re-employment probability (and increases the duration of unemployment). In the remainder of this chapter we shall largely ignore this aspect of the analysis.

Unemployment Flows

If we ignore the flows between unemployment and non-employment ($\varepsilon_t = \tau_t = 0$) we can derive from chapter 2 (assuming a constant labour force)

2.1c $\Delta U_t = D_t^u - H_t^u$

If we further assume a stationary unemployment register we can also derive

2.1d $H_t^u = D_t^u$ if $\Delta U_t = 0$

i.e. the flow rates are equal. Both flow rates can be influenced by workers' job search. As we have seen for an individual worker the re-employment probability is governed by the acceptance probability and the arrival rate of job offers. At the market or economy wide level the outflow rate (H_t^u is obtained using the re-employment probability for unemployed workers as a whole. These aggregate probabilities can be seen as averages taken at each point in time over individual unemployed workers. Clearly they will be extremely sensitive to the composition of unemployment. We have already seen that the acceptance probability and the offer probability help determine the re-employment probability. In the previous chapter we saw how this (θt) varies with personal characteristics, and with the uncompleted length of a current unemployment spell. An increase in the proportion of the unemployed with low re-employment probabilities would clearly affect the aggregate value. If there is a similar increase (as we saw) in the number of long term unemployed, or in the number of older workers this will reduce the aggregate re-employment probability. Some of these effects are considered later in this chapter but we shall ignore them here. At the aggregate level

3.15 $H_t^u/U_t = \theta_t = \kappa_t \beta_t V_t$

(the aggregate re-employment probability)

with $1 \geqslant \kappa_t, \beta_t \geqslant 0$

and therefore

3.16 $H_t^u = \kappa_t \beta_t V_t U_t$

Job search behaviour clearly affects the outflow rate (H_t^u) (and hence both the stock and duration of unemployment) via κ_t and β_t. There are reasons also for believing it might affect the inflow rate (recall $D_t^u = \alpha_t$). If full-time search is relatively efficient as Alchian (1965) has argued, workers will quit their current job to look for an alternative. This will increase the unemployment inflow and therefore the total stock of unemployed. The argument proceeds as follows - the total costs of job search depend significantly on the time spent, and are (4)

3.17 $TC = ct_s$ with $c > 0$

the time spent in optimal search (from the optimal sample size or the sequential search model) also depends on the number of jobs sampled in each time period (μ in equation 3.5). Substituting 3.5 into 3.17 gives

3.18 $TC = c\ S/\mu$

Alchian's argument is that since μ is higher for full-time search it always pays workers to opt for this because the total costs of sampling the optimum number of job offers (S^*) are smaller. However, this ignores the fact that the cost of each unit of full-time job search is greater because of the loss of work income, i.e. c is bigger for full-time search. In order for Alchian's view to hold the extra productivity of, say a week of full-time search has to reduce the total costs by more than the extra cost of the foregone income.

Clearly this is an empirical question which is difficult to resolve in Britain. In the US, Mattila (1974) shows that roughly 60% of those who quit to

change their job, experience no intervening
unemployment. (5) Kahn and Low (1982) confirm that
full-time search is more productive yielding a higher
wage offer per unit of wage time once the individual
characteristics of workers are allowed for. Given
Mattila's work it seems clear that the additional
costs of full-time search more than offset this
effect in the US. In Britain no direct information
exists although indirect information reveals the
same pattern. The data on labour market flows in
Table 1.3 implies that only about a half of
discharges and hires go through the unemployed stock.
If anything, this is likely to be an overestimate of
the actual proportion. Moreover, not all discharges
result from voluntary quitting. Mackay et al (1971)
found the quit proportion of total discharges was as
high as 80% in boom times but fell quite dramatically
in slump. Indeed, data in Bowers, Deaton and Turk
(1982) suggests the quit proportion actually fell to
zero in 1981. (6) On these grounds it seems
reasonable to conclude that most search is part-time
(on the job) and when successful does not involve
intervening unemployment. The work of Shorey (1980)
shows that most search leading to a quit is inspired
by the desire for higher wages and better job
opportunities but this does not shed much light on
these issues.

In any event, initially we shall assume that the
inflow rate is a constant so

3.19 $D_t^u = \alpha$

The usual justification for this is that this inflow
mainly consists of quits <u>and</u> layoffs and these are
inversely related. If, for example, we consider the
inflow rate through time; a period in which quits are
high (usually boom) exhibits a low layoff rate (vice
versa in a slump). In fact the constancy of the
aggregate inflow rate through time is not too
unreasonable an assumption. We saw in chapter two
that although the inflow rate varies by age,
occupation and so on for males as a whole, in Britain
it has remained secularly stable since 1970. Although
this is not true of females, making the assumption of
constancy does not rule out consideration of causes
and effects of <u>changes</u> in the inflow rate which women
workers have experienced. The virtue of the constancy
assumption embodied in 3.19 is that it permits us to
focus on the crucial outflow rate, which has varied a
great deal for men and women alike. Combining
equations 2.1c, 3.16 and 3.19 gives

90

3.20 $\Delta U_t = \alpha - \kappa_t \beta_t V_t U_t$

where recall that U_t and V_t are expressed as proportions of the labour force. In the stationary register case $\Delta U_t = 0$ and therefore

3.21 $\alpha = \kappa_t \beta_t V_t U_t$ and by rearrangement

3.22 $U_t = \alpha / \kappa_t \beta_t V_t = \alpha / \theta_t$

    This gives a relationship between the stock of unemployment and the inflow (α) and the outflow ($\kappa_t \beta_t V_t$) probabilities. Using the data in Table 2.1 we can see how closely the results of performing this calculation (based on steady state assumptions) is to the true unemployment rate (12.5% compared with the actual 12.7%). Using 3.22 we can depict the relationship between U_t and V_t (VU_1) as in Figure 3.4

Figure 3.4

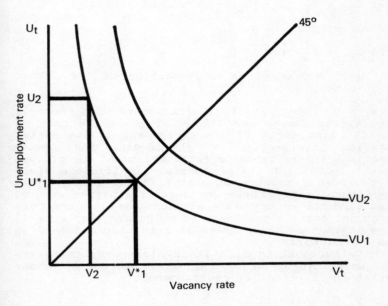

If the inflow rate were to increase ($\Delta\alpha > 0$) or the outflow decrease because of acceptance and/hiring standards increasing ($\Delta\kappa_t$, $\Delta\beta_t < 0$) there would be a shift in the VU curve to VU_2. There would be more unemployment at each level of unfilled vacancies. The VU curve is clearly sensitive to the determinants of the flows through the unemployment register. Changes in the costs and benefits of search, alterations in the expected duration of a job and of the rate at which future benefits from the job are discounted will all shift the stationary register curve. These changes are considered further in chapters seven and eight.

The intersection of the 45° line and the VU curve has a special significance if we assume there is no measurement error in the calculation of vacancy and unemployment statistics. If

3.23 $D_{Et} = E_t + V_t$ (D_{Et} = demand for labour)

and

3.24 $S_{Et} = E_t + U_t$ (S_{Et} = supply of labour)

it follows that

3.25 $D_{Et} - S_{Et} = V_t - U_t$

(all expressed as a proportion of the labour force)

If $V_t = U_t$ then $D_{Et} = S_{Et}$ which occurs when there is zero excess demand for labour. This is the case on the 45° line so U_1^* V_1^* are equivalent to the market clearing intersection of the demand and supply functions in the labour market. The total out of work at this point (U_1^*) is of special significance since it provides a measure of what Friedman (1968) calls the natural rate of unemployment. Alternative ways of measuring the natural rate are considered in chapters seven and eight but all aim to calculate that rate of unemployment at which there is zero excess demand in the labour market.

Using equation 3.22 it is also possible to see why unemployment occurs at this aggregate labour market equilibrium. By rearrangement

3.26 $V_t^* \, U_t^* = \alpha/\kappa_t \, \beta_t$

and since $V_t^* = U_t^*$

3.27 $(U_t^*)^2 = \alpha/\kappa_t \, \beta_t$ and

3.27a $U_t^* = \sqrt{\alpha/\kappa_t \, \beta_t}$

α is the inflow rate and κ_t and β_t determine the outflow rate from the unemployed stock. As long as these flows are positive U_t will be positive. In other words unemployment at zero excess demand occurs because of normal labour market turnover. The slower that turnover proceeds (the lower are $\kappa_t \, \beta_t$) the greater will be the number out of work at the natural rate. Unemployment due to these normal labour market flows is called frictional unemployment but it would be wrong to assume that all unemployment at U_1 is frictional.

There will be some individual workers for whom their own probability of receiving a job offer is close or actually equal to zero. This may be the result of characteristics that make them undesirable employees, e.g. lack of skill, resident in the wrong place or because of their own previous unemployment history (see chapter two for a discussion of these issues). These workers are those we define as the structurally unemployed. Strictly we can define these workers as those who in the current and future time periods have a κ_t value of zero, i.e. they are offered no jobs. The existence of structurally unemployed individuals with a zero offer probability will lower the aggregate offer (the average over all individuals) probability which enters equation 3.27a. Any increase in the extent of structural unemployment will therefore raise the natural rate of unemployment because it lowers κ_t at the aggregate level.

The sum of frictional and structural unemployment (U_1^* in Figure 3.4) is a measure of full employment unemployment. Since it also implies an equality in the current effective demand and supply of labour this adds to its virtue as such a measure. We will return to alternative measures of full employment in chapter seven but we proceed with this definition at this point. U_1^* is however not the only equilibrium level of unemployment. Any point on the VU curve implies a stationary register of unemployed and unfilled vacancies. Recall this was the assumption needed to define the curve in the first place. Given this stationary register assumption inflows and outflows are therefore equal at all points on the VU curve. The VU curve is hence a locus of flow equilibria in the labour market. Consider an unemployment level like U_2 on the VU_1 curve. There is a flow equilibrium ($H_t^u = D_t^u$) but not a full employment (zero excess demand) stock equilibrium. At U_2 unemployment exceeds unfilled vacancies (V_2). Using equation 3.25 if $U_t > V_t$ then $S_E > D_E$ i.e. there is excess supply (negative excess demand) of labour. Unemployment, therefore, exceeds the full employment level by an amount equal to ($U_2 - U_1$) and this we will call non-natural unemployment. The potential causes of this type of unemployment are considered in chapters four, five and six.

Some economists have taken the view that all unemployment at the natural rate is voluntary. This notion emerges from the fact that the labour market is cleared and therefore workers are on their supply curve. Any workers choosing not to work at the market clearing wage do so because that wage does not compensate them for the disutility of work. Moreover, when the natural rate of unemployment is derived from a search model it is sometimes argued that all unemployment is frictional and voluntary. However, those who argue in this way usually have in mind a model based on unconstrained job search by workers, i.e. where all vacancies are open. Once employers' search is incorporated into the search model this is less obvious.

In the case of structurally unemployed workers the situation is unambigious. These are workers who get no offers ($\kappa_t = 0$) and who will have experienced spells of unemployment so long that their acceptance probability is unity or nearly so; they would accept any job offer if only they got one. In this case it is clear that such workers are involuntarily unemployed and will remain so when unemployment is at its natural level. For other workers the involuntary/voluntary dichotomy makes less sense. All will be constrained by the arrival rate of job offers and to that extent some part of their unemployment spell is involuntary in the sense that in the absence of this constraint, they could freely choose the period spent out of work. As a result of this constraint, workers spend more time searching for employment than would otherwise be the case. Some part of their unemployment spell can, therefore, be regarded as involuntary. Equally of course, part of normal job search is voluntary. As long as the acceptance probability is less than one, workers are refusing job offers made to them. Empirically it would be difficult to place precise values on these components of search time. It is clear, however, that some part of search duration may be unwanted by workers and this should be added to the involuntary components of the natural rate of unemployment.

Labour Market Disequilibrium

The analysis so far has focussed on the flow and stock equilibria in the labour market. In reality, of course, even the less demanding flow equilibrium conditions will be met only infrequently. Inflows and outflow rates are rarely equal and in any sequential pair of months some changes in the size of the register invariably occurs. If the register is non-stationary we can no longer calculate the mean completed duration of unemployment using equation 2.6 since it relies upon the stationarity assumption.

Data contained in chapter two has shown that the inflow rate (α) increases in slumps and decreases in booms. This is much less marked for men than women workers and much less than the cyclical variability in the outflow rate (θ_t) but in a slump the inflow rate will exceed the outflow rate and unemployment will increase. We can analyse this process by considering the consequences of a once and for all cyclical increase in the secularly stable inflow rate. This could be the result of especially heavy layoffs, the effects of which are illustrated in Figure 3.5.

Figure 3.5

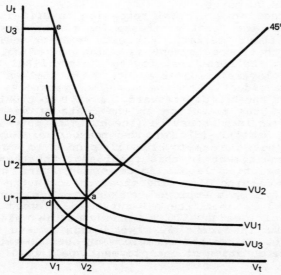

Assume that initially the economy is at full employment U_1^* and there is a once and for all increase in the inflow rate α. Using equation 3.22 it is evident that there will be a shift in the VU curve to VU_2 and an increase in U from U_1^* to U_2 (from position a to position b). If α then falls back to its long run level the VU curve returns to VU_1 and now the combination of unemployment and vacancies is above the stationary register curve. (7) What happens next? With unchanged offer and acceptance probabilities the time taken to fill a vacancy falls. With a greater number out of work applicants per time period increase and vacancies can be filled more rapidly at the given hiring standard. The result is an eventual fall in the stock of vacancies to V_1 (c on VU_1) in Figure 3.5. The adjustment process will be complete at this point with unemployment at U_2 and in excess of the natural level. Only if there is subsequently in a boom a compensating and equivalent once and for all decrease in the inflow rate (α) will the process be set in reverse with a transitory shift in the VU curve to VU_3 and a resulting movement to d. Here vacancies will take longer to fill and the increasing stock of vacancies (to V_2 in Figure 3.5) will eventually restore the labour market to its original position. If cyclical behaviour in the labour market is characterised by these once and for all changes in the inflow rate we should expect to observe this kind of counter-clockwise movement around the VU curve.

In fact in a typical recession in Britain this will not be the first manifestation of the recession in the labour market. A great deal of evidence suggests that unemployment is a lagged indicator of recession. The first response to a slump likely to be on the employers' side is a cut in the numbers being hired by a reduction in the number of vacancies and a raising of the hiring standard. He will do the latter because of the reduction in the costs of search to the employer in a recession (the costs of not filling a vacancy fall). (8) For the reasons explored in chapter one, the employer will prefer to cut his labour requirement in this fashion rather than lay-off his existing labour force or any part of it. Since the raising of hiring standards cuts the offer probability for unemployed workers we can see from equation 3.22 that the VU curve will shift to a higher position (say VU_2). Since vacancies are also cut (to V_1 in Figure 3.5) we initially end up at position d. Since the unemployment outflow rate has fallen the duration of unemployment spells will go up and so will the stock of unemployed. In Figure 3.5 assume it goes up to U_2. Since vacancies have fallen to V_1 the labour market is now at position c. In fact this result requires a particular assumption to be made. The raising of hiring standards will reduce the offer probability (κ_t) and using equation 3.22 will shift the VU curve up to VU_2 in Figure 3.5. In this case unemployment would eventually increase to U_3 (position e). However as we have seen in recession we might expect to observe an increase in the average worker's acceptance probability. If we assume that this increase exactly offsets the decrease in κ_t so as to keep the product $\kappa_t \beta_t$ constant then the VU curve remains in its initial position VU_1. (9) If, on the other hand, it only partially offsets (and this is likely in practice) the VU curve will shift up to some extent and unemployment will eventually exceed U_2 (and also the natural rate U_t^*). (10)

It is most convenient to consider the constant $\kappa_t \beta_t$ case so the VU curve remains at VU_1. The occurrence of a boom simply reverses this process. The increase in vacancies (say to V_2) would shift the labour market from c to b. Since the arrival rate of job offers has gone up and since we are assuming that changes in the offer and acceptance probabilities precisely offset each other, the unemployment outflow will rise and unemployment will fall (remember the inflow rate α is constant through this process) to U_1. Note the clockwise adjustment process in this case.

It is now clear that short run cyclical changes in the level of U^* may occur as the result of transitory movements of the VU curve. Only if α and $\kappa_t \beta_t$ are cyclically invariant will this not be the case. The natural rate is a long run concept, and therefore, requires a form of measurement that eliminates any cyclical variation in its level. How this is done is considered in the next section and in chapters seven and eight. It is also clear that the precise response of workers and employers to recession (and boom) is crucial to the disequilibrium process that is actually observed. Note that we have considered an adjustment mechanism in which there is no role played by changes in the distribution of wage offers. This has enabled the focus of attention to be put upon quantity changes which take place in the labour market in disequilibrium. (11) To incorporate wage offer changes is not difficult. If, for example, firms in recession lowered their offers, reducing wages at all points of the distribution, this would reduce the benefits of search lowering the

97

reservation wage and raising the acceptance
probability <u>as long as</u> workers are aware of this
change in the wage offer distribution. Classical
economists expect workers to be aware of these
changes and in general take the view that the
adjustment mechanism will operate sufficiently fast
that the 'loop' process is also completed very
rapidly so that unemployment different from the
natural rate will exist only transitorily. Other
economists argue the adjustment process is a lot
slower, so that the loops do not disappear 'in the
twinkle of an eye' and that disequilibrium can
persist for very long periods. These arguments about
the speed of adjustment are fully considered in the
next three chapters.

Empirical Evidence

Considerable evidence exists to support the VU
mapping as depicted in Figure 3.4. Dow and Dicks-
Mireaux (1956) showed its existence in the early
post-war period and Gujarati (1972) updated their
study to the early seventies.

Gujarati estimated for the period 1958-1971 for
Britain a relationship of the form

3.28 $\log U_t = \delta_0 + \delta_1 \log V_t + \delta_2 \text{ time}$

and found

$\delta_1 < 0 \quad \delta_2 > 0$

There are econometric problems with this
specification which have been considered and
partially corrected by Foster (1974) and by Warren
(1978). Most of these problems result from the facts
that Gujarati's specification estimates an
equilibrium relationship when the data reveal the
existence of disequilibrium in the labour market.
Although a full disequilibrium estimation has yet to
be done, recent studies allow for a non-stationary
register ($U_t \neq U_{t-1}$) by using a specification similar
to that employed in a recent study of the UK between
1967 and 1979 by Hannah (1984)

3.29 $\log U_t = \delta_0 + \delta_1 \log V_t + \delta_2 \text{ time}$

$+ \delta_3 \log U_{t-1} + \sum_i^n \delta_i \underset{\sim}{z}_i$

where Z_i is a set of exogenous variables and δ the associated coefficients.

Hannah finds (like Gujarati) $\delta_1 < 0$ and $\delta_2 > 0$. He also finds δ_3 to be significantly less than unity <u>and</u> greater than zero. These results suggest that adjustment to equilibrium (where $U_t = U_{t-1}$) takes approximately 6 months. Note that equilibrium here means adjustment to any point on the VU curve NOT to the natural rate.

A further problem is that both U and V in equation 3.28 are subject to serious measurement error. As far as U is concerned this was discussed in chapter one. The recording of vacancies is also notoriously unreliable, particularly in periods of high demand for labour. A survey by the Manpower Service Commission (12) found only 36% of all vacancies were officially recorded. The under-recording was much greater for non-manual workers (24% registered) than manual (47% registered). Estimates observed from 3.19 are likely therefore to be biased (and inconsistent). (13) A further problem is that the VU curve is actually no more than a mapping of stocks in the labour market. It is a summary representation of the underlying dynamic processes in the labour market. No causation is implied by the relationship in equation 3.22. Parikh and Allen (1982) have dealt with this and the measurement problem by arguing that both U and V are determined by the degree of excess demand for labour. Since the excess demand for labour is unobservable, Parikh and Allen use real wages and productivity as instruments to identify the relationship of V, U and excess demand. Although in some of their results the expected relationships between U, V and real wages and productivity are found, the overall pattern is far from convincing.

Parikh and Allen also devote some attention to whether the VU curve for Britain has shifted since 1966. They find an outward shift has taken place which means that the full employment level of unemployment in Britain has increased. Since the gap between total unemployment and this full employment level has also increased they also find that unemployment has increased more than unfilled vacancies. Jackman, Layard and Pissarides (1984) using a similar estimating equation to 3.29 show between 1961 and 1983 the level of unemployment at given vacancies rose substantially. The value of δ_2 (from equation 3.29) is high indicating a two-thirds increase of unemployment at given vacancies over the decade since 1973. Hannah (1984) confirms this

secular increase which was first identified a decade
ago by Bowers, Cheshire and Webb (1972), Taylor
(1972), the Department of Employment (1976) as well
as by Gujarati (1972). (14)

The VU method is not the only means through
which an increase in the natural rate of unemployment
has been identified. Sumner (1978), Batchelor and
Sherriff (1980), Grubb, Layard and Symons (1983) have
all shown this increase in different ways and to
different extents. Recently Minford (1983) has
claimed that the natural rate of unemployment has
risen from 500,000 in the mid-sixties to $1\frac{3}{4}$ million
in 1980. All of this is consistent with the work of
Nickell (1982) who found an increase in the
equilibrium unemployment rate from 2.82% in 1967 to
5.87% in 1977.

The equilibrium level of unemployment is that
level at which the inflows and outflows through the
unemployment register are equal. It is not the same
as the full employment level of unemployment (U* in
Figure 3.4). Nickell's results imply that the point
on the VU curve to which the economy settles in
temporary equilibrium is increasingly higher, i.e.
progressively further up the VU curve depicted in
Figure 3.4. In this sense it is, in part, a study of
the reasons for higher unemployment (i.e. larger
departures from full employment). All of these
studies are considered in more detail in chapters
seven and eight.

Several researchers have made use of the VU
approach to construct a typology of unemployment in
Britain. Cheshire (1973) considers the variation in
unemployment rates by region using this method and
find that inter-regional variation in unemployment
is principally the result of variation in non-natural
unemployment (U-U*) in Figure 3.4. Recently
Armstrong and Taylor (1981) have constructed a
typology of unemployment for Great Britain for each
year from 1963-1978. They sub-divide the structural
unemployment category into 2 groups. They
distinguish those who are structurally unemployed
(receive no offers) because they live in the wrong
place (geographical) from those who are structurally
unemployed because they possess the wrong skill for
the vacancies available (occupational). The main
results of this exercise are shown in Table 3.1. Non-
natural unemployment is seen to be much the most
important category even in the boom conditions of
1973/74 for males though much less for female.
Unfortunately since after 1975 vacancy data is not
recorded separately by sex, it is impossible to

confirm the suspicion that this has changed after 1974.

Table 3.1 Total Unemployment by Category (average) 1979

	Numbers (thousands)	Percentage of total
1. Non-natural unemployment	910.0	78.0
2. Structural unemployment		
(a) geographical	17.7	1.5
(b) occupational	6.3	0.5
3. Frictional unemployment	227.0	20.0
4. Natural unemployment (1)	251.0	22.0

Note (1): (2) + (3) = U* (natural rate of unemployment)
Source: H. Armstrong and J. Taylor 'The measurement of different types of unemployment in Britain' in J. Creedy 'The Economics of Unemployment in Britain', page 113, Table 4.8

Conclusion

We have outlined the basic components of the theory of search in labour markets. We have already briefly considered the use of this framework to assess the view that most unemployment is voluntary. This is considered further in later chapters. Use has been made of the search approach to construct a more general model of stocks and flows in the labour market. We are now in a position to analyse the aggregate stock of unemployment with this analysis in mind. In the following chapters we will consider both theoretical and empirical analysis of the determinants of these stocks and flows. In chapters four, five and six we examine the theory and evidence relating to non-natural unemployment, i.e. in excess of the natural rate. In chapters seven and eight we consider the natural rate itself.

Notes

1. A general survey of search theory is contained in Lippmann and McCall (1976). An excellent textbook exposition can be found in Joll, McKenna, McNabb and Shorey (1983) chapter 4. The particular probability distribution assumed here is considered

in the seminal papers of Stigler (1962) and Alchian (1970).

2. Although the model assumes that no recall of job offers is possible, Chalkley (1982) shows it makes no difference in this case if recall does not occur.

3. See Chalkley (1982) pages 7-11. Chalkley also shows, following Lippmann and McCall (1976) that a continuously falling reservation wage depends on the assumption that no recall of offers is possible.

4. This assumes constant marginal time costs of search. The assumption of rising marginal costs in Figure 3.1 results from (i) falling search productivity through search time (U falls) and (ii) increasing marginal commodity costs like transport and so on.

5. Similar results were obtained by Barron and McCafferty (1977) who found a mean value of the proportion of quitters who experience intervening unemployment as even lower at 21%.

6. Figure 12.1 on page 134 of Bowers, Deaton and Turk (1982) contains the relevant data.

7. This is what we would expect since the register of unemployed has gone up ($\Delta U_t \neq 0$).

8. This can be seen by referring back to Figure 3.3. In recession the total and marginal costs of employer search fall. As a result both the optimal sample size and the hiring standard increase. The same result holds if we assume firms adopt a sequential search strategy.

9. The previously outlined evidence of Lynch (1983) suggests that the re-employment probability will fall in recession so that in practice, the VU curve does shift up. Further evidence is reviewed in chapters seven and eight.

10. A more extensive analysis of these issues is contained in the paper by Bowden (1980). He interprets the VU scatter as a cyclical movement about a stable 'temporary equilibrium' locus (the VU curve itself). Some further developments in theoretical analysis are in Jackman, Layard and Pissarides (1984).

11. Considerably more evidence on these adjustment issues is discussed in chapter six.

12. The results are summarised in 'Engagements and Vacancies Survey Results' DE Gazette, June 1978.

13. Armstrong and Taylor (1981) also show the sensitivity of calculation of U* to the under-recording of vacancies on page 121, Table 4.13. Jackman, Layard and Pissarides (1984) also show this bias has fallen through time.

14. Evans (1977) shows the early mid-sixties shift was confined to male workers.

Chapter Four

MACROECONOMICS OF UNEMPLOYMENT - THE CLASSICAL APPROACH

Introduction

In previous chapters we have considered various aspects of labour market dynamics. In chapter two we examined the flows to and from the stock of unemployed and their relation to the duration of unemployment. In the last chapter considerable emphasis was given to the outflow from unemployment to employment and to the determinants of that flow. The relationship of the stock to these flows has also been considered and in chapter three an equilibrium relationship between the stocks of unemployment and unfilled vacancies was also derived. That relationship can be derived for an individual labour market which is considered in isolation from other markets or for the economy as a whole. (1) In this and the next chapter we will examine the latter by considering alternative macroeconomic approaches to the stock of unemployment. Particular attention will be paid to non-natural unemployment which we defined in chapter three as the difference between actual unemployment and the market clearing or 'natural' level of unemployment ($U-U^*$ in Figure 3.4). In this and the next chapter we will effectively assume that the inflow, acceptance and offer probabilities remain constant so that changes in the stock of unemployment will mirror changes in the vacancy rate. In other words we will examine different positions on the flow equilibrium VU curve. This ignores the flow disequilibrium adjustment process around the VU curve. We will instead concentrate attention on labour market disequilibrium in the sense of a stock of unemployment different from the natural rate (stock disequilibrium). In chapters seven and eight, changes in acceptance and offer probabilities are considered principally from the point of view of their impact on the natural rate.

The approach will be mainly theoretical though relevant empirical work will be considered. It will also emphasise the interaction of the labour market with other parts of the macroeconomy. In this chapter we will consider market clearing approaches to unemployment and in chapter five alternative non-market clearing theories.

The models we consider in this chapter assume market clearing, not in the sense that the labour or any other market in the economy is necessarily cleared and hence in equilibrium. Rather, if it is not actually cleared it is in the process of clearing and any disequilibrium will generally be of a transitory character.

Static Classical Models

Models of this type are invariably associated with economists like Pigou and Fisher. The normal textbook caricature (2) of this style of analysis proceeds in the following way. We assume a labour market in which the individual worker chooses how much labour to supply such that the utility desired from income and leisure is maximised. The aggregate supply curve of labour is the summation of these decisions and if we assume the substitution effect of a change in the wage rate exceeds the income effect in the aggregate then

4.1 $S_E = E(W/P) \quad dS_E/dW/P > 0$

where

S_E = supply of workers
W = money wages
P = price

On the demand side of the labour market, assuming that profit maximising firms operate in product markets that are perfectly competitive, firms will demand labour until the real wage equals the marginal physical product of labour and hence

4.2 $W/P = dY/dE$

where

Y = real output
E = workers

If we assume that firms operate with an employment

105

function of the general form (3)

4.3 $E = e(Y)$ with $dE/dY > 0$ $d^2E/dY^2 > 0$

which exhibits diminishing returns to labour then the demand curve for labour (D_E) is written as

4.4 $D_E = E(W/P)$ $dD_E/dW_P < 0$

Graphically these relationships are depicted in Figure 4.1.

Figure 4.1

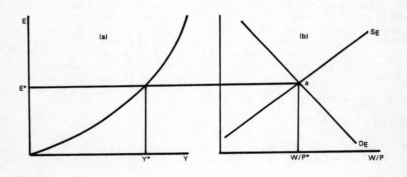

Frame (a) depicts the employment function of equation 4.3 and Frame (b) the supply and demand functions 4.1 and 4.4. Note that all agents are assumed to optimise and hence all decisions are made in real terms. If the real wage is at W/P* the labour market is cleared $(S_E = D_E)$ and the real output level is determined at Y*. There is no involuntary unemployment in the sense that those without jobs are economically inactive because the real wage is too low to compensate them for the loss of their leisure. These are the people on the supply curve above point a in Frame (b). In practice some of these people will be registered as unemployed since they are available for work according to normal (in Britain) government criteria which takes no account of the response of workers to the real wage actually offered. In addition, registration for many unemployed workers is a necessary condition for claiming benefit. The effects of benefits on the supply curve are not included in equation 4.1 but will be considered in later chapters (especially chapter seven). All of these workers are usually described as voluntarily unemployed and a part of the natural rate.

The remainder of this closed economy consists of a goods and a money market. In the goods market the clearing condition requires the equality of aggregate savings and investment (public and private). Savings are assumed to be a positive, and investment a negative function of the real rate of interest. (4)

4.5 $S = s(R)$ $dS/dR > 0$ and

4.6 $I = i(R)$ $dI/dR < 0$

where

I = investment
S = saving
R = rate of interest

In the money market, clearing requires the equality of the supply and demand of nominal money. The former is determined by the Central Bank and the latter by the level of money income and the velocity of circulation of money which in this simple type of model can be assumed to be institutionally determined. This gives

4.7 $M_S = M_0$ and

4.8 $M_d = L(PY)$

or in real terms

4.8a $M_d/P = L(Y)$

M_S = money supply
M_d = money demand
P = price level
Y = real income

The complete model is depicted in Figure 4.2.
Frames (a) and (b) are the labour market
diagrams of Figure 4.1. Frame (c) depicts the
relationship between the price level and real output.
Money income is constant so the PY curve is a
rectangular hyperbola. If the economy is in
equilibrium (E = E* and Y = Y*) then the price level
is determined. If the PY curve is at PY_1, then the
price level is P_1^*. The curve assumes a constant money
stock. If the money supply is increased the PY curve
shifts up to PY_2 (down if the money supply is cut).
If output is at Y^* (full capacity output) an increase
in the money supply leads only to an increase in the
price level (P_2^* in frame (c)). In this case money is
neutral in its effects, it only changes the price
level. In frame (d) the savings and investment
functions are shown with equilibrium at S*, I* and
R*. The economy is in equilibrium when its 3 market
sectors are cleared. It is when the real wage is
W/P*, the rate of interest is R* and the price level
is P*.
When the economy is in equilibrium there is no
involuntary unemployment. Since the demand and
supply of labour are equal we saw in the previous
chapter that unemployment is at its natural level
(i.e. U - U* = 0). The natural level of unemployment
consists in this model of the registration of those
voluntarily unemployed because the real wage is too
low.
What happens in disequilibrium in the labour
market and can this give rise to non-natural
unemployment in the sense we have defined? There is
only one way in which this can happen in the simple
Classical model. Suppose the real wage were W/P_1 >
W/P* then labour supply would be S_E^1 and labour demand
would be D_E^1 in Figure 4.2. There would be excess
supply of labour equal to $S_E^1 - D_E^1$. In this case there
would be unemployment in excess of the natural rate.
Would it persist? The classical market clearing view
was that it would not persist if market forces
operate. In this case the presence of excess supply
of labour would drive down the money wage and the
real wage and equilibrium would be restored at W/P*.
Only if there were impediments to the operation of
this wage adjustment process would this unemployment
not be instantaneously eliminated. The only thing a
government could do was to eliminate these
impediments. If it used an expansionary fiscal policy
to remove the non-natural unemployment any extra
expenditure created would simply 'crowd out'
existing expenditure and leave the demand for goods

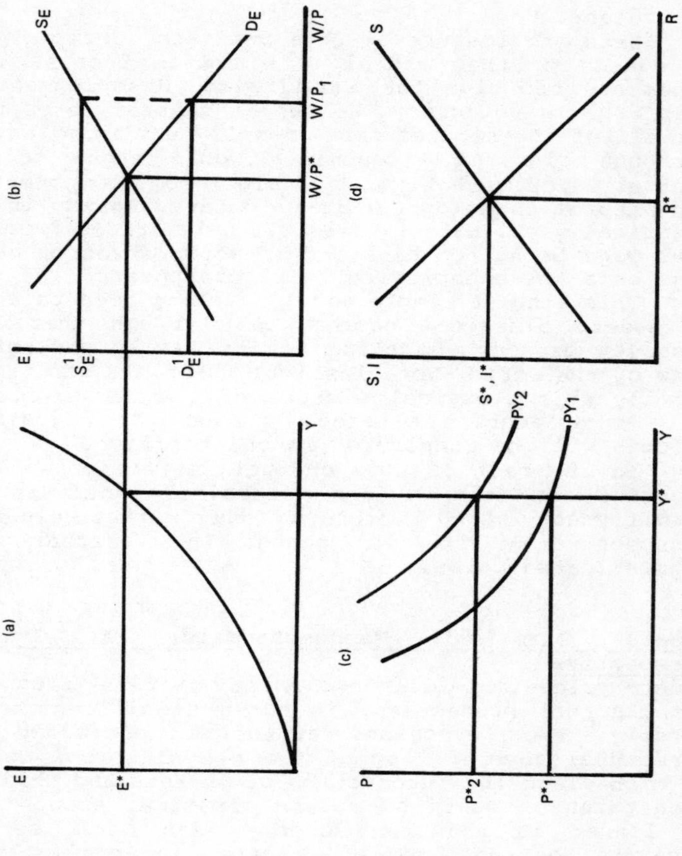

Figure 4.2

unaffected.

There is a role for monetary policy in certain circumstances. If the government increased the money supply, this would shift the PY curve up (say to PY_2) in frame (c) causing an increase in the price level. If money wages stay at the initial (disequilibrium) level, then real wages would fall and move the economy back to equilibrium. If, on the other hand, money wages rose, perhaps as a response to the increase in prices (downward <u>real</u> wage rigidity) then monetary policy would be as futile as its fiscal equivalent.

Note one feature of this analysis. Unemployment in excess of the natural rate arises because real wages are too high for equilibrium. Unemployment of this kind is voluntary. We saw in chapter three that not all of the natural rate unemployment is voluntary although classical economists would argue to the contrary. Equivalently, it is clear some component of non-natural unemployment is voluntary. Again, in the classical view, all of it is. It only arises from the real wage being too high and if workers accept money wage cuts the unemployment will disappear.

This kind of simple model has long been rejected by modern classical economists although there are many lay persons who cling to its easily understood view of the world. Non-classical theorists who reject totally this classical picture of the labour market as a spot auction cleared by a smooth adjustment process will be considered in chapter five.

In the rest of this chapter, attention will be focussed on the modern classical analysis of unemployment which maintains the market clearing perspective of the old though in a rather more sophisticated guise.

Modern Classical Macroeconomics: A General Perspective

Modern classical macroeconomics differs from its intellectual predecessor in three significant ways. Firstly, the Keynesian revolution undermined the structural separability of the old classical model. It emphasised the interaction of markets and this has been taken on board by modern classical economists. No longer is the macroeconomy seen as a set of separate aggregate markets cleared independently by their respective flexible prices (R, W or P) but as an interdependent market clearing system. The crucial Keynesian innovations that provided this interdependence are the consumption function and the theory of liquidity preference which after some initial reluctance has been accepted, modified and improved by modern classical economists. (5)

The second significant departure is in the view of market clearing processes taken by modern classical economists. They acknowledge the logical problems highlighted by Arrow (1959). In perfect competition since every agent is a price taker nobody actually knows the market clearing vector of prices and hence no mechanism for changing prices actually exists. As a result, considerable emphasis is given to incomplete information, uncertainty and the formation of expectations. Extensive use has been made of search theory of the type considered in chapter three. There is a tendency to emphasise the employee's search process at the expense of the employer but it does mean labour market flows and dynamic market clearing processes can be incorporated into classical macroeconomic analysis.

The third and related departure from the traditional classical approach is the break from single period to multi-period analysis. Current decisions made by individuals are not simply dependent upon events in the current time period but also upon their evaluation of future events. The Keynesian consumption function, for example, emphasises the significance of current income but Friedman (1956), one of the founding fathers of Modern Classical Macroeconomics, stresses the role of expected future (as well as present) real income in the determination of consumer expenditure. As a result modern classical economists regard the formation and impact of expectations about future events as central to the macroeconomic analysis of the present.

These departures from traditional modes of market clearing analysis of unemployment character-ise the modern approach which is considered in the remainder of this chapter.

Price Expectations and the Natural Rate of Unemployment

As far as the labour market is concerned the departure point for modern classical macroeconomics is the traditional demand and supply curves. The demand for labour depends on the level of the real wage rate and the supply of labour (also dependent on the real wage) exhibits this same absence of money illusion. Voluntary unemployment will occur as we noted previously when the demand and supply of labour are equal. Agents in labour markets have incomplete information. This leads to search and as we saw in chapter three this may not be completed in a single period of time due to frictions in the search process. Accordingly a positive rate of frictional unemployment is acknowledged to be inevitable and the amount of all unemployment when the labour supply and demand are equal is defined as the natural rate. It was originally defined by Milton Friedman (1968) as:

> the level that would be ground out by the Walrasian system of general equilibrium equations provided there is embedded in them the actual structural characteristics of the labor and commodity markets, including ... the cost of gathering information about job vacancies.

The relation of these ideas to the traditional classical model of the labour market is illustrated in Figure 4.3. Frames (a) and (b) are the conventional labour supply, labour demand and employment/output relationships. Frame (c) is drawn on the assumption that workers in the labour force are either in or out of work. If they are in the latter state we assume they are registered, so we are measuring true unemployment and ignoring the biases discussed in chapter one. It, plus employment, measures the working population at which point the labour supply curve is horizontal in frame (c). Frame (d) is simply the VU curve described in chapter three. The intersection of the VU curve and the 45 line permits the derivation of the natural rate of unemployment as U*. As it happens we can also define the natural employment rate (E*) and the natural (full capacity) output level (Y*) at this point. If unemployment is equal to the natural rate the inflow and output rates into unemployment ($H_t^u = D_t^u$) are also equal and consequently the expected mean length of unemployment can be found as $1/H_t^{u*}$ (or $1/\theta^*$) where H_t^u is the outflow rate when the unemployment stock is at its natural level. In other words it is an integral part of the modern classical approach to define the natural rate of unemployment in a way which incorporates turnover in the labour market using the flow concepts we have considered in earlier chapters.

It is also a critical part of the modern classical approach that the natural rate is not a constant. Indeed empirical work by Hall (1975), for example, has argued that as much as 93% of the variation in US unemployment between 1954 and 1974 was the outcome of variation in the natural rate. We

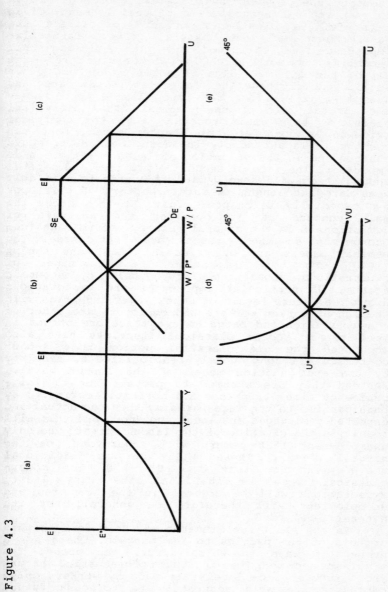

Figure 4.3

113

shall later see that the policy prescriptions for reducing unemployment by classical economists focus on reducing the natural rate of unemployment. Given this, it is clearly important to isolate the determinants of the natural rate. Particular importance is attached to the microeconomic incentives to work which include marginal rates of direct tax and the value of unemployment and other social security benefits. Increases in tax rates and unemployment benefits are both alleged to increase the natural rate of unemployment. The theoretical basis for this claim together with the empirical evidence is considered in chapter seven. Long run changes in labour supply including both demographic changes and in the valuation of leisure (6) are also important. The rate of technical progress and capital accumulation will have demand side effects similarly considered at length in later chapters of this book and especially in chapter eight. At this stage the main concern is to consider the analysis of deviations from the natural rate by modern classical economists so these issues are left aside. The seminal papers are by Friedman (1968) and Phelps (1970) who both emphasise the importance of expectations about the future held by economic agents. Of particular importance are expectations about the future levels of money wages and prices. In the labour market workers and employers are under no money illusion and bargains are therefore struck in real terms. Modern classical theorists have also abandoned the old classical notion that labour contracts are continuously renegotiated as required by the spot auction model of the labour market. Instead they are assumed to prevail for a finite period of time. If prices are correctly estimated by both parties to the wage bargain, then the actual and expected real wages are equal and known and this will result in the clearing of the labour market. The only unemployment that occurs will, therefore, be the natural level. There will be no additional unemployment, so that $U - U^* = 0$. The modern classical view is that, at the very least, expectations will be correct in the long run and unemployment will therefore be generally at its natural level.

In the short run mistakes may be made by either or both of the parties to the bargain. There are a number of ways in which errors can occur. The simplest approach is to assume forecasting errors about future price levels are made by workers only. Employers are able accurately to forecast future price levels because of their superior information about a matter in which they are directly involved. How does unemployment in excess of the natural rate arise? Suppose workers overestimate the future price level. As a result they will believe that the current money wage acceptable to employers (on the basis of their accurate expectations) implies a lower real wage than will actually be the case. Although the actual real wage would equate labour demand and supply in the market, it fails to do so because of the erroneous expectations held by workers. These ideas are illustrated in Figure 4.4 which uses frames (b) and (c) of Figure 4.3.

Figure 4.4

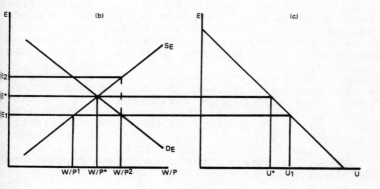

The natural rate of employment (E^*) and unemployment (U^*) will prevail if both workers and employers hold the same (accurate) expectation about the price level over the period to which current wage negotiations relate. If, however, workers believe the price level will be greater than P^* they will also believe the real wage will be lower (W/P^1) in frame (b)). As a result only E_1 workers will work and actual unemployment will be U_1 which exceeds U^*.

Note the important sensitivity of labour supply in these events. This follows from the intertemporal substitution model of labour supply. This says that if households believe the real wage has fallen and is lower than its long run level, then there is an incentive to work less in the current period and more in the future. In other words, households surrender future leisure for current leisure. Unemployment in excess of the natural rate occurs, according to this view, because households choose voluntarily to vary their labour supply through time in response to changes in the expected real wage. Because expectational errors by workers induce these labour supply effects, non-natural unemployment is entirely a voluntary matter for workers who are affected by it. Clearly a conclusion as contentious as this requires empirical verification and this is an issue taken up in chapter six. At this stage we will concentrate on the development of the theoretical ideas.

So far only workers have made errors but although less likely, employers could also overestimate future values of the aggregate price level and agree to a money wage with this in mind. Since the actual market clearing price level turns out to be lower the actual real wage will be greater than expected (W/P^2 in Frame (b) of Figure 4.4). As a result, they will, according to Phelps (1968) interpret this actual price level as a reduction in the relative price of their own product and lay off workers. This also reduces employment to E_1 and U to U_1 (greater than U^*). In this case the unemployment that arises is involuntary in the sense that if the actual wage is W/P^2, E_2 workers will wish to work. This unemployment will be equal to $E_2 - E_1$.

These arguments can now be represented algebraically as

4.9 $U_t = U_t^* + \alpha \ (P_t - {}_{t-1}P_t^e) \quad \alpha < 0$

where

$U_t =$ actual unemployment at time t

$U_t^* =$ the natural rate of unemployment at time t

$P_t =$ the log of the aggregate price level at time t

${}_{t-1}P_t^e =$ the forward looking expectation formed

116

> at the end of period t-1 of the log of
> the aggregate price level at time t

If the price level is correctly anticipated $P_t = {}_{t-1}P_t^e$ and $U_t = U_t^*$ (non-natural unemployment is zero). Only if the price level is overestimated (7) (${}_{t-1}P_t^e > P_t$) will unemployment in excess of the natural rate occur.

Equation 4.9 can be re-written as follows:

4.9a $U_t = U_t^* + \alpha\left(\left(P_t - P_{t-1}\right) - \left({}_{t-1}P_t^e - P_{t-1}\right)\right)$

where P_{t-1} is the log of the previous periods price level. Since $(P_t - P_{t-1})$ is the actual rate of inflation $\dot{P}_t$ and $({}_{t-1}P_t^e - P_{t-1})$ is the expected rate of inflation $\dot{P}_t^e$. This becomes

4.9b $U_t = U_t^* + \alpha\ (\dot{P}_t - \dot{P}_t^e)$

Note the family resemblance of 4.9b to the expectations augmented Phillips curve. In order to see this rearrange 4.9b to give

4.10 $P_t = 1/\alpha\ (U_t - U_t^*) + \dot{P}_t^e$

If unemployment is below U_t^* the actual inflation rate exceeds the expected rate (recall α is negative). If unemployment is equal to the natural rate the actual inflation rate is perfectly anticipated ($\dot{P}_t = \dot{P}_t^e$) and as we have seen, if unemployment exceeds U_t^* the inflation rate is overestimated and actual inflation is less than expected.

We have now seen the consequences of an overestimation of the price level in modern classical analysis. However, the unemployment that results will not persist as expectations are revised to the correct level and errors are eliminated. If the inflation rate is constant these errors could be eliminated within a single period. If it is variable it might take longer but critical to the speed at which the non-natural unemployment is eliminated, is the way in which expectations are formed and these are considered in the next two sections of this chapter.

Before this is considered we need to consider the classical exposition of the macroeconomic context in which the labour market functions. The basic structure employed might best be described as modified Keynesian. In the monetary sector the emphasis is placed on Fisher's (1930) distinction between the nominal and the real rate of interest.

Algebraically this distinction can be written as

4.11 $i_t = R_t + \dot{P}_t^e$

where

i_t = nominal rate of interest

R_t = real rate of interest

$\dot{P}_t^e$ = expected rate of inflation based on the forward looking expectation of the price level formed at the end of period t-1

In the textbook Keynesian model, the demand for real cash balances is interest elastic. Classical economists emphasise that the cost of holding money is not simply the real rate of interest but also the rate of inflation which governs the rate at which the real value of a given money holding is depreciating. The demand for real money function is therefore

4.12 $Md_t/P = L(Y_t, R_t, \dot{P}_t^e)$ with

$\partial Md_t/P\big/\partial R_t < 0 \quad \partial Md_t/P\big/\partial \dot{P}_t^e < 0$

$\partial Md_t/P\big/\partial Y_t > 0$

Contrast this equation with equation 4.8 to see the recognition by modern classical economists of influences other than real income on the demand for real cash balances. In determining desired real cash holdings at the beginning of the period of analysis expectations are formed by money holders about the rate of price inflation. Hence 4.12 includes the expected rate of price inflation ($\dot{P}_t^e$) as an argument.

In the goods sector of the economy the Keynesian IS curve of aggregate demand is represented algebraically by

4.13 $Y_t = c(Y_t, R_t, M_t/P) + Z_t$

where

Z_t = autonomous demand
M_t/P = real cash balances

The whole system can be put into logs and linearised

4.14 $M_t - P_t = L_1 Y_t - L_2 \left(R_t + (_{t-1}P_t^e - P_{t-1})\right)$

with $L_1 > 0$
$L_2 > 0$

This is the familiar LM equation. The modified IS equation for the aggregate demand for goods is

4.15 $Y_t^d = Z_t + c_1 Y_t - c_2 (R_t) + c_3 (M_t - P_t)$

with $c_1, c_2, c_3 > 0$

where $R_t = (i_t - (_{t-1}P_t^e - P_{t-1}))$ and

Y_t^d = demand for goods

Equation 4.9 is reconstituted by most modern classical theorists as the Lucas-Sargent (8) aggregate supply equation. The natural rate of unemployment U^* implies a natural level of output Y^* (see Figure 4.3). Departures from the natural rate of unemployment are mirrored by output so equation 4.9 can be written after log-linearising as

4.16 $Y_t^s = Y_t^* + \beta (P_t - _{t-1}P_t^e)$ with $\beta > 0$

If the price level is overestimated ($_{t-1}P_t^e > P_t$) then output will be less than its natural level. In the simplest case where only workers make such errors this will occur because employers are unable to get the workers they need to produce Y_t^*. They are constrained by workers who opt to take current leisure rather than work. They will also be constrained by the demand for goods if overestimation of the price level occurs in the goods or monetary sector of the economy. This is considered more fully in the next section. This is essentially the system employed by Sargent (1976) and will form the basis of the analysis of the next two sections.

Adaptive expectations and unemployment

A critical question, both theoretically and empirically, for modern classical macroeconomics is the way in which expectations are formed. Some empirical work (9) has avoided this question by employing directly observed expectations available from surveys. The problem with the surveys that exist is incomplete coverage - they do not extend to all agents in the economy and the period over which they are collected is often too short for thorough-going time series analysis. As a result alternative methods are invariably used. Initially we will consider the

adaptive expectations approach, introduced by Cagan
(1956). This assumes that expectations are formed by
economic agents as follows:

4.17 $_{t-1}X_t^e = \lambda X_{t-1} + (1-\lambda)_{t-2}X_{t-1}^e$ $0 < \lambda < 1$

where X is the economic variable about which
expectations are being formed. The procedure assumes
agents compare the previous period's expectations
with the outturn and adjust their current forecast by
a fraction of the previous period's forecasting
error. In the previous period the expected value of X
is obviously

4.18 $_{t-2}X_{t-1}^e = \lambda X_{t-2} + (1-\lambda)_{t-3} X_{t-2}^e$

By recursive substitution to eliminate the
unobservable X^e we obtain:

4.19 $_{t-1}X_t^e = \lambda X_{t-1} + \lambda(1-\lambda)X_{t-2} + \lambda(1-\lambda)^2 X_{t-3}$

$$+ \ldots \lambda(1-\lambda)^n X_{t-n-1}$$

$$+ (1-\lambda)^{n+1} {}_{t-n-2}X_{t-n-1}^e$$

If n is large enough the influence of the final
unobservable term can be made infinitesimally small.
Equation 4.19 shows that the current expectation is a
geometrically declining weighted average of past
values of X.

Consider now the impact of an expectations
forming mechanism of this type on the unemployment
equation 4.9b. Recall this tells us that only if the
rate of price inflation is overestimated will non-
natural unemployment result. Suppose the actual rate
of price inflation stays constant, what will happen?
We shall call that constant rate of inflation $\bar{P}$. If
we substitute this into 4.19 we get:

4.20 $_{t-1}\dot{P}_t^e = \bar{P} \left(1 + (1-\lambda) + (1-\lambda)^2 + (1-\lambda)^3 \ldots\right) \lambda$

$$= \lambda\bar{P}/1-(1-\lambda)$$

$$= \bar{P}$$

In other words if the inflation rate stays constant
it will eventually be perfectly anticipated and when
it is, any non-natural unemployment will disappear.
The period over which this unemployment disappears

will be governed by the speed at which expectations
are revised. In the real world in these circumstances
of constant inflation the process is likely to be
quite short. If, on the other hand, the inflation
rate is highly variable the period is bound to be
longer.

Are there any circumstances in which
unemployment in excess of the natural rate can
persist indefinitely? The analysis of the previous
section indicates the classical view that this can
only happen if the inflation rate is persistently
overestimated. Under the adaptive expectations
mechanism this happens if the inflation rate
decelerates each period. Only part of the previous
period's forecast error would be made up in the
current period, as equation 4.18 shows, so that
economic agents would persistently overestimate the
rate of inflation and non-natural unemployment would
persist. This argument is, of course, exactly that
outlined by Friedman (1968) except that he placed
greater emphasis on the <u>acceleration</u> of inflation
that would need to accompany any persistent tendency
for unemployment to be <u>below</u> the natural rate. When
this happens the inflation rate is underestimated.

Within the monetary and goods sectors of the
economy where aggregate demand and portfolio balance
take place the position is a little more ambiguous.
Overestimation of the rate of inflation leaves the <u>ex
post</u> demand for money at a higher level which drives
up the real interest rate. This reduces the demand
for goods which confirms the forces in the supply
side of the economy that cause unemployment to occur.
On the other hand, real cash balances are at a higher
level than expected and this increases the demand for
goods unless we make the special assumption that the
LM curve is vertical. In this case the unexpected
rise in real cash balances causes an upward shift in
the IS curve but it has no effect on the aggregate
demand for goods. No conflicting signals that might
undermine the rise in unemployment occur in this
case. An assumption of this type requires the
interest elasticity of the demand for money to be
zero which is precisely the view of old classical
economists. In the face of the empirical evidence,
modern classical economists are reluctant to rely
upon an assumption of this kind. Sargent (1973)
argues that these special restrictions required on
the slope of the IS/LM curves for the use of the
adaptive expectations framework are too stringent
and can only be overcome by the alternative rational
expectations approach.

121

The implication that non-natural unemployment can, in principle, persist under adaptive expectations if inflation is decelerating has also proved rather unpalatable for modern classical economists. The character of the expectations formation mechanism implies in general, systematic mistakes which classical economists believe will not occur. Optimising individuals are bound, they believe, to take corrective action to prevent this happening so that such unemployment cannot persist. If it did persist the labour market would not clear and this goes against the whole classical tradition of analysis. The classical macroeconomics of the 1970s has also scorned the notion that the expected value of an economic variable is forecast simply by the use of its own past values. Such a simple mechanism is rejected in favour of a procedure that allows for system-wide influences on the variable to be forecast. It is for these reasons that modern classical macroeconomists now rely upon the assumptions of rational expectations for their analysis of unemployment.

Rational Expectations and Unemployment

Basic to the use of rational expectations is the view that the subjective expectations of the future movement of an economic variable held by an economic agent coincides with the objective conditional mathematical expectations of such a time path occurring. Algebraically

$$4.21 \quad {}_{t-1}X_t = {}_{t-1}EX_t$$

where X_t is the subjective expectation and ${}_{t-1}EX_t$ is the conditional mathematical expectation of X_t formed using all available information at time $t-1$. Advocates of this approach do not argue that economic agents actually perform the calculations necessary to arrive at ${}_{t-1}EX_t$. Rather they believe:

> an expectation would be rational, if the expectation arrived at by instinct, intuition or judgement, based on past experience, turned out to coincide with the expectation based on a careful recording of previous experience and the calculation of a conditional expectation from those data
>
> (Parkin and Bade (1982))

It also does not mean that economic agents do not

make mistakes. Mistakes are unavoidable given imperfect information but any errors that are made are assumed to be random and serially uncorrelated, so there is no relationship between mistakes in the current period and mistakes in previous periods. Systematic error, which is a central feature of the adaptive expectations approach, is therefore ruled out by rational expectations. As we have seen, of critical importance to the analysis of non-natural unemployment is the expectation of the price level and its rate of inflation. Classical economists like Sargent (1973) posit that expectations about the logarithm of the price level are rational and 4.21 can be particularised as

4.22 $\quad _{t-1}P^e_t = {}_{t-1}EP_t$

In order to specify the terms on which 4.22 is conditioned requires use of a stochastic version of equations 4.14, 4.15 and 4.16.

4.14a $\quad M_t - P_t = L_1Y_t - L_2\left(R_t + ({}_{t-1}P^e_t - P_{t-1})\right) + \mu_t$

(LM equation)

4.15a $\quad Y^d_t = Z_t + C_1Y_t - C_2(R_t) + C_3(M_t - P_t) + \varepsilon_t$

(IS equation)

4.16a $\quad Y^s_t = Y^*_t + \beta\ (P_t - {}_{t-1}P^e_t) + \eta_t$

Recall all the variables are in logs. The exogenous variables in this system are Z_t (autonomous expenditure), Y^* (the natural rate of output) and M_t (the nominal money supply). Z_t, Y^* and all the random variables (μ_t, ε_t, η_t) in 4.14a, 4.15a and 4.16a are assumed by Sargent (1973)) to be governed by an autoregressive process of the type

4.23 $\quad g_t = \rho_g\ g_{t-1} + \gamma_{gt}$

where g is the random variable in question. The γ's are mutually uncorrelated, serially uncorrelated, normally distributed random variables with a mean of zero. The money supply is determined partly by a randomly determined part of its own plus a systematic part dependent upon distributed lags in all of the exogenous variables (M_t, Y^* and Z_t) and of the random terms (μ_t, ε_t, η_t) in the model. Using these further assumptions we can write

123

4.24 $_{t-1}P_t^e = \underset{t-1}{E} (P_t/\emptyset_{t-1})$

where $\emptyset$ includes all observations on M, Y*, Z, ε, μ and η dated t-1 and before.

Economic agents are assumed to prepare a forecast <u>as if</u> they knew the structure of the model and the properties of the exogenous and random variables shown above <u>and</u> assuming the economy is in equilibrium so that the goods, money and labour markets all clear. (10) The rational expectation of the price level, therefore, will be the equilibrium level that will be that expected at full employment ($Y_t^s = Y_t^d = Y_t^*$). It is easy to show (Lucas (1972)) that the prediction error in the forecast of the price level which economic agents make is

4.25 $P_t - \underset{t-1}{E} (P_t/\emptyset_{t-1})$

The regression of the prediction error on $\emptyset_{t-1}$ is

4.26 $\underset{t-1}{E} (P_t - \underset{t-1}{E} P_t/\emptyset_{t-1}) | / \emptyset_{t-1})$

$= \underset{t-1}{E} (P_t/\emptyset_{t-1}) - \underset{t-1}{E} (P_t/\emptyset_{t-1}) = 0$

Since the expected value of the prediction error is zero we can see from equation 4.16a that the level of output and hence unemployment will normally be the natural rate. It will only depart from that level when the error η_t is non-zero. On average η_t will equal zero given the statistical assumptions that have been made so that any tendency for non-natural unemployment (Y ≠ Y* or U > U*) to occur will be purely random and will be quickly corrected and probably within a single period.

The meaning of these formal statements can also be stated intuitively. The rational expectations view assumes that workers and employers produce a forecast of the price level. This forecast assumes they know the structure of the economic system (the IS, LM and aggregate supply relationships in our example) and the value of exogenous variables, like government expenditure and the money supply. The forecast also assumes that markets in the economy are cleared - it is an equilibrium forecast. In the labour market the price level that is expected by workers (and employers) will be the one that ensures the equality of supply and demand (W*/P in Figure

4.4). Not surprisingly (and tautologically?) the rational expectations model predicts that <u>generally</u> the labour market will be in equilibrium, so that unemployment will be equal to the natural rate. This, however, will not <u>always</u> be the case. Errors can be made in the preparation of forecasts in much the same way as they are by the Treasury, the London Business School and other professional economic forecasters in Britain. In the rational expectations world these errors have a mean of zero so that on <u>average</u>, unemployment will not exceed the natural rate. Only when a random error is made will the price level be overestimated and will this occur but it will not last.

A conclusion as strong as this has important implications for policy to reduce unemployment and these are considered in the next section.

Modern Classical Macroeconomics and Unemployment Policy

Given the theoretical analysis of unemployment it is no surprise that modern classical economists take a generally sceptical view of the capacity of fiscal and monetary policy to affect the level of unemployment. In that respect they bear a close resemblence to their intellectual predecessors in the Classical tradition.

The standard Lucas-Sargent supply equation (4.16) assumes as we have seen, that non-natural unemployment results from an overestimation of the rate of price inflation. Under the adaptive expectations assumption this can persist in general and if it does there is a clear role for the government at least in the short run. It can pursue policies designed to affect expectations directly through an interventionist prices policy or it can eliminate the unemployment by an expansionary fiscal or monetary policy. This will not simply create demand in the conventional Keynesian fashion but will drive up the actual rate of inflation to the expected level. This process will increase the expected rate itself but under an adaptive expectations scheme will do so less than in proportion. Eventually the actual and expected rates of inflation will coincide and unemployment will return to the natural level. The problem with this type of policy is that it necessarily leads to a permanent increase in the actual rate of inflation.

In fact, classical economists would argue that the error in expectations can be relied upon to correct itself and no policy is needed. This view relies upon the adoption of the rational expectations framework. Since departures from the natural rate are random occurrences that will correct themselves no remedial action to remove non-natural unemployment is necessary. The argument is further strengthened by examining what might happen if the government were to adopt a systematic expansionary policy for unemployment. The rational expectations framework assumes this policy is recognised by economic agents who revise their price expectations with consequent effects on the price level itself. Real decisions that govern the demand and supply of goods and labour are unaffected and the expansionary policy has no effect on employment except in the very short term. Begg (1982a) summarises the argument thus:

> While it would be difficult to maintain that all systematic policy changes are immediately understood by the private sector, the spirit of this analysis is that demand management at best can only have very temporary effects. Individuals observing data on government behaviour and taking account of government statements of its policy intentions quickly infer the policy rule in operation.

Not only do modern classical economists deny the need or the value of demand management to remove unemployment in excess of the natural rate they also assert its total inadequacy in forcing unemployment below its natural level or changing the natural level itself where it is thought to be too high. The former of these two arguments has been called by Begg (1982a) the weak neutrality argument and the latter the strong neutrality argument. The former is basically the argument of Friedman (1968) that attempts to drive unemployment below its natural level can only succeed if economic agents are persuaded to underestimate the rate of inflation. If the rate of inflation is perfectly anticipated then the aggregate supply and demand relations will maintain output at its natural level. This is illustrated diagramatically in Figure 4.5.

Frame (a) represents the conventional IS/LM aggregate demand sector as described by equations 4.14 and 4.15. Frame (b) is the familiar employment function relating real output to employment. The rest of the labour market is not shown in Figure 4.5 but to see the implications of the analysis for that sector, simply requires Figure 4.3 to be plugged into

Figure 4.5   Figure 4.6

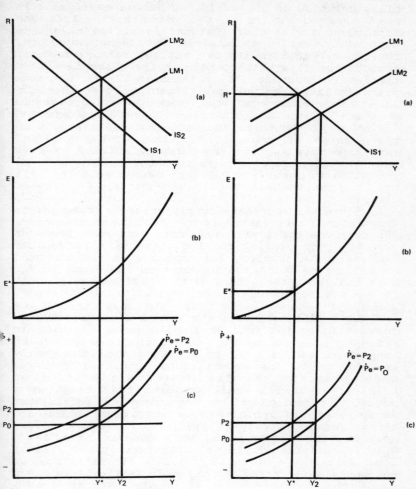

Figure 4.5. Initially in the spirit of the modern classical view of the world, we assume employment is at E* and output is at Y*. Since both output and employment are at their natural levels we also know the labour market is cleared and unemployment is, therefore, equal to its own natural rate. Frame (c) depicts the relationship between the price level and the level of output. It is shown in Figure 4.5 as a price inflation/output relationship. It depicts the Lucas/Sargent aggregate supply relationship shown in equation 4.16. With a given level of expected inflation it shows the amount firms will supply with given rates of actual inflation. If the expected inflation rate is zero the curve labelled $\dot{P}_e = 0$ is the aggregate supply curve. If the actual rate of inflation is zero ($\dot{P} = P_0$) then output supplied will be Y* (the natural rate) as equation 4.16 makes clear.

Since the aggregate supply curve in Frame (c) is drawn on the assumption of constant price expectations there will be a curve for each level of expected price inflation. The curve $\dot{P}_e = P_2$ depicts the aggregate supply relationship when the expected rate of price inflation is positive and equal to P_2. Note that when the actual rate of inflation is equal to P_2 output supplied equals Y*. In other words, since, in general, actual and expected price inflation will coincide, the normal aggregate supply curve will be vertical at Y*. The curve depicted in Frame (c) only occurs when expectational errors (with respect to prices) are made. Note, also the family resemblance to the expectations augmented Phillips curve. Frame (c) can also be seen as a depiction of that curve. In its familiar form it is drawn as a negative function of the unemployment rate. Here unemployment is replaced by real output (which are themselves negatively related) so the curve slopes upwards. The basic ideas are, however, the same. Only if inflation is imperfectly anticipated will it look like $\dot{P}_e = 0$ or $\dot{P}_e = P_2$. If inflation is perfectly anticipated the curve is <u>vertical</u>. In other words the normal ($\dot{P}_t = \dot{P}_t^e$) Lucas-Sargent supply equation is no more than the long run vertical Phillips curve.

Now consider the effects of the government adopting an expansionary fiscal policy which moves the IS curve from IS_1 to IS_2. We can see that if output were to rise price inflation would also rise to P_2. If workers and employers know of the government's policy change and anticipate its effects the aggregate supply/Phillips curve will

Figure 4.7

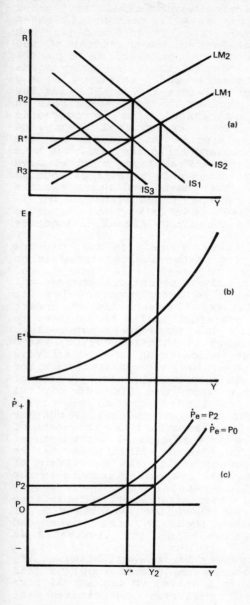

shift upwards to $\dot{P}^e = P_2$. If these events are perfectly anticipated output would remain at Y* (and unemployment would stay at U*). That still leaves excess demand for goods (Y_2 - Y* in Frame (a)) but this will not remain. In the demand sector of the economy the increase in prices would lead to the belief that the real value of the fixed money stock would fall and the LM curve would shift up to LM_2. Aggregate demand would therefore stay at Y*. (11) The basic result for an increase in the money supply is the same. A fully anticipated rise in aggregate demand and the price level leaves real output and employment (and unemployment) unaltered. Had the rise in aggregate demand and the price level not been anticipated then output and employment would have risen to Y_2 and E_2. This can only persist as long as the increase in aggregate demand and price remains unanticipated. Under rational expectations, individuals cannot be 'fooled' in this way and therefore attempts to expand the economy by fiscal or monetary policy will fail.

The strong neutrality argument is also of some importance. The analysis so far implies there is no need for a policy to deal with non-natural unemployment which is only a transitory phenomenon. Moreover attempts to drive unemployment below its natural level are futile. The emphasis of modern classical economists therefore shifts to the need to reduce the natural rate of unemployment. The strong neutrality argument suggests that convention demand management is impotent in achieving this objective.

The starting point for the analysis is the observation that in the long run the natural rate of output depends partly upon the rate of capital accumulation because of its effects on production capacity. The critical issue, therefore, is whether fiscal or monetary policy can affect the real rate of interest and hence the rate of capital accumulation. The crucial proposition (Sargent (1973)), as far as monetary policy is concerned, is the invariance of the real interest rate with respect to changes in the nominal money supply. Increases in the money supply will increase nominal rates of interest because they increase the actual and hence the expected rate of inflation. This reduces both the real demand and supply of money balances. This is illustrated in Figure 4.6

Initially the economy is in equilibrium at Y*, R* and E*. An increase in the normal supply shifts the LM curve to LM_2. This drives up the actual rate of inflation and if perfectly anticipated the expected rate of inflation, shifting the $\dot{P}_e$ curve to P_2. The increase in the actual rate of inflation would reduce the real money supply and push the LM curve back to its original position, restoring real interest rates at R* although the nominal rate will have gone up by P_2. If this change in the money supply is perfectly anticipated by agents, neither investment nor Y* will therefore be affected by this policy. In some versions of this argument (e.g. Begg (1982a)) investment is lagged a single period at the end of which the constancy of the real rate of interest is known to investors so that real investment and hence Y*, E* and U* are unaffected. The story with fiscal policy is a little different and this is shown in Figure 4.7.

Again we start at Y*, E* and R*. An increase in government expenditure, for example, will shift the IS curve to IS_2. This stimulates a domestic inflation of P_2 which if perfectly anticipated will shift the LM curve to LM_2 (see the argument relating to Figure 4.5). This will shift the aggregate supply curve to $\dot{P} = P_2$. If the inflation is perfectly anticipated this will restore output to its original level. There has been no change in the actual <u>or</u> natural level of output (or unemployment). However there is an important difference compared with monetary policy. Where fiscal policy is used in a (futile) attempt to lower the level of U* the real interest rate ends up higher at R_2 in Frame (a) of Figure 4.7. As a result the increase in government expenditure will 'crowd out' private sector investment which, in the long run, will reduce capacity output hence reducing Y*, E* and increasing U*. If fiscal policy is to be used to cut the natural rate, therefore, it must lead to cuts in the real interest rate to, say, R_3 in Frame (a) of Figure 4.7. This requires a downward shift in the IS curve to IS_3 and this will only be achieved by <u>cuts</u> in public expenditure which 'crowds in' private sector investment and increases Y*. The implication that long run reductions in the natural rate of unemployment requires these cuts has been seized upon with glee by right wing politicians seeking an economic justification for the application of what, for them, is political ideology. (12)

It is important to re-emphasise that these results depend upon the inability of the government consistently to 'fool' economic agents. Under rational expectations this is no problem since systematic fooling simply cannot take place. The results also depend upon some specific restrictions about the structure of the macroeconomy. Sargent

(1973) confesses in a footnote that, rather surprisingly, the real balance effect must be excluded from the aggregate demand (IS) schedule to derive some of these results. This is particularly important for the 'strong neutrality' of monetary policy. If a real balance effect is included in the IS curve, increases in the rate of inflation reduce real cash balances which shifts the IS curve down resulting in a lower real rate of interest in Figure 4.6 even if inflation is perfectly anticipated. Although unemployment rises in the short run it is quickly eliminated as the fall in R* causes investment to rise and Y* and E* to increase and U* to fall in the longer run. The results with fiscal policy depend upon the extent to which the reduction in consumption resulting from reduced real balances 'crowds in' private sector investment. In other words, the outcome depends on the extent to which the wealth effects of higher prices shift the IS curve down. If the IS curve is shifted back to its original position the long run increase in U* does not take place if an expansionary fiscal policy is adopted. Indeed if the wealth effects are sufficiently strong to force the IS curve back to IS_3 a long run decrease in the natural rate will occur. In practice the most likely outcome is for the real balance effects on consumption to leave the IS curve between IS_1 and IS_2 and the real rate of interest between R* and R_2. The inclusion of the real balance effect is likely, therefore, to weaken the conclusion about the 'strong neutrality' of fiscal policy. In the case of monetary policy it totally overturns it. The general pessimism about the value of demand management in changing the level of unemployment conforms with the old classical view of the general futility of governmental attempts to regulate a free enterprise capitalist economy. Note, however the government is not completely powerless in influencing the level of unemployment. Apart from the possible effects of demand management on the long run natural rate it is also possible for the government to influence upwards or downwards the level of non-natural unemployment. For this to happen the government must 'surprise' the private sector by making an unanticipated change in policy which gives rise to errors that are not speedily corrected. Although the rational expectation approach says this will not, in general, happen consider the effects of the policy changes made since 1979 and designed to reduce the rate of inflation in Britain.

The classical view would be that the major

change of policy regime that was required to meet this objective would be quickly learnt and so the downward impact on employment and output would be short lived. This has not been the case. One explanation is that economic agents do indeed learn a good deal more slowly than the classical models (which assume market clearing) would have us believe. An alternative explanation is that the models themselves are severely inadequate descriptions of a western industrial economy. This is a more sceptical view, the basis of which is considered later in this and throughout the whole of the next chapter. At this stage we shall consider the implication of modern classical macroeconomics for the control of unemployment in an open economy.

Rational Expectations and Unemployment in the Open Economy

The analysis so far has assumed a closed economy, but for Britain with its heavy involvement in international transactions, this may be inappropriate. Since the early seventies the exchange rates in the western world have been flexible and this has been a major ingredient of the modern classical analysis of the open economy. (13) We shall firstly consider the fixed exchange rate case. The analysis of the causes and cures for unemployment is not strikingly different from the closed economy case. Rational expectations of the domestic price level are influenced by additional variables like the foreign price level and changes in the level of fixed exchange rate. The real economy is vulnerable to shocks from the outside world. However, if the changes are fully anticipated and no mistakes are made in the calculation of the expected price level, unemployment and output will remain at the natural level. Fluctuations in the world output or price level could lead to an overestimation of the price level which will cause unemployment. Under a rational expectations regime these mistakes cannot persist despite the more complex nature of the information relevant to the formation of expectations. Similarly, any attempt to remove unemployment by fiscal policy will only succeed if the price level effects of the policy are less than fully anticipated. Substantially, the results are the same as for the closed economy. Expansionary demand management increases the price level but leaves unemployment unaffected. The only additional effect is that with fixed exchange rates the increase in the domestic price level makes domestic industry less competitive. The result will be a worsening of the current account balance which has further repercussions on the domestic economy.

The full sequence of events is shown in Figure 4.8. Frames (b) and (c) are the same as those used before in this chapter. Frame (a) is the conventional IS/LM relationship augmented by a Mundell/Fleming external balance schedule (14) which assumes

4.27 $X = x(\gamma)$ $dX/d\gamma > 0$

4.28 $F = f(Y,\gamma)$ $\partial F/\partial Y > 0$ $\partial F/\partial \gamma < 0$

4.29 $KI = k(R)$ $dKI/dR > 0$

where

γ = $Pf/\tau Pb$ (index of competitiveness)
Pf = foreign price
Pb = home price
τ = rate of exchange of foreign currency for domestic currency
KI = the net capital inflow
F = imports
X = exports

4.27 and 4.28 imply that as output increases the current account of the balance of payments worsens. If the overall balance is to be maintained this requires a compensating improvement in the capital account which equation 4.29 shows can be achieved by an increase in the domestic interest rate. This is the reason for the positive slope of the XB curve. (15)

Now consider the consequences of an unanticipated fiscal expansion designed to drive output above the initial level (Y*) and unemployment down. Initially, assume we are at the intersection of LM_1, XB_1 and IS_1. The unanticipated fiscal expansion shifts the IS curve to IS_2 and Y to Y_2. This increases the rate of interest and price inflation to P_2. The increase in the price level reduces the real money supply although this will be offset by the effects on the money stock of an increase in foreign exchange reserves resulting from the balance of payments surplus in this new situation. The surplus results from the capital inflow induced by the higher rate of interest. The increase in reserves occurs because we are assuming a fixed exchange rate.

The increase in the price level has another

Figure 4.8

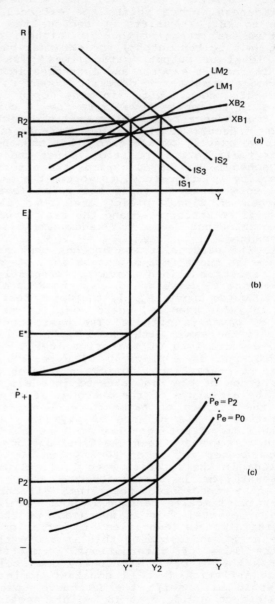

important effect. It worsens international competitiveness, which shifts the external balance function to XB_2. It shifts up because the loss of competitiveness means either a higher rate of interest (with given output) for external balance or a lower level of output (with given R) is needed. Because it reduces exports and increases imports, it also reduces demand for domestic goods so the IS curve shifts down. Note in the open economy, increases in the price level move the IS curve down even in the absence of domestic wealth effects (like the Pigou effect). If the various effects on the IS and LM curve exactly offset each other then both will return to their initial position. Since the external balance schedule has moved upwards the effect of the fiscal policy is, therefore, to worsen the balance of payments as well as to raise the price level. Once the changes in fiscal policy are known all these effects will be anticipated and the real economy will revert to an output level of Y* and unemployment will not be changed.

Note the particular assumptions that have been used to derive the effect on the balance of payments. Had the effects outlined above not precisely offset each other the IS curve would have ended up above IS_1 and the LM curve above LM_1. If the net effect were at LM_2 and IS_3, for example, there would be no adverse balance of payments effects. The basic conclusion, however, is the same. With fixed exchange rates and rational expectations of the price level, no change in real output or employment will be achieved by using expansionary fiscal policy in an open economy. The invariance of the real rate of interest may not, however, be a feature of the outcome. If it does not change, the balance of payments will worsen. If a deterioration in the balance of payments is not to occur the rate of interest has to rise at least as high as R_2. As we have seen the final outcome depends on the parameter values of the system. In general, some change in the interest rate is likely and this is different from the closed economy case.

We have considered the final effects of an unanticipated fiscal expansion without examining the intervening events. This is necessary so that final rate of inflation is identified. If inflation were to continue at P_2 and assuming this is above the world level the loss of international competitiveness would push the IS curve eventually down below IS_1. The price inflation (with a constant nominal money stock) would also shift the LM curve upward. The combined effect would be an IS/LM intersection below

Y*. This overshooting below Y* could cause the actual and expected rate of inflation eventually to fall to zero (or to the world rate of inflation if that is positive). In this model a once and for all fiscal expansion will always raise the price level but not necessarily the rate of price inflation. In the closed economy both will occur according to the classical model.

So far we assumed a fixed exchange rate but what happens if the rate of exchange (τ) is flexible? This is interesting not merely since exchange rates have been more flexible over the last decade but also prominent classical economists like Friedman (1968) have been principal advocates of floating exchange rates. In this case a rational expectation of the domestic price level requires the formation of an expectation about the exchange rate itself. Superficially it might be thought that this complicates the information problem for economic agents but this does not take account of the fact that the exchange rate itself contains relevant information which it is rational for economic agents to use in forming expectations about the domestic price level.

Consider the effects of an unanticipated increase in the money supply (16). Initially assume the economy is producing at the natural rate and expected values of P and τ are derived on that assumption. The unanticipated rise in the money supply shifts the LM curve to LM_2 in Figure 4.9. This reduces R to R_2 causing a capital outflow and increases Y, E and P (to Y_2, E_2 and P_2). This leads to a worsening in the current balance, reinforcing the overall trend to balance of payments deficit. The deficit and the unexpected rise in prices will cause the exchange rate to fall below its expected level. This will shift the XB curve (downwards) to XB_2. If we assume the boost to competitiveness offsets the effect of higher prices the IS curve stays at IS_1. The rise in price will, however, reduce the real value of the nominal money stock so the LM curve will move back to a position like LM_3. This leaves the economy with a higher inflation rate (P_3) but with output still above and unemployment still below the natural level (Y_3 in Frame (c) of Figure 4.9).

How long will this fall in unemployment persist? If the increase in the rate of inflation to P_3 is perfectly anticipated then the normal Lucas-Sargent aggregate supply equation will cause supply side forces to push Y down to Y*. What happens on the demand side of the economy depends on the way in

Figure 4.9

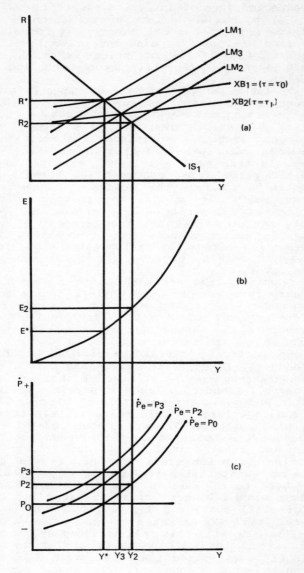

which the rational expectation of the exchange rate is formed. Since the rate of inflation ($\dot{P}$) is positive the LM curve will continue to drift upwards to its original position. At the exchange rate τ_1 this will lead to a balance of payments surplus and an appreciation of the exchange rate to its original level with the external balance schedule at XB_1. If all of this enters the rational expectation of τ then the economy will return to its 'natural' position although the nominal interest rate and the price level will be higher. In order to get inflation back to its original level, output will need to 'overshoot' to below its natural level. The eventual effect of the policy change will have been an increase in the domestic price level with no affect on real output or employment which is just the same result as in the closed economy.

This is consistent with the general approach of the modern classical economist. In an open economy adjustment may be more complex and slow moving than in the closed but the conclusion is the same. In general unemployment can only be reduced transitorily below the natural level by unanticipated monetary growth or by fiscal expansion. Permanent cuts in unemployment can only be achieved by cuts in the natural rate. This has all been summarised by Minford (1981):

> The essence of our approach is easily summarised. We reject the assumptions of 'disequilibrium' analysis, instead we suppose that markets always clear in the operational sense that some agent, or set of agents (be it a union or a government or competitive agents) always remove excess demands for any given market. Individuals then make voluntary maximising decisions subject to the market structure of the economy and the prices they face ...
>   When shocks hit this system, mistakes are made and adjustments allowed to be made, which take time to carry out. Monetary shocks ... are no exception.

This view of the world has not gone unchallenged and in the next section some of the principal criticisms are reviewed. The alternative disequilibrium approach is considered in the next chapter.

The Modern Classical Approach - A Preliminary Critique

The rational expectations approach has been the subject of considerable criticism from economists who believe that unemployment in excess of the natural rate can persist. The first and most obvious criticism is that economic agents do not form expectations in a rational manner. Kaldor and Trevithick (1981) have put this forcefully:

> The assumptions of rational expectations which presupposes the correct understanding of the workings of the economy by all economic agents to a degree which is beyond the grasp of professional economists is not science, nor even moral philosophy, but at best a branch of metaphysics.

Firstly, this asserts that it is impossible in the current state of economic knowledge to discover the correct model to use for the formation of rational expectations of a variable. Secondly, that even if there were a 'correct model' economic agents would not have the computational skill to find the solution. Those who advocate the rational expectations approach argue that the first problem which is one of econometric specification can be applied to most kinds of analysis. To the second point they reply that the modern classical approach does not assume agents actually perform the necessary calculation but they construct expectations as if they did. This is a familiar <u>riposte</u> often associated with Milton Friedman. These, however, are not such serious objections to the classical approach.

An associated objection to the rational expectations approach is its assumption that all economic agents have the same model and have access to the same information sets in constructing expectations. (17) This assumption is unlikely to be empirically supportable but it does enable the classical economist to sidestep the issue of what happens when economic agents, (employers and union negotiators for example) have different expectations rationally formed from different models or with different data. This seems a more profound objection to the modern classical approach. The view of rapid market clearing might take something of a jolt if conflicting expectations had to be resolved. This highlights the most fundamental objection to the modern classical approach to unemployment and its cure, and that is its reliance on market clearing.

This not only confounds the empirical facts but also the theoretical expectation that markets will clear at significantly different rates. The clearing process may indeed be so slow that markets may be regarded as never in equilibrium. There may also exist mechanisms which cause markets to stick in a disequilibrium state.

Why should we expect markets not to clear? Firstly there is the logical difficulty of who actually clears the market in a competitive model which assumes all economic agents are price takers. This leaves nobody with knowledge of the market clearing vector of prices and markets with a tendency to quantity adjustment. A further problem arises with the existence of market power, in the hands of monopolistic firms. As Hahn (1982) observes:

> When market power is present, the Smithian vision of the invisible hand is lost. Instead of the machine-like responses of agents to prices, the agents will find themselves engaged in a game.

The objectives they pursue in the 'game' may differ from those expected in the market clearing paradigm. Industrial economists (18) have shown how the growth of monopoly and oligopoly is associated with the abandonment of profit maximisation and the adoption of alternative maximands. We will consider these questions more fully in the next chapter but it is already clear that there are sufficient things to cause anxiety about the market clearing analysis of unemployment for it to be necessary to examine non-market clearing approaches.

Notes

1. The problems of aggregation are complex and are inadequately explored in the literature. One important paper in this respect is that of Hansen (1970).

2. See for example, Branson (1979).

3. There is an extensive empirical literature which is surveyed in Killingsworth (1971) and more recently by Hazledine (1981) and Nickell (1984a). Note that this formulation assumes a constant technology, capital stock and utilization rates of labour and capital.

4. The rate of interest clears this sector of the economy.

5. Many of the significant papers of modern

classical macroeconomics are included in two books by
two of the intellectual leaders of this approach,
namely R. Lucas and T. Sargent (1981) and R. Lucas
(1981).

6.   Hall (1980), for example, found a large
propensity for intemporal substitution of leisure in
the US and this affects the natural rate.

7.   If the price level is underestimated these
conclusions are reversed. This was the major concern
of Friedman (1968) who argued that unemployment could
only be forced below the natural rate if the price
level was underestimated. For this to happen,
inflation has to accelerate, he argued, so that the
Phillips curve trade-off is actually between the rate
of acceleration of inflation and unemployment, not
the inflation rate and unemployment.

8.   An excellent discussion of this (and other
associated matters) is contained in Begg (1982a) pp.
137-139.

9.   A study which aims to explain unemployment
in Britain and make use of survey data is Batchelor
and Sheriff (1980). Some of the problems are
discussed in Carlson and Parkin (1976).

10.   Strictly, forecast errors are only
serially uncorrelated in the one period horizon used
in the text if current information is full.

11.   This would be reinforced by the presence of
a real balance effect in the goods sector of the
economy which would cause a downward shift in the IS
curve if inflation equalled P_2.

12.   Note this argument assumes there is no
change in the relationship of Y* to U* and E*. A
shift from public current or capital expenditure to
private sector investment could increase Y* but not
increase E* as much or at all if the private sector
is more capital intensive than the public. In this
case the gain in private sector 'natural' employment
is to some extent offset by the loss in the public
sector. In principle this 'offset' could be total. So
U* is invariant to fiscal policy although Y* is not.

13.   Recent papers analysing rational expectations in an open economy include Minford (1983) and
Minford and Peel (1980).

14.   The original papers are Mundell (1962),
and Fleming (1962). For a textbook exposition see
Levacic and Rebmann (1982) pp. 165-174.

15.   The XB schedule is drawn flatter than the
LM curve, i.e. the interest elasticity of the capital
inflow exceeds the interest elasticity of the demand
for money. In the classical case it is not an
important issue but in non-market clearing

(Keynesian) models this will affect the comparative efficiency of fiscal and monetary policy, see Levacic and Rebmann (note (14) above).

16. The effects of an unanticipated increase in the money supply in the fixed exchange rate world are similar to that of fiscal expansion.

17. Asymmetric information of this kind has some powerful effects on the operation of markets. For an excellent discussion of this and other issues too, Hahn (1982).

18. For a good textbook review see Sherer (1973).

Chapter Five

MACROECONOMICS OF UNEMPLOYMENT - THE NON-MARKET CLEARING APPROACH

Introduction

Several objections to the market clearing approach to unemployment have already been raised in chapter four. In this chapter we will explore some alternative approaches to non-natural unemployment which rely upon the notion that market disequilibrium is not only the normal state of affairs but also that correcting forces may be so weak or even non-existent that non-natural unemployment persists over a sufficiently long period for it to be a matter of concern to policymakers. Initially we consider the traditional Keynesian approach to unemployment but later in this chapter more recent disequilibrium analysis is examined.

Traditional Keynesian Unemployment Theory: Closed Economy

The conventional IS/LM model is the basis of this approach. Incorporating the real balance effect the equation for the IS curve in the closed economy gives

5.1 $Y = C + I + Z$ with

5.2 $C = c(Y, M/P)$ $1 > \partial C/\partial Y > 0$ $\partial C/\partial M/P > 0$

5.3 $I = i(R)$ $dI/dR < 0$

where

I = fixed investment
C = real consumption
Z = autonomous expenditure
M/P = real cash balances

The LM curve is

144

5.4 $M_s/P = L(Y,R) = M_d/P$ with

$\partial M_d/P \big/ \partial Y > 0$ $\partial M_d/P \big/ \partial R < 0$

where

P is the aggregate price level
Y and R are real income and real interest rate respectively
M refers to nominal money the supply (M_s) of which is fixed.
      The conventional employment (production) function is also assumed, in an identical form to that used in Chapter 4.

5.5 $E = e(Y)$ $dE/dY > 0$ $d^2E/dY^2 > 0$

This system is illustrated in Figure 5.1 which also includes in Frame (c) a price adjustment relation

5.6 $\dot{P} = p(Y - Y^*)$

where

Y^* = the full employment level of output and
$d\dot{P}/d(Y-Y^*) > 0$

      Assume the economy is initially producing at the natural rate E^* and Y^*. Unemployment can arise in this model via an upward shift of the LM curve or a downward shift of the IS curve. We will consider the latter. This fall in aggregate demand for goods leads to a fall in output to Y_1 and employment to E_1 (below the natural level). [1] Non-natural unemployment appears, and, with a constant labour force is equal to $(E^* - E_1)$. In order to see the full labour market effects, reference should be made to Figure 4.3. How can this unemployment be eliminated? A necessary condition is the restoration of aggregate demand to the Y^* level. This could happen if the LM curve shifted down or the IS curve up or both happened. In the absence of government intervention this would happen if the price level fell (to $\dot{P} = P_1$ in Frame (c)). A fall in the price level ($\dot{P} < 0$) would increase the real value of the nominal money supply shifting the LM curve down and since the real value of money balances rises the stimulus to consumption is reflected by an upward shift in the IS curve. This is shown in Figure 5.1 with the IS curve at IS_3 and the LM at LM_2. This would be the normal market clearing state of affairs. If there were a liquidity

Figure 5.1

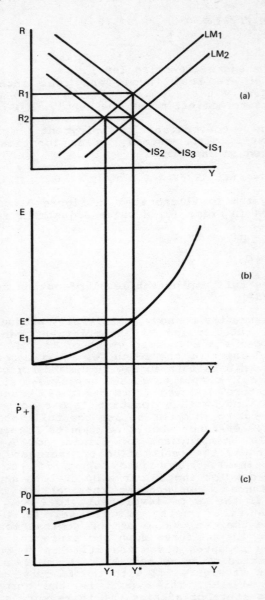

trap ($\partial M_a/\partial R = \infty$) in the economy the LM curve would be horizontal (1) the monetary stimulus to full employment would disappear and the full burden of adjustment would fall on the real balance effect. Many economists have argued that, in practice, the real balance effect would not be large or quick acting (2) so that the restoration of full employment demand for goods could be a long-winded affair. In principle, however, falls in the price level would do the job in the end, reducing interest rates (to R_2 in Frame (a)) thereby increasing investment and stimulating consumption directly. If falls in the price level are necessary they may not be sufficient to restore full employment because of constraints on the supply side of the economy. Standard Keynesian theory opts for the same profit maximising, competitive model of firm behaviour as its classic counterparts. This means that employers will only hire labour if the real wage is less than or equal to the marginal product of labour ($W/P \leqslant dY/dE$). If the price level falls with a given money wage the real wage rises. In other words the stimulus to aggregate demand given by the fall in the price level would only affect actual output and actual employment if the <u>money wage</u> falls to match the fall in the price level and restores the <u>real wage</u> to its initial full employment level. If the money wage does not fall then non-natural unemployment will be positive and persistent because the real wage is too high.

Reductions in both prices and money wages together are in general sufficient for the elimination of unemployment in this simple Keynesian model. The adoption of a classical market clearing assumption with rational expectations would provide this flexibility. In contrast Keynesian economists have always emphasised the weakness of the classical market mechanism. It is not the structure of macroeconomic models as much as differing assumptions about their dynamic functioning that divide classical from Keynesian economists.

Keynesian economists rely heavily on either or both the downward inflexibility of money wages and prices to explain non-market clearing and the persistence of non-natural unemployment. This leads to the conclusion that "For all practical purposes, we would speak of the economic system as having an equilibrium' even when employment might be less than full" Ackley (1961). As a result according to the Keynesian view unemployment in excess of the natural rate ($E^* - E_1$ in Figure 5.1) can exist and persist unless the appropriate policy remedies are adopted by

147

the government. The policy prescriptions from this analysis are well known and straightforward. If aggregate demand could be stimulated to the full employment level directly by either or both an expansionary fiscal and monetary policy then the IS curve could be shifted to IS_3 in Figure 4.1 and the LM curve to LM_2. Falls in the price level would no longer be necessary and with a given wage level this would mean that real wages would stay at the full employment level. No supply side constraints would appear. Some Keynesians placed greater emphasis on fiscal policy as an instrument of demand management for the removal of unemployment because of scepticism about the effectiveness of monetary policy.

This was the orthodox view of economic policy in both the US and Britain until the 1970s, since when it has come under increasing attack from both modern classical economists and their political counter-parts. Despite these attacks the view has by no means been abandoned. A controlled expansion of aggregate demand remains an ingredient of many packages to reduce unemployment but even hardened Keynesians now argue that, although necessary a policy of this kind will not be sufficient to reduce permanently the level of unemployment. This will be considered further in chapter nine.

There are a number of severe criticisms that have been made of Keynesian models of this kind. Firstly, the policy prescriptions rely upon the assumption of a closed economy. In an open economy, especially with flexible exchange rates, the conventional Keynesian analysis has been found to be deficient. Secondly, the model is excessively static and in the fifties and sixties this led to the proliferation of growth models. In the seventies the acceleration of inflation has been an important feature of the experience of western economies and many argue that the conventional Keynesian approach is ill-equipped to deal with it. Thirdly, since it is single period analysis it fails to take account of the formation and influence of future expectations (unlike the modern classical approach) on current behaviour. In this respect (as in others) Keynesianism departed from Keynes himself who placed considerable emphasis on expectations formed in the face of uncertainty about the future. Finally, its heavy reliance on non-market clearing is based upon a series of ad hoc assumptions about market behaviour, which however valid from an empirical point of view stick in the throat of many economic theorists. We will examine (in subsequent sections of this chapter) each of these criticisms in more detail and see how this has stimulated major developments in the non-market clearing (disequilibrium) approach to unemployment in recent years.

Keynesian Economics, Unemployment and the Open Economy

We can introduce an international sector by employing the assumptions of the previous chapter (equations 4.27-4.29) namely

5.7 $\quad X = x(\gamma) \quad \dfrac{dX}{d\gamma} > 0$ (export function)

5.8 $\quad F = f(Y,\gamma) \quad \dfrac{\partial F}{\partial Y} > 0 \quad \dfrac{\partial F}{\partial \gamma} < 0$ (import function)

5.9 $\quad KI = k(R) \quad \dfrac{dKI}{dR} > 0$ (capital flows function)

where

X = exports
F = imports
γ = index of competitiveness
KI = net capital inflow

This is depicted in Figure 5.2 with the XB schedule drawn in the same way as in Figure 4.8. Initially we assume that the exchange rate is fixed. Consider the impact of the same downward shift in the IS curve (to IS_2) discussed in the previous section. The effects on the domestic economy are the same, namely a fall in Y and E and the appearance of positive non-natural unemployment equal to $(E^* - E_1)$. The fall in output improves the current balance of payments $(X - F)$ but the fall in the interest rate to R_2 causes a greater deterioration in the capital account and so the balance of payments moves into deficit. Under a fixed exchange rate regime that will reduce the level of foreign exchange reserves. This will have an effect on the money supply since in an open economy (3)

5.10 $\quad M_S = FER + DC = D + Mc$

where

FER= foreign exchange reserves
DC = domestic credit (total domestic assets of the banking system)

Figure 5.2

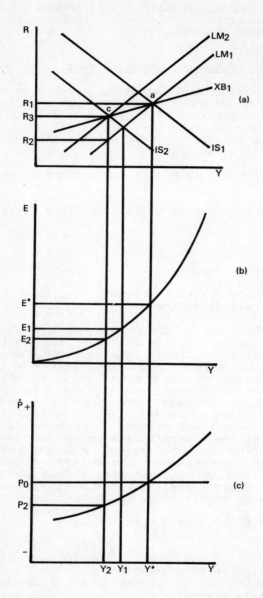

D = bank deposits of the public
Mc = currency in circulation with the public

The fall in the foreign exchange reserves will reduce the money supply causing the LM curve to move up and to the left (to LM_2) causing the interest rate to rise to R_3. In Figure 5.2 this shift and the accompanying rise in the interest rate which improves the capital balance is sufficient to eliminate the balance of payments deficit even though the interest rate is still below its initial level. However the level of non-natural unemployment is higher than in the closed economy $((E^* - E_2)$ compared to $(E^* - E_1))$ because of the induced fall in the money supply.

Just as the effects of a fall in aggregate demand are magnified in an open economy so is the beneficial effect of a fall in money wages and prices that much greater. If both were to fall leaving real wages unchanged, unemployment in excess of the natural level would be eliminated. Note the similarity of this to the classical model. This is shown in Figure 5.3 which shows an enlarged version of Frame (a) in Figure 5.2. The initial position is at the intersection of IS_2, LM_2 and XB_1 (c in Frame (a) of Figure 5.2).

A fall in wages and prices improves international competitiveness (γ increases) and this stimulates the production of exports and import substitutes. This reinforces the real balance effect so the IS curve moves up (to IS_3 in Figure 5.3). The external balance schedule also shifts because of the boost to competitiveness (to XB_2). It shifts down because of the improvement to the current balance at each level of real output. This means a lower rate of interest is required to ensure overall external balance. In other words, the capital balance can deteriorate to offset the current balance improvement. The LM curve also shifts down to LM_3 as the real money supply increases following the improvement in the external balance. Employment (and unemployment) will (eventually) be restored to their natural levels (Output at Y*) with a lower rate of interest (R_4) than that experienced in the first instance (R_1 in Figure 5.2). Only if the rest of the world experiences the same response to the same unemployment causing the world price level to fall in line with the domestic (keeping competitiveness constant), will this sequence of events not occur.

However, if wages and prices do not fall as the Keynesian non-market clearing approach assumes, then a fiscal and monetary expansion along the XB_1 curve

151

Figure 5.3

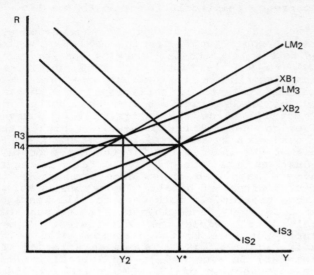

curve (to avoid external imbalance) is the essential
and appropriate policy. Mundell (1962) argues that
fiscal policy should be concerned with the
elimination of unemployment while monetary policy
should be used to ensure that external balance is
maintained (where it exists as in Figure 5.2) or
secured where it does not. In a fixed exchange rate
world the traditional Keynesian analysis of the cause
and cure for unemployment is, if anything,
strengthened.

Once we assume exchange rates to be flexible,
conclusions are a little different and of particular
relevance to the economic experience of the seventies
and eighties. A downward shift in the IS curve has
the same initial effects as in the fixed exchange
rate world. The critical difference is that under a
floating exchange rate it is the rate of exchange not
the foreign reserves that bears the burden of
adjustment. The deficit that arises as the economy
moves from position a to position b in Figure 5.4 now
leads to a depreciation of the currency that shifts
the XB schedule downwards. Since the depreciation
also improves international competitiveness, this
stimulates exports and the production of import
substitutes and the IS curve also shifts upwards to
intersect the XB and LM curves at a position like c

152

Figure 5.4

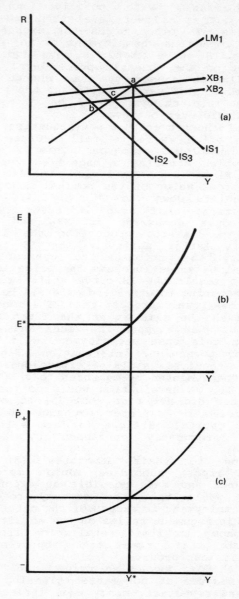

in Figure 5.4. The economy ends with output less than the natural rate, with positive non-natural unemployment but at a lower level than under fixed exchange rates. In other words the exchange rate cushions the impact on unemployment of the downward shift in the IS curve. Note we have ignored any upward impact on the domestic price level, of the rate of inflation caused by this change in the exchange rate. If this were significant the effect of the exchange rate changes would be a good deal smaller and could even be zero.

What would happen in this new situation if wages and domestic prices were to fall because of the presence of unemployed resources? This is shown in Figure 5.5 which contains a magnified version of Frame (a) in Figure 5.4. The lower price level would increase the real value of the nominal money supply so the LM shifts down (to LM_2 in 5.4). It also increases international competitiveness, shifting the XB schedule downwards to XB_3 and by its stimulation to domestic production the IS curve upwards. This latter shift in the IS curve is reinforced by the stimulus to consumption of increased real balances (because the price level has fallen). As a result the IS curve shifts to IS_4 in Figure 5.5 restoring internal and external balance at Y* but at a lower real interest rate. The conclusions are pretty much the same as in the fixed exchange rate world but what happens if prices and wages do not fall. In this case unemployment will only be eliminated by government intervention. Figure 5.5 shows what is required: a mix of expansionary policy needs to be complemented by measures to shift the XB schedule to XB_3. A devaluation would do the job if domestic prices did not rise, but import controls, export subsidies or stricter exchange control to reduce gross capital outflows (4) are all obvious alternatives frequently canvassed by Keynesian economists.

According to their advocates (5) import controls or export subsidies would improve the current balance and make possible an expansion of demand that would take the economy to Y* and eliminate unemployment in excess of the natural rate. Of course, this argument relies on the ability of the domestic economy to limit retaliation from other economies so that some net improvement in competitiveness can occur.

The orthodox Keynesian view can now be summarised. Because of non-market clearing arising from price and especially money wage inflexibility,

Figure 5.5

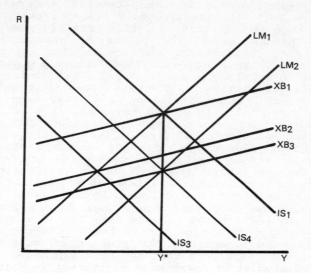

non-natural unemployment can exist and persist. It therefore requires correction by government intervention. In an open economy an expansion in aggregate demand will be necessary but not sufficient for the removal of non-natural unemployment. This requires further direct measures to ensure external balance.

A Rationale for Non-Market Clearing

So far we have examined the consequences of non-market clearing within the framework of the conventional Keynesian model of the macroeconomy. On what basis is the assumption of non-market clearing justified? Keynesians have traditionally tended to refer to a variety of ad hoc justifications for this assumption. In the product market the failure of prices to fall in recession is attributed to market imperfections and non-profit maximising behaviour. A common rationale for price stickiness is the kinked demand curve associated with oligopolistic market structure. In this case a cut in price by a firm is followed by its competitors so that little change occurs in product demand or in the firm's market share. If the oligopoly is collusive, producers will enter into overt or covert agreements not to cut

155

prices so the effect will be the same. Product markets, particularly in the private sector of the British economy (6) are typically oligopolistic over a wide range of industries and this lack of incentive to cut prices is likely to be of considerable significance in practice. Evidence on this point is not easy to obtain. Domberger (1979) shows a positive association between the speed of price adjustment and oligopoly but as he notes "the estimates are based on a period of rising inflation and therefore are related essentially to upward movements in prices".

As far as money wages are concerned the assumption of downward flexibility is frequently justified by the action of trade unions resisting money wage cuts on behalf of members suffering from a severe dose of money illusion. Other institutional features of wage bargaining like Wage Councils are thought to reinforce that outcome. Keynes himself (7) emphasised the fact that money wage cuts might be resisted by workers not because they feared a cut in their absolute real wage but in their relative real wage. This resistance to the erosion of customary differentials is a fact that has been supported by a number of studies of money wage adjustment in Britain and the US, although, once again, these studies relate to a period in which nominal money wages have consistently risen. On the other hand, Keynes did not believe that there were no circumstances in which real wages could fall. Indeed he argued, that this could happen but only through the occurrence of a price increase because "it would be impracticable to resist every reduction in real wages due to a change in the purchasing-power of money which affects all workers alike" Keynes (1936).

Although reference to the institutional features of wage and price setting behaviour have satisfied some economists, others have been concerned to explain the apparent downward inflexibility of money wages and prices within a more conventional microeconomic model of maximising behaviour. Most of this analysis has in practice been concerned with the labour market and with theoretical explanations of money wage stickiness which leads to non-market clearing because real wages are then too high. Some of the ideas are novel but many build upon notions long familiar to economists specialising in the analysis of labour markets.

The first approach relies upon imperfect information about market conditions. Leijonhufvud (1968) utilising the ideas of Stigler (1962) and Alchian (1970) abandons the assumptions of short run market clearing on the grounds that the absence of a Walrasian auctioneer in labour markets means nobody knows the market clearing level of wages. Given the costs and benefits of search it is also obvious from the analysis of chapter three that no agent has the incentive to know the market clearing conditions. If, for example, a worker adopts the 'optimal sample size' strategy there will remain many unsampled vacancies if he/she equates the marginal costs and benefits of search. These arguments led Leijonhufvud to emphasise quantity adjustment in the labour market. The consequences of quantity rather than wage and price adjustment in the labour (and other) markets are examined in the next section.

A related aspect of the labour market which provides disequilibrium models with sounder theoretical foundations is the existence of asymmetric information with a heterogeneous labour force. The notion that excess supply of labour will lead to a fall in money wages rests on the belief that unemployed workers are perfect substitutes for those currently employed. However, workers are not uniform in their endowment of talents, training and experience. Employers may either conclude that unemployed workers are not substitutes for the employed worker or take the view that it is not worth undertaking extensive search among the unemployed to find out because of the costs of identifying the potential performance of an unemployed worker in employment within the firm. This is the asymmetric information problem which employers might resolve by the selection of what Spence (1973) has called indices and signals. One such signal might be the wage demand itself. If unemployed workers offer themselves at a lower wage than that currently paid the employer might conclude they are low skill/low quality workers, and reject them without further intensive search. In this case the wage signal has a perverse effect and fails to affect employment, so the market fails to clear even in the presence of flexible acceptance wages by unemployed workers.

More recently theorists have emphasised the role of uncertainty about future events. This is the principal ingredient of the implicit contract theory of Azariadis (1975), Baily (1974) and Gordon (1974). The starting point is the fact that the labour market is not a spot auction market but what Okun (1981) has called a 'customer market' in which long run contractual relationships between buyer and seller predominate. Azariadis puts it thus:

in uncertainty, labor services are not auctioned off in quite the same way fresh fruit is. Rather, they are exchanged for some implicit set of commitments, hereinafter called an <u>implicit labor contract</u>, on the part of the firm to employ the owner of those labor services for a reasonable period of time, and on terms mutually agreed upon in advance.

The labour contract to which Azariadis refers provides risk averse workers with a level of income which is stable over the cycle. In other words the contract prevents the fall in money wages in recession, which market clearing models require. Of course, this stability of income can only be obtained at a price and this is charged by the employer. Essentially, risk netural firms enter into the implicit contract by selling insurance to their workers. Workers are assumed to want income stability and would like insurance against fluctuations in their income. The problem is that normal insurance companies do not provide this type of cover at least partly because they do not possess the information available to the actual employer. As a result, employers themselves are assumed to offer this kind of insurance as part of the normal employment contract. The premium for the insurance reduces the wage but firms who provide this income stability guarantee have no trouble attracting workers to their firm.
The simplest contract framework proceeds as follows. Assume
(a) there are 2 states of nature observable by employers and employees. Each state of nature has a probability of occurrence of 0.5
(b) in state 1 a proportion (ϵ) of workers are employed, so $0 < \epsilon < 1$. They would receive in the absence of a contract the market clearing wage which is less than that paid in state 2 in which it is assumed
(c) all workers are employed
(d) <u>enforceable</u> contracts are made to eliminate this unwanted variability of income.
What are the terms of contract? We assume the firm offers a contract (ϕ) to E workers employing ϵE in state 1 and E in state 2. The utility of this contract to workers ($V(\phi)$ is

5.11 $V(\phi) = 1/2 \left(\epsilon u(W_1) + u(W_2) \right)$

We can form a conventional isoutility indifference

curve relating to W_1 and W_2. The slope of the indifference curve will be dictated by the ratio of the marginal utilities in state 1 and state 2, i.e.

5.12 $-\epsilon \dfrac{\partial u}{\partial W_1} \Big/ \dfrac{\partial u}{\partial W_2}$

Figure 5.6 shows this indifference curve (II) assuming diminishing marginal utility of both W_1 and W_2. It also depicts the employer's isoprofit line ($\pi\pi$) with a slope obtained from the differentiation of π (profits) w.r.t. W_1 in equation 5.11a.

5.11a $\pi = \pi_1 + \pi_2 = (P_1 e(\epsilon E) - W_1 \epsilon E) + (P_2 e(E) - W_2 E)$

where P_1 and P_2 are product prices prevailing in states 1 and 2 respectively. This gives the slope of the linear isoprofit line (dW_2/dW_1) as a constant ($-\epsilon$). Efficient risk sharing requires that the marginal rates of substitution between wages in both states be the same for both parties. This is shown as the tangency between the workers isoutility curve (II) and the employer's isoprofit curve. If we equate the slopes of II and $\pi\pi$ ($-\epsilon$ with 5.12) we find $\partial U/\partial W_1 / \partial u/\partial W_2$ is equal to 1. Given the nonlinearity of the utility function these marginal utilities are equated ($\partial u/\partial W_1 / \partial u/\partial W_2 = 1$) if $W_1 = W_2$.

Figure 5.6

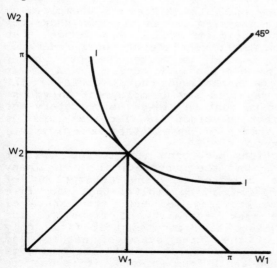

159

Hence the tangency in Figure 5.6 is on the 45° line, (8). Wages in both states are the same ($W_1 = W_2$) despite the fact that in state 1 some workers are unemployed. Workers receive an insurance indemnity (the wage paid exceeds the market clearing level) in state 1 and pay a premium in state 2 (the wage is less than the market clearing level). Money wages are rigid and in a recession adjustments take place via quantity rather than through money wages. Hours of work and/or employment will fall but the fall in wages necessary for the restoration of aggregate demand to a full employment level will not take place. In other words, in recession unemployment greater than the natural rate will appear and persist until every contract has been renegotiated. An obvious problem with this kind of analysis is the assertion that workers desire wage stability but have no objection to the consequent employment (and hours) instability. For this to be true in the employment case it is helpful to assume that wholly unemployed workers become eligible for unemployment compensation. However, if the $1-\epsilon$ workers who are unemployed are to accept the contract, the system of compensation for temporary layoff must ensure that unemployment benefit is equal to the difference between the wage and the marginal utility of leisure experienced while unemployed. The problem then is that this explanation of wage rigidity and non-natural unemployment makes very special institutional assumptions about the system of unemployment pay. Without such a system it can be shown under the assumption of the basic implicit contract model that the quantity adjustment consists of hours reduction across all workers and no worker becomes wholly unemployed, so no unemployment occurs. Even if it does it should be emphasised that because of the benefits regime required any unemployment in excess of the natural rate must be viewed as voluntary and the theory does not as Gordon (1974) claims, provide a neoclassical theory of involuntary unemployment, on Keynesian lines.

Other objections have been made to the implicit contract model. On the theoretical side many economists have objected to the assumptions of symmetric information, which implies that both firm and workers have knowledge of the 'true state of nature' and the risk neutrality of firms. In its place some theorists have assumed that firms only have knowledge of the 'true state of nature' and cannot be relied upon to tell the truth. If employers act to conceal the truth from workers, it is easy to see that the wage paid will be lower in both states of nature. They could convince workers the isoprofit curve (ππ in Figure 5.6) was lower and force workers on to a lower indifference curve (and wage). It is more difficult to see how this would give rise to greater unemployment in the 'bad state'. Indeed, if anything it is more likely to lead to overemployment. Moreover, if firms do exploit their current informational advantage to cheat, then if they are found out by workers (as is likely with repeated cheating) the ensuing loss of reputation would have a profound effect on the credibility of their guarantee of income stability. Workers will insist upon contract clauses that induce employers not to cheat. For example, a limitation of employment (E) clause will be costly to a firm in a good state and if made large enough will induce the firm to tell the truth. In a recent survey of these models, Stiglitz (1984) has argued:

> At the very least, however, it can be argued that the assymetric information theory of implicit contracts does not provide a robust explanation of unemployment: whether there exists underemployment is sensitive to special assumptions concerning the nature of the utility function and the degree of risk aversion of firms.

In practice, of course, firms also will not know the 'true state of nature'. Some limited use is therefore made of contingent contracts in which some part of pay (usually a bonus) depends upon profits or upon the market valuation of the firm but any such contracts are explicit and frequently collectively negotiated. In fact, neither these nor implicit contracts are a widespread feature of the British labour market at all. Partly, this is to do with the enforceability of implicit contracts. Implicit contract theorists tend either to assume the enforceability of the contract or refer to the possibility that firms who renege or cheat, lose their reputation and find hiring harder and more costly as a result. They may also suffer a loss of effort and commitment on the part of their existing labour force. This is unlikely to be enough so in practice workers have found it necessary to negotiate <u>explicit</u> contracts which are enforced by sanction both legal and collective.

The essence of the implicit contract approach is to emphasise quantity adjustment in a labour market characterised by long term attachment, and multi-period contracts. Empirically, the implicit contract approach requires layoffs to be temporary and hence not to breach the long term relationship of the employee and the employer. Feldstein (1978) has shown in the US that the temporary layoff in recession is an important labour market phenomenon. He calculates that 50% of all US unemployment is of this form in his sample period and 75% of those temporarily laid off return to their former employers, though more recent work by Clark and Sumners (1979) suggests the proportion is lower (50-60%). Medoff (1979) confirms this figure but he also shows the greater incidence of temporary layoffs in the unionised sector of the economy. In this sector, contracts are explicit and as Freeman (1980) shows, attachments (job tenures) are much longer in the US. In fact, the contracts described above as 'implicit' make much more sense in the one-period renegotiated explicit contract/long job tenure context of the unionised sector of the US economy than elsewhere.

Work by Gordon (1982) and Moy and Sorrentino (1981) has also shown that the incidence of temporary layoffs in accordance with an implicit contract view of the world is a peculiar feature of the US labour market. Gordon, for example, in a study of the US, Great Britain and Japan finds quantity adjustment in recession much less in the latter two economies than in the former. Moy and Sorrentino's results suggest the implicit contract/temporary layoff view is inconsistent with labour market behaviour in Britain. Gordon argues that this is the result of differences in the system of unemployment benefit in the countries he studies. A further problem, as Flanagan (1984) points out is that much of this literature rationalises real, rather than money wage rigidity. This is because both parties to the contract are assumed to know the future movement of prices so that contracts are struck in real terms. This obviously limits the usefulness of theories designed to explain involuntary non-natural unemployment arising from the failure of money wages to adjust to excess labour supply even when prices have fallen.

Although long run relationships are central to the implicit contract explanation of wage stickiness it is also the case that much of the literature "does not explain long term attachments between firms and workers but rather assumes their outcome" (Gordon (1982)). As a result, to explain long term attachments that inhibit wage flexibility and lead to the kind of quantity adjustments that do take place requires an alternative approach.

Recently macroeconomic theorists have begun to make use of the long familiar (to labour economists) ideas of Oi (1962) referred to in chapter one. Particularly important in this respect is the work of Okun (1981) who acknowledges that investments made by both employer and employee lead to the kind of long term attachment actually observed in Britain and elsewhere by Main (1981) and Metcalf (1984). Okun argues this attachment leads to the development of a career labour market. Similar ideas have been advanced by Wachter (1975) who emphasises the importance of investment in human capital to the existence of internal labour markets. These concepts of the labour market refer to the rules that characterise the modern corporation (public and private) and govern such matters as promotion, the age-experience-earnings relationship, layoff procedures and so on. From a neoclassical point of view, Carmichael (1981) has shown, using a human capital model in a world of imperfect information, that seniority rules for layoffs and promotions are optimal for both the workers and the employers. From a different perspective, radical economists have also emphasised the importance of the internal labour market and job stability to the effective discipline, control and performance monitoring of workers in the large bureaucratic enterprise that dominates both the public and private sector of the British economy. The provision of agreed rules of conduct within the internal labour market ensures the attachment of workers to firms who gain not only by their ability to amortise their initial investment but also because workers acquire significant job specific skills and knowledge during the course of their employment. Costly labour turnover is also reduced. This makes jobs examples of what Williamson, Wachter and Harris (1975) call idiosyncratic exchange. Learning by doing which increases productivity enhances this gain to employers.

As well as the benefits of tenure the modern theory of labour demand emphasises the transaction costs associated with the retention of workers. Hiring (including search) and firing costs reinforce the tendency towards long term attachment. A stable labour force saves turnover costs.

Hence as Okun (1981) observes: "there are more reasons than we need to explain why real-world employers care about retaining experienced workers". However the fact and efficiency of long term attachment does not, of itself, explain the downward stickiness of money wages. Recently, some economic theorists have revived the efficiency wage argument to complement the fact of long term atachment. The idea is that labour productivity is an increasing function of the wage paid. If firms cut their wages this will adversely affect the morale of workers, so that the productivity enhancing effects of long term attachment will be jeopardised and reduced. As a result labour costs may, in principle, actually rise.

In a recent paper Akerlof (1982) has argued, using the wealth of sociological literature, that an individual's work effort is constrained by the norms of his or her work group. Akerlof's 'gift exchange model' suggests a cut in money wages persuades a work group to reduce the excess of their effort over the minimum possible. In other words, workers will restrict output in the way depicted by the Hawthorne researchers (Roethlisberger and Dickson (1939)) in their study of Western Electric Company in the US in the thirties. Labour productivity will then fall.

A similar argument characterises the so-called 'shirking model' proposed by Bowles (1981), Shapiro and Stiglitz (1984) and others. The idea is that no payment system or any labour contract terms can permit an employer rigidly to control all aspects of a worker's performance in the firm although a considerable degree of individual monitoring is clearly possible. As a result firms have an incentive to pay a money wage in excess of the market clearing wage to stop workers 'shirking'. Moreover, cuts in money wages would increase the incentive to shirk which lowers labour productivity and by increasing employment would also reduce the effectiveness of unemployment in excess of the natural rate as a discipline device on employed workers. Some economists have denied (Lazear (1981)) that it is totally impossible to devise a contract that provides a penalty for shirking and permits the firm to cut wages. In practice such a contract rarely exists though the central feature of Lazear's model which is the payment of wages in excess of the marginal product to senior workers is a feature of most pay structures in Britain and elsewhere.

A further problem with Lazear's model is that the incentive not to cheat is only relevant to non-senior workers. Since the promise of higher pay cannot be made to senior workers who are on the top rungs of the pay ladder they may shirk. Employers could fire them but fear of loss of reputation or explicitly negotiated 'last in-first out' rules (a feature of the US and British labour markets) may prevent them. As a result there is a disincentive to cut money wages which might encourage shirking among senior workers and lower their productivity in the firm.

Other sorts of reasons have also been suggested to justify the use of the efficiency wage argument in a developed economy. (9) Weiss (1980), for example, considers the case of a labour market with heterogeneous workers who cannot be distinguished by a potential employer. He argues that if a firm lowers its wage rates it will attract lower productivity applicants to fill the vacancies that arise (even in recession) because of death, retirement and so on. This will lower average productivity levels within the firm. Of course, this would persuade firms to maintain relative rather than absolute wages at their present level. However, as long as individual firms believe any wage cut will worsen their relative position and have this effect on productivity, absolute wage levels in all firms will be maintained. Given the degree of imperfect information and the weakness of collusive arrangements in the labour market this is likely to be the outcome. A further problem with this 'adverse selection' model is that it assumes either firms do not recognise lower productivity workers once they are employed, or cannot fire them if they do. This seems a little far fetched. The analysis of employer job search in chapter three suggests that firms formulate a hiring strategy which attempts to reveal a worker's true characteristics at the hiring stage.

If productivity and wage levels are positively related as these theoretical arguments imply, wages will not be cut in the presence of excess supply of labour and involuntary non-natural unemployment will occur. No firm will have an incentive to cut money wages. The argument is illustrated in Figure 5.7. This shows the relationship between labour productivity and the wage paid. Labour productivity is at a maximum at W* which is the efficiency wage. It minimises costs per unit of labour employed. If W* is above W* (the market clearing wage) firms will not cut the wage to permit the removal of excess supply. Involuntary unemployment will, therefore, exist. (10)

The fact of long term attachment and the payment of efficiency wages in labour markets not only explains the rigidity of nominal wages but also helps to provide a theoretical rationale for the adjustments that do take place when output falls

Figure 5.7

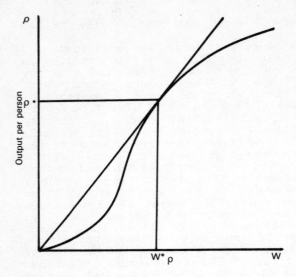

below its natural level. The benefit to firms of long term attachment explains the fact that in Britain, a major burden of the adjustment to disequilibrium takes place via changes in the hours and the intensity of work. It also helps to explain the composition of falls in employment and rises in unemployment that do take place. We saw in chapter two the concentration of the unemployment stock and the inflow on certain workers (the manual, the unskilled, the young and women) in whom firms invest less and for whom the benefit (to the firm) of long term attachment is less.

The benefits of long term attachments also explains why firms might enter into long term contracts. The gains of long term attachment make the potential costs of failing to agree a contract high for both employers and employees. As Gray (1978) shows the optimal length of a contract increases the greater are the costs incurred each time the contract is renegotiated. Where long term attachment is important the gain may be jeopardised by frequent disputes about the terms of contract. On the other hand, Gray also shows that the optimal length of contract falls as the expected level of uncertainty about the future increases so that long term attachment is not the only consideration.

It is clear from the empirical point of view that the contractual fixing of money wages is a dominant characteristic of British labour market institutions and there are good theoretical reasons for it being so. Moreover, as Williamson, Wachter and Harris (1975) argue, there are substantial savings in transaction costs from collectivising the contractual relationship especially where long term job tenure is the norm. In fact, in Britain 80% of workers are covered by an explicit collectively negotiated contract. Instantaneous changes in the terms of these contracts do not occur, at least at the national level. Nominal wage rigidity which arises for the reasons we have considered becomes institutionalised. Unlike the traditional Keynesian view it is not the mere existence of the institutions of collective bargaining that explain nominal wage rigidity. The institutions themselves reflect the same underlying economic forces that produce nominal wage rigidity as a feature of the labour market. The contractual fixing of money wages and its effect on disequilibrium processes in the labour market has become a cornerstone of the modern Keynesian approach to the analysis of unemployment. This is considered later in the chapter. We will also examine later the important role of trade unions. At this stage and in the next section we will consider models which assume downward nominal wage (and price) rigidity and which focus attention on quantity adjustment in aggregate markets.

Modern Disequilibrium Models of Unemployment

The starting point for modern disequilibrium models is the proposition that markets do not clear and more specifically that market adjustment involves changes in quantities via inventories or employment, for example, rather than via wage or price changes. In this respect they do not differ from older Keynesian models considered earlier in this chapter. The seminal work was done by Clower (1965) and Leijonhufvud (1968) but further advances have been made, especially by Barro and Grossman (1976) and Malinvaud (1980). A major point of departure from more traditional non-market clearing models is the considerable emphasis given to the microeconomic basis of the theory. Economic agents are assumed to optimise in line with the tenets of standard neoclassical theory but are also assumed to be constrained by macroeconomic events, particularly the failure of markets to clear. This leads to

Figure 5.8

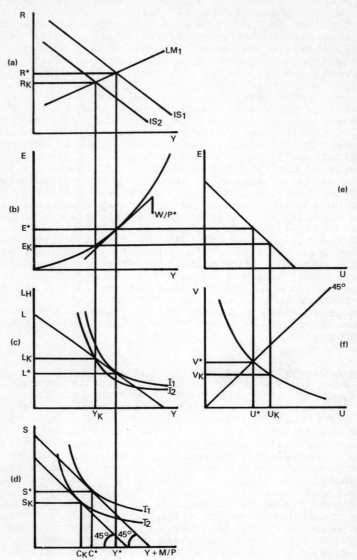

transactions being conducted at non-market clearing prices and wages. As a result a special kind of equilibrium can be attained which is not Walrasian and where (involuntary) unemployment in excess of the natural rate can exist and persist. Actual economic magnitudes may therefore differ from the desired or optimising levels. Consumption may be less than desired given normal neoclassical decision making procedures, and similarly employment and/or hours worked may be less than desired.

In the terminology of Clower, effective (actual) magnitudes may differ from the notional (desired) levels dictated by conventional micro theory. Given that economic agents may be prevented from attaining their notional targets rationing will be widespread and given that actual decisions are made on this basis, it is possible to develop an alternative notion of equilibrium. The kind of equilibrium that results from the behaviour of rational agents is called a temporary equilibrium.

Figure 5.8 illustrates these ideas. Initially we assume the economy is in full employment equilibrium with employment (E*), unemployment (U*) and output (Y*) at their natural levels. In Frame (a) the IS/LM curves intersect at full employment aggregate demand. In Frame (b) we can see that output is produced at the point of tangency of the employment function and the real wage, so profit maximising firms are producing on their downward sloping labour demand curves. In Frame (c) the position of utility maximising workers is shown. This shows the conventional indifference curve indicating the constant utility preference between leisure (L_H) and income. It is helpful to think of L_H as measured in terms of working hours per year. Full-time unemployment leads to a reduction in L_H for any individual worker and for workers as a whole. Note that drawing Y in Frames (b) and (c) on the same axis implies that all profits are distributed to households in the economy. (11) For the equivalent analysis (from which Figure 5.8 is derived) that allows the value of output to differ from the income of wage earners, see Stoneman (1980). At Y* there is a point of tangency between the indifference curve and the budget line, the slope of which is given by the real wage. In other words in full employment equilibrium the real wage ensures the labour market is cleared and workers and employers are on their supply and demand curve respectively. In Frame (d) we show the allocation of income and current wealth (in the form of real money balances) between current

169

consumption and saving (future consumption). The indifference curve I_1 reflects the constant utility preferences of consumers as between present and future consumption. The slope of the budget line indicates that all income and wealth (M/P) is either consumed or saved. Full employment consumption is at C* and saving at S*, which is again an optimal position, so notional consumption equals effective consumption. In frames (e) and (f) are shown the labour market relationships derived in chapters three and four. At full employment vacancies (V)* = unemployment (U)* and inflows into unemployment = outflows from unemployment. Note in frame 'f' the axes have been reversed to that of previous chapters. However this makes no difference to the argument here.

Now consider the impact of an autonomous reduction in some component of real spending which shifts the IS curve to IS_2. This reduces output to Y_K with no change in W or P. This accords with the basic assumptions of this model. Layoffs reduce actual employment to E_K, hours of work to $(L - L_K)$ and increases leisure to L_K. Inspection of frame (b) shows that although firms are using the cost minimising number of workers (they are on the employment function), this is not the profit maximising employment level (E*). Actual (effective) labour demand is less than desired (notional) labour demand. Similarly on the supply side of the labour market. Workers are forced away from a point of tangency to the intersection of the lower indifference curve I_2 with the wage line. Effective labour supply $(\bar{L} - L_K^2)$ is lower than notional labour supply $(\bar{L} - L*)$. Workers experience rationing (of work) which forces them into a sub-optimal position. Strictly, we assume all workers experience a spell of unemployment during the course of a working year so that they work fewer hours over the course of a year than they desire. Since it ignores all differences between workers, this analysis fails to capture the concentration of unemployment we saw to be a fact in chapter two.

The reduction in income shifts the budget constraint in Frame (d) inwards, because consumers have a smaller amount to allocate between consumption and saving. Consumers reduce the levels of their consumption to C_k and saving to S_k as a result of the drop in their income. This reduces effective demand for goods contributing to the fall in output to Y_K. This is essentially the Keynesian multiplier process. Frames (a) and (d) then depict a new temporary equilibrium brought about by the inflexibility of money wages and prices. The adjustment of quantities creates constraints for economic agents who find themselves forced to make suboptimal decisions which confirm the unemployment that arises as a result. This is shown in Frame (e) of Figure 5.8 where actual unemployment (U_K) is now above the natural (U*) level. We have assumed in Frame (f) that neither firms nor workers alter their offer/acceptance standards so the probability of a hire is unaltered for these reasons. (12) If this were not assumed, the VU curve itself would shift as the analysis of chapter three demonstrates. The mean probability of being hired (the re-employment probability) is reduced, however, because of the fall in vacancies to V_K. This means that although unemployment inflows and outflows are equal in this new temporary equilibrium, the duration of a spell of unemployment increases because of this reduction in the arrival rate of job offers caused by a fall in vacancies. Workers find themselves constrained by the drop in job opportunities and are involuntarily unemployed as a result.

Can this temporary equilibrium persist or will wage and price cuts eventually occur to eliminate this so-called Keynesian non-natural unemployment? Hahn (1980) tackles this question and argues that the equilibrium will persist. Hahn argues that although agents may know the effect on the quantity constraint of a change in wages or prices, they may "calculate that the cost of removing or reducing a quantity constraint is too high". There is no incentive for economic agents to make the decisions that will take the economy back to full employment.

An example of this 'cost of reducing a constraint' comes from the idea of efficiency wages discussed in the previous section. If firms pay efficiency wages there is no incentive to cut money wages because of the consequent adverse effect on labour productivity in the firm. As a result the economy can get locked in to a position like Y_K, E_K and U_K in Figure 5.8. Even if money (and hence real) wages were to fall the effect would be to reduce non-natural unemployment but at the expense of higher levels of natural rate unemployment. Consider Figure 5.9 which depicts a conventional labour supply and demand curve. Suppose there is a fall in the aggregate demand for goods of the kind depicted in Figure 5.8. In Figure 5.9 this is shown as a shift in the _effective_ demand for labour move to $E_1 D_E^1$. Note the horizontal section of the curve from E_1 to the

171

notional (D_E^1) labour demand curve. This shows the maximum amount of labour demanded given the constraint of the aggregate demand for goods. Initially at E*, the real wage paid is the efficiency wage (W^*_ρ) deflated by the price level (P_1). Suppose firms cut the money wage to W_1. This does nothing to reduce the constraint imposed by aggregate demand unless prices are also cut. Assume they are not so the effective demand curve stays at $E_1 \ D_E$. The cut in money wages causes a fall in labour productivity so the notional (D_E) curve shifts down. What actually happens depends on the extent of this shift. If the shift is to D_E^2 non-natural unemlpoyment falls (to E_2^* - E_1) but the level of natural rate unemployment rises by (E_1^* - E_2^*). Even if the shift in the demand curve were less or more does not matter. As long as money wage cuts lead to lower levels of labour productivity as the efficiency wage hypothesis implies any cuts in non-natural unemployment are offset by increases in the natural rate. (13)

Figure 5.9

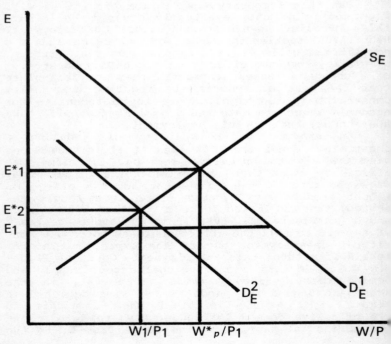

Similar results may also be obtained if we assume increasing returns in the production technology. Weitzman (1982) constructs an increasing returns model in which attempts to cut money and hence real wages would increase equilibrium unemployment. Since labour productivity rises as output increases, real wages should also <u>rise</u>, not only to satisfy the marginal productivity conditions but also to create the additional aggregate demand necessary to permit firms to dispose of the additional output derived in this increasing returns context.

The activity of unions may also inhibit spontaneous market adjustment back to Walrasian equilibrium. Recently some attempts have been made to construct models of rational trade union behaviour that result either in money (and hence real) wage rigidity or perverse real wage movements in recession which lead to the persistence of 'temporary' equilibria. One way to examine the effect of unions is to utilise the monopoly model first suggested by Fellner (1951) and Carter (1959) and recently formalised by Oswald (1982). The union is assumed to possess a utility function

5.13 $u = u(W,E)$ with $\partial u/\partial W > 0$ $\partial^2 u/\partial W^2 < 0$

$\partial u/\partial E > 0$ $\partial^2 u/\partial E^2 < 0$

in which the marginal utilities of both wages (W) and employment (E) are positive and declining. The union is assumed to maximise this utility function subject to a conventional labour demand curve

5.14 $E = e(W,\eta)$ with $\partial E/\partial W < 0$ $\partial E/\partial \eta \lessgtr 0$

where η is a shift parameter. The maximum obtained is wholly conventional and is found where the unions marginal rate of substitution is equal to the slope of the demand curve. This is shown diagramatically in Figure 5.10.

I_1 is the unions indifference curve reflecting its wage employment preferences. Oswald (1982) assumes unions determine the wage level at W* in Figure 5.10 which is the point of tangency of the indifference curve with the demand curve (D_E). Firms set the level of employment at E* (14). Contrast this with the competitive solution which is also shown on Figure 5.10. Relevant here is the conventional supply curve S_E which ceases to be appropriate when an economy is unionised. The effect of monopolistic

173

Figure 5.10

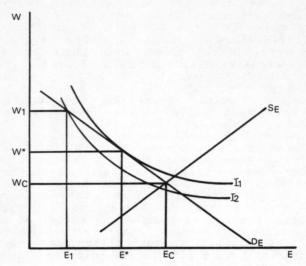

and employment is reduced from E_C. Note that this identifies a once and for all effect.

Note also that the monopoly model can be used to explain the failure of wages (money and hence real) to fall in a recession caused by a fall in demand. If firms are faced with a demand for goods constraint and, as a result cut employment to, say, E_1 in Figure 5.10 the wage agreed with the monopoly union will actually go up. Unions can no longer achieve an optimum position. They are constrained in the Keynesian unemployment situation just like other agents. The best solution is on the lower indifference curve I_2 which intersects the demand curve at W_1. In other words if unions can't achieve the level of employment they want, they compensate by 'setting' an even higher wage. (15) This they are able to do because of their monopoly power.

Similar results are obtained if we assume that unions and employers negotiate 'efficient bargains'. This is a matter recently pursued by McDonald and Solow (1981). In this case employers and unions agree a bargain that involves workers being paid more than their marginal product. The basic assumptions, however, are the same as the union monopoly model and are illustrated in Figure 5.10a.

The outcome of bargaining using the union

Figure 5.10a

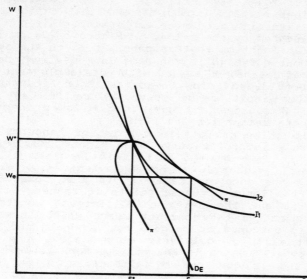

Figure 5.10b

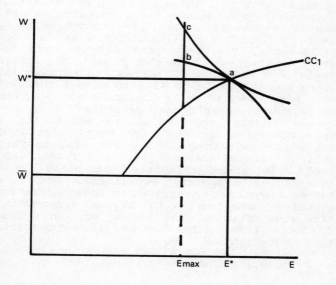

monopoly model is W* and E*. In contrast the 'efficient bargain' model assumes that employers do not unilaterally determine employment. This can also be influenced by the union. In Figure 5.10a $\pi\pi$ is an isoprofit function that reaches a peak on the demand for labour curve (D_E). The same (non-maximum) profit could, of course, be earned with more employment than E*. McDonald and Solow treat the isoprofit curve as the firms indifference curve. Since for any E a smaller W creates a bigger profit lower isoprofit curves are better for the firm.

The union can attain a point of tangency with the firm's isoprofit curve on a higher indifference curve (I_2 in Figure 5.10a). This involves a lower wage but a higher level of employment at W_e and E_e than in the monopoly case. It is also possible to derive the locus of these points of tangency of the isoprofit and the union's indifference curves and this is called the contract curve which shows the possible outcomes of bargaining. McDonald and Solow show it will be positively sloped above a minimum wage level W, which is the minimum acceptable to the union and is governed by alternative wage levels available elsewhere in the economy. This is shown in Figure 5.10b where the contract curve is CC_1. Initially assume a settlement at 'a' with a wage of W* and employment at E*. Now consider the effect of a fall in aggregate demand that creates a sales constraint for the firm that cuts employment to E_{max} in Figure 5.10b. The initial bargain at 'a' is no longer tenable. The best that can be done is a bargain that implies a wage that lies in the interval bc. Employment falls to E_{max} from its initial level but wages not only fail to fall to offset this, they actually rise above W* as in the union monopoly model and so Keynesian unemployment persists.

These models are useful in explaining any perverse movements in real and money wages which inhibit market adjustment. They are less useful in explaining nominal wage rigidity itself which combined with price rigidities can lead to the persistence of temporary equilibria. One recent attempt at doing that integrates a model of rational trade union behaviour with Keynes' emphasis on relative wage effects. This is the work of Gylfason and Lindbeck (1984). They amend the union utility function (equation 5.13) to

5.13a $U_i = u(W_i, E_i, W_j)$

and the labour demand curve to

5.13a $E_i = e(W_i, W_j, \eta)$

where the subscript i refers to the union in the ith sector and the j subscript refers to other sectors of the economy. The marginal utility $(\partial u_i/\partial W_j)$ is negative and increasing with W_i. The refusal to accept money wage cuts is shown within this 'Cournot style' model of union behaviour. In the simplest case there are two competing unions in the economy who each maximise a utility function (5.12a) subject to the constraint of a labour demand curve (5.13a). This gives the familiar Cournot reaction curves which show the utility maximising wage upon which each union will settle <u>given</u> the wage of the second union. The important assumption is made that each union does not expect the <u>other</u> union to react to its <u>own</u> wage demand. The argument is illustrated in Figure 5.11.

TU_1 and TU_2 are the reaction curves of each of the two trade unions. They indicate the value of the utility maximising wage of each union <u>given</u> differing values of the other union's wage level. The Cournot equilibrium occurs where the reaction curves intersect.

In Figure 5.11 this happens where TU_1 and TU_2 intersect to give equilibrium wage levels of W_1^* and W_2^*. The rigidity of money wages follow from the stability of the Cournot equilibrium. If, for example, an attempt were made to cut money wages in sector 1 to say, W_1^2 this would lead to a cut in money wages acceptable to union 2 (to W_2^2). So far so good. However, this reaction of union 2 would cause a counter-reaction by union 1 raising its optimal wage to W_1^3. This would provoke a further reaction from union 2 raising its wage to W_2^3.

This reaction and counter-reaction goes on until the Cournot equilibrium is restored. In other words once a pattern of relative wages is established money wage cuts are resisted by rational trade unions. There are a number of obvious objections to this model. The assumption that unions do not <u>expect</u> a reaction from other unions seems odd given that reaction and counter-reaction <u>actually</u> take place in the adjustment to equilibrium. Industrial economists have done a good deal to patch up Cournot theory but although Gylfason and Lindbeck acknowledge this, the matter is not pursued. Whether it is appropriate to model union behaviour as if unions were profit maximising oligopolists or duopolists is contentious. Nonetheless, despite these obvious problems, this approach helps to provide some theoretical support for the view that in an economy with many

Figure 5.11

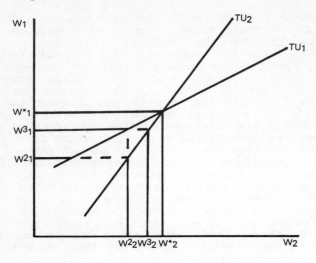

trade unions concerned with relative wages, there will be substantial resistance to money wage cuts as Keynes argued. This will sustain a temporary equilibrium with Keynesian unemployment greater than the natural rate.

The story told by Figure 5.8 is essentially that of standard Keynesian unemployment. The mode of analysis differs, the micro foundations are more detailed but unemployment in excess of the natural rate arises because of a fall in the aggregate demand for goods and persists because of the failure of the Classical market adjustment mechanism. This, however, is not the only cause of non-natural unemployment (U > U*) that can be handled by this disequilibrium model. Malinvaud (1980) in particular has given considerable emphasis to the analysis of classical style unemployment within a disequilibrium framework. In this case we examine the consequences of a once and for all increase in the money wage. The increase in the money wage has its immediate effects on the supply side of the economy. It increases the real wage above the market clearing level (recall P is assumed to be fixed in this model) so all changes (or no changes) in the level of money wages imply equivalent changes in direction for real wages. Union activity may be responsible for the higher money

178

wage. We have already seen how in the union monopoly model wages are raised when unionisation takes place. If sectors are being unionised then this could lead to an increase of the kind we wish to consider. We need to assume that the increase in wages in the unionised sector does not depress wages in the non-union sector as unemployed (and previously unionised) workers enter and create excess supply in that sector. As a result money and real wages in the economy as a whole are clearly and unambiguously raised by union action.

What effect does this increase in money and real wages have on the rest of the economy? This is shown in Figure 5.12. The initial equilibrium position is at Y*, E* and U*. The profit maximising level of employment is cut to Y_C and employment falls to E_C (see Frame (b)) because of the wage increase. It also shifts (outwards) the budget line that determines the labour supply decision. The new optimal position for workers in Frame (c) remains at L* (income and substitution effects of the increase in the real wage exactly cancel each other out). However, the actual work available puts them at position L_C so actual labour supply is less than notional (full employment) supply. There is excess supply in the labour market in exactly the same way as in the case of Keynesian unemployment. Non-natural unemployment ($U_C - U*$) exists and in this case is called Classical unemployment. In one important respect it differs from the Keynesian equivalent. If it arises from union activity or some other worker induced change, it can no longer be regarded as involuntary. It is voluntary in the sense that it is the outcome of worker's collective behaviour. Another important difference is in the goods sector of the economy. Although there is a reduction in consumer demand (see Frame (d)) because of the fall in household income as output is cut, there is net excess demand for goods. This is shown in Frame (a) of Figure 5.12. If we assume the money market clears then the rate of interest will be R_C. At this rate of interest the demand for goods will be Y_{CN}. In fact the supply is only Y_C so there exists excess demand for goods of ($Y_{CN} - Y_C$). What has happened is that at R_C there is substantial extra demand for investment goods which are not produced because it is unprofitable for capital goods producers to meet the demand at the wage level W/P_C. Even if the money market did not clear and the rate of interest remained at R* there would still be excess demand for goods.

There are fundamental differences as we saw

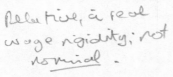

Relative, a real wage rigidity; not nominal.

179

Figure 5.12

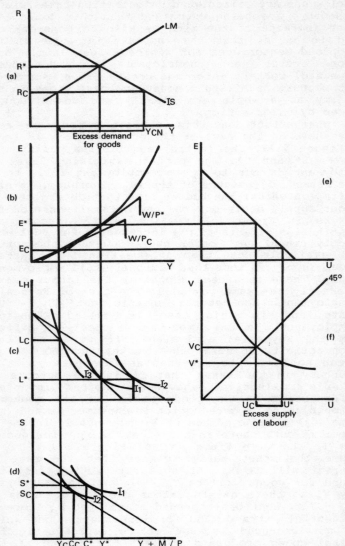

above between Keynesian and Classical unemployment
and this is illustrated in Table 5.1. This shows the
various combinations of excess supply (X_S) and excess
demand (X_D) in the labour and goods market of the
economy. It includes two combinations (repressed
inflation and underconsumption) which we will
ignore. We will concentrate on the two unemployment
cases where there is excess supply in the labour
market. Table 5.1 demonstrates a major advantage of
the modern disequilibrium approach, namely that it
does not rely on any single cause of unemployment.
Correspondingly, it does not imply any single
solution to the existence of non-natural
unemployment, unlike conventional Keynesian economics. Consider the impact of an expansionary fiscal
policy which is a critical ingredient of the
Keynesian cure for unemployment. If unemployment is
Keynesian and caused by a fall in aggregate demand as
in Figure 5.8, then an expansionary fiscal policy
will shift the IS curve back to its original position
and unemployment in excess of the natural rate will
be removed. If, however, an expansionary fiscal
policy were to be adopted when unemployment is
classical then the shift in the IS curve would add to
aggregate demand for goods, increasing the excess
demand for goods, but do nothing to relieve the
constraint on the supply side caused by money (and
real) wages being too high. The solution in this case
would require a general control on wages and prices
leading to a reduction in money and real wages. The
problems involved in achieving this are unlikely to
be modest given the way in which efficiency wages and
union rivalry constrain the downward flexibility of
money wages. One implication of the Gylfason and
Lindbeck (1984) model is that a successful incomes
policy requires that unions are persuaded to
cooperate and collude if money wages are to fall. If
this fails to occur allowing prices to increase ahead
of wages might be appropriate as long as the pattern
of relative wages is not disturbed.

Table 5.1

| | | Goods Market | |
		X_S	X_D
Labour	X_S	Keynesian Unemployment	Classical Unemployment
Market	X_D	Under-Consumption	Repressed Inflation

Because this would also shift down the IS curve (via real balance or other wealth effects) and shift the LM curve up by reducing the real value of the money supply the level of aggregate demand required for unemployment to be restored to its natural level would not be attained. The government would therefore need to adopt an expansionary fiscal and monetary policy to offset the real effects of the increase in prices. Malinvaud (1982) discusses in detail the case for an incomes policy operated in tandem with expansionary demand management when unemployment is Classical.

What is clear about the disequilibrium, non-market clearing approach, however, is that unlike the modern classical view active government intervention is necessary. There is no presumption that non-natural unemployment will correct itself. An interesting feature of this analysis is that the Classical unemployment story provides an alternative interventionist rationale to policies pursued in Britain by the Thatcher government. In chapter six we will consider the empirical case for the adoption of such a view of the British economy. Next we will consider unemployment in long run models of the closed economy.

Unemployment and Growth

Recently Malinvaud (1982) has extended the non-market clearing analysis of Classical unemployment to the longer run. A necessary condition for long run equilibrium is the equality of the rate of growth of output $(\dot{Y}/Y)$, capital $(\dot{K}/K)$ and the natural rate of growth determined by the sum of the growth in the labour force $(\dot{L}/L)$ and Harrod-neutral (labour saving) technical progress (σ) namely

5.14 $\dot{Y}/Y = \dot{K}/K = \dot{L}/L + \sigma$

If 5.14 holds and unemployment is initially at the natural rate it remains there. Malinvaud explores the possibility that inappropriate values of real wages and/or the user cost of capital may lead to non-natural unemployment $(U > U^*)$ in the long run. Of course, this is an issue well known in the growth theory literature. The basic Harrod/Domar model of economic growth explains long run unemployment of this type by the fact that the rate of growth of demand (the warranted rate) is lower than the growth of capacity $(\dot{L}/L + \sigma)$. This situation persists either because of a fixed coefficient technology that prevents firms adopting a more labour intensive method of production which would take up the unemployed workers or because non-market clearing in the monetary sector leaves interest rates at too high a level. In addition in a non-clearing labour market real wages fail to fall in the presence of unemployment so even if the elasticity of substitution is non-zero, firms have no incentive to adopt the more labour intensive technology necessary for the removal of unemployment. This is like Classical unemployment in the sense that the level of the real wage inhibits the adoption in the long run of the technology appropriate for full employment, although, of course, this situation could also arise for the other reasons considered above.

Malinvaud's (1982) model is essentially an extension of these ideas. Firstly he defines the level of investment in the economy as

$$5.15 \quad I = \bar{y}\dot{k} + k\dot{\bar{y}}$$

A putty clay technology is assumed so that productive equipment is represented by its capacity $\bar{y}$ and its capital intensity k where

$$5.16 \quad k = K/\bar{y}$$

Equation 5.15 says that investment occurs to increase the capital intensity of capacity output ($\bar{y}\dot{k}$) and to increase capacity output at a given degree of capital intensity ($k\dot{\bar{y}}$). The growth in capacity ($\dot{\bar{y}}$) is given by

$$5.17 \quad \dot{\bar{y}} = |a(\pi^e/R) - b(1-v^e)|\bar{y} \quad \text{with } a>0 \ b>0$$

where

v^e = expected level of capacity utilisation

π^e = expected profit rate

R = user cost of capital

Equation 5.17 shows that the growth of capacity depends negatively on expected excess capacity ($1 - v^e$) and positively on expected profitability (π^e). In exactly the same way as the conventional Harrod-Domar model, unemployment can arise in Malinvaud's because of too high a level of capital intensity. Insofar as this is the result of too high a level of real wages this unemployment is Classical in character and

183

cause. The additional ingredient is Malinvaud's
argument that long run classical unemployment can
exist and persist in a non-market clearing model, as
a result of a shortage of capacity. Equation 5.17
shows that if there is a squeeze on profitability
then $\bar{y}$ (the rate of growth of (capital) capacity)
will fall. (Recall a > 0). Formally to derive this
result Malinvaud assumes a, b, real wages and R are
constant and V is at its maximum value so there is no
spare capacity. The desired capital intensity of
production is then constant because relative costs
are fixed or Malinvaud further assumes that if actual
k (capital intensity) differs from its desired level
it is moving towards it. With these assumptions,
Malinvaud then shows (pages 5-6) that if remuneration
rates are too high this will: "lead to a sustained
decrease of productive capacities, which may be
called a classical depression. In order to cure it,
one must lower remuneration rates".

Malinvaud gives some attention to the policy
necessary to correct a classical depression. An
incomes policy which cuts the real wage rate and
restores profitability would be necessary but not
sufficient to remove non-natural unemployment. This
is because in the short run a reduction of the real
wage rate would reduce consumption and investment.
The latter happens because the reduction in real
wages encourages the use of a labour intensive
technology discouraging investment. The direct
effect of this on employment is, Malinvaud argues,
offset by the reduction in output caused by the fall
in consumption demand and investment. In the long run
the stimulus to profitability will encourage
investment via the effects described in equation 5.17
and 5.15. In the short run, however, Malinvaud argues
that incomes policy will need the support of
expansionary demand management policies. In other
words if one adopts the long run perspective favoured
by Malinvaud there remains a scope for demand
management at least in the short run even if
unemployment is Classical. This is, of course,
similar to the cure for Classical unemployment
considered in the previous section of this chapter.

Although neoclassical in style there are
elements of Malinvaud's analysis of unemployment
which overlap with Marxian theory. Marxist analysts
also prefer to take a longer run perspective on the
performance of a free enterprise economy.
Considerable emphasis in Marxist theory is given to
the tendency of capitalist economies to experience
periods of crisis. The most important signal of

crisis is the falling rate of profit. Traditional Marxist analysis attributes this falling rate of profit to the organic composition of capital or, very loosely speaking, increasing capital intensity in production. Alternatively or additionally there may be a fall in the rate of exploitation caused by a rise in real wages in a period of rapid capitalist accumulation. Such a process is accompanied by rapid depletion of labour reserves. This strengthening of labour's position lies at the basis of the reduction in the rate of exploitation. Glyn and Sutcliffe (1972) argue, for example, that the fall in profitability in Britain can be attributed partly to increased collective power by workers squeezing profits at a time when intensive overseas competition prevented employers from exploiting their domestic market power. Smith (1981) analyses the fall in profitability in ten capitalist economies and concludes: "The evidence seems to show that the decline in the rate of profit is due more or less equally to a fall in the rate of exploitation and a rise in the organic composition of capital". The consequences of this fall in profitability will be a fall in the rate of capital accumulation (as Malinvaud argues). This will be accompanied by rising unemployment in excess of the natural rate. Marxist economists, however, strengthen this tendency for unemployment to rise during capitalist crises. They argue that the resolution of capitalist crisis requires the creation of a 'reserve army of labour' to restore the balance of class forces. This follows partly from the view that the depletion of labour reserves actually contributes to the falling rate of profit by strengthening the power of organised labour, but also reflects the notion that a fall in real wages is necessary for the resolution of capitalist crisis and that the creation of a reserve army will assist this process. (16) This is not dissimilar from the views expressed by Malinvaud. In a similar way Glyn (1982) has recently argued (like Malinvaud (1982)) that British capitalism is now in a position where low profitability means a shortage of the capital necessary for full employment. Rising non-natural unemployment is, therefore, for Marxists a symptom of capitalist crisis but also a necessary part of the process of restoring profitability. Its removal is bound, therefore, to be a slow, drawn out process like in the 1930s. The actual speed of adjustment depends critically upon the other ingredient of the Marxist analysis of capitalist crisis, namely the restructuring of production to

achieve a higher level of factor productivity. Partly
this can be achieved by closure of low productivity
plants and factories which assists in the creation of
a reserve army. It also involves the exploitation of
productivity enhancing technical progress. In the
1980s in Britain this argument has particular force
with the increasing use of microelectronic
technology. This role of technical progress in
creating unemployment is explored more fully in
chapter eight. In fact it is not simply the selection
of technologies on purely technical grounds that
underpins the Marxist analysis. Of crucial
importance is the selection of technologies that
increase the employers' control of the work process.
The employer seeks methods of production that enhance
his control over the pace at which workers work, and
hence over their productivity per unit of time. The
adoption of assembly line production in the thirties
is an example of this process which has received
particular attention. In this respect microelectronic technology has distinct advantages to the employer
which are over and above the simple employment saving
benefits. The use of payment systems that reduce
'shirking' and ensure maximum effort is also part of
this process.

However, the restructuring of capitalist
production does not only involve alterations in
machinery with which employees work and in payment
systems. It also requires the adoption of
organisational forms which facilitate and improve
the employer's control of the work process. The
growth in divisionalised systems of management in
Britain can be viewed in this light. (17) Merger
which enhances product market power weakens
organised labour by giving employers greater control
over their own environment. These structural changes
are, however, very slow and if they are a necessary
accompaniment to the resolution of capitalist crisis
without destruction to the system then the speed with
which non-natural unemployment (the reserve army in
Marxist technology) is removed will be very slow. Of
course Marxist economists urge, as a result, the
adoption of a socialist system of production which,
they argue, will greatly speed up the process. Most
economists in Britain have been reluctant to accept
this type of analysis, partly because of the emphasis
it gives to institutional factors in explaining both
the cause and the cure for high unemployment. An
alternative and much less radical approach is to
incorporate the rational expectations assumptions of
the modern classical economist within a non-market

clearing model. This is the subject of the next section.

Rational Expectations Contracts and Non-Market Clearing

Non-market clearing models provide an alternative to the analysis and prescription of modern classical economics considered in chapter four. This has recently been strengthened by the emergence of a new Keynesian theory. Seminal papers are those by Fischer (1977) and Taylor (1979) and recently in Britain the work of Begg (1982b) amongst others.

The starting point for this approach to unemployment is the use of the theory of contracts considered earlier in this chapter. The economists involved in the development of these ideas are very concerned not to adopt an approach that is totally at variance with that of modern classical economics. They share the concern for strong micro (optimising) foundations for macro theory. They do not wish to reject the standard neoclassical approach but rather to emphasise the theoretical and policy weaknesses of a market clearing perspective. Their pragmatic and moderate approach to economic policy makes them true successors to the Keynesian tradition, which repeatedly draws attention to the inadequacy of models and policies based on the assumption that markets (particularly the labour market) actually clear.

The first and basic assumption is that the labour contracts are made (for reasons considered earlier in this chapter) for a finite period of time. Money wage rates are set for that period on the basis of the expected levels of supply and demand.

In the US institutional arrangements justify the assumption of a fixed term contract with invariant terms. In Britain contracts are shorter, likely to be variable in length and a good deal less detailed. The greater degree of bargaining decentralisation in Britain makes possible local (plant level) amendments to the basic contract which would not occur in the US. Although basic money wage rates are usually centrally determined there is considerable scope for the adjustment of effective money wage rates through the manipulation of the factor level component. The so-called 'drift' component of pay in Britain makes for much greater variability in wages, as Gordon (1982) has recently shown. The empirical validity of the approach adopted by Fischer (1977) and others may therefore be greater in the US than in Britain. The second important assumption is characteristic of other non-market clearing models already considered, namely that <u>actual</u> demands and supplies are equal. This means that rationing is an important feature of the labour market. When there are unemployed resources in the labour market, for example, there is job rationing and workers have to content themselves with supplying less than they would at the current money wage over the period of the contract. Finally, some attention has been given especially by Taylor (1979) to the fact that in the economy as a whole contracts are staggered. They are concluded on different days for different durations.

Initially, Fischer (1977) constructs a model with one period contracts which are not staggered so that all workers settle on the same date for the same single period. Output supplied is a decreasing function of the real wage which is fixed by negotiation on the basis of a rational expectation of the price level. The rational expectation is formed using the knowledge of the next period's money supply which is possessed by all economic agents. The real wage agreed will be that which ensures employment is at the natural rate and the nominal wage simply adjusts to the expected price level. Any departures from the natural level will be purely random. In other words this model has exactly the same properties and predictions as the conventional modern classical model. (18)

Fischer then explores the same model but assumes labour contracts run for two periods and are not indexed to the price level. In this case during period t half the firms are operating under a contract agreed at the end of t-1. The other half have a contract drawn up at the end of t-2. Each of these contracts was negotiated on the basis of rational expectations but these were formed at different times in the past. Agents get locked into these expectations by the contractual fixity of the money wage. This fixity of the money wage comes about, it should be emphasised, by contractual commitments that prevent the revision of money wages in the light of new information like an unexpected cut in the aggregate demand for goods.

The aggregate supply equation also requires modification to allow for the influence of older (than t-1) expectations about the price level. This is done by rewriting the aggregate Lucas-Sargent supply equation (equation 4.16) for the two group/two period case as

$$5.18 \quad Y_t^s = Y_t^* + \frac{1}{2} \sum_{i=1}^{2} (P_t - _{t-i}P_t^e)$$

Using the same assumption as before Fischer shows that non-natural unemployment can arise and persist because money wages are fixed for the period of the contract. It also can be reduced by monetary changes. Government policy can react to new information about the economy which those affected by contracts two periods ago cannot anticipate. They cannot therefore take this into account in forming their own expectations. In a sense the existence of an older fixed contract enables the government to make changes which are unanticipated by the affected group. Since the changes are unanticipated there are real effects in the same way we considered in the last chapter. Once the real world fact of long term contracts are considered even within a rational expectations framework, unemployment in excess of the natural rate can persist for at least the period of the contract, unless the government acts to correct it.

Fischer also shows that when contracts are indexed to the price level in a way which duplicates the effect of one period contracts, non-natural unemployment disappears and government policy is both unnecessary and futile. However, the indexing formula is "unlike anything seen in practice". Fischer attributes this to the fact that:

> calculation of their terms would be difficult since industry and firm specific factors omitted from this simple model are relevant to contracts that duplicate the effects of a full set of spot markets.

Begg (1982b) has recently outlined a model similar to that of Fischer in which non-natural unemployment exists and persists. Begg assumes the same money wage is paid in both sub-periods of the contract. Firms are assumed to maximise profits in a competitive world subject to a conventional neoclassical function

$$5.19 \quad Y_t = 1/a \, E_t \quad 1 < a < 0$$

Aggregate demand is given by

$$5.20 \quad Y_t = cY_t + b(M_t/P_t) + Z_t \quad 0 < c < 1 \quad b > 0$$

where

189

Z_t = autonomous demand
M_t/P_t = real cash balances

In the same way as Fischer, Begg assumes that the price level clears the goods market. He justifies this assumption on the grounds that the transaction costs of changing prices are less than wages and so we should expect to see greater flexibility in the former than the latter. Begg then considers the effect of a downward shift in autonomous demand at time t. One group (A) of workers who settled their contract at t-1 are locked into the previously agreed money wage (group A). Begg assumes that group B who settle at the time autonomous demand falls ($\Delta Z_t < 0$) takes this into account and settle for a money wage that ensures their continued full employment. It is important to emphasise the assumption that both groups are producing the same good. In this case group B does not have to accept a cut to the full employment wage for both groups. This is because they can secure their own full employment by cutting their wages below that of Group A and taking some of their share of the market. In other words they shift the unemployment to Group A. In the next period, Group A, whose contract is being renegotiated, cut their wages to ensure their full employment and unemployment increases for Group B. This process continues, Begg argues, until the economy moves back to full employment with lower wage levels. This could take a good deal of time, but the existence of long term contracts slows the market adjustment down to such an extent that the government should feel it must act to remove the unemployment, even though the model assumes individuals do not make systematic errors, because expectations are formed rationally.

Begg also considers the role of demand management. He shows that even with a lag if the government reacts to the fall in aggregate demand by an offsetting change in its own level of real demand, then full employment will be restored. In his recent book, Begg (1982a) has summarised his results as follows:

> Rational Expectations can be applied in models which do not impose continuous market clearing and conventional stabilisation policy will then have the conventional Keynesian effects, even though the policy is understood and incorporated into the process of expectations formation.

Our discussion of modern non-market clearing models has so far been largely concerned with the closed economy. In the next section we examine the open economy.

Disequilibrium Models in the Open Economy

Some interesting extensions to the basic temporary equilibrium model can be made by considering the open economy. The main difference is that disequilibrium shows itself as a balance of payments surplus or deficit rather than as rationing in the goods market of the economy. In fact if we assume that producers face perfectly elastic demand curves in the world economy (empirical evidence suggests they do not), then producers of goods cannot be quantity constrained. The excess supply of goods that characterises Keynesian unemployment will be taken up by exports. Similarly in the labour market, given this assumption about export demand elasticities, non-natural unemployment can only be Classical. If this unrealistic assumption regarding export demand elasticities is dropped then Keynesian unemployment can occur but the strength of expansionary demand management is weakened (as we have seen already) by the fact that the balance of payments deteriorates as excess supply of goods and labour is eliminated. What is necessary in this case is a cut in real wages to make export and import substitutes more competitive and thereby to improve the balance of payments and reinforce the stimulation of output achieved by the expansionary policy. If this is done by a devaluation, the problem is that the beneficial effects may not last as the evidence of Ball, Burns and Laury (1977) shows. The solution then is a direct cut in real wages by the use of an incomes policy or some other means. However it is done, the treatment of Keynesian unemployment in an open economy may well require the use of some of the instruments necessary for the cure of Classical unemployment.

In the presence of Classical unemployment itself the excess demand for goods that is not satisfied by domestic production will be met by imports. Attempts to remedy this type of unemployment by an expansionary fiscal policy will not only fail to reduce unemployment but the addition to the aggregate demand for goods will spill over into imports, causing a deterioration in the balance of payments. The case against fiscal policy is therefore even more powerful in the open economy where unemployment is Classical. Only a cut in real wages will help to reduce the unemployment in excess of the natural rate.

The presence of an external sector also permits us to consider a further cause of unemployment which some economists consider to be of considerable importance in explaining the current high levels of unemployment in Britain and the rest of the industrial world. Stagflation theories of non-natural unemployment are based upon the response to shocks like a change in the rate of productivity growth of western economies or major increases in the prices of imported energy and raw materials. A productivity growth slowdown and increased input (especially oil) prices is exactly what happened in the seventies as unemployment increased in most western economies.

Consider, for example, the effect of the oil price increases of the mid and late seventies. The effect of these increases was to raise the domestic price level in an industrial economy like Britain. In the presence of a real balance (or other wealth) effect this depresses aggregate demand. This is reinforced by the adverse effects of a higher domestic price level on the competitiveness of domestic goods. With a given nominal money supply this domestic price increase would also reduce the real value of the money supply. The IS curve shifts down and the LM curve shifts up. The effect would be to reduce aggregate demand and create Keynesian unemployment in the manner considered for the closed economy earlier in this chapter and shown in Figure 5.8. This, however, is not the end of the story in an open economy and this is why the standard demand management remedies for Keynesian unemployment may be inappropriate in this case.

The starting point is a crucial amendment to the neoclassical closed economy theory of labour demand appropriate to the open economy, which can be written as

5.21 $D_E = e(W/P, P_m/P)$ with $\partial D_E / \partial W/P < 0$

$$\partial D_E / \partial P_m/P < 0$$

where

P = the domestic price level
P_m = the price of imported raw materials (including oil)

There is a standard and normal negative relation

between labour demand and the real wage ($\partial D_E/\partial W/P < 0$). The amendment to the normal labour demand function is the inclusion of the relative price of imported inputs (P_m/P). It also has a negative relation with labour demand. The reason is that labour and raw materials (and energy) are assumed to be net complementary inputs particularly in the short run. As a result, an increase in the price of imported inputs reduces their usage <u>and</u> cuts the demand for labour ($\partial D_E/\partial P_m/P < 0$). Work by Berndt and Wood (1975) demonstrates the existence of such an effect in the US in the long run. A 10% fall in energy use which would follow an increase in energy prices lowers the marginal product of labour by 1% in the long run while comparable falls in <u>materials</u> use have an even bigger effect reducing the marginal product of labour by 10%. Any substitution effect of a rise in input prices that encourages <u>greater</u> labour demand is apparently more than offset by these strong income effects. Indeed many economists argue that the depressing effect on employment is even stronger in the short run. (19)

Since the marginal product of labour falls so will the real wage employers are willing to pay any given number of employees (the notional labour demand curve shifts down). If the real wage fails to fall, (because of contract, efficiency wage or union effects) therefore, employment will fall and unemployment will rise. Since this unemployment results from too high a level of real wages it is Classical in cause and character and requires the remedies outlined earlier in this chapter.

These (and other) effects are shown in Figure 5.13 which utilises Frames (a), (b) and (c) of Figure 5.8 but includes in Frame (a) the external balance schedule for an open economy (see Figure 5.2). Frame (b) is the conventional employment function and (c) depicts the labour supply and real wage relationship. Initially we assume Walrasian equilibrium at R*, E* Y* and L*. The balance of payments is also in equilibrium. The aggregate demand effects of a rise in imported input prices are shown in Frame (a). The IS curve moves down to IS_2 and the LM curve up to LM_2. Output falls to Y_K and Keynesian unemployment of E* - E_K occurs. Unemployment therefore exceeds the natural rate.

As we have seen this is not the end of the story. The effect of the increase in input prices will be to shift the employment function so that less labour is desired for the production of any level of output. Since there is also assumed to be a fall in

193

the marginal product of labour, the slope of the employment function depicted in Frame (b) will also change. It will become steeper reflecting the fact that a fall in the marginal product of labour will increase the extra labour required for the production of any extra unit of output. The employment function will shift to T_2 and if the real wage remains unchanged the point of tangency will be at a lower level of employment. In Frame (b) employment falls to E_C so that the economy experiences Classical unemployment of $E_K - E_C$. Workers are forced even further off their supply curve and on to an even lower indifference curve to L_C in Frame (b). Only if real wages fall will this important component of unemployment be removed.

Stagflation theorists place great emphasis on the downward rigidity of <u>real</u> wages in some (especially European) Western economies. They reverse the view of Keynes that nominal wages are rigid and real wages flexible in the face of increases in prices and assert that nominal wages are flexible while real wages are rigid. Their view is that increases in prices caused by increases in material prices will cause a rapid increase in domestic prices and lead to a matching adjustment of money wages. The argument is that in the inflationary world of the seventies, Keynes' view of the flexibility of real wages is wrong. If the inflation that results from higher imported input prices is perfectly anticipated and adjusted to in money wage settlements (as some modern Classical economists argue) then <u>real</u> wages will be rigid downwards. The result will be that increases in imported input prices cause Classical unemployment of the type depicted in Figure 5.13.

So far we have ignored the balance of payments effects of a rise in import prices. On the current account there is a clear deterioration. Apart from the direct effect on the import bill the induced increase in domestic prices and money wages (because of real wage rigidity) reduces the international competitiveness of the domestic economy with adverse effects on exports and imports. This moves the XB schedule upwards. In Figure 5.13 we have assumed a shift to XB_2. Since interest rates are assumed to remain at R^* this means the worsening of the current account is not offset by any improvement on the capital account. This means an overall deficit in the balance of payments arises. Note this conclusion depends on the assumption that the shift in the IS and LM curve leave the interest rate unchanged at R^*.

Figure 5.13

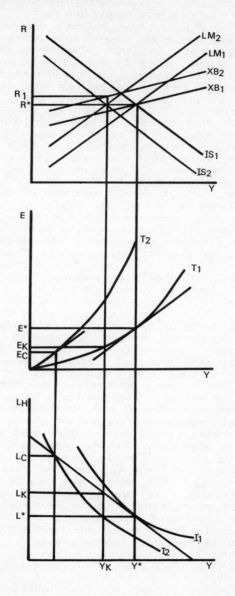

This may not be the case and an interest rate (IS, LM intersection) at R_1 for example, would not mean a worsening of the balance of payments.

The experience of the British economy in the 1970s, however, was that an eventual worsening of the balance of payments did take place and so we will confine our attention to this case. If the exchange rate is fixed in the analysis of Figure 5.13 real wage cuts will greatly assist in the removal of Keynesian (E* - E_K) as well as Classical unemployment. This is because of the boost to international competitiveness given by these cuts. This boost shifts the IS curve up and the XB curve down to their initial position.

If on the other hand exchange rates are flexible the overall deficit in the balance of payments depicted in Figure 5.13 will drive the exchange rate down. This will shift the XB and the IS curves back to their initial position. If, however, the fall in the exchange rate induces further increases in prices and money wages little change will take place. Real wage rigidity will prevent the movement in the exchange rate assisting in the removal of non-natural unemployment.

Stagflation theorists argue, therefore, for cuts in real wages as a necessary condition for the reduction of all unemployment in excess of the natural rate. If the labour market fails to facilitate this by a reduction in real wages as the non-market clearing models considered in this chapter suppose, then incomes policy is essential. The position has been put clearly by Layard and Symons (1984): "Wage restraint looks like a necessary ingredient of any recovery programme. The alternative is to wait, perhaps for a very long time, until unemployment itself reduces the real wages". The empirical evidence in support of these assertions and of non-market clearing in general, is considered in the next chapter. Since, as the models we considered earlier in the chapter show, unions may actually bring about an increase in real wages in recession the case for an incomes policy to secure this wage restraint is even greater in a unionised economy. Not surprisingly those who emphasise the stagflation theory of Classical unemployment also argue forcefully for incomes policies to permit the reduction of large scale unemployment.

Conclusion
This chapter has outlined non-market clearing

approaches to unemployment. This type of analysis justifies the view that non-natural unemployment (U > U*) exists and will persist in the absence of government intervention. In addition in most of the models it is not inappropriate to describe much of this unemployment as involuntary, and as the result of unwanted constraints on the actions of economic agents. It has also made clear that the theoretical case of the modern classical economists rests not upon the assumption of rational expectations, but on the far more important claim that markets (especially labour) clear. The task of providing firm theoretical foundations for the non-market clearing paradigm has already made significant progress, particularly in the labour market. The empirical case for the adoption of this framework is considered in the next chapter.

Notes

1.   This is fully explained in any standard text. For example Branson (1979), pages 132-135.
2.   Recent empirical evidence on wealth effects in Britain has been reviewed by Grice in Artis and Miller (1981).
3.   A full discussion of the money supply in the open economy can be found in Levacic and Rebman (1982), chapters 9 and 11.
4.   The most extensive justification for the adoption of import controls has been provided by the Cambridge Economic Policy Group. A concise statement of its position can be found in Ward (1981).
5.   In Britain the abolition of exchange controls by the Thatcher government has increased the gross capital outflow. Again, only in the absence of retaliation would the net effect of their reintroduction be the same as the gross effect.
6.   Some comparative data on this point has been provided by George and Ward (1978). See also Cable (1982).
7.   There is an interesting discussion of this in Keynes (1936), page 14.
8.   This is the result obtained by Azariadis (1981).
9.   This efficiency wage argument or the economy of high wages is usually considered in developing economies where the positive relationship of pay and productivity depends on the positive correlation of both with nutrition. For a survey of the recent literature on the application of efficiency wages to industrialised economies, see

Yellen (1984).

10. A formal analysis of this argument is in Malcolmson (1981). He shows wage rigidity and involuntary unemployment will exist in perfectly competitive sub-markets of the economy subject to the assumption that the <u>individual</u> productivity of different workers cannot be discriminated <u>perfectly</u> by observation at work.

11. Strictly the profits are assumed to be paid as a supplement to hourly wages so that the wage rate includes a profit component. If this were not the case Frame (c) would need to allow for non-labour incomes as a lump sum. This is not difficult but its complication adds little to the argument in the text.

12. This assumption is made throughout this and the previous chapter. We consider the effect of long and short run changes in the offer and acceptance probabilities in chapters seven and eight.

13. This also happens because the cut in wages which reduces productivity will reduce the offer probability for unemployed workers searching for a job. This is considered further in chapter eight.

14. This currently popular model is used for illustration to show how unions might affect wages and unemployment. It has a great many drawbacks. Industrial relations specialists would argue like Ross (1948) that maximisation models are totally inappropriate to the analysis of unions. They (and many economists) would also take issue with the monopoly view of the trade unions. Union members (and leaders) are assumed to share the same preferences and internal dispute within the union is totally ignored. A further problem is that the assignment of roles in the model leaves no real scope for bargaining or conflict to occur. Wage negotiation consists of the firm making sure the union knows the position of the demand curve so it can fix wages. Few empiricists believe employers play such a passive role.

15. This rather odd result arises from the ability of the union to fix wages once the demand curve is known and firms have fixed employment. It is also assumes that the demand function does not shift isoelastically (see McDonald and Solow (1981), page 899) in recession when W will then be <u>rigid</u>.

16. The validity of this argument is considered in K.G. Knight (1984).

17. An extended version of these arguments can be found in P.A. Geroski and K.G. Knight (1984).

18. The details are in Fischer (1977), pages

265-268.

19. Grubb, Jackman and Layard (1982) for example argue this way in Annex 1 of their paper (page 724). The argument in the text could be supplemented by adding a general terms of trade effect to the labour demand function. If import prices rise relative to export prices in a common currency for any reason this could shift the demand curve downwards. For an argument along these lines see Minford (1983).

Chapter Six

NON-NATURAL UNEMPLOYMENT - EMPIRICAL EVIDENCE

In the two previous chapters the alternative approaches to the analysis of aggregate unemployment in excess of the natural rate have been outlined. The market clearing approach favoured by the modern classical economists suggests any such unemployment is a random occurrence requiring no government intervention. In general the labour market like other aggregate markets will be in equilibrium. The disequilibrium approach, on the other hand, implies non-natural unemployment can exist and persist and requires corrective action by the government although the form of that action depends upon the causes of the unemployment that occurs. Knowledge of the latter is required before selection of the appropriate corrective instrument. In this chapter we will consider the empirical evidence that has been advanced to support these alternative ways of examining unemployment. This is mainly in Britain, although we will refer to evidence from other countries where appropriate.

Economic Policy and Non-natural Unemployment

In Chapter 4 we saw that modern classical economists believe that demand management is neither necessary nor effective. In part this belief rests on the assumption that expectations are formed rationally but also as we saw in Chapter 5 depends on the further assumption that markets in the economy continuously clear. With both of these assumptions expectational errors are quickly corrected and as a result we can infer the neutrality of demand management in terms of its effects on real magnitudes in the economy as a whole. One obvious test, therefore, of the whole classical approach to the cause and cure for unemployment is to examine whether in practice economic policy changes are neutral unless they are unanticipated by the private sector.

Sargent (1976) has tested this proposition regarding demand management within the context of a macroeconometric model of the US economy. This involves estimating an equation of the form

$$6.1 \quad U_t = \sum_{j=1}^{m} \alpha_j U_{t-j} + \sum_{j=1}^{n} \beta_j z_{t-j} + \sigma_t$$

where in the empirical work the vector z includes a variety of policy variables like real government expenditure, and the nominal money supply. If the natural rate assertion of modern classical economists holds up we should expect the parameters β_j, $j=1,\ldots n$ to equal zero and the actual unemployment rate will be the natural rate and will be (statistically) a weighted average of its own past values and invariant with respect to monetary and fiscal policy variables. Sargent uses US data from 1952 to 1972 to estimate equation 6.1. Employing the Granger (1969) (1) test Sargent finds the β coefficients are in fact non-zero for two variables, the money supply and the nominal money wage. Some contradictory results are obtained using other tests and although Sargent claims that his results overall suggest that demand management does not affect unemployment, the evidence against the hypothesis that they do is by no means unambiguous.

Indeed if such evidence were clearly available it would contradict the conclusion of earlier studies of the US, some of them by economists sympathetic to Sargent's (1976) view of the superiority of fixed rules (like a constant rate of growth in the money supply) over contingent rules (which respond to current circumstances) in fixing policy instruments. Andersen and Jordan (1968), for example, in an influential study of the US found that although fiscal policy changes had little effect on output (and unemployment) over the period they study, monetary changes had a significant impact although with a lengthy lag. This result has been confirmed by several other studies in the US which showed the lag was also variable and uncertain. Before rational expectations became a central feature of the classical approach this empirical fact was important to classical economists like Milton Friedman because

In such an environment, even a well-informed and well-intentioned policy maker is likely to have a difficult time determining the optimal feed back rule. Real world governments are frequently neither well informed nor well intentioned. It is therefore preferable to constrain the policy authorities options by committing them to simple fixed rules such as a constant growth rate for the money supply or a balanced budget. (Buiter 1981).

In Britain, Artis and Nobay (1969) undertook similar tests to those performed by Andersen and Jordan and found some rather different results. Not only did fiscal policy exert a significant impact on output and employment but monetary had little, if any, effect. Goodhart and Crockett (1970) came to a similar conclusion, as do Andrews and Nickell (1982) in their empirical study of unemployment in Britain for 1950 to 1979. One explanation may be that the channels of monetary influence are weak in Britain compared with the US. Savage (1978) in a review of the empirical evidence shows how, in all but a few sectors, the direct influence of money on spending is small in Britain. Much also depends on the time period chosen for the study. Active monetary control was not a feature of the period studied by Artis and Nobay. Mills and Wood (1978) show rather stronger effects in the 1970s, when British governments have not relied simply on fiscal instruments for demand management policy. The conclusion from this evidence is that in both the US and Britain fiscal and monetary policy both influence real output and employment although there are significant differences between the countries.

In fact the position of the modern classical economists is rather more subtle than that of the more traditional monetarists like Friedman. They do not deny (see Chapter 4) that policy changes can have effects on the real sector of the economy but they argue for this to be the case the policy changes must not be anticipated by the private sector. If the policy change is known its effects are predicted and discounted so that no real changes take place. In order to test this hypothesis it is necessary to distinguish between anticipated and unanticipated changes in policy instruments. This is the empirical question to which the American economist Barro has given considerable attention in Barro (1977, 1978) and Barro and Rush (1980). Similar work for Britain has been conducted by Attfield, Demery and Duck (1981a and b) using data from 1963 to 1978. The first stage in the empirical work which is concerned with assessing the impact of monetary policy on the real economy is the estimation of a nominal money supply rule. The version of this rule employed by Attfield, Demery and Duck (1981b) using quarterly data is

$$6.2 \quad \Delta M_t = \delta_0 + \delta_1 \Delta M_{t-1} + \delta_2 \Delta M_{t-2} + \delta_3 \Delta M_{t-3}$$
$$+ \delta_4 PB_t + \delta_5 S_{t-1} + \varepsilon_t$$

where $\Delta M_t = \log M_t - \log M_{t-1}$, PB_t = the real value of the central government borrowing requiring, S_{t-1} = the lagged real value of the current balance of payments surplus. The actual specification is slightly different from that employed by Barro and Rush (1980) for the US but the differences are not significant. Attfield, Demery and Duck find δ_1, δ_4 and δ_5 to be statistically significant (2). Both δ_4 and δ_5 had the expected sign (positive in both cases).

The next stage in the study is to estimate an equation for real output (Barro and Rush use unemployment as the dependent variable in this equation) which employs the forecasting errors from 6.2 above, namely

$$6.3 \quad \Delta MR_t = \Delta M_t - {}_{t-1}\Delta M_t^e = \Delta M_t - \Delta \hat{M}_t$$

where $\Delta \hat{M}_t$ is obtained from the estimates of 6.2 and ΔMR_t is therefore the residual from that equation. $\Delta \hat{M}_t$ is also the rational expectation of the growth in the money supply. The output equation is

$$6.4 \quad Y_t = \beta_0 + \beta_1 t + \beta_2 V_{Pt} + \beta_3 \Delta MR_{t-1} + \beta_4 \Delta MR_{t-2}$$
$$+ \beta_5 \Delta MR_{t-3} + \beta_6 \Delta MR_{t-4} + \beta_7 \Delta MR_{t-5} + \beta_8 \Delta MR_{t-8} + \mu_t$$

where t = time and V_{Pt} is the log of the variability of the inflation rate. The latter variable is not included in the specification employed by Barro and Rush (1980) for the US but Attfield, Demery and Duck advance a number of reasons for its inclusion and for their expectation that β_2 will be negative. Basically these arguments rely upon the belief that price uncertainty (high V_{Pt}) will lower the natural level of output (Y_t^*) (raise U_t^*) and hence actual output Y_t. It turns out that β_2 is indeed significantly negative when equation 6.4 is actually estimated. Using ΔMR_t as the estimate of unanticipated monetary growth, Attfield, Demery and Duck find β_1, β_5, β_6, β_7 and β_8 to be positive and statistically significant and

Their summed value of approximately 3.0 suggests that a quarterly unanticipated growth rate of 10% per annum which persists for six quarters will raise output by about 7% above its natural level.

This is consistent with the Barro and Rush (1980) study which finds that only unanticipated monetary changes can affect unemployment. It is also consistent with the classical perspective on unemployment that demand management will only have an effect as long as the private sector can be 'fooled'. However it is worth recalling that this view also suggests that the costs of such a policy will be increases in the price level (and its rate of inflation). The curious feature of Attfield, Demery and Duck's work is that when they estimate a price equation their results suggest that in these circumstances the price level will actually fall! - a Keynesian paradise indeed. Some comfort is derived by the authors from the fact that the estimated standard error is sufficiently large for the expected classical result to be possible. Such crumbs of comfort are unlikely to satisfy the sceptic who may also be worried by other aspects of the methodology. It is a critical part of the method that the estimates obtained from equation 6.2 have the statistical properties outlined in Chapter 4. Of particular importance is that the errors should be serially uncorrelated. In their initial estimates, Attfield, Demery and Duck were unable to reject the hypothesis that the errors were serially correlated, although further tests confirm that this was not a problem which seriously undermines their results. It is also important to establish the stability of coefficients in equation 6.2. Attfield, Demery and Duck split the data into two subsets corresponding to the periods of fixed and floating exchange rates in Britain. They find the estimates are stable across these two subperiods. Begg (1982) has also highlighted some problems with the Attfield, Demery, Duck approach. He notes that equations 6.5 and 6.7 can be written in a form that suggests that only past unanticipated growth in the money supply matters and he concludes 'this procedure will never shed light on the efficacy of the stabilisation policy'. As far as fiscal policy is concerned, Attfield, Demery and Duck's work also provides some insights. In estimating equation 6.2 they use an estimate of the real value of the central government's borrowing requirement rather than PB_t itself. If the actual value of PB_t is greater than this estimate this could be interpreted as an unanticipated expansionary fiscal policy which is associated with an unanticipated expansion in the money supply assuming that the increment to PB_t is not totally debt financed. In this case subject to the limitations of the methodology outlined above, Attfield, Demery and Duck's results could be seen as a test of the capacity of fiscal 'surprises' to affect the real economy. Consequently, the problem arises that if unanticipated changes in policy have real effects it is not clear whether fiscal or monetary changes are ultimately responsible. More directly the study by Andrews and Nickell (1982) indicates that unanticipated increases in government spending do reduce the unemployment rate in Britain so fiscal 'surprises' may work as well as the monetary equivalent.

Recently, further studies have been conducted that confirm these doubts about the neutrality of demand management in Britain and the US. Mishkin (1982) shows that Barro's results for the US depend critically upon the length of the lag that is assumed in the modelling of the influence of money on output. Pesaran (1983) has also subjected the neutrality hypothesis to close critical scrutiny using US data. He argues that a proper test of the neutrality of demand management requires consideration of 'at least one genuine alternative'. Pesaran employs a Keynesian alternative in which <u>anticipated</u> changes in monetary and fiscal policy are able to alter the level of output and employment during the period 1946-73. He finds that <u>both</u> monetary and fiscal stimuli do, in fact, increase real output but the latter acts more rapidly than the former. (3) He also finds that this conventional Keynesian equation, in which no significant independent effects of unanticipated policy changes are found, explains the data at least as well as the Classical alternative. Pesaran also performs tests that indicate that the Keynesian and Classical alternatives are strong rival hypotheses with no clear superior. Pesaran offers reasons for believing the Keynesian model is in fact superior during the period covered by his empirical work. He shows that the kind of model estimated by Barro and Rush in the US and Attfield, Demery and Duck in Britain can be obtained by assuming that the government employs an active fiscal policy and an accommodating monetary policy. If, as was the case in Britain until the mid-seventies, the government pegs the nominal rate of interest and

205

allows the money supply to change to ensure this then the measure of the unanticipated growth in the money supply actually reflects changes in the stance of the active fiscal policy. In other words an expansionary fiscal policy, for example, shows up as an increase in money supply greater than expected (by the monetary authorities) and hence the results of Barro and Rush actually can be viewed as evidence 'for', not against the Keynesian explanation of unemployment. This argument is not too dissimilar from that employed before in the context of fiscal 'surprises' in the discussion of the results of Attfield, Demery and Duck. Pesaran concludes that the results of Barro and Rush replicated for Britain by Attfield, Demery and Duck

> do not form any empirical basis whatsoever for the abandonment of the Keynesian explanation of unemployment and the 'activist' policy implications that accompany it.

Recent studies of Britain confirm this scepticism of the modern classical view of economic policy and of the economic structure and functioning which underlie it. Bean (1984) undertakes some tests of the hypothesis that unanticipated money supply changes are no different in their effects from those that are fully anticipated. His results confirm this when a narrow definition of money (M1) is selected but neutrality (only unanticipated changes have an effect) is not rejected by the data when a broader (M3) definition of money is used.

Demery (1984) has provided rather more clearcut time series evidence for Britain between 1963 and 1982. Like Pesaran (1982) he argues that a proper test of the market clearing/rational expectations view must involve the comparison of alternative models of the economy. Demery employs (4) a model proposed by Gordon (1982) that assumes a gradual and non-instantaneous market clearing process in contrast with the classical model that underlies his previous work with Attfield and Duck (1981a, b). He finds considerable evidence for this gradual adjustment hypothesis in contrast with the instantaneous market clearing model which is rejected by the data. In particular he finds fiscal and monetary policies which increase anticipated or unanticipated nominal output growth both significantly increase real output and employment. Note that this effect does <u>not</u> depend on the policy change surprising the private sector. This is counter to the

lassical view. Demery concludes from his empirical
nalysis that if an increase in the rate of
nticipated monetary growth has failed to affect real
utput in Britain, as his previous work indicates,
his arises out of the failure of monetary policy to
ffect aggregate demand rather 'than the failure of
nticipated aggregate demand to influence real
utput'. In practice British monetary policy may have
een ineffective in changing real output and
mployment but in principle it could be used to
roduce reductions in the level of unemployment. Not
urprisingly Demery concludes his results 'provide
n old-fashioned Keynesian interpretation of part of
he existing empirical literature'. With this
vidence in mind we can conclude that modern
lassical economists who rely on market clearing have
ailed to demonstrate that demand management is
either necessary nor effective. We can also infer
hat the lack of strong policy evidence for this
eutrality proposition in both Britain and the US
rovides indirect support for the superiority of a
on-market clearing approach to unemployment and of
he consequent existence of positive and persistent
on-natural unemployment. We will consider more
irect tests of this view in the remainder of this
hapter.

xpectations, Labour Supply and Unemployment
s we have seen disequilibrium can occur in the
lassical market clearing framework because of
xpectational error. Of course since the error is
ssumed to be rapidly corrected this is not an
mpediment to market clearing. This suggests a
urther test of the classical view. Departures of
nemployment from the natural rate should clearly
ccur only if the price level is over or
nderestimated. We have seen non-natural unemploy-
ent occurs in the former case. A direct test of this
proposition) for Britain, using survey data on
xpectations has been conducted by Batchelor and
heriff (1980). They estimate an equation of the form

.5 $\quad U_t = U_t^* + \alpha(\dot{P}_t - {}_{t-1}\dot{P}_t^e) + \mu_t$ with $\alpha < 0$

here $\dot{P}$ = price inflation rate. μ_t = error term. The
atural rate of unemployment U_t^* is not a constant but
s specified as

.6 $\quad U_t^* = \beta(W/P) + \underset{\sim}{\delta}'\underset{\sim}{X}$

207

where W/P = the real wage and X is a vector of othe
labour market characteristics with δ a vector o
related coefficients. This specification permits Batchelor an
Sheriff to allow for the variation in U_t^* which wa
referred to at the end of Chapter 2 and will b
considered more fully in Chapters 7 and 8. Usin
monthly unemployment data to estimate equation 6.
they find α to be consistently negative and with
value of 0.2. This is consistent with the basi
theory that if $_{t-1}\dot{P}_t^e$ is more than $\dot{P}_t$ (inflation i
overestimated) unemployment will rise above th
natural level. Recall that this happens because mone
wages are assumed to be fixed on the basis of an e
ante forecast of the price level made by employer
and workers. If workers alone make an error ex ant
labour supply will be reduced so (voluntary
unemployment in excess of the natural rate occurs
(5) If employers make the same kind of error, the
will ex post lay off workers when they realise th
actual real wage is higher than expected. In fact
the effect of expectational error on unemployment i
quite small. The maximum error in the period 1950-7
used by Batchelor and Sheriff was 8% and the maximu
error sustained over 12 months was 4%. (6) Th
writers conclude:

> Within the 1960s and early 1970s period th
> maximum deviation of the unemployment rate fro
> its equilibrium level which could be attribute
> to expectation errors was consequently les
> than 1 percentage point.

However, Batchelor and Sheriff conjecture that th
impact of overestimation of inflation by firms an
consumers in 1977 had a far more significant effec
on unemployment. Presumably the same could be said o
1980 but it is mere conjecture. The assertion abou
1977 relies upon the coefficients of the X variable
estimated for the period 1950-74. If thes
coefficients were changed by the addition of th
observations from 1974 to 1977 (not unlikely) the
Batchelor and Sheriff's conjecture (and their model
would be invalidated. The problem with th
specification used in this study is that it assume
non-natural unemployment can only arise throug
expectational error. It contains no test of th
capacity of alternative specifications to explai
the data and no test of the superiority of th
specification actually chosen. For example, th
actual model estimated contains no variable tha

would proxy the impact of deviations in the level of aggregate demand for goods that, conventional Keynesian analysis implies, should be included.

Batchelor (1982) has provided confirming evidence for four European nations over a similar period (1965-1977) and Minford (1983) has also provided evidence for a British time series ending in 1979. Minford notes the equivalence of equation 6.5 (Lucas-Sargent supply equation) to his own wage equation which includes an expectations term. Minford remarks:

> Of course the derivation and true meaning (of the wage equation) is quite different from that in the Lucas equilibrium model. But the family resemblance is striking, were someone to use the Lucas model - for the UK he should obtain reasonable results (e.g. Batchelor and Sheriff (1980)).

Despite this the interesting thing is that Minford's empirical work finds the 'errors in inflation expecations' variable to have consistently the wrong sign and to be statistically insignificant. This difference in results might be due to the inclusion of the latter years of the 1970s in Minford's study. Further evidence for this view is provided by Layard and Nickell (1985) using data up to 1983. They confirm the unimportance of expectational errors in explaining unemployment. We are forced to conclude on the basis of this evidence that in the period since 1974 when unemployment has increased substantially in Britain there is little reason to believe this is the result of persistent overestimation of the price level. To the non-classical economist this fact is no surprise since unemployment in excess of the natural rate arises from other sources (like deficient aggregate demand) in a world in which markets fail to clear. Of course these results are also <u>not</u> inconsistent with the classical view of unemployment. If expectations are formed rationally and markets clear there should not be any persistent error with which to explain unemployment in excess of the natural rate anyway. Unemployment will be equal to the natural rate. Any variations in unemployment which are observed are, therefore, the result of variations in the natural rate.

Crucial to this equilibrium view of unemployment is the seminal empirical work by Lucas and Rapping (1970). They estimate a log linear labour supply model for the US from 1930-1961 of the following form. (7)

$$6.7 \quad S_{Et} = \alpha_0 + \alpha_1 \frac{W}{P}t + \alpha_2 \frac{W^*}{P}t + \alpha_3 (i_t - {}_{t-1}\dot{P}^e_t)$$

$$+ \underset{\sim}{\beta}' \underset{\sim}{Z} \quad \varepsilon_t$$

where

$\dot{P}_t$ = rate of inflation

S_{Et} = labour supply

i_t = nominal interest rate

W/P_t = real wage

ε_t = error term

${}_{t-1}\dot{P}^e_t$ = expectation of the current inflation rate formed at the end of t-1

Current labour supply is assumed to be a positive function ($\alpha_1 > 0$) of the actual current real wage (W/P_t), derived from an accurate forecast of the current price level in money bargaining between workers and employers, (8) and a negative function ($\alpha_2 < 0$) of the <u>future</u> expected real wage (W/P^*_t) or 'normal' real wage. If current real wages go down with expected <u>future</u> wages constant, labour supply will decrease and (voluntary) unemployment will go up. This response is measured by a transitory labour supply elasticity (α_1 in equation 6.7). If we regard expected <u>future</u> real wages as the 'normal' or 'permanent' level, then the coefficient α_1 also measures the response of labour supply when real wages are thought to be abnormally high or abnormally low. The long run labour supply elasticity can be found by ($\alpha_1 + \alpha_2$) and is of indeterminate sign because of the conflicting income and substitution effects of a change in 'permanent' real wages. (9)

This intertemporal substitution model of Lucas and Rapping is completed by the inclusion of a positive effect ($\alpha_3 > 0$) of the real interest rate ($i_t - {}_{t-1}\dot{P}^e_t$). Workers are assumed to substitute current leisure for future leisure when the real interest rate falls and hence labour supply decreases. Voluntary unemployment can therefore increase if there is any change in real interest rates. (10) The only additional (Z) variable specified by Lucas and Rapping in their theoretical

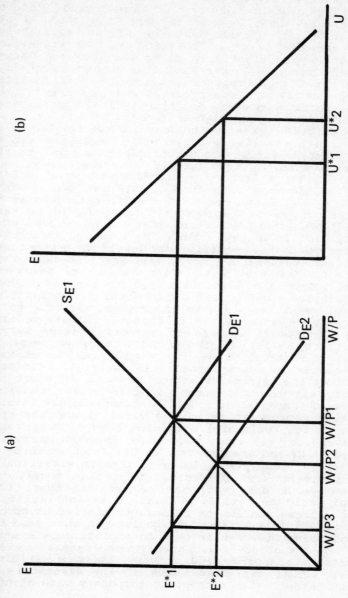

analysis is real non-human wealth but this drops ou
in the empirical work.

The classical theory of unemployment assume
non-natural unemployment is generally zero so al
variation in unemployment is of an equilibriu
character ($U_t = U_t^*$). This requires the transitor
labour supply elasticity to be positive and large
(11) In order to understand this argument conside
Figure 6.1 which depicts in frame 'a' the familia
labour supply and demand curves and in frame 'b' th
relationship between employment and unemploymen
(assuming a constant labour force).

Initially, assume the demand curve for labour i
at D_E^1 with the real wage at W/P_1, employment at E
and unemployment at U_1^*. Unemployment is equal to th
natural rate in this market clearing story. No
consider the effect of a demand shock which shift
the demand curve down to D_E^2. This can occur for
variety of reasons but Hall (1980) attributes it t
shifts in public employment. The equilibrium rea
wage falls to W/P_2 so that real wages mov
procyclically in this model. The level of employmen
falls to a new equilibrium level E_2^* as worker
withdraw voluntarily from employment because th
current real wage has fallen below the permanen
level. Note the flexibility of real wages. Sinc
equilibrium employment has fallen equilibriu
unemployment has risen to U_2^*. This course of events
however, depends on the fact that in frame 'a' th
supply curve is assumed to possess a large suppl
elasticity. (12) If the supply curve possesses
small elasticity the ability of this model to explai
movements in unemployment is severely limited
Consider the extreme situation in which the short ru
supply elasticity is zero. In this case the suppl
curve in frame 'a' of 6.1 will be horizontal. This i
because employment is on the vertical and the rea
wage on the horizontal axis. The demand curve shif
will reduce real wages to W/P_3 but employment remain
fixed at E_1^* and unemployment at U_1^*. In other words i
the labour supply elasticity is zero no variation i
unemployment is predicted by this model. I
unemployment does vary (as we know it does) thi
model would be totally useless at explaining it.
less extreme conclusion follows if the labour suppl
elasticity (α_1) is found to be low. In this case th
equilibrium view can be seen to explain only a smal
part of the observed variation in employment. In fac
Lucas and Rapping find a very large elasticity
Their actual estimated value of the elasticity o
labour supply with respect to temporary wage change

(α_1) is very high at 4.6. (13)

Surprisingly this view of the world (14) has until recently been subject to little further empirical testing. Altonji (1982) has to some extent remedied this deficiency. He updates the US data to 1976 and employs a rational expectations version for the computation of permanent real wages (W/P^*) which Lucas and Rapping estimated within an adaptive expectations framework. This is, therefore, a more precise test of the classical ideas. Unlike Lucas and Rapping, Altonji's results provide little or no support for the intertemporal substitution model. He does find small and significant short run supply elasticities (never more than a quarter of the size of those found by Lucas and Rapping) but with the opposite (negative) sign. Recent evidence for Britain by Andrews (1984) also confirms these doubts about the strength if not the direction of the intertemporal substitution mechanism and hence of the viability of this element of the classical view of unemployment. Andrews finds a short run labour supply elasticity with the right positive sign but it is extremely small (less than 10% of the Lucas and Rapping value). (15)

It is also possible to derive an unemployment stock equation from this Lucas-Rapping labour supply model within a market clearing framework. This involves the estimation of a log linear equation of the form:

6.8. $U_t = \beta_0 + \beta_1 (W/P_t - W/P_t^*) + \gamma_t$

where γ_t = error term

If real wages are thought to be below their long term level and hence abnormally low, unemployment should increase according to the intertemporal substitution model. β_1 must therefore be significantly positive and large if much of the variation in unemployment is to be explained by the market clearing model. A model similar to 6.8 which also allows for revisions in W/P_t^* through time has been estimated for Britain by Altonji and Ashenfelter (1980) and Hannah (1984). Hannah uses quarterly data for a more up to date period (1967-1980) than Altonji and Ashenfelter and he also allows for an upward trend in the natural rate of unemployment (β_0 in equation 6.8). Their results are, however, broadly similar giving little support to the intertemporal substitution hypothesis and the classical explanation of unemployment. Hannah, (16) for example, finds β_1 to be

213

statistically insignificant and with the wrong
(negative) sign.

Andrews and Nickell (1982) find a somewhat
stronger impact in their study of unemployment in
Britain between 1952 and 1977. A 1% fall in real
wages relative to normal is associated with a rise of
between 0.14 and 0.28 percentage points in one year
with a further rise in the second year. They point
out that this could arise because of effects on the
unemployment inflow and/or outflow rates. The paper
by Nickell (1982) which models aggregate inflow and
outflow rates confirms this. However Andrews and
Nickell also show that the implied unemployment
duration elasticity of real wages derived from their
estimates is implausibly high. They conclude their
discussion in a sceptical way. 'All in all therefore,
we do not feel that this kind of competitive model is
consistent with the data'.

This contrasts with Lucas and Rapping who
confirm the classical view that if current wages are
lower than the 'normal' level unemployment will rise
in the US. However, this also has been subject to
further examination by Altonji (1982) who finds
exactly the reverse with a coefficient on the
departure of the real wage from its long run value
having significant coefficients with the opposite
sign to those obtained by Lucas and Rapping. As a
result of this and also the tests of the inter-
temporary substitution hypothesis he conducts,
Altonji concludes (on the basis of US evidence) 'the
results ... raise serious doubts about the empirical
viability of the intertemporal substitution market
equilibrium view of the labour market'. (17) Our
survey of the relevant British evidence confirms that
this variant of the classical view of unemployment is
also of little value in explaining unemployment in
Britain. This, however, does not finally dispose of
the market equilibrium models of Chapter 4. We need
to consider further evidence which considers
directly the case for a market clearing view of
unemployment and this is the subject of the next
section.

Market Clearing in Labour Market Models

We saw in Chapter 5 that the crucial assumption of
classical models is that of market clearing. Even if
expectations are formed rationally it is possible to
construct a disequilibrium model in which
unemployment can exceed the natural rate. One way of
rejecting the classical model is to reject the

rational expectations assumptions on the grounds
that agents do not possess the necessary information
or that agents have different information and have
different expectations. Evidence produced by Ormerod
(1982), Pesaran (1982) and Whitley (1983) suggests
price expectations, in practice, are not formed
rationally. These studies reject the forward looking
nature of rational expectations in favour of a
backward looking or compensation approach. Whitley
conjectures:

> This may reflect the uncertainty over future
> projections of inflation so that the least-risk
> solution for wage bargainers (both employers
> and workers) is compensation for past changes
> rather than the anticipation of future prices.

The implication of this is that non-natural
unemployment can occur but only in the slightly
larger interval of time that this backward looking
(adaptive expectations, for example) behaviour takes
to correct errors. However, although this empirical
work weakens the classical view it does not reject
it. The crucial assumption in the classical analysis
of unemployment is market clearing and it is this
issue upon which we focus in this section.

The market clearing analysis of unemployment
requires that at the end of each period workers and
employers in the labour market are <u>both</u> on their own
respective supply and demand curves and therefore at
the intersection of <u>both</u>. In order to test an
assertion of this kind one approach would be to
estimate aggregate labour supply and demand curves
and test whether employment and unemployment are
normally at their natural rates.

This is the approach of Minford (1983) who
constructs a model of an open economy in which the
labour market clears. There are two sectors in the
labour market, one of which is unionised and the
other is not. Goods are sold in competitive product
markets by firms who face the same production
function. In the unionised sector trade unions are
utility maximising monopolies. As we saw in Chapter 5
that means that wages in the unionised sector are
raised above and employment below the competitive
level. Recall also that unions fix money wages which,
given the price level, determines the real wage and
employers set employment in this model. Once the
level of employment in the union sector is determined
the real wage adjusts so as to clear the non-union
sector of the economy. This is shown in Figure 6.2

Figure 6.2

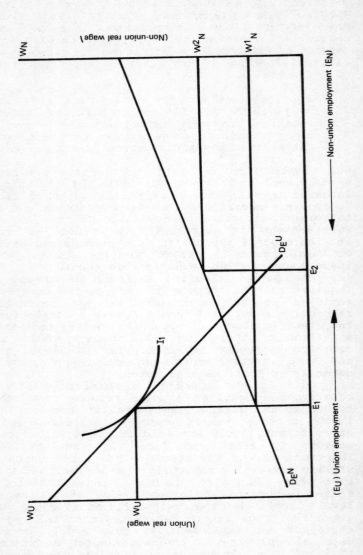

using a diagram of Oswald (1982).

In the union sector the point of tangency of the union's indifference curve (I_1) with the demand for union labour curve (D_E^U), is at a wage of W_u and a level of employment E_1. Note that union employment is measured from left to right in Figure 6.2. In the non-union sector employment is measured from right to left along the horizontal axis of Figure 6.2. If the entire labour force ($E_u + E_N$) is to be employed, the real wage in the non-union sector needs to be W_N^1 for market clearing. This will only be the case, of course, if W_N^1 lies on the labour supply curve at the point it intersects the labour demand curve in the non-union sector (D_E^N). The reasons advanced by Minford for believing this actually happens are considered in Chapter 7. The crucial feature of the analysis at this stage is that since the non-union labour market is cleared all outcomes in the market must be on the labour supply curve. Suppose the labour supply curve intersects the D_E^N curve at a wage W_N^2. In this case the market will clear but employment will be less than necessary to employ the entire labour force. The shortfall ($E_1 - E_2$) will produce voluntary equilibrium unemployment of that amount.

In order to make this analysis empirically operational Minford firstly derives a labour demand curve. Detailed discussion of this specification is reserved until later in this chapter but it is entirely conventional, so that movements up and down a cost minimising employment function of the type we considered in Chapter 1 can arise either because of the changes in expected real output or in expected real labour costs. A specification of this kind assumes that increases in expected output shift the aggregate labour demand schedule upwards. The only unusual feature of Minford's specification is that he employs unemployment rather than employment as the dependent variable. This involves a transformation of the kind shown in frame 'b' of Figure 6.1. Since unemployment is negatively associated with employment the normal signs in a labour demand function are reversed. The labour demand (unemployment) equation actually estimated is (all variables except T_F are in logs)

6.9 $\quad U_t = \delta_0 + \delta_1 (\frac{W^e}{P}_t + T_{Ft}) + \delta_2 Y^e_t + \delta_3 t + \delta_4 U_{t-1} + \varepsilon_t$

where

T_{Ft} = employer's national insurance contributions as a percentage of male manual earnings

Figure 6.3

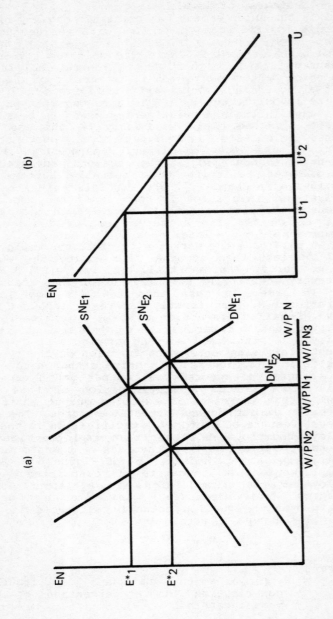

$\dfrac{W^e}{P}t$ = expected real wages

Y^e_t = expected output

ε_t = error term

This equation is estimated simultaneously with a real wage equation which Minford regards as a labour supply equation, although he says this procedure 'is in principle arbitrary and unsubstantive'. In fact the specification he adopts is a natural consequence of assuming that the labour market clears and hence that workers are always on their labour supply curve. In this case all movements along the labour supply curve and all shifts in it will lead to changes in the real wage, so changes in the latter reflect labour supply side effects. To clarify this point consider Figure 6.3.

Since this depicts the market clearing non-union sector of the economy, the demand and supply curves in frame 'a' have 'N' superscripts to represent this. Similarly with employment and the real wage. There is no superscript on the horizontal axis of frame 'b', since this refers to the economy as a whole. Initially assume the labour market is in equilibrium at E^*_1, W/PN_1 and U^*_1. If there is a move along the supply curve resulting from, in this case, a demand curve shift to D^N_{E2} the real wage falls to W/PN_2 and so does employment to E^*_2. Unemployment rises to U^*_2. Any move along the supply curve will result in a negative association of the real wage with unemployment. This is a feature of Minford's labour supply (real wage) equation. In addition if there is a shift in the labour supply curve there will be a different wage associated with each employment level. In frame 'a' of Figure 6.3 the supply curve shifts to S^N_{E2} and the real wage associated with employment E^*_2 and unemployment U^*_2 rises to $W/PN3$. In other words as a result of market clearing in the non-union sector we can write the real wage equation as a negative function of unemployment and of a vector of supply curve shift variables.

6.10 $\dfrac{W_N}{P}_t = \phi(U_t, Z^S_t)$

where Z^S_t is a vector of labour supply variables. (18)

The problem with estimating 6.10 is that W/PN_t is an unobserved variable. We only have data on real wages in the economy as a whole. However, since this is a weighted average of real wages in the union (W/Pu) and non-union sector (W/PN)

6.11 $\frac{W}{P}_t = C_a \frac{W}{P} u_t + (1-C_a) \frac{W}{P} N_t$

where C_a = the coverage of collective agreements

and

6.12 $\frac{W}{P} u_t = (1 + z) \frac{W}{P} N_t$

where z is positive and is the union markup on non-union real wages. Combining 6.11 and 6.12 gives

6.13 $\frac{W}{P}_t = C_a(1 + z) \frac{W}{P} N_t + (1-C_a) \frac{W}{P} N_t$

so we can write the aggregate real wage in terms of the non-union wage alone. In order to derive a model for the aggregate real wage use can be made of equation 6.10 together with variables which proxy C_a and z. Although direct measures of z are available for time series analysis in Britain, this is not the case for C_a. In the event Minford estimates (in logs except T_L)

6.14 $\frac{W}{P}_t = \beta_0 + \beta_1(\dot{P}_t - {}_{t-1}\dot{P}^e_t) + \beta_2 q_t + \beta_3 UNR_t + \beta_4 L_t + \beta_5 T_{Lt}$

$+ \beta_6 B_t + \beta_7 U_t + \beta_8 W/P_{t-1} + \mu_t$

where

$\dot{P}_t - {}_{t-1}\dot{P}^e_t =$	=	expectational error
UNR_t	=	unionisation rate
q_t	=	unemployment benefit disqualification rate
L_t	=	labour force
B_t	=	a measure of real unemployment benefits
T_{Lt}	=	percentage of national gross earnings repaid in tax and national insurance contributions
μ_t	=	error term

The first two variables ($\dot{P}_t - {}_{t-1}\dot{P}_t^e$ and UNR_t) are intended to proxy the impact of the union on the aggregate wage level. The remainder reflect movements along the non-union sector supply curve (U_t) and shifts of the curve (B_t, T_{Lt} and L_t). Equations 6.9 and 6.14 are estimated using a variety of annual, quarterly and industry level data for periods ending in 1979. Results are presented for all the coefficients of 6.9 but because of the persistent statistical insignificance of the expectational error and benefit disqualification variables, no estimates for β_1 (19) and β_2 are presented by Minford. Details of these results are further discussed in the following chapters. At this stage we are particularly interested in two coefficients of the labour supply equation (β_7 and β_8 in 6.14) and most of all in the calculation of the natural rate of unemployment using the two equations 6.9 and 6.14. In the labour demand equation all the coefficients have the expected sign ($\delta_1 > 0$ $\delta_2 < 0$ $\delta_3 > 0$ $1 > \delta_4 > 0$) so expected real wages and output changes have the conventional effects on employment (negatively in the former case and positively in the latter). However, only δ_4 is statistically significant using annual data. Using quarterly data the results are much improved with all the coefficients possessing coefficients significantly different from zero. In the real wage (labour supply) equation β_7 is negative as expected but significant only in the quarterly estimates while β_8 is significantly positive only in estimates derived from both quarterly and annual data.

In order to calculate a series for the natural rate, Minford calculates the long run coefficients of the quarterly estimates of 6.9 and 6.14 (20). In order to complete the calculation Minford uses estimates of expected output and real wages from the rest of the Liverpool model, in which the long run relationship between real wages and output is constrained by the condition that the current account is in balance. Combining equations 6.9 and 6.14 it is then possible to construct a series of the (long run) natural rate of unemployment. This shows the natural rate to have been on a 'dizzying rise' since 1965. Comparison of this estimate with the actual unemployment rate shows a close correspondence of the two series. Departures from the natural rate are generally small and between 1968 and 1980 there is no evidence of non-natural unemployment except between 1975 and 1978. In 1980 the natural rate of unemployment is estimated to be $1\frac{3}{4}$ million, which is almost identical to the natural rate. Note no evidence is presented for the 1980s.

On the face of it, this is impressive evidence in favour of the Classical model. Unemployment does seem to reflect movements in the natural rate itself. If this is true, policy clearly needs to be directed to the determinants of the natural rate and not to departures from it. However, recall that to derive Minford's model, market clearing is part of the maintained hypothesis. Given this assumption perhaps we should not be surprised at the results. In other words Minford does not really demonstrate the viability of the classical model of the labour market - he assumes it. Less serious criticism of the Minford approach centre on the details of his estimation procedure. Examples of this include his use of retail prices rather than producer prices in the labour demand equation, the combination of long run coefficients from the quarterly data with values of expected output and real wages obtained from an annual model. (21) More substantially Minford attempts little in the way of exploration of the dynamic behaviour of real wages. If the classical view is to be supported by the evidence, it is necessary to explore the behaviour of real wages to see if market clearing is possible.

In order to consider more direct <u>tests</u> of the classical market clearing view in Britain, we need to consider the work of Andrews (1984) and Ashenfelter and Altonji (1980). The latter study examines the dynamic behaviour of the real wage in Britain between 1949 and 1978 and obtains evidence that is not consistent with a market clearing model. Andrews (1984) estimates a structural model of the labour market which provides explicit tests of the market clearing view. He uses a slightly modified standard Lucas-Rapping supply model discussed earlier in this chapter, namely (in logs)

$$6.7a \quad S_{Et} = \alpha_0 + \alpha_1 \ W/P_t + \alpha_2 \ W/P^*_t$$

$$+ \ \alpha_3 \ (i_t - \dot{p}^e_{t+1}) + \underline{\beta}' \ \underline{Z} + \varepsilon_t$$

The vector of exogenous variables (Z) includes the ratio of unemployment benefits to income (the replacement ratio), the labour force and a dummy variable that takes the value of unity after 1967. The real wage variable is constructed net of direct and indirect taxes. The demand equation is (in logs)

$$6.15 \quad D_{Et} = \delta_0 + \delta_1 \frac{W}{P}t + \delta_2 \frac{W}{P}t-1 + \delta_3 \frac{Pm}{P}t + \delta_4 \frac{Pm}{P}t-1$$
$$+ \delta_5 K_t + \delta_6 K_{t-1} + \delta_7 E_{gt} + \delta_8 E_{gt-1} + \delta_9 t + \epsilon_t$$

where

Pm = imported input prices

E_{gt} = government employment

K_t = capital stock

ϵ_t = error term

The estimated version of the demand equation also includes lagged dependent variables. The real wage is defined as the product wage (unlike Minford) and is calculated inclusive of labour taxes which add to labour costs. Conventional arguments predict δ_1 and δ_2 will be negative. Since imported inputs are assumed to be complementary to labour, increases in their prices will depress labour demand (δ_3, δ_4 < 0). The capital stock and time trend are intended to pick up the effect of capital accumulation and technical change. Since the data is for the whole economy and the demand function is more appropriate to a (competitive) private sector, the government employment terms enter. This follows the procedure of Andrews and Nickell (1982). As it turns out δ_7 and δ_8 are insignificantly different from zero in the empirical work. Similar results occur for δ_9 because of the high degree of collinearity of t and K_t which has a marked upward trend over the period for which Andrews estimates this model.

Detailed discussion of this type of labour demand function takes place later in this chapter but note the exclusion of any output or aggregate demand variable in the model. This provides a strongly classical view of the world. Such a specification derives naturally from a profit maximising, competitive model of firm behaviour. This is not to say, however, that there are no links with the product market. Although the model used by Andrews has a strong supply side feel about it so that labour demand shifts reflects output supply changes there is a role for the influence of aggregate demand policy as well. The reason is the presence of the real interest rate in the labour supply curve and the relative price of imported inputs in the labour demand equation. An increase in aggregate demand for goods, for example, can in Andrews' theoretical model

223

raise the real rate of interest raising labour supply at any real wage and reduce the relative price of imported inputs which has a similar upward effect on labour demand. Labour market equilibrium would then be altered by this aggregate demand shock. In other words this classical type model does not embody the structural separability of traditional classical macroeconomics although it possess other characteristics.

The model is estimated on data from 1950 to 1979. The results in the demand equation are as expected. The long run elasticity of labour demand with respect to the product wage is -.57 and with respect to the relative price of imported inputs is -.09. δ_1 and δ_2 are both negative and although the initial effect of a rise in imported input prices is to increase labour demand ($\delta_3 > 0$) the longer run effect is for it to fall as input complementarity requires ($\delta_4 > \delta_3$ in absolute size). There are also substantial positive effects of the capital stock on employment. We have already outlined the results from the supply side earlier in this chapter. Recall they show the expected Lucas-Rapping effects but they are small in size. The replacement ratio has the expected negative sign but the coefficient is small in line with most of the evidence. The dummy variable has a significant negative sign indicating a marked downward shift in labour supply since 1967. This would be consistent with a rise in voluntary unemployment if only we could interpret the meaning of a variable of this kind in this way. In fact, Andrews also shows that market clearing depends on the inclusion of the post-1967 dummy variable. Once it is excluded the evidence in favour of market clearing disappears because, as Andrews argues, the dummy variable allows the labour market to clear after 1966 when it should not. This is a matter we examine further in the next section. Andrews also performs further tests which actually confirm the unstable dynamic nature of real wage adjustment which prevents long run labour market equilibrium in Britain.

Andrews' results are an important rejection of the market clearing paradigm and hence of the classical model of unemployment. They confirm the earlier results of Andrews and Nickell (1982) (22). Some light is also shed by the work of Beenstock and Warburton (1982). In the latter study supply and demand functions for total person hours are specified. The structure is extremely simple with real wages appearing in both equations. The output level has a positive effect on labour demand (23) and growth in the population raises labour supply. Beenstock and Warburton calculate (24) equilibrium employment by equating the labour and supply demand curves they estimate. Algebraically (in logs) these are

$$6.16 \quad D_{Et} = \delta_0 + \delta_1 Y_t + \delta_2 \frac{W}{P}t \quad \text{(labour demand)}$$

$$6.17 \quad S_{Et} = \alpha_0 + \alpha_1 L_t + \alpha_2 \frac{W}{P}t \quad \text{(labour supply)}$$

in person hours

from which by equating 6.16 and 6.17 we can obtain values of the equilibrium real wage and employment. When this equilibrium model was subject to output and population growth shocks the dynamic adjustment process took a considerable degree of time (up to six years). This suggests that the transition to long run equilibrium is, at best, in the aggregate labour market in Britain, a very long process even if market clearing is assumed. Market clearing models, therefore seem appropriate only, perhaps, for the analysis of the very long run (25) which is not very useful for practical policy making.

The evidence surveyed so far in this chapter suggests there is not a strong empirical case for accepting the classical analysis of unemployment in Britain. The implication that there can be no persistent non-natural unemployment problem, that stabilisation policy is futile unless it is a 'surprise' to the private sector and as far as unemployment is concerned can only succeed at the expense of higher inflation is, at best, unproven. Consequently any government that relies upon its precepts to guide the conduct of economic policy is undertaking what remains in Britain, an act of faith.

In the next section we will consider the evidence for accepting a non-market clearing explanation of unemployment that permits unemployment to exceed the natural level.

Non-Market Clearing - Empirical Evidence
Insofar as the evidence reviewed so far provides only very weak support for adopting a classical labour market clearing approach to the analysis of unemployment there is already a strong case for the adoption of the alternative non-market clearing perspective of Chapter 5. Non-natural unemployment

is not only possible but likely and hence some kind of interventionist policy by the government will be necessary. Before we can draw this conclusion we will also examine direct and indirect evidence for believing that a disequilibrium approach to unemployment is the most satisfactory. The indirect evidence largely relates to the observed behaviour of wages and quantities in the labour market. For completeness we will also refer to evidence on the degree of price flexibility that characterises product markets.

The market clearing model requires the rapid and convergent adjustment of wages and prices to their market clearing level in labour and product markets. We have already reviewed in the previous section some of the evidence that suggests the dynamic behaviour of real wages is inconsistent with market clearing, but is it consistent with a non-market clearing approach? We saw in Chapter 5 that positive and persistent non-natural unemployment can arise because the real wage is at an inappropriate (for market clearing) level. This can result from nominal wage rigidity so unemployment in excess of the natural rate persists even if prices are falling. In a period in which prices are rising it can also arise from real wage rigidity so that unemployment occurs in response to adverse shocks like imported input price increase, a slowdown in productivity growth or cutbacks in public investment programmes.

What is the evidence for nominal and real wage rigidity? To clarify the analysis it is useful to write down a conventional kind of money wage equation (without time subscripts)

$$6.18 \quad \dot{W} = \alpha_0 + \alpha_1 (D_E - S_E) + \alpha_2 \dot{P}^e + \underset{\sim}{\alpha w}' \underset{\sim}{Z w}$$

where Z_w is a vector of exogenous variables with associated αw coefficients. In a period in which prices are constant or falling, money wage rigidity will prevent the labour market clearing. In equation 6.18 this will show up as a low or perverse value of α_1 which theory suggests should be strongly positive. This general unresponsiveness of money wages should also lead to small values of α_2 which measures the response of money wages to price expectations (recall α_2 is positive according to conventional theory and unity according to classical theory). In fact these are precisely the results usually found in studies of money wage movements in the 1930s. Hines' (1968) study is typical. Both α_1 and α_2 are insignificantly different from zero. Hines uses unemployment as a

proxy for excess labour demand to obtain an estimate
of α_1. Money wages only fell in the intense recession
of the 1930s in the face of stern opposition from
workers and then to only a modest extent.

In the post-war period the situation is
different because, in general, prices have risen.
Most econometric studies find in the estimation of
6.18 significantly larger values of α_2 than for the
1930s. This is the case, for example, with Hines, who
finds for the period 1949-61 that α_2 is approximately
0.4. Studies which incorporate the high inflation
period of the more recent post-war years tend to find
much larger values of α_2 which are often
insignificantly different from unity. Sachs (1979)
is an example. He finds an average value of α_2 of
1.075 for an annual analysis of France, West Germany,
Italy and Britain between 1963 and 1978. The contrast
of the late post-war with the early post-war and pre-
war results may simply reflect the fact that the
value of α_2 is dependent (positively) on the rate of
inflation. If price increases are small, zero or
negative, they do not figure in money wage
bargaining. If, on the other hand, price inflation is
large, α_2 will be large.

In the light of Sach's results for the value of
α_2 we can rewrite 6.18 as a real wage equation

$$6.19 \quad \dot{W} - \dot{P}^e = \alpha_0 + \alpha_1 (D_E - S_E) + \underline{\alpha}w' \underline{Z}_w$$

Small (insignificant) values of α_1 should then be
interpreted as real wage rigidity that arises from
the flexibility of money wage to changes in the price
level. Typical are the results of Grubb, Jackman and
Layard (1983). They use unemployment as a measure of
excess labour demand $D_E - S_E$ and find an average
estimate for α_2 for EEC countries as a whole of .98.
Hence equation 6.19 applies. They find a correctly
signed, significant but small value of α_1. The
results for Britain are typical of EEC nations as a
whole. We conclude, therefore, that if real wages are
above their market clearing level this was more
likely to be the result of money wage rigidity in the
intense recession of the 1930s. In the 1980s it is
the flexibility of money wages to price inflation and
the rigidity of real wages to equally intense
recession that make non-market clearing a more
appropriate perspective to adopt.

Confirmation for this view comes from the
successful attempts in Britain to explain money wage
movements with the aid of a 'real wage resistance'
model. The idea of these models is that workers are

backward looking, so if the past value of the real wage falls short of their aspirations they will in the current period make pay demands (and secure pay increases) that will make good some of this shortfall. Favourable results for models of this kind are reported by Henry, Sawyer and Smith (1976), Whitley (1983) and others. If price inflation (or any other factor like direct taxes) erodes the real consumption wage of workers money wages will, to some extent, adjust through collective bargaining. (26) A mechanism of this kind can easily inhibit the adjustment of real wages to the market clearing level so that unemployment in excess of the natural rate can exist and persist.

There is, however, evidence of significant cross country variations in the pattern of wage rigidity we observe. Most significant is the difference between the US and Europe (including Britain). Sachs (1979) (27), for example, finds α_2 to be only .11 in the US, so that it would be more appropriate to regard the US as characterised by money wage rigidity since it also has low values of α_1 (insignificantly different from zero in Sach's study). The inclusion of a lagged dependent variable in Sach's equation confirms the greater degree of nominal wage sluggishness in the US. This is also the conclusion of Gordon (1982) who also finds quantity adjustment to be more rapid in the US than Britain. Gordon attributes these cross country differences to labour market institutions. Longer term contracts and an unemployment benefit system that encourages temporary layoffs are important aspects of these differences. It also means that the contract/temporary layoff paradigm favoured by US and US educated theorists and discussed in Chapter 5, is most appropriate in the US.

In Britain it would appear that although money wages are no less rigid downwards than they were in the intense recession of the 1930s for the reasons we explored in Chapter 5, the high degree of flexibility of money wages to price inflation conceals it and gives rise to direct real wage inflexibility which also and equally inhibits market clearing. In the US the traditional pattern remains. Money wages are rigid in recession but in the face of adverse shocks that also raise prices (like imported input price increases), real wages will fall so in this case unemployment in excess of the natural rate is unlikely to be such a severe problem in the US. The passive acceptance by US unions of erosion of real wages by inflation means a market clearing perspective is less inappropriate in the US than in Europe. Whether it has meant less unemployment in practice is an issue to which we return in the next and last section of this Chapter. (28)

Further light can be shed on the causes of wage rigidity by examining differences between sub-sectors of the aggregate labour market. Different-ials between sectors, between the union and non-union worker and between the skilled and unskilled, all tend to widen in recession. This implies nominal wage rigidity is greater in certain industries especially where a unionised and skilled labour force is employed. There is also evidence that the response of money wages to inflation is higher in the unionised sector of the economy (Pierson (1966)) and in certain industries. If this is the case real wage rigidity will be a more prominent feature of the unionised sector of the economy. Clearly any attempt to explain wage rigidity without referring to union behaviour is unlikely to be empirically useful. In the previous chapter we outlined some of the modern theories which emphasise the role of unions in the explanation of wage rigidity. Hall (1975), for example, in a study of wage rigidity in the US finds several of the rigid wage industries he identifies are highly unionised, while none of the clearly wage flexible industries are substantially unionised.

However, the theory also suggests that employers may have a vested interest in maintaining the rigidity of wages especially where long term attachment is important. Hall finds wage rigidity to be greatest in the non-entrepreneurial sector of the US economy. Although Hall attributes this to the lack of product market competition in this sector it could equally be the result of the greater importance of long term attachment. In Britain there is a clear need for further empirical enquiry to identify the causes (as opposed to the consequences) of wage rigidity. Some evidence is provided from the cross country study of McCallum (1983). McCallum finds that those countries characterised by slow adjustment of real wage aspirations and hence by a high degree of real wage rigidity also exhibit a low degree of social consensus and a high level of social and industrial conflict. McCallum uses strike data to support his hypothesis, which may not be entirely appropriate in all countries. In Britain a high degree of strike activity cannot be explained without a model of union behaviour and in this sense McCallum confirms the general importance of collective behaviour by workers.

The evidence considered so far relates to the labour market (on which we have concentrated) and it does suggest a substantial degree of wage rigidity which is consistent with the modern disequilibrium analysis of unemployment. On the goods market side the administered price hypothesis favoured by Means (1935), suggests that price inflexibility may also be a problem in recession. Sachs (1980) shows in an analysis of the twentieth century as a whole that this problem is a good deal more severe in the post-war period than in previous decades. However, the evidence also suggests that what is observed is partial but not total or complete price rigidity. In other words price adjustment is very sluggish rather than being completely non-existent and this contributes to the slowness of response of the macroeconomy to exogenous shocks. Attempts have been made by Blinder (1982) and others to construct a theory to explain price stickiness. The essence of the analysis is to derive a price smoothing policy from a long run theory of profit maximisation. Even profit maximising competitive firms will not equate marginal cost with marginal revenue at each point in time because it does not pay to do so. It is more profitable to adjust inventories or output. Blinder concludes: 'sticky prices will tend to emerge when it is not very costly to vary inventories, and when demand shocks are very transitory'. The adoption of price smoothing policy by firms leads to other commonly observed patterns of behaviour. Firms will carry buffer stocks, offer contracts to customers of differing length which guarantee price stability and adopt a pricing policy that takes account of long run costs and demand. Product differentiation and the need to maintain customer attachment and loyalty will (analogously to the labour market) reinforce this tendency to price stability. The product market, in other words, is no more an auction market than the labour market upon which we have focussed.

The degree of price stickiness varies a good deal across industries and analysis of these differences sheds some light on the causes of price stickiness and its greater importance in the post-war period. A recent study by Encaoua and Geroski (1984) sheds some light on these issues. In a time series study of five OECD countries they show price adjustment is slower in the less competitive part of the economy. Firms in this sector are slower to absorb new information relevant to the pricing decision as well as being slower to act on it. In contrast, in the competitive sector demand has a significant and rapid impact on prices. Price stickiness also seems to be greater in those sectors not exposed to intense international competition. There is a striking similarity between these results and some of the tentative conclusions we made about wage inflexibility. If this association of price stickiness and market concentration is true, it is also no surprise that as industry has become less competitive through merger and firm growth in the post-war period price stickiness has grown in importance.

Encaoua and Geroski also find significant cross country differences that to some extent, mirror the degree of wage inflexibility. Japan, for example, is the country in which prices appear to exhibit the greatest degree of price flexiblity while Britain (which is highly concentrated by international standards) has a very large degree of price stickiness. The US, Canada and Sweden lie in between.

The conclusion of this survey of the evidence is that the degree of wage (real and money) and price rigidity in Britain is sufficiently great for a disequilibrium approach to unemployment to be appropriate. (29) This view is confirmed if we also examine the evidence of the speed at which quantities adjust in the labour market. There is a tendency in the theoretical analysis of disequilibrium unemployment to suppose that the slowness with which price and wages adjust is matched by a rapid adjustment of quantities (hours and employment) in the labour market. As we have seen Gordon (1982) finds this view is not unreasonable in the US, partly because of the widespread use of temporary layoffs in recession but in Britain quantities also adjust rather slowly. This is confirmed by Beenstock and Warburton (1982) who examine the impact on employment of exogenous shocks. The reaction is very slow. Similar results are obtained from the estimation of employment functions. Deaton (1982), for example, has estimated for the period 1970 to 1981 that the typical manufacturing firm takes 5 quarters to adjust actual employment to its desired level. Not only is adjustment slow but given that desired employment usually changes each quarter, firms are rarely, if ever, actually operating on their cost minimising employment function let alone their profit maximising demand curve. This is, of course, consistent with the existence of labour hoarding which we considered in Chapter 1, and inconsistent with the classical notion of market clearing which requires firms to be operating on their demand curve at the end of each period. This apparent slowness of the employment/unemployment transition in Britain is confirmed by the data on unemployment duration we considered in Chapter 2. Recall that the duration of a typical spell of unemployment currently exceeds 40 weeks and according to some estimates is more than a year. In these circumstances it is difficult to believe in a spot auction market clearing view of the labour market. Transitions in the labour market are slow and even if prices and wages did adjust rapidly this will lead to non-market clearing with agents frequently off demand and/or supply curves.

More direct evidence on the superiority of the non-market clearing approach is also available. Firstly, we consider attempts to measure the extent of non-natural unemployment using the VU approach outlined in Chapter 3. Recall the results of Armstrong and Taylor (1981) who find unemployment in excess of the natural rate to be much the most important component of unemployment even in the boom period of 1973/74. The problem with the approach adopted in this study is the methods through which U_t^* is estimated. Armstrong and Taylor treat non-natural unemployment as a residual after deducting U_t^* from measured unemployment. U_t^* is obtained by fitting a VU curve against time series data. Once the coefficients of the VU curve are obtained the intersection of the curve with the 45° line can then be calculated. The first problem is that the theoretical relationship between U and V is likely to be estimated with serious measurement error present. As we saw in Chapter 3 the main point is that the under-recording of vacancies is a more serious problem than the under-recording of unemployment (crudely, $\frac{1}{3}$ are reported compared with $\frac{3}{4}$ for unemployment). This means that the level of true and recorded unemployment at which V and U are equal is likely to be greater than estimated by Armstrong and Taylor. Since they underestimate U_t^* they also overestimate unemployment in excess of U_t^* in Table 3.1. Armstrong and Taylor show that if vacancies are adjusted upwards by a factor of 3 then non-natural unemployment for males and females is actually zero. Given the sensitivity of this estimate it would be reckless to rely solely upon this evidence as proof of the existence of unemployment in excess of U_t^*.

More satisfactory is the direct evidence obtained from structural models of the labour market. One approach is to model labour market flows and to obtain estimates of the equilibrium rate of unemployment. This is the method of Nickell (1982).

Both the aggregate inflow and outflow rates are explained by secular and disequilibrium variables. The secular variables determine the equilibrium flows. The disequilibrium variables used by Nickell include aggregate demand variables, the vacancy rate, a real wage variable, an index of non-competitiveness and expectational error variables. The results show that these disequilibrium variables have a significant effect on unemployment flows and hence (as we saw in Chapter 2) on unemployment stocks. (30) By setting the value of these disequilibrium variables to zero Nickell calculates the equilibrium flow rates and by equating the inflow and outflow rates calculates the equilibrium unemployment rate. The problem with this methodology is that flow equality is only a necessary condition for identifying the natural rate of unemployment as defined in Chapter 3. It is not sufficient. (31) Moreover, unless the secular variables used by Nickell are purged of any disequilibrium component the estimate of U_t^* obtained by this method is likely to be on the high side. Nonetheless Nickell finds that for seven years between 1967 and 1979 there is significant (non-natural) unemployment in excess of his equilibrium rate in all but one of those years (1973). However, it is also worth noting at this stage that most of the increase in unemployment over the 1967-79 period was due to increases in the equilibrium not the disequilibrium level of unemployment. Note again, however, that Nickell's estimate of the equilibrium rate is likely to be an overestimate of the natural rate so this conclusion should be treated with care.

A further method for establishing the existence of non-natural unemployment arising from a failure of markets to clear, is to construct a structural model of labour market stocks which does not presume market clearing. One way of doing this is to specify a real wage equation which does not assume that the real wage adjusts instantaneously to clear the labour market. Rather the real wage equation should contain independent variables which reflect the kind of forces (like trade unions) which prevent the real wage from attaining its market clearing value. This follows naturally from the view that to suppose a competitive economy with a union sector is a less accurate picture in Britain than a model that assumes a non-competitive economy with widespread collective bargaining. This is the perspective adopted by Andrews and Nickell (1982) and Nickell and Andrews (1983). The specification of the crucial real wage equation is an augmented version of that employed by Minford (1983) which we have examined earlier (equation 6.14). The additional variables pick up further union, demand and productivity effects. We will consider the details later in this and the next chapter but significant differences in the results from those of Minford (1983) do emerge as a result of the adoption of this augmented real wage equation.

In a recent paper Nickell and Layard (1985) extend this type of model of a non-competitive economy and estimate it with the aid of a time series that ends in 1983. The model consists of three structural equations for labour demand, real wages and prices which reduce to an unemployment equation of the form

6.20 $U = u(\sigma, \dfrac{K}{E}, \underset{\sim}{Z}, \dfrac{P}{pe}, \dfrac{W}{We})$

where

σ = aggregate demand
$\underset{\sim}{Z}$ = vector of exogenous variables
K/E = capital/labour ratio

Note the presence of disequilibrium variables (σ, P/Pe and W/We) in this specification which is used in collaboration with coefficient estimates from the three equation model to analyse the components of the change in unemployment since 1956. However, in equilibrium the inflation error variables (P/Pe, W/We) disappear. Since the level of aggregate demand is a free variable only in the short run this means that it can only deviate from the natural level when expectational errors are made. Since these errors are zero in equilibrium the level of aggregate demand also disappears in the equilibrium natural rate equation

6.21 $U^* = u(K/E, \underset{\sim}{Z})$

Using this Friedmanite definition of the natural rate Layard and Nickell are able to construct a time series of the value of U^* with which actual unemployment can be compared. They find (like Minford (1983)) no evidence until 1979 of positive non-natural unemployment. However since that time they find that a major component of total unemployment (about one quarter) is of this type. The high value of the natural rate throughout the period considered by Layard and Nickell may be surprising but it follows fairly naturally from a non-accelerating inflation rate (NAIRU) definition of equilibrium. (32) In a sense the real difference between these models and the market clearing equivalent is not that they do not assume market clearing in the long run, but that they do not presume it in the short. Real wages will eventually adjust to clear the market but in the meantime governments can and should do something to reduce unemployment.

A more explicitly non-market clearing approach is that pioneered by Rosen and Quandt (1978) in a study of the US labour market from 1930 to 1973. In this case market disequilibrium is assumed to be normal though market clearing is encompassed as a special case. The labour supply and demand functions are modelled in a way very similar to those we have seen in this chapter, namely (in logs)

6.22 $S_{E_t} = \alpha_0 + \alpha_1 \frac{Wd}{P}t + \alpha_2 L_t + \alpha_3 A_t + \varepsilon_{1t}$

6.23 $D_{E_t} = \delta_0 + \delta_1 \frac{W}{P}t + \delta_2 Y_t + \delta_3 t + \varepsilon_{2t}$

where

$\frac{Wd}{P}t =$ net (of tax) real wages

$\frac{W}{P}t =$ gross real wages

$A_t =$ non-labour income (rent, interest, dividends)

$\varepsilon_{it} =$ error terms

The real innovation is to abandon the equilibrium assumption that employers and workers are both on their demand and supply curves respectively and replace it by the condition that employment is given by the short side of the market. Algebraically

6.24 $E_t = \min (D_{E_t}, S_{E_t})$

If demand exceeds supply, then the latter determines actual employment. When supply exceeds demand (the non-natural unemployment case) employment is determined by the demand curve. In Figure 6.4 this argument is illustrated. Actual observed employment will only lie on the bold parts of the supply (S_E) and demand (D_E) curves and not only on broken sections.

Figure 6.4

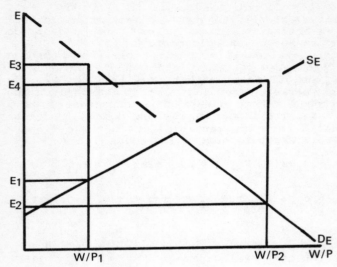

At W/P_1 there is excess demand for labour (E_3-E_1) so employment will be on the supply curve at E_1. At W/P_2 there is excess supply of labour (E_4-E_2) so employment will be on the demand curve at E_2. Estimates of the parameters of the labour supply and demand curve using this method yield sensible and significant results. As expected α_2, α_3 and δ_2 are significantly positive. δ_1 and δ_3 are both negative although the latter is not statistically significant. The labour supply elasticity (α_1) is insignificant (and negative). In equations of this kind this is not an unsurprising result since it implies the income and substitution effects of a wage change cancel out. The model is also tested against an equilibrium version where labour supply and demand are equated and is clearly superior.

Rosen and Quandt also estimate a real wage equation of the form

6.25 $W/P_t - W/P_{t-1} = \beta_1 (D_{E_t} - S_{E_t})$

236

Real wages are assumed to adjust to excess demand and supply and eventually to clear the market. Rearranging 6.25 gives

$$6.26 \quad \frac{1}{\beta_1}(W/P_t - W/P_{t-1}) = D_{E_t} - S_{E_t}$$

If $1/\beta_1 = 0$ then we have the instantaneous market clearing case ($D_{E_t} - S_{E_t} = 0$). If $\beta_1 = 0$ no change in real wages will restore equilibrium. This is the strict rationing cases where cuts in real wages do not increase employment, so the effective labour demand curve is horizontal at E_2 in Figure 6.4. In fact the results show $1/\beta_1$ is significantly positive and less than infinity. The US labour market adjusted slowly to equilibrium over the period analysed by Rosen and Quandt; sufficiently slowly for excess supply ($U > U^*$) to exist and persist for very long periods of time.

This, however, is the problem for this model. Rosen and Quandt find that most of the early post-war years are in a period of excess supply. Several of the inter-war years (1930, 1932, 1936-40) are found to be periods of excess demand. This counter-intuitive result casts something of a shadow over Rosen and Quandt's results. Yatchew (1982) finds more sensible results by restricting the estimation to the post-war period. With the exception of 1958-63 and 1970-1 there is excess demand in the labour market. Only in those years did non-natural unemployment occur. Romer (1982) also found the dropping of non-labour income (A_t) from the supply curve overcomes this problem and greatly improves the predictive power of the model.

Of course, disequilibrium in this model still occurs because of real wage stickiness rather than absolute rigidity. In this sense, therefore, the model is not a test of the kind of theory that relies on the absence of any real wage response and to the existence of binding constraints that prevent a return to full employment.

In Britain the most successful attempts to model the labour market from a non-clearing point of view have taken place in the analysis of the aggregate labour market for young workers. Wells (1983) estimates a supply and demand equation for young workers which is not dissimilar from the Rosen and Quandt (1978) framework. He finds that the youth labour market was in excess demand until 1969 for males and 1971 for females and has been in a state of continuous but variable excess supply ($U > U^*$) ever

since. Unfortunately Wells' much publicised study
has some severe flaws. The selection of switching
point for the transition from excess demand to excess
supply is exogenously and arbitrarily determined by
the author. The point of the Rosen and Quandt
methodology is that whether we have negative, zero or
positive non-natural unemployment should be
determined endogenously by the data. This has been
done by Rice (1984) and Junankar and Neale (1985) who
confirm that unemployment in excess of the natural
rate has characterised the youth labour market for
most of the last fifteen years but they employ more
reliable methods than those of Wells.

Nickell (1984) sets out a methodology for
estimating a non-market clearing model of the UK
labour market as a whole which relaxes the assumption
of a single labour market. Preliminary results are
reported in Andrews and Nickell (1984). They find
that market clearing ($1/\beta_1 = 0$ in equation 6.26), is
rejected by the data. A disequilibrium interpretation of events is more appropriate. The model
endogenously selects the excess demand and/excess
supply regime. This exercise suggests that the UK
labour market was in equilibrium until the late 1960s
and has been characterised by unemployment in excess
of the natural rate (excess supply) ever since. This
result appears inconsistent with those of Layard and
Nickell (1985). There are, however, substantial
modelling differences to explain this. One obvious
explanation is that the equilibrium variables used to
retrieve U* in Layard and Nickell includes
disequilibrium components so its value is
consistently exaggerated and unemployment in excess
of the natural rate underestimated as a result.

Although by no means overwhelming, the direct
and indirect evidence we have surveyed provides a
strong support for the adoption of a non-market
clearing view of unemployment and against the
equilibrium view. Although there is no overwhelming
support for the notion of absolute and permanent
rigidity in real wages it is clear that, in
principle, unemployment in excess of the natural rate
can exist and persist for very long periods of time
because of real wage stickiness. In addition this
evidence creates a clear case for remedial action by
the government. The form and extent of that action
depends on the scale and cause of non-natural
unemployment. These are questions considered in the
next section.

Keynesian v. Classical Unemployment

The balance of evidence favours the notion that unemployment in excess of the natural rate can exist and persist. The analysis of Chapter 5 suggests that this can occur either because of a fall in the aggregate demand for goods (Keynesian unemployment) or because of a generally supply side induced increase in real wages (Classical unemployment) or both. A necessary condition for each of these forms of unemployment to arise is the existence of a significant response of labour demand to aggregate demand for goods (in the former case) and to real wage changes (in the latter case). Therefore initially we will examine empirical evidence on the demand for labour. The basic approach involves the estimation of a single labour demand equation of the type we have already considered in this chapter.

In general functional form (33) it is (without time subscripts)

6.27 $\quad D_E = \delta(Y, \frac{W}{P}, \frac{Pm}{P}, t)$

The demand for labour is a positive function of output and a negative function of real wages and of relative input prices. Real wages in this equation means real product wages so the money wage is deflated by a product price index. It should also take account of labour taxes imposed on the employer (like National Insurance contributions). The effects of technical change and capital accumulation are proxied by the time trend in 6.27. It is negatively related to labour demand if technical change and capital accumulation are labour saving. Models of this kind have usually been estimated with an adjustment relation. This means actual employment moves towards desired employment with a lag. (34)

Typical results are obtained by Morgan (1979) for the period 1963-76. The relative price of imported inputs are ignored in his formulation of 6.27. He finds the real wage elasticity for male workers in manufacturing to be insignificantly different from zero. Examining manual males separately he does find the expected significant negative real wage elasticity but the short run output elasticity is thirty times larger and it also implies increasing returns. For females the real wage elasticity is significantly negative and the relative size of the output elasticity is much less approximately ten times).

This specification has, however, been

criticised on a number of grounds. One important objection is that it fails to take account of the variation of hours of work or of the impact of capital and its degree of utilisation. This objection can be overcome by the use of the Nadiri-Rosen (1969) model. This involves the estimation of a four equation model with the number of employees, the hours of work, the capital stock and its degree of utilisation as the four independent variables. Using this more complex formulation Briscoe and Peel (1975) find that both the long run and short run elasticity of employment is also significantly greater (six times) than the real wage elasticity. Although the difference is not as marked, again, the results suggest employment is relatively insensitive to the cost of labour compared with its sensitivity to output. Similar conclusions are reached in the US. Clark and Freeman (1979) find a real wage elasticity of $-\frac{1}{2}$ for US manufacturing for 1950-76 (compared with Briscoe and Peel's estimate of -2 for Britain 1955-1972). Solow (1980) uses these estimates to argue that the labour market is unlikely to clear given these small estimates. They also suggest that the unemployment creating effects of a rise in the real wage are likely to be small so that classical unemployment is likely to be comparatively unimportant.

One further problem with these conventional models of labour demand that use actual output rather than aggregate demand measures as an independent variable in the labour demand equation is that they are structurally unstable. Knight and Wilson (1974), Briscoe and Roberts (1977) and more recently Wren-Lewis (1984) demonstrate this weakness which implies a serious mis-specification. Their theoretical basis is also somewhat ambiguous to the point at which some economists have argued they are 'devoid of economic content', (Nickell (1984)). This scepticism has helped to reawaken new interest in the specification of the labour demand equation. Some of the recent developments in empirical analysis have been inspired by the work of Sargent (1978) and these challenge the view that real wage changes have little effect on unemployment.

Much of the work proceeds using a profit maximising assumption. In this case output is endogenous. We only observe points along the production (employment) function if the real wage changes and gives different points of tangency along it. This is shown in Figure 6.5. A fall in real wages from W/P_1 to W/P_2 raises both employment to (E_2) <u>and</u>

output (to Y_2). Since output changes are endogenous and have no effect on labour demand equation 6.27 is estimated without the inclusion of an output variable. Only if the real wage (and relative imported input prices) change will there be a change in output. Output supplied and labour demand are jointly determined. The only role for aggregate demand is via the nominal price level. If a fall in aggregate demand causes the real wage or the relative price of imported inputs to change then the demand for labour changes. Given the short run insensitivity of the price level to changes in aggregate demand this leaves precious little scope for the occurrence of Keynesian unemployment. This highly classical view with its associated supply side notion of output determination has been tested for Britain and elsewhere in a series of papers by James Symons. In Symons (1985) and Layard and Symons (1984) empirical support is found for this view. In Symons (1985) a large but slow acting effect of real wages on employment on labour intensity (capital/labour ratio) is found in British manufacturing industry. The real wage elasticity of employment is found to be -2.4. This implies that a rise in real wages of 1% in the early 1980s would have reduced employment by approximately 140,000. This is a very large change. Symons and Layard (1984) show that this elasticity is also large by international standards. Only in Canada is the estimated elasticity larger and in Germany and France it is substantially smaller (less than .5).

Figure 6.5

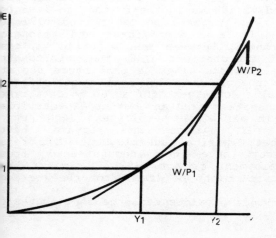

A crucial feature of the specification is that Symons and Layard include the relative price of imported inputs as an additional explanatory variable in their labour demand equation. As well as possessing a significant negative long run elasticity of its own in Germany, Canada and Britain, its inclusion has a profound effect on the significance and size of the real wage effect. For example excluding input prices changes the estimated real wage elasticity for Britain from -1.8 to $+.1.$ Symons (1985) and Symons and Layard (1984) also find no direct role for aggregate demand except in France and the US.

The latter conclusion (not least for Britain) is somewhat surprising. In manufacturing industry both Nickell (1984c) and Wren-Lewis (1984) have found that output expectations are critical determinants of manufacturing employment (and hence unemployment). Since aggregate demand factors are a crucial feature in the formation of such expectations this seems to contradict the results of Symons and Layard. Wren-Lewis generates output expectations (35) using

$$6.28 \quad Y_t^e = \sum_{i=1}^{T} \alpha_i Y_{t-i} + \sum_{i=1}^{T} \beta_i' Z_{t-i} + \mu$$

where Y is actual manufacturing output and Z is a vector of variables containing the real exchange rate, the real public sector budget balance and relative oil prices. Note the latter since it raises the possibility that the imported input price variable used by Layard and Symons may be a proxy for output expectations. If it is, then the failure of aggregate demand variables in their study is less of a surprise. In results based on the period 1972 to 1983 Wren-Lewis finds a significant and strongly positive relationship between manufacturing employment and output expectations. (36) The unfortunate features of Wren-Lewis's paper is that there are no tests of the strength of the real wage effect. However its results do suggest for an up to date time series that aggregate demand and output expectations are important in explaining employment (and hence unemployment). If Symons and Layard have demonstrated that Classical unemployment is a real possibility they have not demonstrated that Keynesian unemployment is not. (37) A similar but opposite conclusion might be drawn from the work of Wren-Lewis.

Nickell (1984c) provides evidence that suggests

hat both sources of higher unemployment are <u>possible</u>
iven the response of labour demand in manufacturing
o both aggregate demand and real wage changes.
ickell constructs a theoretical model of the demand
or labour at the <u>industry</u> level. Even if aggregate
emand has no effect on the firms in a competitive
ndustry it will certainly have effects at the
ndustry level. Modelling labour demand at the
anufacturing industry level (like Symons and Layard
1984) incorporating only relative prices as
egressors is clearly inappropriate. Aggregate
emand shifts the industry labour demand curve
positively) even in the competitive industry. In
act Nickell goes a stage further moving towards the
eality of most British manufacturing industries by
ssuming a non-competitive product market.

Note that the statistically estimated labour
emand curve is actually the <u>effective</u> demand curve
hich determines <u>actual</u> employment. This is shown
iagramatically in Figure 6.6.

igure 6.6

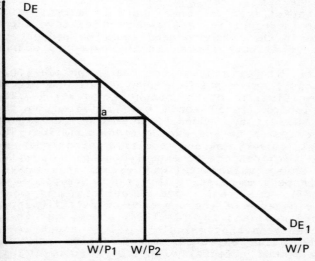

The notional demand curve when firms are not
ationed by product market conditions is $D_E D_{E1}$.
uppose initially the real wage is W/P_1 and current
ggregate demand keeps employment at a maximum of E_1.
he effective labour demand curve is then $E_1 D_{E1}$.

243

Suppose there is a fall in aggregate demand so that the maximum employment level is E_2. The effective labour demand curve is now E_2D_{E1}. If the real wage stays at W/P_1 there will be a reduction of employment at that real wage. Note also that since position 'a' is inside the demand curve workers are being paid less than their marginal product. Aggregate demand shifts and the output expectations they induce are bound therefore to be of some importance in explaining employment.

Of course this still leaves a role for real wages. In the initial situation where the effective demand curve is E_1D_{E1} a rise in real wage above W/P_1 would reduce employment. In the case of the demand curve E_2D_{E1} a rise above W/P_2 would have the same effect. Nickell allows for both these effects. He derives within an imperfectly competitive framework a labour demand curve of the same form as 6.2 except that like Wren-Lewis he also incorporates output expectations, not output itself. The Z vector of variables that determine these expectations in an equivalent equation to 6.28 include real share prices, aggregate demand variables (the money stock, the price level, manufacturing investment, real and nominal interest rates) <u>and</u> relative input prices. Nickell's specification means that the substitution effects of increases in real wages or relative input prices are in the labour demand equation proper and their output effects appear in the expected output term.

Nickell reports results that include only lagged output, share prices, money stock and prices in the specification of the output expectations. The other variables listed above were rejected on the grounds that they added little in terms of explanatory power to the expectations equation. The result was a very strong positive elasticity of employment with respect to expected output of +1.11. The long run equivalent real wage elasticity is -0.15 and with respect to relative imported input prices is -0.13. (38) The real wage elasticity is well determined because of the presence of relative input prices as Symons and Layard (1984) argue, but it is much smaller than they calculate (-1.8) and is much smaller than the expected output (which includes aggregate demand effects) elasticity. According to this evidence induced changes in real wages have to be very large to have much effect on employment. In 1980/1, for example, real wages would have to have risen by 54.2% (!) to explain all of the decline in employment in British manufacturing. Clearly (<u>gross</u>

real product wages actually grew by 4.9% in 1980/1)
other factors dominate in that period. Expected
output and therefore aggregate demand are the obvious
candidates. Our conclusion from these single
equation labour demand studies is that the necessary
conditions exist for <u>both</u> the occurrence of Keynesian
(aggregate demand falls) and Classical (real wage
increases) non-natural unemployment. However,
changes in the latter need to be a good deal larger
than the former to bring about a given reduction in
employment and (with a constant labour force) an
equivalent increase in unemployment.

One of the problems with the studies we have
surveyed so far is that they model only the demand
side of the market. This gives rise to a number of
difficulties that might create some unease in
accepting the precise estimates obtained. An obvious
problem is that rather than identify a demand curve
the estimates might be consistent with a supply
curve. Consider the work of Symons and Layard. Their
real wage/employment estimate could be what we might
obtain from a long run backward bending supply curve.
We could be sure we had identified the demand curve
if we knew the labour market was in disequilibrium
and characterised by excess supply. To that extent
single equation estimation from the 1970s and 1980s
(like Wren-Lewis) might be more acceptable. The
obvious alternative solution is to estimate a
structural model of the labour market and examine the
effects of real changes on labour demand so that any
possible supply side effect is removed.

We have already considered a number of models of
this type so all that is required now is to review
the evidence they provide on real wage/labour demand
elasticities. In general significant real wage
effects are found in these models. Andrews (1984)
using an equilibrium model of the labour market finds
a real wage elasticity of -0.51. The labour demand
equation is highly classical in character and fails,
therefore, to take account of expected output and
aggregate demand effects. This is remedied by Layard
and Nickell (1985) who also, as we have seen, adopt a
model that does not assume market clearing and allows
for the effect of product demand on labour demand.
They adopt a labour demand function, derived from a
model of a firm operating in an imperfectly
competitive environment. In this case the firm's
downward sloping product demand curve is displaced by
changes in aggregate demand. Similar effects are to
be found on the labour demand curve which is (in
logs) (39)

6.29 $D_{E_t} = \delta_0 + \delta_1 \frac{W}{P}t + \delta_2 \sigma_t + \delta_3 K_t +$

$\delta_4 E_{t-1} + \delta_5 E_{t-2} + \varepsilon_t$

where

$W/P_t =$ real product wages (tax effects included)

$K_t =$ capital stock

$\sigma_t =$ aggregate demand variable

$\varepsilon_t =$ error term

The aggregate demand variable is a compendium of three components (i) a public sector deficit variable (ii) deviations of world trade from trend (iii) a measure of trading competitiveness. Large public sector deficits, positive deviations of world trade from trend and increasing competitiveness should all increase employment in Britain. Using annual data from 1954-83 for the whole economy Layard and Nickell show they do and significantly so. They also show, using both a single and three equation estimation format, a significant long run real wage elasticity of between -.6 and -.9 (about half the value of the long run total demand elasticity). They also show that 'a simple competitive model where only K and W/P would appear is not an adequate representation of the data'. Omitting the aggregate demand variables leaves the real wage coefficient less well determined and models that do are, hence, less reliable.

Although different estimates are obtained for whole economy compared with manufacturing data and for different time periods we can conclude that cuts in aggregate demand and increases in real wages can both, in principle, increase unemployment. Similar conclusions have been reached from studies of the youth labour market in Britain. (40) Early studies by the Department of Employment (1978) showed only a significant effect of aggregate demand on youth employment and unemployment but the recent study by Wells (1983) has changed that. Wells estimates a demand equation (and a supply equation) separately for the period 1953-69 in which he believes there is excess demand and for 1969-81 in which he believes there is excess supply. We will concentrate on the latter period in which youth unemployment has increased so dramatically. The demand equation used by Wells in (in logs)

6.30 $D_{E_t} = \delta_0 + \delta_1 RW/P_{t-i} + \delta_2 CYC_t + \epsilon_t$

where

RW/P_{t-i} = relative labour costs (inclusive of tax effects) of youths (males under 21, females under 18) relative to adults

CYC_t = male unemployment rate excluding school leavers

It is difficult to make a lot of sense of this equation in terms of conventional theory. There is no term to allow for the effects of technical change, or the usage and the cost of other inputs. Presumably the inclusion of CYC_t is intended to represent the behaviour of non-profit maximising firms in a non-competitive environment. That is not made clear by Wells. If this is the underlying theoretical model, then the use of the male unemployment rate is inappropriate. We have seen most studies use a measure of output, aggregate demand and/or output expectations to capture these scale effects. Even if unemployment were appropriate, account has to be taken of the fact that its current value reflects past aggregate demand fluctuations. It is, however, clearly inappropriate. Recall that Wells argues that post-1969 the male youth labour market exhibits excess supply (post-1971 for females). Since unemployment is the difference between the labour force and actual employment (on the demand curve) a decrease in youth employment will cause an increase in total unemployment unless the labour force falls to compensate. This is exactly the reverse causation to that required by Wells' specification.

There are other objections to Wells' model. We have already indicated the unsatisfactory way in which disequilibrium regimes are classified. Junankar and Neale (1985) carry out a variety of specification, structural stability and robustness tests that significantly weaken Wells' results. Wells finds (post-1969) a large significant relative wage elasticity and for males no significant coefficient for the CYC_t variable for males, though some of the usual results were found for females. Since this result seems to suggest that high youth unemployment is the result of young workers being 'priced out of their jobs' by high relative wages this study received more than the normal degree of publicity (page 2 lead in The Times) for a piece of economics research. It is evident, however, that the study is seriously flawed. Junankar and Neale show that if the CYC_t variable is defined as an index of GDP (excluding North Sea Oil) then the significance of relative labour costs in explaining youth unemployment collapses in almost all equations estimated by Wells.

A much more satisfactory indication of real wage and aggregate demand (via output) effects is in the study by Hutchinson, Barr and Drobny (1984). They assume excess supply and estimate a demand curve of the conventional form depicted in equation 6.27 except that relative wage variables enter the specification. They find young males are a complementary input to adult males and a substitute for female labour in general. They also find a (diminishing returns) output elasticity greater than unity, which confirms (see Chapter 2) that employment (and unemployment) amongst the young is especially cyclically sensitive in Britain. However, Hutchinson, Barr and Drobny assume excess supply - they do not demonstrate it. In their work Junankar and Neale (1985) and Rice (1984) attempt to deal with this problem. Both studies endogenise the selection of disequilibrium regime as we saw in the last section. Employing an index of aggregate output, Junankar and Neale find a significant large and positive output elasticity (especially for females) and a significant negative real wage elasticity (for females only). Rice, on the other hand, finds significant effects of both demand and relative wage changes on youth unemployment.

Confirmation of the view that, in principle, non-natural employment can be Keynesian or Classical also comes from the studies of unemployment flows. Junankar and Price (1983) show negative deviations of output from trend increase unemployment inflows and decrease outflows. Increases in real wages increase inflows and decrease outflows. Nickell (1982) uses demand variables and finds reductions in aggregate demand reduce outflows and increase inflows. In his results, increases in real wages only significantly affect inflows (positively). In the outflow equation the coefficient is correctly signed (negative) but it is insignificant.

There is abundant evidence, therefore, that either or both cuts in aggregate demand or increases in real wages can cause higher unemployment. Which, in practice, has been dominant? An answer to this question may also shed light on the cures to unemployment which we consider in Chapter 9. Some clue can be obtained by inspection of the relevant

aggregate statistics. Unemployment in Britain has
risen (employment fallen) to a significant extent at
four points in time since the mid-1960s namely 1967,
1971, 1976 and 1980-2. In 1967, 1971 and 1976 and
1980 the increase in unemployment followed a major
increase in real product wages in the preceding year.
In 1975, 1981-2 real wages had either fallen or risen
to a very small extent in the preceding year. The
increase in unemployment was also significantly
larger in the early 1980s although the increase in
real wages was more modest than at previous points in
time. On the face of it these crude statistics
suggest that Classical unemployment caused by rising
real wages is important. However, the data for the
1980s also suggest it is a less important feature of
recent unemployment. In addition, 1967, 1970, 1976
and most significantly 1980-2 were also preceded by
falls in aggregate demand. Only in 1975 is this not
the case (largely because of an increase in the
budget deficit in 1974). On this basis Keynesian
unemployment caused by falls in aggregate demand is
also likely. Moreover its relative importance is also
likely to have increased significantly in the 1980s.
(41)

Some confirmation for this view comes from
Layard and Nickell (1985). They find that about a
quarter of the total increase in unemployment
(natural and non-natural) between 1966 and 1979 can
be attributed to falls in aggregate demand whereas
almost three quarters (73%) is explained by this
cause since 1979. This is confirmed by Junankar and
Price (1983) who find that between 1979 and 1981, 67%
of the total increase in unemployment was explained
by falls in aggregate demand. Increases in real
labour costs account for considerably less. The
conclusion from this is that non-natural
unemployment is now principally Keynesian in
character. This does not, however, appear to be quite
so strongly the case in the preceding fifteen years
when Classical unemployment may have been,
relatively, more important. Nickell (1982), for
example, finds that of the increased male
unemployment in Britain between 1969 and 1977 only
just under 40% can be attributed to a decline in
demand. Of course, exogenously caused increases in
real wages can also have effects on aggregate demand.
This has been given some emphasis recently by
government economists in Britain. Although such
increases induce an upward jump in consumer spending
they may also (depending on the reaction of the
exchange rate) cause a loss of international

competitiveness which figures in Layard and Nickell's demand variable. In addition, they may also squeeze company profits and induce a major fall in investment. We will consider this further in Chapter 9 but clearly this is an important <u>caveat</u> in the interpretation of these results.

As we saw in Chapter 5 there are several ways in which non-natural unemployment can arise directly through too high a level of real wages. One occurs when real wage rigidity prevents adjustment to an adverse real shock. One important shock of this kind is the oil and raw material price increases of 1973 and to a lesser extent 1979. We have already reviewed the considerable body of evidence that suggests these input price increases will reduce the demand for labour. If this demand curve shift is not matched by falls in the real wage level we saw in Chapter 5, that this will lead to higher (Classical) unemployment. There is abundant evidence in favour of this view for the 1974-80 period. Layard and Nickell (1985), for example, find the rise in relative import prices explains about one third of the total rise in unemployment in this period. On the other hand, in the decade before 1974 and also since 1980, the effect of the observed movement in real import prices is actually to reduce unemployment.

Confirmation of this important cause of Classical unemployment in the 1970s is also to be found in the work of Sachs (1979), Bruno (1980), Grubb, Jackman and Layard (1983) and others. Grubb, Jackman and Layard, for example, find for EEC countries as a whole that the same (one third) proportion of the increase in unemployment in the 1970s is accounted for by the combination of a rise in relative import prices and real wage rigidity. Interestingly this study also finds the slow down of productivity growth in the 1970s which would have decreased the feasible rate of growth of real wages in all EEC countries, also contributed substantially to the rise in unemployment in the 1970s. In Britain all of the increase in unemployment that took place is explained by this cause. However, the model used by Grubb, Jackman and Layard seriously overpredicts the increase in unemployment, so care needs to be taken in accepting this numerical estimate too precisely. This body of evidence, however, suggests real wage inflexibility was a potent source of rising (non-natural) unemployment in the 1970s.

Rises in real wages above the 'feasible' equilibrium rate of growth may also occur through the action of trades unions. In combination with other factors this may cause a rise in the natural as well as the non-natural rate of unemployment. We will consider this further in the next chapter. Its potential importance in the 1970s could be considerable given that in that decade we observed in Britain, an increase in the coverage of collective agreements and in the union differential. The proportion of workers unionised in Britain went up from 47.3% in 1969 to 59% in 1979. According to data in Metcalf and Nickell (1985) the differential in average earnings between union and non-union male manual workers went up from 5.5% in 1969 to 8% in 1979. The impact of unions on unemployment via their effect on real wages is generally found to be small, but in the 1970s non-trivial. Nickell and Andrews (1983) calculate the impact of unions on unemployment since the war has been of the order of 400,000. Somewhat higher estimates are obtained by Minford (1983). In contrast, Layard and Nickell find that only 8% of the rise in unemployment since 1979 can be explained by union activity. However in the 1970s the comparable figure is 27%. Note again that these estimates combine the total effect of trade unions on both U^* and unemployment in excess of U^*_t.

Relative earnings movements were also a factor in the rise of youth unemployment in the 1970s. Rice (1984) shows about a third of the rise in male youth unemployment and a quarter of the comparable rise in female unemployment occurred for this reason. Since that time this will have become less important because the relative wage of young workers has actually fallen. The bulk of the evidence, however, continues to suggest that falls in aggregate demand are the principal cause of high youth unemployment. However, factors which contribute to the rise in the natural rate of unemployment as a whole will also have their impact on youth unemployment. This rise is considered in more detail in the next chapter.

Conclusion

The evidence we have reviewed in this chapter is broadly in favour of the rejection of the market clearing equilibrium view of unemployment. The notion that unemployment is consistently at its natural equilibrium level is not confirmed by the bulk of the evidence.

Although the evidence is not totally overwhelming it clearly favours the adoption of a non-market clearing approach to the analysis of unemployment in Britain. Unemployment in excess of the natural rate will, therefore, occur and will persist. This unemployment can arise through falls in aggregate demand or rises in real wages. Both seem to have been a feature of rising unemployment in Britain in which the demand for labour is sensitive to both kinds of change. The evidence suggests falls in aggregate demand are consistently important in explaining non-natural unemployment. In the 1980s this may be the total explanation for any changes in unemployment in excess of the natural rate that have taken place. In the previous decade this is much less evident with real wages increases and real wage rigidity playing a more critical role. Whether cuts in real wage levels or merely the rate of growth are a necessary condition for reducing unemployment in the next decade is considered in Chapter 9, after we have considered the natural rate of unemployment itself.

Notes

1.   This is a test of causality. According to Granger (1969) "... we say that y_t is <u>causing</u> x_t if we are better able to predict x_t, using all available (past) information than if the information apart from (past) y_t had been used".

2.   Alogoskoufis and Pissarides (1983) estimate price equations for Britain using unanticipated changes in the money supply as an independent variable. This requires them to estimate an equation similar to 6.2. However they find no significant link between the real PSBR and the growth of the money supply. This may be the result of the use of lagged values of the PSBR unlike Attfield, Demery and Duck, who use unlagged values (see equation 6.12 in the text).

3.   Contrast this result with that obtained by Andersen and Jordan (1968) for an earlier period.

4.   Demery's results 'strikingly replicate' the findings of Gordon (1982) for the US.

5.   A further mechanism is provided by Lucas and Rapping (1970). In their model of labour supply if the price level is overestimated, workers expect a lower real rate of interest. This causes a substitution of current for future leisure so labour supply falls and unemployment rises. In fact Andrews (1984) finds this effect to be small in Britain so it is ignored in the text at this point although the entire Lucas-Rapping model is considered later in this chapter.

6.   Studies in the US have shown that survey

data is not always consistent with the classical view. Using data from the Livingston survey, Figlewski and Wachter (1981) show expectational errors are serially correlated <u>and</u> do not have a mean of zero as the statistical assumptions of the rational expectations hypothesis require.

7.   This model is derived from a utility function in which current and future goods and leisure are the arguments. It is maximised subject to a budget constraint which assumes a perfect capital market. In order to derive the signs of the coefficients discussed in the next it is necessary to assume that future goods and leisure are substituted for current leisure and leisure is not inferior. (See Lucas and Rapping (1970) pp.264-5).

8.   Note this assumption that in the fixing of money wages in the <u>current</u> period no expectational error is made. The assumption that the current price level is correctly anticipated is necessary to depict the equilibrium (market clearing) view of unemployment we obtained from the intertemporal substitution model of Lucas and Rapping (1970). If this were not true we would have non-natural (disequilibrium) unemployment.

9.   We can rewrite this part of equation 6.7 as α_1 (W/Pt - W*/Pt) + (α_1 + α_2) W*/Pt. Since the variables are in logs (W/Pt - W*/Pt) is actually the <u>ratio</u> of the current real wage to the long run expected wage. If W/Pt exceeds W*/Pt more labour is supplied and if W/Pt is less than W*/Pt less labour is supplied. α, therefore, measures the response of labour supply to transitory departure of the real wage from its permanent or long run level.

10.   Non-natural unemployment can also occur if the inflation rate is over-estimated (see footnote (5)).

11.   This is shown formally by Andrews (1983) pp. 2-3.

12.   Note that if the supply curve possesses an infinite elasticity it is vertical in the frame 'a' of 6.1. This means that real wage movements are not necessary so the procyclical pattern of real wage changes will not occur.

13.   Some US studies especially for women workers (Heckman and MaCurdy (1980), for example) confirm this large labour supply elasticity.

14.   They also find α_3 to be significantly positive. This is important since it provides a direct link between the goods and the money markets of the economy (where real interest rates are determined) and the labour market. Labour supply,

therefore, can respond to the aggregate demand in a way Figure 6.1 ignores.

15. Altonji also tests for the impact of real interest rates on labour supply. He finds the relevant coefficient (α_3) typically has the wrong sign (negative rather than positive) but the effects observed are, in many cases, very small. In contrast for Britain, Andrews finds significant positive coefficients as the Classical theory requires but the observed response of labour supply to changes in real interest rates is also very small (see footnotes (5), (10), and (14). This is why the dependence of labour supply on aggregate demand is ignored in Figure 6.1.

16. The basic method is to define W/P_t^* as

$$\sum_{K=1}^{m} \delta_K \hat{W}_{t+K} \text{ where } \Sigma \delta_K = 1$$

and $\hat{W}_t$ are generated from an auto-regressive forecasting equation. Hannah estimates

$$\hat{W}_t = \alpha_0 + \alpha_1 W_{t-1} + \alpha_2 W_{t-3} + \alpha_4 W_{t-4}$$

+ seasonals from quarterly data. The weights (δ_K) were chosen to decline geometrically over a two year time horizon.

17. This is consistent with the work of Ashenfelter and Card (1982) who use autoregressive and moving average (ARMA) representations of labour market variables as a test of alternative models of the labour market. They conclude 'the intertemporal substitution hypothesis by <u>itself</u> is not capable of describing the aggregate time series data on wages, prices, interest rates and unemployment' in the US.

18. This real wage equation can be seen to be a family relation of equation 6.7. Andrews (1985) shows that if 6.7 is inverted and if we include L_t as an independent variable entering the labour supply equation with a unitary coefficient, we can derive the market clearing real wage equation used by Minford.

19. Note that this result confirms the general conclusion of the previous section that expectational errors are of minor importance in explaining unemployment in Britain.

20. Minford says (p.238) these are calculated using the lagged dependent variables from the annual equation. However the estimates presented appear to use the coefficients of the lagged dependent variables from the quarterly equations. The method of

retrieval is very simple. If we assume in the real wage equation, for example, that

(i) $W/P_t \big/ W/P_{t-1} = \left[\dfrac{W/PLR}{W/P_{t-1}} \right]^{\lambda}$

where W/P_{LR} is the long run value of W/P and λ is the rate of adjustment to that value then (in logs)

(ii) $W/P_t = \lambda(W/P_{LR}) + (1-\lambda)(W/P_{t-1})$

Since we can calculate λ from the coefficient of the lagged dependent variable in 6.13 we can work out the long run coefficients of all the variables in 6.13 by simply dividing the estimated coefficients of the variables that determine W/PLR (UNR_t, U_t etc.) by λ.

21.   The demand equation used by Minford also is inconsistent with his assumption that product markets are competitive and firms maximise profits. In this case at the firm level the level of output is endogenous and should not feature in the labour demand equation at all.

22.   They conclude after an examination of three theoretical models that 'the equilibrium (i.e. classical) model does not really fit the facts implying that at least some of the unemployed are off their supply functions'. Ashenfelter (1980) in a study of the US labour markets confirms that workers are displaced from their optimising supply curves as a result of demand side constraints in the labour market. This is consistent with the analysis of disequilibrium models in Chapter 5 and in particular with the concept of Keynesian unemployment.

23.   This specification is not wholly consistent with the classical approach to labour demand.

24.   This is done to derive both equilibrium real wages and person hours. Beenstock and Warburton use an 'error correction' framework for the analysis of disequilibrium. This assumes the labour market does adjust to equilibrium following an external shock.

25.   This sluggish adjustment process is confirmed in an analysis of a more up-to-date version of the Beenstock and Warburton model by Wallis (editor) 1985.

26.   The real wage resistance models of money wage determination can easily be regarded as the reduced form of a wage bargaining model. Evidence on the causes of union activity like strikes and

membership issues suggests that erosion of real wages is a powerful positive force. If this (as the evidence suggests) results in higher money wages then the real wage rigidity we observe is very much the consequence of (rational) collective action by workers.

27. Grubb, Jackman and Layard (1983) confirm a small and insignificant value of α_2 for the US and a small, correctly signed but insignificant value of α_1.

28. This pattern of real wage rigidity combined with money wage flexibility and vice versa is very much in line with Sachs (1979). Grubb, Jackman and Layard take a different view arising from the different ways in which they define real and money wage rigidity. This means it is possible to observe the coexistence of both types of wage rigidity. They adopt a Friedmanite view of the natural rate which assumes in the face of an adverse shock that inflation has to return to the original level. If it fails to do so we observe higher unemployment and the measure of real wage rigidity is obtained from measuring that extra unemployment in the face of adverse shocks. The actual definitions they use are $1/\alpha_1$ (for real wage rigidity) and $[(1 - \alpha_2),/\alpha_2] \, 1/\alpha_1$ (for money wage rigidity). Their calculations[1] confirm the high degree of money wage rigidity in the US (low α_2) but also show a higher degree of real wage rigidity (low α_1, also) as they define it.

29. Alogoskoufis and Pissarides (1983) also produce evidence for this price sluggishness in the British economy as a result of which 'anticipated monetary policy may have a significant role to play in the short run'. Price stickiness, in other words, also undermines the classical view of the ineffectiveness of demand management policies to reduce unemployment.

30. These results, together with those of Junankar and Price (1984), are considered in more detail later in this chapter and in Chapters 7 and 8.

31. Recall the flow equilibrium condition identifies a position on the VU curve. Although the natural rate of unemployment is on the VU curve the flow equilibrium unemployment rate could actually be in excess of the natural rate. The argument in the text is that this may be the case for Nickell's estimates.

32. We consider the issue of the definition of U_t^* in the next chapter. Recall however that if the secular (equilibrium) variables have a transitory

(disequilibrium) component the Layard and Nickell estimates of U_t^* will be biased upwards.

33. Strictly speaking, the exact form of the labour demand function adopted differs in each study from equation 6.27 in accordance with the precise assumptions that are made. 6.27 should, therefore, be interpreted as an equation some of the principal determinants of the demand for labour but not in any precise way.

34. The usual form is $E_t/E_{t-1} = (E_t^*/E_{t-1})^\lambda$ where E_t^* is desired employment (labour demand). This gives a lagged dependent variable in a log linear version of equation 6.27.

35. Since output expectations more than one year ahead are also important Wren-Lewis generates these expectations as well. This requires equations for expected Z variables also. This is done in an analogous way to equation 6.28, namely

$$6.28a \quad Z_t^e = \sum_{i=1}^{T} \delta_{\sim i}' Z_{t-i} + \sum_{i=1}^{T} \partial Y_{t-i} + \gamma_t$$

36. Wren-Lewis also finds a strong positive link between company liquidity and manufacturing employment. Wadhwani (1984) also finds a link between financial distress, bankruptcy and job loss in the manufacturing sector. Insofar as these are related to high nominal interest rates in a depressed economy, there is a clear additional link between the product and the labour market.

37. Indeed in a footnote Layard and Symons say 'our main conviction is that real wages matter rather than demand shift variables do not'. A further difficulty with the work of Symons (1985) is that it exhibits some of the instability that characterises earlier work. The model breaks down during the late 1970s. Symons attributes this to the transitory effects of the Social Contract and to the caution of firms faced with high real interest rates. The omission of a product demand variable in what is then a misspecified equation is an alternative explanation although Symons performs some tests that do not support this view.

38. Nickell also estimates the demand equation without the relative price effects. The estimated expected output elasticity is a little smaller (+.9). Tests of structural stability which are very important in view of the notorious instability of labour demand equations in Britain show this version to be superior. Some researchers (e.g. HM Treasury

1985) have suggested Symons (1985) estimate of the real wage elasticity is high because he uses data from manufacturing. Outside manufacturing, it is asserted firms are less responsive to real wage changes. Nickell's estimates (also for manufacturing) suggest it may be the omission of aggregate demand effects from his equation that gives Symons his rather large estimates of the real wage elasticity.

39.   The long run elasticity of the capital stock is imposed to be unity in the estimates so the coefficient on the capital stock in 6.29 is actually $(1-\delta_4-\delta_5)$. Note also the absence of a relative input price variable. In the Layard and Nickell system this features in the real wage equation and its effects on employment comes via this route.

40.   There is also growing literature about the aggregate labour market in the inter-war period. Smyth (1983), Hatton (1983) and Broadberry (1983) have conducted disequilibrium studies of this period. There is also a lively debate on the cause of high unemployment in the early 1930s and the recovery later which considers the role of real wages (see Dimsdale (1984), Worswick (1984)).

41.   Note also that since the mid 1960s in only two years has male unemployment fallen significantly (1973 and 1979). In the year preceding these there were major _increases_ in real wages and more modest increases in aggregate demand (less so in 1973 than 1978).

Chapter Seven

THE NATURAL RATE OF UNEMPLOYMENT: THE SUPPLY SIDE

Introduction

In the previous three chapters we have considered the
theory and evidence relating to unemployment in
excess of the natural rate. We have seen that some
modern classical economists believe no policy is
necessary for the removal of such unemployment since
it is self-eliminating. However, that does not mean
that such economists believe no policy is necessary.
On the contrary there is a great emphasis placed on
the need to reduce the natural rate of unemployment.
In order clearly to detail an appropriate policy it
is necessary to outline an empirically satisfactory
theory of the natural rate. Indeed even for those who
accept the theoretical and empirical case for non-
natural unemployment the calculation of the natural
rate of unemployment is necessary to assess its
residual extent. Moreover, few economists believe
that the reduction of unemployment to its natural
level will leave no substantial unsolved problems.
Policies for reducing U^* are likely to be just as
important in reducing unemployment as policies to
reduce the non-natural level. Consideration of the
determinants of the natural rate and of forces that
increase (and decrease) its level is therefore
necessary. This is the purpose of this and the next
chapter.

A Theory of the Natural Rate

A theory of frictional unemployment derived from a
search framework was developed in Chapter 3. The
natural rate was defined as the point at which actual
vacancies are equal to actual unemployment. We have
already outlined some of the difficulties involved in
its calculation but the analysis of Chapter 3 implies
three critical factors that determine the size of U_t^*.
Firstly, on the employee side is the probability of a

job offer being accepted. (β_t). Secondly, on the employer side is the offer probability (κ_t) and the vacancy rate (V_t) that together determine the arrival rate of job offers. It is the combination of the acceptance probabilities with the arrival rate of offers that determines the chances of a hire taking place. Thirdly, U_t^* is influenced by the rate of inflow to the unemployment stock (α_t). Changes in this inflow rate affect both the VU curve and the natural rate (U_t^*) of unemployment. As we saw in Chapter 3 short run variations in β_t, κ_t and α_t can and do take place. In chapters 4 and 5 on the other hand, we assumed that the value of U_t^* was cyclically invariant so that the natural rate was a constant. Non-natural unemployment can then be calculated as the residual difference between the total actually unemployed and U_t^*. We shall now abandon this assumption and allow β_t, κ_t and α_t to vary freely. In a slump a searching worker can expect that the productivity of search time will fall since he will encounter a greater number of job contacts in which no offer will be made. The reason for this is that during a slump firms will cut vacancies and/or raise their hiring standard. In the latter case this will reduce the offer probability κ_t. This happens because, in a slump, the total and marginal costs of not filling a vacancy falls since there is less (or even zero) foregone output and profit. This shift in the employer's search cost function leads to longer search and a raising of the hiring standard. This lowers the offer probability (κ_t).

A further rationale for this course of action in the cost minimising firm has been provided by Mortensen (1970). The starting point for his analysis is the 'supply' relationship.

$$7.1 \quad \Delta E_i = \phi(W_i, \rho_i^*) \text{ with } \frac{\partial \Delta Ei}{\partial \frac{Wi}{W}} > 0$$

$$\frac{\partial \Delta E_i}{\partial \rho_i^*} < 0$$

where ΔE_i is the change in employment in the ith firm (or industry) $W_i/\bar{W}$ is the relative wage of the firm (or industry). ρ_i^* is its hiring standard (reservation productivity or labour quality level) applied in a labour market in which workers differ in terms of their experience, abilities and training. The partial derivatives indicate that the flow of acceptable workers to a firm will increase with its relative wage and decline with its hiring standard. Mortensen argues that firms have to construct a hiring strategy that takes account of the fact that the positive marginal inflow declines the higher is the relative wage and the lower is the hiring standard. Any hiring strategy becomes less productive the more (relatively) a firm relies upon one of the options (relative wage or hiring standard). This gives rise to the curvature of the ΔE_i curve in Figure 7.1. It slopes up because to maintain a constant labour force ($\Delta E_i = 0$), for example, can be achieved by a high relative wage/high hiring standard strategy or a low value of both. This the firm has to decide. If it wants to decrease its labour force the firm can cut its relative wage, raise its hiring standard or both. Whichever it decides the firm will be on the $\Delta E_i < 0$ curve which lies below the original level. Using similar arguments if an increase in employment is desired this takes the firm on to the $\Delta E_i > 0$ curve. What actually happens depends on the cost implication of the two alternative policies open to the firm. A firm at position a on $\Delta E_i = 0$ and wishing to change its labour force can opt for a change in its relative wage or its hiring standards or both. What governs the choice that firms make? The cost minimising firm will obviously take account of the relative costs of each strategy. Mortensen takes a relatively narrow view of the costs involved emphasising the straight wage costs of changing $W_i/\bar{W}$ and the training and net search cost effects of altering ρ_i^* in the way we considered in Chapter 3. If the labour force is to be cut, for example, this can be achieved by a cut in the relative wage (which reduces wage costs) or by an increase in the hiring standard (which reduces training costs). Note no account is taken of additional costs like collective resistance or loss of morale of retained workers in the face of relative wage although it is not difficult to introduce these kinds of costs.

In order to define the optimal strategy for the cost minimising firm Mortensen derives the isocost (CC) lines shown in Figure 7.1 on the assumption that the marginal cost of lowering hiring standards increases the lower is the initial level. The training cost and performance effects of accepting lower quality workers become more serious for the firm. Consequently larger relative wage cuts are necessary to maintain constant costs for a firm with a low hiring standard. Hence the curvature of the CC curve. The cost minimising firm will choose a point of tangency of the ΔE_i and CC lines. The HH line is the locus of these points of tangency. Changes in desired employment will move firms along the HH line so that a mixed strategy requiring a change in hiring standard will occur. If the savings of a wage cut are overestimated by Mortensen (because of the offsetting resistance and movement costs resulting from the long run attachment of firms and workers) then the curve will be a good deal flatter than in Figure 7.1. In this case changes in hiring standards (a form of quantity adjustment) will be even more pronounced and wage changes less so. Arguments of this type show how the rigidity of wages and the adjustment of quantities characteristic of non-market clearing models can be seen within models of labour market flows as well as the stocks we have emphasised in Chapters 4 and 5.

Figure 7.1

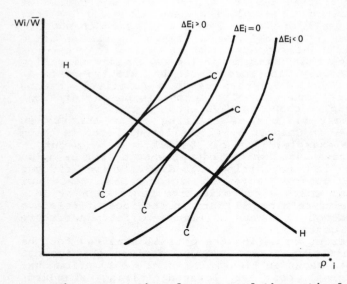

There are, therefore, sound theoretical grounds for believing firms will not only cut vacancies but also raise hiring standards in recession and vice versa in boom. This will tend to raise U_t^* in recession but there will be offsetting factors from the workers' side that are likely to mean U_t^* is unaffected. In the short run workers' expectations are likely to be inelastic. However, a decline in vacancies, plus the increase in hiring standards will reduce the productivity of search time, raise both the marginal and total costs of search and reduce the reservation wage. In other words, the acceptance probability (β_t) is likely to rise in recession. This is shown in Figure 7.2 which reproduces the sequential decision model diagram used in Chapter 3.

Figure 7.2

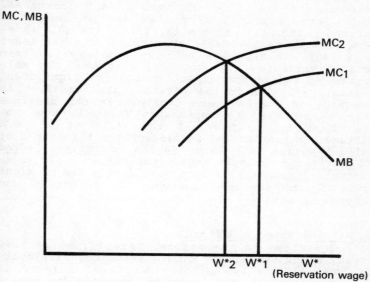

MC, MB

MC2

MC1

MB

W*2   W*1   W*
(Reservation wage)

Initially assume the relevant cost curve is MC_1. The optimising worker will choose a reservation wage of W^*_1. In recession marginal costs of search for all jobs sampled rise, and hence the marginal cost curve shifts to MC_2. The reservation wage falls to W^*_2. If the recession is thought to be permanent (or nearly so) by workers and/or if the mean duration of spells of unemployment rise dramatically the acceptance probability may be close or even equal to unity. In Britain, for example, in 1984 as we have seen, mean unemployment duration for males is 41 weeks. The re-employment probability calculated by Atkinson, Micklewright, Gomulka and Rau (1984) at this duration is significantly less than 5%. This is consistent with a value of the acceptance probability of the average unemployed worker which is close to unity.

263

In recession it would seem that acceptance probabilities are likely to be so high that for the average unemployed worker the notion of 'voluntary' unemployment is almost meaningless. Of course there will be some short term unemployed workers for whom this is not true. In boom, on the other hand, we can expect β_t to fall significantly and voluntary unemployment in increase.

The inverse movement of κ_t and β_t is therefore quite likely to make the value of U_t^* cyclically invariant. However the natural rate could increase in recession if the rate of inflow (α_t) increases. Recall from Chapter 2 that the rate of inflow is governed principally by the layoff and the quit rate. Since these move inversely the inflow rate (at least for males) exhibits, as we have seen, very little cyclical variation. The conclusion is that for male workers we should not expect to observe significant cyclical variation in the natural rate itself. This view has, of course, been implicit in the previous three chapters where non-natural unemployment was defined as $U_t - U_t^*$ as if the value of U_t^* were constant. In the case of female workers the degree of cyclical variability in α_t (which is underestimated by registered unemployment statistics) will mean that this assumption is less justifiable and we might expect U_t^* to increase somewhat in recession and decrease in boom.

The Natural Rate in Britain

The calculation of the natural rate is, as we have already seen, bedevilled with statistical difficulties. The alternative methods we have reviewed in Chapters 3 and 6 all provide potentially biased measures. The VU method employed by Armstrong and Taylor (1981) and Hannah (1984) suffers from the problems of under recording of both vacancies and unemployment. In order to see the scale of the measurement problem, consider Armstrong and Taylor's measure of U_t^* in 1973 using recorded vacancies and unemployment. This is 375.6 thousand compared with the 604 thousand when vacancy registration bias is allowed for, and 500 thousand when unemployment registration bias is also accounted for. Given this lack of precision there is clearly a long way to go before we can rely on the VU estimates of U_t^*.

One thing, however, is clear from these estimates, and that is that there has been a major increase in U_t^* since the mid-sixties. Other methods of estimating the natural rate are also flawed in one

or more respects. The flow equilibrium unemployment
rate adopted by Nickell (1982) is an example. It
suffers from the drawback mentioned in the last
chapter that if the secular variables used to
calculate it contain a disequilibrium component the
measure of the natural rate will be biased upwards.
Nickell, for example, initially presents estimates
of U_t^* which suggest that between 1969 and 1979 the
natural rate rose by 3.22 percentage points. This,
however, includes the product wage and an
international competitiveness variable as secular
variables used to compute the natural rate. Since,
for example, the real product wage has a
disequilibrium component its effect should be
excluded. Nickell does this and his estimate of U_t^*
falls from 5.82% in 1979 to 5.35% and the increase
since 1969 to 2.64 percentage points. A similar point
can be made in respect of the calculation of Minford
(1983).

Some recent estimates of the natural rate use
the so-called NAIRU method. In general these give
bigger estimates of the natural rate and of the
increase that has taken place since the mid-sixties.
The method relies upon Friedman's (1968) prediction
that if unemployment is below its natural rate,
inflation accelerates and vice versa if unemployment
is above the natural rate. Since inflation is stable
at U_t^* if the value of unemployment at which this
happens can be calculated this could be regarded as
the natural rate. Not surprisingly as inflation
reached higher levels in the 1970s so do the
calculated value of the NAIRU. Sumner (1978), for
example, calculates the value of unemployment
consistent with a constant growth in money wages
(equal to productivity growth) and a zero growth in
prices. This produces rather high estimates of U_t^* at
2.4% in the mid 1960s and 5.1% in the mid 1970s.
Grubb, Jackman and Layard (1982, 1983) also make use
of the NAIRU method. They estimate a wage and price
inflation equation and use this to compute the value
of unemployment at which their inflation rate is
stable. (1) Basically their view is that the feasible
rate of growth of real wages fell in the 1970s
principally because of the rise in import prices, and
the fall in labour productivity growth.

If workers pursue wage claims that require a
growth in real wages above this level employers are
forced to raise the rate of price inflation to bring
real wage growth down to the feasible level. This
could lead to further wage and price inflation. One
way this process could be corrected would be a rise

in unemployment since this will enforce a downward revision of real wage expectations to the 'feasible' level. NAIRU will then rise because it is the unemployment rate needed to contain the inflationary pressure resulting from these unrealistic real wage aspirations. These ideas can be shown within the context of a money wage inflation model. Algebraically

7.2. $\dot{W}_t = \alpha_1 \dot{P}_t^e + \alpha_2 (U_t - U_t^*) + \alpha_3 (W/P_t^* - W/P_t)$

Money wage inflation depends positively ($\alpha_1 > 0$) on the expected inflation rate, negatively on the excess of unemployment over the natural rate ($\alpha_2 < 0$). It also depends on the gap between the desired real wage level (W/P_t^*) and its actual value (W/P_t). The greater is the discrepancy between real wage aspirations and the actual value ($W/P_t^* > W/P_t$) the greater will be the increase in money wages ($\alpha_3 > 0$). If we assume that inflation is correctly anticipated ($\alpha_1 = 1$) we can derive the following

7.3 $\dot{W}_t - \dot{P}_t^e = 0 = \alpha_2 (U_t - U_t^*) + \alpha_3 (W/P_t^* - W/P_t)$

and

7.4 $U_t - U_t^* = \dfrac{-\alpha 3}{\alpha_2} (W/P_t^* - W/P_t)$

Since α_3 is positive and α_2 is negative this means that if real wage aspirations exceed the actual level ($W/P_t^* > W/P_t$) unemployment must exceed the natural rate ($-\alpha_3/\alpha_2 > 0$). The revision of expectations which results will eventually bring real wage aspirations into line so that unemployment will eventually equal the natural rate. However, both natural and non-natural unemployment will have risen in the short run and may also persist in the long run. As a result estimates of the natural rate from this method are generally too high and show a larger increase since the 1960s than the alternative available. It is easy to show this diagramatically. Consider Figure 7.3. Initially the economy is in equilibrium at W/P_1, E_1^* and U_1^*. There is positive growth in labour productivity or negative growth in imported input prices (and other relevant factors) that shift the demand curve to D_E^2. Employment could rise but if it does not an increase in real wages to W/P_2 is feasible. If workers' real wage aspirations shift the labour supply to S_E^2 there is no problem. Real wages will rise to W/P_2 and the natural rate is undisturbed at U^*_1. Suppose, however, real wage aspirations shift the labour supply curve to S_E^3. In this case labour market equilibrium will be reached at a lower level of employment (E^*_2) and a higher natural rate of unemployment (U^*_2). Note however the real wage has risen above the 'feasible' level (to W/P_3) achieved by an acceleration in the rate of wage inflation. The non-accelerating inflation rate gives a lower real wage of W/P_2. Clearly if aspirations are not revised downwards price and wage inflation will continue to accelerate. It is quite likely (and consistent with historical experience) that the government will step in and reduce the inflationary pressure. This may be done by cuts in the fiscal deficit, for example. This will shift the <u>effective</u> demand curve downwards so that it intersects the supply curve S_E at W/P_2. Employment falls to E_3 and unemployment rises to U_3 which exceeds the natural rate U^*_2. Two changes therefore take place in the level of unemployment. The natural (equilibrium) rate of unemployment has risen from U^*_1 to U^*_2. Non-natural unemployment has also risen from zero to $U_3 - U^*_2$. The extra unemployment necessary to contain the inflation pressure which results from 'non-feasible' real wage aspirations is partly natural and partly non-natural. The NAIRU method assumes all of it to be increases in the natural rate so not surprisingly it tends to exaggerate the size of U^* and the extent of its increase in Britain where governments, especially in the last decade, have responded in the way we have supposed.

Figure 7.3

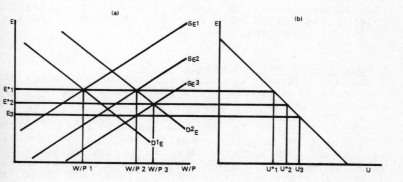

267

With this in mind we can now consider the up-to-date estimates of Layard, Basevi, Blanchard, Buiter and Dornbusch (1984). They estimate a NAIRU version of the natural rate and the results are shown in Table 7.1.

Table 7.1: The Natural Rate in Britain

	1966–70	1971–75	1976–80	1981–83
U_t^* (%)	2.2	4.0	5.5	9.0

Source: Layard et al (1984)

Although these estimates are likely to be generally on the high side, it is, nonetheless, clear the U_t^* has risen significantly in Britain since the mid-1960s. In fact all the evidence confirms this whatever the method of calculation. There may be some uncertainty as to the extent of the rise but the evidence confirms the view that if a successful policy to reduce non-natural unemployment were devised, the target level of unemployment to be reached by such a policy is bound to be higher now than twenty years ago. Given the error in the estimates that we have for the value of U_t^*, we cannot be too precise but it is difficult to believe unemployment in Britain can be lowered much below two million without policies which are designed to reduce the natural rate itself. This requires the determination of the significant variables which explain the natural rate and the spectacular rise in its level since the mid-1960s. The remainder of this chapter concentrates on the supply side factors in the labour market. In Chapter 8 we will examine the role of the demand side forces in the determination of the natural rate.

Labour Supply and the Natural Rate
A secular rise in the natural rate of unemployment can occur as a result of an increase in the rate of growth of the labour supply. In Figure 7.4 this is shown by considering employment and unemployment stocks. In frame 'b' a rise in the labour force shifts the EU mapping outwards and the horizontal section of the S_E curve upwards if the equilibrium level of employment stays the same the natural level of unemployment will rise to U_2^*. In effect there is

an increase in the degree of voluntary unemployment since we have assumed the supply curve itself does not shift. The increase in the labour supply simply increases the number of workers unwilling to work at W/P_1. In terms of our flow analysis an increase in the rate of growth of the labour supply or its level would show up in permanent or once-for-all changes in the aggregate unemployment inflow rate (α_t).

Figure 7.4

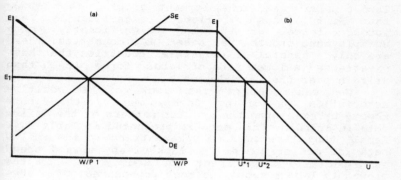

There is, however, little evidence to suggest this is a significant feature of rising unemployment in Britain. Metcalf and Nickell (1985) collate and present some relevant data.

Table 7.2: Labour Supply and Unemployment in Britain

	1959–66	1966–71	1971–77	1977–84
ΔL_t (change in the labour force)	+1456	–513	+1153	+789
ΔU_t (change in unemployment)	–139	+443	+726	+1580

Source: Metcalf and Nickell (1985)

We can see that in the period in which the labour force increased to the greatest extent (1959-66) unemployment actually fell. In addition in the late sixties when U_t^* started its upward shift, the labour force fell (in size). Recently (1977-84) the increase in employment overall and in U_t^* is the most pronounced and yet the increase in the labour force is modest compared with 1971-77 and 1959-66. Evidence from the 1930s confirms that increases in the labour supply do not necessarily increase unemployment. In that decade the labour supply went up by 11% and unemployment was halved. International comparisons confirm this lack of association between labour supply and unemployment growth. This shows that Britain has experienced significantly less labour force growth and significantly more unemployment growth than other OECD countries. There are only a handful of industrial countries that have experienced a lower rate of labour force growth than Britain over the last decade.

We can confirm the lack of a positive association of rising unemployment with labour supply by examining the secular pattern of the inflow rate in Britain. This data is presented in Table 2.7. Recall that it showed no upward trend in the inflow rate for men or women. The lack of any upward trend is especially significant for women for whom the growth in labour supply is most pronounced. Of course the inflow rate is also influenced by other flows (quits and layoffs), so some caution is needed. However, it would be surprising if some upward trend in α_t did not occur if an increase in the labour force did cause higher unemployment and a higher natural rate because these flows tend to move inversely giving an otherwise constant value of α_t. In other words any trend in α_t is most likely to reflect the effect of labour force growth. Since there is no upward trend there seems little reason to believe labour force growth has led to higher values of U_t^*. In fact if there is any association between labour force size and unemployment the causation is likely to be in the opposite direction with a negative association between the two. This is because of the 'discouraged worker' effect. Labour supply studies in Britain have shown how important this is. (2) Rising unemployment deters potential workers from entering the labour force because of the greater probability of failure in job search. In Chapter 1 we considered the scale of the discouraged worker effect in Britain. It is clearly positive and this is confirmed (crudely) by the data in Table 7.2 which, if anything, shows the negative association of changes in the labour force, and changes in unemployment which we would expect if the 'discouraged worker' effect were important.

It seems clear that we can safely reject the notion that excess growth in the labour force has caused the rise in the natural rate of unemployment in Britain.

Unemployment Benefit and the Natural Rate

A rise in the natural rate can occur as a result of the operation of an unemployment benefit system. In the analysis of labour market stocks this is depicted as a shift in the labour supply curve (downwards in Figure 7.3) which raises equilibrium real wages, reduces equilibrium employment and raises the natural rate. In the search and flow analysis this is tantamount to a reduction in the acceptance probability (β_t) and an associated rise in the average reservation wage in the economy. We have seen in earlier chapters that for the individual worker the acceptance probability rises and the reservation wage falls during a spell of unemployment. At the aggregate level we need to assume a constant structure of unemployment spell lengths in order to draw sharper conclusions for the macroeconomy from studies of individual behaviour. One factor that determines the individual's acceptance probability (and the aggregate mean probability) is the cost of undertaking job search. Since these costs are significantly influenced by an unemployment benefit scheme we should expect some kind of relationship with individual and economy wide unemployment experience. Theoretically, there are two main ways in which the existence and generosity of a benefit system can affect the acceptance probability (β_t). Firstly, unemployment benefit lowers the most important cost of search (lost work income). Consider Figure 7.5. Initially we assume marginal search costs and benefits curves which are the same as those in Figure 3.2. Marginal costs and benefits of search are equated at W^*. Suppose the unemployment benefit system becomes more generous in its scale of payment or more lax in its administration. Both will lower the marginal (and total) costs of search and will raise the reservation wage to W_2^* which lowers the acceptance probability at each stage of an unemployment spell. In the aggregate the unemployment outflow probability will fall and the natural rate will therefore rise. Secondly, the

271

payment of unemployment benefit increases the value
of leisure (by decreasing its cost) so that we should
expect increased consumption of leisure which
prolongs optimal search periods and reinforces the
reduction in the acceptance probability. These
effects should not be regarded as necessarily
inefficient. On the one hand they represent a
desirable intertemporal substitution of leisure for
work for the worker who contributes to the
unemployment scheme. In addition the prolongation of
job search prevents the 'snatching' of jobs which
leads to a highly unstable labour force. Prolonged
search is more likely to lead to more permanent
matching. This not only reduces turnover costs for
the firm but also creates benefits for the economy as
a whole.

Figure 7.5

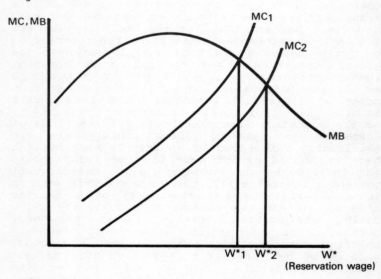

These arguments suggest that β_t (the acceptance
probability) will vary inversely with the generosity
of unemployment benefits.

The natural rate at the aggregate level could
also be changed because of the impact of changes in
the unemployment benefit system on the inflow rate
(α_t). If the system reduces the total costs of job
search it increases the incentive to workers to quit

their current job and search full-time. Full-time search is efficient but more costly. (3) A reduction in its cost makes it a more attractive strategy to the worker seeking alternative employment. Individual (and aggregate) inflow probabilities will, therefore, rise with positive effects on the natural rate of unemployment.

Initially we will consider the evidence for these propositions at the individual level. This work has concentrated on the effects of unemployment benefit on the acceptance probability (β_t) and, hence, on the individual re-employment probability (θit). The literature is extensive but the basic methodology is similar and involves the estimation of the re-employment probability for an individual i at time t during an unemployment spell. This is discussed in Chapter 2 but we recall it here as

7.5 $\quad \theta it = e^{\beta' X_i}_{at} t^{a-1}$

where X_i is a vector of characteristics and β a vector of associated coefficients.

We have already seen in Chapter 2 the importance of a as an indicator (in 7.5) of duration dependence in unemployment experience. Our interest here is, however, in the estimated effect of unemployment benefit and other unemployment income on θi_t <u>given</u> the impact of individual characteristics, duration dependence, and so on.

The calculation of unemployment income is a critical empirical issue. Most data sources used to estimate 7.5 do not contain a direct measure of unemployment income, so a variable has to be constructed. This is done, for example, by Nickell (1979) using 1972 GHS data which does not contain direct measures of unemployment and income. The basic measure constructed by Nickell is the sum of unemployment benefits, supplementary benefits, rate rebates, family allowances, free school meal allowances, wife's income and post-tax unearned income. He calculates alternatives which allow for the use of information on benefits and previous earnings. This ensures a more accurate calculation of the earnings related supplement which was paid as a component of unemployment benefit until its abolition under the 1980 Social Security Act. The level of benefits is then compared with the income which an unemployed male would receive while in work. Since previous income estimates may not be

satisfactory or available Nickell fits an earnings
function to estimate an individual's expected work
income given his characteristics - age, education,
skill, and so on. To this is added wife's income,
unearned income and other benefits (like family
allowance) to which the unemployed individual
remains entitled while in work. Taxation and national
insurance are then calculated and deducted. The ratio
of the calculated benefit and income is then used as
an explanatory variable of the re-employment
probability.

Using this estimate of unemployment income,
Nickell finds a significant negative relationship
with the re-employment probability with an
elasticity of duration lying between 0.6 and 1.0
depending on the specification and the particular
method of measurement selected. Significantly
Nickell also finds that the impact of the
benefit/income ratio on the re-employment probability is much reduced once an individual has been
unemployed for six months or more. Once workers have
been unemployed for this time it would seem they have
exhausted the voluntary component of their
unemployment spell (actual duration exceeds desired
duration) and optimal search considerations no
longer apply. Nickell considers the impact of his
estimates upon unemployment in the late sixties and
early seventies. He finds that of the increase in
unemployment between the boom years of 1963 and 1973
only 14% can be attributed to the impact of
unemployment benefit on durations. He also
calculates that the introduction of the earnings
related supplement in 1966 added only 10% (less than
50,000) to the unemployment rate. The conclusion from
Nickell's work is that the impact of unemployment
benefit schemes of unemployment is modest and that
there is little in these calculations to justify the
recent abolition of ERS. (4) The problem remains,
however, that even sophisticated methods of
calculating unemployment income are bedevilled with
difficulties as Dilnot and Morris (1983) and
Micklewright (1985) clearly demonstrate. Micklewright concludes his study as follows:

> economists modelling the effects of unemploy-
> ment benefit on labour supply need access to
> information on actual benefits, or need to
> construct more realistic simulation models than
> has hitherto been the case.

One piece of work that does have access to

information on actual benefits received is that of Narendrenathan, Nickell and Stern (1985) which uses the DHSS cohort study of 1978/79. We have already considered some of their results from the estimation of equation 7.2 using the same data source in Chapter 2. Since the data used by Narendrenathan, Nickell and Stern is provided by the DHSS, it was possible to obtain a direct measure of benefit paid to the 2332 males in the cohort using DHSS computer records. This was supplemented by interview data on other forms of unemployment income like Family Income Supplement, housing and tax rebates, wife's income and so on. This direct information is then deflated by a measure of earnings derived from an earnings function of the type employed earlier by Nickell (1979).

It turns out that this measure is negatively related to the re-employment probability via the reservation wage/acceptance probability effect. Increases in benefit and more generally unemployment income increase reservation wages, decrease acceptance probabilities and increase the duration of unemployment. The estimated elasticity of unemployment duration is in the range 0.35 - 0.47 which is slightly lower than Nickell's (1979) estimate using GHS data. (5) Narendrenathan, Nickell and Stern also confirm Nickell's earlier results which suggests the unemployment income effect only has an impact on the search behaviour of those unemployed for less than six months. Contrary to most other studies (Lynch (1983) for example), they also find the elasticity of duration is highest for those aged less than 20. For those aged 44 and over the estimated elasticity is actually zero.

At the aggregate level these results imply that abolition of ERS has reduced the natural rate of unemployment by, at most, a modest 120,000 (about half a percentage point reduction in the unemployment rate). Atkinson, Gomulka, Micklewright and Rau (1984) use Family Expenditure Survey data with which it is also possible to get close to a direct measure of unemployment income. Their results confirm this modest impact of unemployment benefits on job search and unemployment duration. In fact their estimate for 1975-77 is statistically insignificantly different from zero. For the earlier 1972-75 period they obtain an estimate very close to that of Nickell (1979). There is, therefore, a remarkable degree of consensus on the effects of unemployment benefit on the acceptance probability. The effect is significant but small. At the aggregate level only a small part of the increase in U_t^* and an even smaller part of the increase in unemployment as a whole can be explained in this way. The abolition of ERS has had a very modest effect in reducing the natural rate.

Aggregate time series evidence can also be examined to detect the effect of increases in benefit. Table 7.3 contains data on the replacement ratio (6) obtained from Layard and Nickell (1985).

Table 7.3: Replacement Ratio 1963–1983

	1963	1967	1971	1975	1979	1983
Replace-ment Ratio	43.9	52.6	50.6	49.2	46.0	54.4

Source: Layard and Nickell (1985b), page 86.

Note the jump in the replacement rate in the mid-1960s caused by the introduction of ERS. After that there is a notable downward trend until the 1980s, when the replacement ratio rises again despite the abolition of ERS.

The studies of aggregate flows by Nickell (1982) and Junankar and Price (1983) provide evidence on the effect of these movements in unemployment benefits upon both the inflow and outflow rates. It is possible, therefore, to examine whether the greater incentive to full-time search afforded by benefit increase has had any effect, as well as to test for the effect on outflows. Nickell finds no evidence for the former effect (on inflows) (7) but does confirm the negative effect of increases in the replacement ratio on the outflow (via β_t) probability. Junankar and Price do, however, find a significant inflow effect but somewhat bizarrely find that increases in benefit _increase_ outflows. One explanation may be the inclusion in their sample period (Nickell's ends in 1977) of years in which benefit was falling as unemployment outflows were also falling. Whatever the explanation, there is scant evidence here of a significant effect of the replacement ratio on unemployment. In fact Nickell finds in a decomposition of the rise in unemployment between 1969-1977 that the movements in the replacement rate over that period actually _reduced_ the natural rate of unemployment.

However, most of the time series evidence uses unemployment stock rather than the flow data used by Nickell (1982) and Junankar and Price (1983). In general it confirms the idea that increases in unemployment benefit (especially because of ERS) raised the natural rate of unemployment. There is, however, some disagreement as to the scale of the effect. The seminal paper for the post-war period is that of Maki and Spindler (1975). They estimate an ad hoc equation of the form

7.6 $\quad \log U_t = \alpha_0 + \alpha_1 B/Y_t + \alpha_2 z_{1t} + \alpha_3 z_{2t} + \alpha_4 z_{2t-1}$

$\qquad \alpha_1 > 0 \ \alpha_2 > 0 \ \alpha_3 < 0 \ \alpha_4 < 0$

where

B/Y is the benefit/income ratio

z_{1t} is a measure of labour supply

z_{2t} is the ratio of GNP to trend

All the signs when estimated for a sample period that stretches from the 1950s to the early 1970s are as expected, and are all significantly different from zero. The coefficient α_1 is large and implies an increase in U_t^* as a result of the introduction of the earnings related supplement in 1966 of 110,000. Some confirmation for their view can be found from the study of Batchelor and Sheriff (1980). We have already considered the evidence they advance which supports the idea that departures from U_t^* result from expectational errors. In order to test this hypothesis they specify some determinants of U_t^* itself which include a benefit/income variable. In fact they do not use the B/Y series but instead employ a dummy variable which takes the value of unity only during those years in which ERS was paid. The results are not entirely robust but they do imply the introduction of ERS had a once-for-all effect (upwards) on U_t^* in the mid-1960s that has not subsequently increased. However, it does suggest that its abolition should have reduced U_t^*. The verification of the Maki and Spindler result is therefore a matter of considerable empirical and policy interest.

In fact, the Maki and Spindler study has been widely criticised. The coefficient of B/Y was reduced to insignificance by Taylor's (1977) use of a time trend and by Cubbin and Foley's (1977) inclusion of a permanent income variable in equation 7.6. Junankar (1981) introduces variables that reflect structural changes in the British economy indicating the relative decline of the manufacturing sector which not only reduce the B/Y coefficient for the period 1952-1975 (and 1952-65, 1952-70) to statistical insignificance but also reverses its (insignificantly) sign. Sawyer (1979) has also indicated the substantial degree of instability in Maki and Spindler's results. Junankar (1981) confirms this instability all of which has led to some well-founded scepticism about the Maki and Spindler results.

The study has also been criticised for the ad hoc nature of its estimating equation and in particular the relationship of unemployment to employment, labour demand and supply. The micro behavioural aspects are obscure. More satisfactory are the estimates obtained from structural models of the labour market by Minford (1983), Andrews and Nickell (1982), Nickell and Andrews (1983), Andrews (1984) and Layard and Nickell (1985). Most of these studies reveal a small but significant effect of increasing unemployment benefit on the natural rate of unemployment. The impact appears no greater in some models that assume market clearing from others that do not make these assumptions. Andrews (1984), for example, using an equilibrium model of the labour market finds that the coefficient on the replacement ratio in the labour supply equation is negative but small in size. Andrews and Nickell (1982) on the other hand find a relationship between unemployment and the replacement ratio which is similar in sign and scale to that found in cross section studies using data for unemployed individuals. Their results suggest the maximum effect of the introduction of ERS in the mid 1960s was to increase the natural rate by 80,000 with a lower bound of 55,000. That is slightly less than the Maki-Spindler estimate. Even if we accepted the upper estimate it looks small in comparison with a total rise in unemployment of 3 million and in the natural rate of at least 1½ million. (8)

The most up-to-date time series work is that of Layard and Nickell (1985) which includes the recent period in which the replacement ratio appears to have risen slightly. They use a three equation model for prices, wages and employment, in which benefits shift the labour supply curve and lead to higher real wages. Through the labour demand equation this leads to higher unemployment in the manner shown in Figure 7.2. In a sense making the benefit system more generous helps to create 'non-feasible' real wage levels and raises NAIRU. Layard and Nickell's empirical results found that this was the case in the mid-1960s. Their maximum estimates shows that nearly 30% of the increase in unemployment between 1956-66 and 1967-74 can be accounted for by the rise in the replacement ratio in the mid 1960s. However this represents only .54 of a percentage point on the unemployment rate (125,000 workers). The effect in the 1970s and 1980s, however, was to reduce unemployment by a modest amount - less than .2 of a percentage point. There seems little evidence here to attribute more than a modest proportion of the increasing unemployment at the natural rate over the last twenty years to the impact of unemployment benefit.

However, Minford (1983) argues that the consensus view underestimates the true benefit effect. The theoretical arguments revolve around Minford's use of a model of the labour market which has a union and a non-union sector. The details are laid out in the previous chapter but we reproduce here the relevant diagram (Figure 6.2) as Figure 7.6 to show the effect of raising the unemployment benefit level.

Figure 7.6

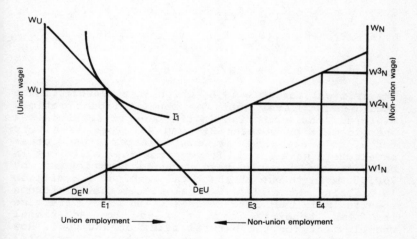

The real wage in the union sector is W_u with employment at E_1. If the entire labour supply is to be employed, the real wage needs to be W_N^1. Then non-union employment equals $L-E_1$ (L is the labour supply). If the real wage is above W_N^1 there will be unemployment. This is the effect of raising unemployment benefit. Suppose the benefit level is initially above W_N^1 and equal to W_N^2. Since this shifts the labour supply curve (as in Figure 7.3) and leads to a 'non-feasible' real wage, the market clears with E_3-E_1 unemployed. Since the labour market is cleared (recall Minford assumes this), E_3-E_1 represents the increment to the natural rate (market clearing rate) of unemployment. If the benefit level is raised (by EBS, for example) the equilibrium real wage rises to W_N^3 and the natural rate increases by E_4-E_3. Of course the effects are much exaggerated in Figure 7.6, but it explains Minford's view that it is the combination of a highly unionised economy <u>with</u> a generous system of unemployment benefits that is crucial in explaining high unemployment in Britain. As we saw in Chapter 6, Minford (1983) tests this assertion by estimating a labour demand (unemployment) equation and a labour supply (real wage) equation. The details are discussed in the previous chapter, but we reproduce them here for convenience (both are in logs except T_L and T_F).

6.9 $\quad U_t = \delta_0 + \delta_1(\frac{W^e}{P}t + T_{Ft}) + \delta_2 Y_t^e + \delta_3 t + \delta_4 U_{t-1} + \varepsilon_t$

6.14 $\quad W/P_t = \beta_0 + \beta_1(P_t - P_t^e) + \beta_{2qt} + \beta_3 UNR_t + \beta_4 L_t + \beta_5 T_{Lt}$

$\qquad\qquad + \beta_6 B_t + \beta_7 U_t + \beta_8 W/P_{t-1} + \mu_t$

The critical variable is B_t which is a measure of the real benefit level (not the benefit/income ratio). Minford finds a 1% rise in the benefit level raises unemployment by between $2\frac{1}{4}$% and 4%. This is a very large estimate and is much larger than other researchers have found. It suggests that a 10% cut in benefit levels would have reduced unemployment by 700,000 when it was at the total level of 2.8 million in Britain. Nickell (1984) calculates that Minford's results imply that between 1967-8 and 1978-9 the rise in real benefits of 14% led to additional unemployment (on the natural rate) of 980,000!. How does Minford get such large and untypical results? One explanation might be in the calculation of the benefits variable. Minford's calculations use benefit rules so they do not refer to actual benefit received. We have already referred to Micklewright's (1985) stricture on this point. Minford also uses benefit levels rather than the ratio of benefits to income (the replacement ratio) widely used in other studies. The ratio has fallen in the 1970s while real benefit levels have risen. At least the variable is trending in the same direction as unemployment (upwards) and this might help explain Minford's result. This, however, does not seem crucial. Nickell and Andrews (1983) use a similar variable and find it only has a 'marginal effect on employment' and unemployment which is in stark contrast to Minford's results.

Nickell (1984) provides some alternative clues as to the explanation. He points out that the large long run effect of all the variables in the real wage equation (6.14) result from the large size of the coefficient on the lagged value of real wages (β_8). In order to retrieve the long run coefficients we have to divide the estimated coefficients from 6.14 (including β_6) by $(1-\beta_8)$. (9) Since $1-\beta_8$ is small the long run effects are bound to be large. Nickell also attributes the large size of β_8 to the exclusion from 6.13 of several key variables. In particular Nickell argues that because 6.13 contains no variables that can explain the upward movement of real wages over time the coefficient on the lagged value of real wages (β_8) is spuriously large. Nickell and Andrews (1983) in contrast obtained estimates from the fully specified wage equation which does contain relevant variables and, as we have seen, these give only small effects of increased benefit levels on unemployment. It also uses annual data.

Minford (1984) argues for the superiority of results which use quarterly data. He estimates an equation suggested by Nickell (1984) which includes key variables (including the capital labour ratio and relative imported input prices) omitted from 6.14. In the results the value of the lagged real wage coefficient (β_8) remains large, contrary to Nickell's assertions. However the coefficient on unemployment benefits (β_6) actually becomes insignificantly different from zero in this extended version of 6.14. Similar things happen with annual data although here β_8 is actually zero and so the long run coefficients are those actually obtained from estimating 6.14. (10) In the light of these results it would seem that Minford's results are seriously flawed. From an empirical point of view he has failed to make out a case for the credibility of his estimates. (11) It would seem, therefore, the consensus view is appropriate - raising unemployment benefits does raise the natural rate. The effect, however, is small and is largely confined to the

1960s in Britain. It has little or nothing to do with the increase in unemployment over the last decade. (12)

Some researchers have also considered the stringency with which the unemployment benefit system is administered. Clearly the more stringent is the administration the greater is the probability of a worker accepting a job offer and the lower will be U_t^*. Layard (1983) presents some evidence that from the late 1960s social security became more easily available in Britain. This, together with changes in social attitudes to receiving benefit, may have contributed to the rise in the natural rate since that time. Some evidence for the importance of the former effect is contained in the papers by Nickell (1982) and Minford (1983). The variable used is the number of unemployed benefit recipients who are denied benefit for refusing work expressed as a proportion of new benefit claimants. The ratio is divided by the number of unfilled vacancies on the grounds that disqualification would clearly vary positively with that number. Nickell finds that there was a marked downward trend in this measure with the 1977 measure less than a quarter of its 1968 value. This relaxation of pressure on the unemployed had an upward effect on outflows from unemployment (no evidence for any effect on inflows is found) adding half a percentage point to the unemployment rate between 1969-1977. However these results are ambiguous because the relevant coefficient is just insignificant. Minford's evidence does not confirm this result (13) but nevertheless the evidence rather weakly suggests that the stringency with which the benefit system is administered may have had a more marked effect on U_t^* in Britain (at least until 1977) than the degree of generosity which has been given so much attention in the literature. That, however, in the 1970s is not to claim a great deal.

The Natural Rate - Other Supply Side Determinants

The acceptance probability and the natural rate of unemployment are both influenced by a variety of other supply side factors. In his study of the shift in the vacancies/unemployment relationship in the mid-1960s in Britain, Gujarati (1972) placed considerable emphasis upon the role of statutory redundancy payments introduced in 1975 in explaining the mid-sixties increase in U_t^*. Unfortunately he presents no direct evidence. Subsequently Mackay and Reid (1972) and Andrews and Nickell (1982) have shown the effect to be small. In the former case significantly smaller than the effect of the rate of unemployment benefit and in the latter about the same. Using individual level data Narendrenathan, Nickell and Stern (1985) also show this small effect. A man receiving redundancy pay of £5000 has a lower acceptance and hence re-employment probability but the effect is to raise his expected unemployment duration by only 2 weeks. There are good theoretical reasons for expecting the effect to be small. The redundancy payment is a lump sum payment so we can expect a possible income effect on leisure and hence a negative effect on the acceptance probability. On the other hand it does not affect the relative costs of leisure, work and search. There is no substitution effect. Since the marginal costs of job search are unaffected, in principle the acceptance probability should also be unaffected by redundancy payments. Indeed it was this property that led Hammermesh (1977) to argue for the replacement of conventional unemployment benefit by a lump sum payment to the unemployed. He calculates, using Mackay and Reid's (1972) results, that a lump sum equivalent to ninety times the average weekly unemployment benefit would have the same effect on the acceptance probability.

Some evidence also exists on the impact of direct and indirect taxes on unemployment. Here we concentrate on their effect on the supply side of the labour market. Since the mid-1950s there has been a marked increase in both the average direct and indirect tax rate. The imposition of these taxes reduces the net real consumption wage received at any given value of the real product wage. This so-called 'tax-wedge' can create upward pressure on gross real product wage aspirations as workers seek to maintain and advance their own standard of living (net real wage). Effects of this kind exist in model of money wage adjustment in Britain (like equation 7.2). Henry, Sawyer and Smith (1976) for example, find gross money (and hence real) wage increases are larger as a result of a rise in the direct tax rate. Clearly this could also induce a shift in the labour supply curve which would lower the equilibrium level of employment and raise the natural rate of unemployment. This is shown in Figure 7.7. Initially equilibrium is at a gross real wage of W/P_1 with equilibrium employment at E^* and unemployment at U^*. Suppose there is an increase in the direct tax rate. In order to achieve the same net real wage workers require an increase in the gross real wage to W/P_2. The labour supply curve shifts to the right.

Equilibrium employment is now at E_2^* and the natural rate has risen to U_2^*. In terms of the search model framework we have employed an increase in the tax rate raises the reservation gross real wage and reduces the acceptance probability for any gross wage offer. Since β_t falls the natural rate of unemployment rises. This is because workers refuse wage offers because the net pay is insufficient to compensate them for the disutility of work. In other words voluntary unemployment is increased by upward movements in tax rates.

Figure 7.7

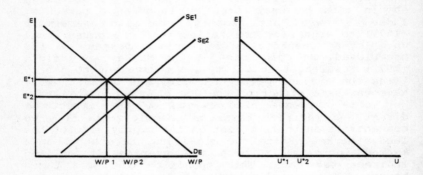

A number of attempts have been made to isolate an effect of this kind within structural models of the labour market. Clearly its existence is of some importance to those who argue that the labour supply side effects of cuts in taxes will reduce unemployment. This is something we will examine further in Chapter 9. In fact most studies show the effect to be small, ambiguous, or even non-existent. Nickell and Andrews (1983), for example, find a statistically insignificant link between tax rates and employment. In their recent study Layard and Nickell (1985) conclude: 'Our estimates suggest that the rise in these taxes has had no impact on unemployment'. These results are not really a surprise. Conventional single equation labour supply modelling has not been able to identify a significant effect on labour supply using individual or aggregate data. Andrews (1983), for example, finds a small net real wage supply elasticity in his study of the aggregate labour market (14). Shifts in the supply curve in the manner of Figure 7.7 are likely to be small or non-existent. The main exception to this consensus is again Minford (1983). He finds very large effects. Using Minford's estimates Nickell (1984) calculates that direct tax increases caused an increase in unemployment of 780,000 between 1967-9 and 1978-9. In fact the reasons for this high estimate are the same as in the case of unemployment benefit. The specification of the real wage equations assumes the same coefficient on unemployment benefits as the direct tax rate. Since the specification omits several key variables this and/or the coefficient on the lagged real wage variable will be biased. Minford's (1984) quarterly estimates using the full specification proposed by Nickell (1984) confirm this. Although the coefficient β_8 in equation 6.14 on lagged real wages is almost unchanged, that on the direct tax variable (income tax rate) is reduced to statistical insignificance. In view of this it would seem there is no robust evidence to support the view that increases in taxation have had significant effects on unemployment via the supply side of the labour market. Neither labour supply nor the related job search decision appear to have been significantly affected by tax changes. From this aspect of the matter tax cuts to reduce the tax wedge seem unlikely to reduce unemployment significantly in Britain.

Trade Unions and the Natural Rate

So far we have largely concentrated our discussion on the effects of individual labour supply decisions. Now we will turn our attention to the collective decisions made by trades unions. We saw in Chapter 6 that from a theoretical view trades unions can cause unemployment by using monopoly power to drive up the real wage or to prevent it adjusting to the market clearing level. In the former case this is tantamount to shifting the industry or aggregate labour supply curve in a fashion which causes lower equilibrium employment and a higher natural rate. We can also depict this as a rise in reservation wages in the economy as a whole which reduces the mean acceptance probability and raises the natural rate. In the latter wage rigidity case union behaviour causes disequilibrium (non-natural unemployment) to occur and persist. The theoretical basis for the former case is rather stronger than the latter. The popular union monopoly and efficient contract models demonstrate wage rigidity only under some rather stringent assumptions, unless we introduce union rivalry into the analysis. On the other hand the empirical case for the view that unions impede market clearing, is, as we have seen, a little stronger.

Since, in principle, unions can affect both the natural and non-natural rates of unemployment, there is a difficulty in measuring the scale of the union effect on either of these two magnitudes. This is a problem we have encountered already. In practice most empirical work assumes union behaviour has its impact only on the equilibrium natural rate. Since this procedure is bound to exaggerate the scale of the natural rate effect, we cannot pinpoint precisely the impact of trades union behaviour. However, the total impact of union behaviour on all types of unemployment can be measured by this procedure and this is, of course, useful. The effect of unions in the models used by Minford (1983), Nickell and Andrews (1983) and Layard and Nickell (1985) is a little more subtle than simply supposing shifts in the aggregate labour supply curve or in the average reservation wage in the economy take place. As we have seen in Minford's model unions push up wages in the union sector. This causes a reduction in employment in that sector which results in excess supply in the non-union sector. Full employment market clearing real wages are driven down below the unemployment benefit level. As a result the labour market in the non-union sector clears at a higher natural rate than would otherwise be the case. Note that unions cause higher unemployment among non-members and that this results both from their behaviour and, as we saw in the previous section, the workings of the benefit system. Minford's empirical procedure is, as we have seen, to estimate a real wage equation (6.14) in which the national unionisation rate appears as an exogenous variable. Clearly the coefficient (β_3) on this variable is expected to be positive. The higher level of real wages then increases equilibrium unemployment. This is what Minford finds. He also finds the effect to be very large. Every rise in the unionisation rate of 1 percentage point raises unemployment by 170,000 according to Minford's calculations. The actual rise in unionisation between the late 1960s and early 1980s would have raised unemployment by a massive 1½ million according to this estimate.

Nickell and Andrews (1983) adopt a slightly different framework. They assume a fully unionised economy justifiable on the grounds that most workers are paid a wage rate negotiated by a trades union. They also allow for wage bargaining between employer and employee. Recall that in the simple union monopoly model the union sets the wage unilaterally. They specify a real wage equation which contains more than one variable to capture the effect of unions. They acknowledge that the aggregate unionisation rate is a rather crude measure and augment it with a time series of the union/non-union differential. The argument they employ to justify the use of this variable is that an increase in union power leads to a higher differential and so it is a good proxy. Their results show (like Minford) the relevant coefficient (β_3) in an extended version of equation 6.13 is positive where both unionisation and the differential are used. In fact they find only the coefficient on the latter variable statistically significant. The long run impact on real wages and hence on employment of the upward movement in those union power variables is computed for Britain for the period 1951-1979. This reveals that between 1958-8 and 1974-9 the union action reduced employment (and raised unemployment) by a maximum of 400,000. Nickell and Andrews conclude:

> Given that employment is currently about four million below potential labour supply this suggests that the union effect, although substantial is hardly overwhelming.

Why is the Nickell and Andrew's estimate so much below that of Minford? (15) The answer is the same as we saw in the case of unemployment benefit. Minford's real wage equation is misspecified. Once we include the key variables he omits, the unionisation effect dwindles. Minford (1984) shows this himself in a real wage equation estimated for a longer time period (1951-81) using annual data (like Nickell and Andrews) and also using quarterly data. These reveal that when the real wage equation is fully specified the coefficient on the national unionisation rate not only becomes smaller it is also statistically insignificantly different from zero. Again we must conclude that the scale of the effect claimed by Minford is much exaggerated by the form of the real wage equation he estimates.

Confirmation that the impact of unions on real wages and unemployment is rather small comes from the recent work of Layard and Nickell (1985). In their model unions are the agency through which 'non-feasible' real wage expectations are articulated. This, as we have seen, raises the value of NAIRU. Although not a totally reliable indicator of the effects on U_t^*, it provides an estimate of the total unemployment effect of union action. The results suggest that between the early 1950s and the late 1970s union action increased the percentage unemployment rate by 1.7 points. This is very similar to the estimates of Nickell and Andrews (1983). For the period 1975-7 to 1980-3 the effect was to raise unemployment by about one-half a percentage point in a period when unemployment overall went up by 7 percentage points. These studies, therefore, seem to suggest that the growth in unionisation, in union organisation and strength especially since the 1960s, have had a definite but modest impact on total unemployment. The effect on the natural rate, though smaller, is bound nonetheless to be significant on the basis of these estimates.

However, considerable caution should be exercised before accepting these results. All the studies assume that unions have no effect on the labour demand curve so if unions raise wages they also reduce employment. If there is an efficiency wage effect so wages and labour productivity are positively related, the demand curve for labour will shift up. There are reasons for believing this to be a possibility. The introduction of unions into a plant leads to the emergence of a set of rules and judicial system necessary for the management of conflict in the plant. The existence of a union, especially in large plants, provides workers with a voice (16) which can be used to air and remedy grievances. The alternative for discontented workers in a non-union plant is to quit. As a result we should also expect job tenure to be greater in the union sector. This is what Freeman (1980) finds in the US. If job attachment increases labour productivity perhaps by 'learning by doing' effects, the labour demand curve will shift out. This might be reinforced if employers adopt forms of work organisation and management or employ machines which lead to higher productivity in the union plant. The effect is shown in Figure 7.8.

Figure 7.8

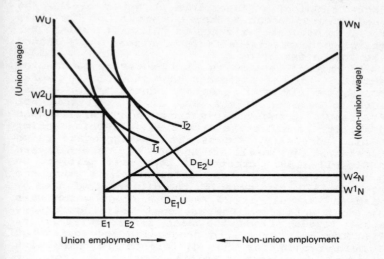

If we do not allow for these positive demand curve effects the union sector wage will be W_u^1. If the non-union labour market is to be cleared the wage is W_N. If unemployment benefit shifts the non-union labour supply curve market clearing will take place at a wage W_N with unemployment of (E_2-E_1) and a level of employment of E_2. Suppose that unions also cause an upward shift in the labour demand curve to $D_{E_2}U$. Tangency with the higher (I_2) indifference curve gives a wage of W_u^2 and employment of E_2. Now the non-union labour market clears at W_N^2 and E_2. There is no additional unemployment as a result of the unions. The effect on marginal products and hence on the demand curve offsets the impact of unions on real wages. Of course unions could have the reverse effect, so the estimates of Nickell and Andrews (1983) for example, could also be biased downward. Clearly this is an empirical matter. Aggregate labour market estimates need to take account of the effect of unions on the demand curve for us to be sure that the impact of unions on unemployment is correctly measured. Empirical work in the US by Brown and Medoff (1979), Clark (1982), Allen (1984) and others has shown a positive relation of trade union presence with labour productivity although a slightly more sceptical note has recently been struck by Clark

(1984). If such effects were found in Britain even the modest Layard and Nickell (1985) estimates of the effect of unions on unemployment would clearly be biased upwards because they do not allow for this effect. No adequate evidence on this point exists for Britain so the precise effects of unions on U_t^* cannot therefore be assessed.

Additional caution is also necessary because of the proxies for union effects used in empirical work. Unionisation may be a necessary condition for trades unions to have an effect, but it is certainly not sufficient. Strong organisation and a willingness and ability to undertake effective collection action are also necessary. The use of the aggregate union differential by Nickell and Andrews (1983) and Layard and Nickell (1985) creates further difficulties. On the whole the calculated differential is much too large. In 1975, for example, the differential used by Layard and Nickell is 24.7%. In a study which uses individual data from the National Training Survey, Stewart (1983a) finds the mean differential to be 7.7%. This only refers to production industries but the main reason for the difference is that with individual data more complete, correction for the characteristics of workers is possible. (17) In addition Stewart (1983a) and Geroski and Stewart (1985) find substantial variation in the average differential. There are many parts of the production sector where the measured differential is very small indeed.

A further difficulty with the use of unionisation or the differential in the real wage equation is that in practice neither is exogenous. Studies of unionisation and its rate of growth by Bain and el Sheikh (1976) and others and of union activity by Shorey (1976), Geroski and Knight (1983) and many others show this to be the case. Increases in real wages may also, for example, cause unionisation to increase. This possible reverse causation and endogeneity is clearly recognised by Nickell and Andrews (1983) and Minford (1983). However, no substantial attempt is made to deal with this problem, at least partly because of problems created by data availability and so on. For all of these reasons it is difficult to be totally convinced by the empirical work on the impact of the unions on unemployment. Clearly much research needs to be done. In the meantime we are forced cautiously to conclude that because of their (small) effect on real wage levels unions have contributed, but only to a relatively trivial extent, to the rise in unemployment (and in the natural rate) in Britain.

Conclusions

In this chapter we have emphasised the importance of modelling the natural rate of unemployment to economic policy. The evidence that has been reviewed shows the value of U^* has increased in Britain and that some of the increase can be attributed to supply side factors. However, with the important exception of Minford (1983) most of the evidence suggests the importance of supply side variables in determining the natural rate and in explaining its increase in Britain is quite small. Consequently the reduction in unemployment likely to result from cuts in unemployment benefit, weakening union influence over labour supply and so on are also likely to be quite small. The implication is that demand side aspects of the British labour market are rather more important and these are considered in the next chapter.

Notes

1. The method involves the estimation of a wage equation

(a) $\quad \dot{W} = \alpha \dot{P} + (1-\alpha)\dot{W}_{t-1} - \beta \ell n U_t + \delta t + \text{constant}$

and a price equation (b)

$$\dot{P}_t = S(\tfrac{1}{2}\dot{P}m_t + \tfrac{1}{2}\dot{P}m_{t-1}) - \dot{\rho}_t + \theta \dot{W}_t + (1-\theta)\dot{W}_{t-1} - \gamma \dot{U}_t$$
$$+ \text{constant}$$

where ρ = trend labour productivity and all other variables have the notation used in the text. From (a) and (b) an equation for the rate of acceleration of wage inflation ($\ddot{W}$) can be obtained as follows

(c)
$$\ddot{W} = \frac{\alpha}{1-\alpha\theta} \; [S \tfrac{1}{2}\dot{P}m_t + \tfrac{1}{2}\dot{P}m_{t-1} - \dot{\rho}_t - \gamma\dot{U}_t]$$

$$+ \frac{1}{1-\alpha\theta} - \beta \ell n U + \delta t$$

$$+ \text{constant}$$

from which the value of U at which $\ddot{W} = 0$ can be retrieved given the values of the other exogenous variables.

2. A recent example is Joshi, Layard and Owen (1983) who find that recession in the labour market (manifest in lower vacancies) significantly reduces the number of women in the labour force. Other studies are surveyed in Greenhalgh and Mayhew (1981).

3. Recall the discussion in Chapter 3. The relevant equation is 3.18 TC = CS/μ. The total costs of job search depend on the cost per vacancy sampled (C) and the time productivity of search (μ). μ is larger for full time search but so is C. A reduction in C (μ unchanged) clearly increases the incentive to full-time search.

4. Nickell's estimates are similar to those obtained by Mackay and Reid (1972) for the 1960s, and Lancaster (1979) for the 1970s using alternative data sets.

5. Narendrenathan, Nickell and Stern (1985) also test for potential bias in the effects resulting from unobserved heterogeneity (difference between individuals not observed in the data). The estimate of the elasticity of duration with respect to unemployment income is highly stable in the face of these tests. The fact that the estimated elasticity is lower than Nickell (1979) probably reflects the higher unemployment in the late 1970s.

6. This is calculated from data contained in the DHSS 'Abstract of Statistics'. This gives relevant unemployment income for different family types who are weighted by a set of fixed proportions. This is annualised and deflated by an estimate of average earnings.

7. In an earlier working paper version Nickell does find a positive effect of benefits on inflows. Inclusion of a real wage variable appears to reduce its impact to zero in Nickell (1982).

8. Evaluating elasticities at the sample mean of unemployment gives the elasticity with respect to benefits at around .6 for cross section studies. Andrews and Nickell get estimates between .75 to 1.1 which is very close to those of Maki and Spindler but, of course, using a superior modelling framework.

9. The method and reasons are discussed more fully in footnote (20) of Chapter 6.

10. Recall again that long run coefficients are found by dividing coefficients in 6.13 by $1-\beta_8$ which in this case equals unity.

11. Henry, Payne and Trinder (1985) also subject Minford's results to a variety of tests which employ data up to 1982. These confirm the scepticism about Minford's results.

12. There is also a large and growing literature on the inter-war period. The seminal paper here is Benjamin and Kochin (1979) who claim that a significant part of unemployment in inter-war Britain was due to high unemployment benefit. This rather surprising view has been subject to a great deal of critical comment, some of which was published in a symposium in the Journal of Political Economy (1982).

13. At the individual level Narendrenathan, Nickell and Stern also find no relationship between an individual's re-employment probability and benefit disallowance in their analysis using the 1978/9 DHSS Cohort study.

14. The small scale of the effects of taxation on labour supply is confirmed by a number of cross section studies. The effect for males is especially small. A survey of this literature is contained in Brown (1980).

15. Henry, Payne and Trinder (1985) also conclude: 'By using revised data for unionisation ... we find the empirical support for the main parts of the Minford model is questionable'.

16. These ideas are fully developed in Freeman (1976) and Freeman and Medoff (1984).

17. Many other reasons can be advanced for this bias. For a comprehensive critique of the macro estimates of the union/non-union differential, see Lewis (1983).

Chapter Eight

THE NATURAL RATE OF UNEMPLOYMENT: THE DEMAND SIDE

Introduction

In the previous chapter we have examined the determinants of the natural rate and the cyclical movements in these factors which lead to changes in U_t^*. We also considered at some length the acceptance probability (β_t) and the supply side aspects of the inflow rate (α_t). As a result it was possible to assess the contribution of supply side factors to the value of U_t^* we observe in Britain. In this chapter we will concentrate on the demand side forces which emanate from employers and which also, in principle, have an effect on the natural rate. This analysis will also suggest policies which will be considered in the concluding Chapter 9. The theory set out in Chapters 3 and 7 reveals two ways in which the natural rate of unemployment is influenced by employers assuming a given value of vacancies. Firstly, any change in the offer probability (κ_t) will change the natural rate. Specifically, a secular fall in κ_t will cause a secular rise in U_t^*. Empirically we shall examine the basis for this interpretation of events in Britain. Secondly, any change in layoffs will affect the inflow rate. An increase in layoffs will increase the natural rate of unemployment via its effects on α_t. In order to consider these issues we will adopt the framework suggested by Mortensen (1970) and outlined in the first part of Chapter 7 and also the employer search theory described in Chapter 3. Together this suggests a number of possible causes of changes in κ_t and α_t. Initially we will concentrate on the offer probability and its determinant, the hiring standard.

Changes in the hiring standard can be explained in a variety of ways within these frameworks. Firstly, any change in the desired level of

294

employment (of persons) will alter the hiring
standard except in very unlikely and extreme
circumstances. This can be seen by referring to
Figure 7.1. Any shift in the EE function ($\Delta E \neq 0$)
alters the hiring standard (ρ_t^*) except in the extreme
and unlikely circumstances that the HH line is
vertical. Secondly any change in the underlying
labour cost structure will alter the optimal strategy
for the firm. This causes a change in hiring
standards. This could happen because changes in
search costs have a direct and immediate effect. It
would also happen for other reasons and these are
considered in the remainder of this chapter.

Employment and Hiring Standards: Hours v. Persons

In Chapters 3 and 7 we have seen that if falls in
aggregate desired employment take place, vacancies
will fall and generally hiring standards will rise.
The opposite will happen if desired employment
increases. A fall in vacancies will reduce the
arrival rate of job offers and will increase non-
natural unemployment as we have defined it. This is
because recession causes a shift along the VU curve
away from the market clearing equality of vacancies
and unemployment. If hiring standards rise this also
will have a further effect causing a decrease in the
offer probability. This will shift the VU curve
outwards and change the natural rate itself. These
two effects are shown in Figure 8.1.

Figure 8.1

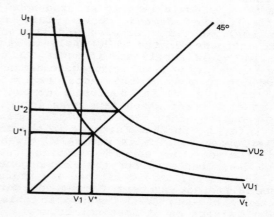

Initially we have a VU curve at VU_1 with vacancies equal to $V*$ and unemployment at the natural rate (U_1^*). The fall in the aggregate offer probability will shift the VU curve to VU_2 so the natural rate of unemployment will rise to U_2^*. Since vacancies have also fallen to V_1 non-natural unemployment will occur and equal $U_1 - U_2^*$. Both of these effects will lead to the pro-cyclical movement of the unemployment outflow rate which we have already observed. In practice, of course, as we saw in the last chapter the acceptance probability also increases in recession. This will offset the downward movement in the offer probability. If it exactly offsets it the natural rate of unemployment will remain constant at U_t^*. An opposite sequence of events will characterise a boom though here also U_t^* will remain approximately constant. Since, in general, this appears to be the case (as we saw in Chapter 7), cyclical variation in aggregate demand and desired employment lead mainly to non-natural unemployment. In view of this and the concern with the secular long run value of the natural rate, we will focus in this chapter on hiring standards and the offer probability. In particular we will examine the extent to which shifts in the VU curve in Britain are caused by a secular increase in hiring standards.

It is important to note again the difference between this analysis and that (like Layard and Nickell (1985)) which relies on a NAIRU definition of the natural rate. In that case aggregate demand changes can actually result from changes in secular variables. Suppose, for example, there is an exogenous reduction in the offer probability. In stock terms this is equivalent to an exogenous shift down of the labour demand curve. This causes equilibrium employment to decrease and the natural rate (U_t^*) to increase. In the NAIRU analysis wage and price inflation would accelerate if aggregate demand remained at its existing level. Aggregate demand must therefore be cut to prevent this acceleration. This leads to a further shift in the labour demand curve and a fall in employment which causes an increase in equilibrium unemployment. In the NAIRU analysis, therefore, there is a further increase in the natural rate of unemployment, which is why NAIRU gives such large estimates of the market clearing rate of unemployment (see Chapter 7 for the same argument in a different guise). NAIRU calculations are useful but they produce different numbers from those deriving from the theory of Chapter 3 because in this case this secondary effect on U_t^* does not occur.

Initially we will look at the employer's decision concerning the desired composition of the labour input and then later turn to the desired labour input itself on determinants of labour demand and the offer probability (κ_t).

There are three dimensions of the labour input which governs its composition

(a)   employment (persons employed)
(b)   the hours of work of each employee
(c)   effort per hour of labour time

Our concern is with employment but clearly secular change in desired employment can take place as a result of changes in hours of work, effort or both. Increases in long run average hours of work or effort per hour of work will both, for example, reduce desired employment and affect hiring standards. Assuming no change in effort per hour it is possible to focus on the employment/hours mix of the labour input and the choices that firms have to make. The basic ideas can be easily understood with the aid of Figure 8.2. The person/hours function (EH) is depicted so all points along it represent a constant labour input, i.e. if we assume a constant rate of substitution between employment and hours of work.

Figure 8.2

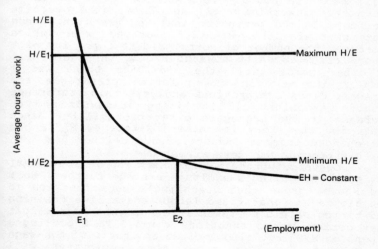

The employer faces constraints on his choice between person and hours, which impose maximum and minimum values of H/E. These can be viewed as supply side constraints imposed by workers individually or collectively, or by statutory intervention. The employer can choose any person/hours mix between $H/E_1 E_1$ and $H/E_2 E_2$. Any secular movement towards $H/E_1^- E_1^-$ clearly causes a fall in desired employment and hence a rise in hiring standards and in U_t^*. What might cause such a movement to take place? Brechling (1965) considered this issue as part of an analysis of employment in British manufacturing. He argued that the choice between person and hours is governed by the desire by firms to minimise the wage bill

$$8.1 \quad W = (H/E_s \, W_1 + H/E_0 \, W_2) E$$

where

H/E_s = standard hours

H/E_0 = overtime hours

W_1 = basic wage rate

W_2 = overtime wage rate

On minimising this expression for the wage bill Brechling shows that both the demand for persons and the demand for hours depend on H/E_s (the length of the standard working week) and W_2/W_1 (the overtime premium). In the period he analysed Brechling finds that cuts in the standard working week which increased the number of hours paid at a premium wage caused firms to shift towards $H/E_2 E_2$ in Figure 8.2. In other words until the mid-1960s there was a secular increase in the relative preference for persons. Given our previous analysis this preference caused a secular fall in hiring standards and an increase in the aggregate offer probability. Since that time the story is rather different. W_2/W_1 has not changed in most industries and neither has H/E_s so this process has been arrested.

However, further work by Hart and Sharot (1978) has taken Brechling's analysis a stage further. Hart and Sharot argue that Brechling's wage function is too simple and that fixed labour costs like training and hiring should be taken into account. As a result they derive demand functions which like Brechling's depend on H/E_s but also include the ratio of non-wage to wage costs. They argue that employment will decrease and hours of work will increase if the ratio of non-wage to wage costs increases. Hart and Sharot examine employment in British Manufacturing from 1961 to 1972 and find some evidence for the view that increasing fixed costs of employment persuaded firms to move towards an hours intensive mix of persons and hours. Given the continued rise of fixed costs (1) as a proportion of total labour costs in the 1970s, this trend would lead to general increases in hiring standards, falling offer probabilities and rising U_t^*.

Further support for this proposition giving particular attention to the role of the employers' national insurance contribution has been provided by several recent studies. Symons and Layard (1984), using a single equation approach and the various structural models of the labour market all produce remarkably consistent results. Minford (1983), for example, can retrieve the effect of labour taxes via his demand (unemployment) equation (6.9). He obtains results that suggest that increases in employers' labour taxes between 1967-8 and 1978-9 increased unemployment by 300,000. Over the longer period 1956-66 to 1980-83 Layard and Nickell (1985) find the possible effect of increased employer labour taxes to be about 400,000 on the natural rate and more on NAIRU. This consensus (2) confirms that increased fixed labour costs, especially employers' labour taxes, have added significantly to the natural rate of unemployment by altering the optimal hours/persons combination chosen by employers. (E_2 to E_1 in Figure 8.2). In the light of this the gradual reduction in these taxes (continued further in the 1985 Budget for low paid workers in Britain) is not surprising. Neither is the general welcome these changes have received.

So far we have only considered hiring and employment costs especially those resulting from employer taxes. There is also some evidence on the effect of increased firing costs. Nickell (1982) estimates the impact of a variable that reflects this, namely the number of unfair dismissal cases brought under the terms of the employment protection legislation in Britain. He finds a significant negative effect on the unemployment outflow rate (θ_t). The explanation for this is that the risk of incurring future firing costs causes employers to raise hiring standards. This contributes to the rise in the natural rate. However Nickell also finds that the risk of incurring current firing costs as workers invoke their employment protection rights reduces the unemployment inflow rate. Since employers are also more reluctant to lay off workers (Junankar and Price (1983) confirm this result for a more up-to-date time series) as a result of this legislation it may offset the effect on hiring standards. This is what Nickell finds. He calculates that the net effect of the legislation was to <u>reduce</u> unemployment by just under one percentage point over the period 1969-1977. Using unemployment stocks data Andrews and Nickell (1982) do not confirm this but the positive effects on unemployment of the unfair dismissal case variable is small. It is difficult to avoid the conclusion of Layard and Nickell (1985):

> This result is very tentative since the variable used to capture the effect of the (unemployment protection) legislation is very feeble. Given existing evidence we must therefore remain agnostic on this question.

We might also explain the positive effect found by Andrews and Nickell (1982) of redundancy payments on unemployment as a demand side phenomenon. Insofar as it eases the processes of layoff and redundancy by reducing the individual and collective resistance of affected workers the redundancy payments system reduces firing costs and by so doing increases the natural rate by its effect on the inflow rate α_t. The effect is, however, very small (generally less than one half of a percentage point on the unemployment rate).

Overall it would seem there is evidence for believing that changes in fixed labour costs including employers' labour taxes have increased the natural rate of unemployment mostly through their short and long run effects in raising the average hiring standard (κ_t) in the economy as a whole. However, the overall effect seems unlikely to have added more than two percentage points to the natural rate but this effect is clearly non-trivial.

Hiring Standards and Employment: Work Effort and Technical Change

Until recently there has been little interest amongst economists in the third dimension of the labour input, namely work effort. The emphasis has been on the person/hours choice. Only radical economists more deeply immersed in the traditional Marxian concern with the labour process have considered this issue. Their view is that as part and parcel of the process of production employers are always seeking ways to secure labour productivity enhancing increases in effort per hour. The effect of this (if successful) is to reduce the employment (and hours) required to produce a given level of output. The demand curve for persons shifts downwards which reduces the natural rate of employment (increasing U_t^*). In flow terms since employers require fewer workers, hiring standards rise and the offer probability falls, which has the same positive effect on the natural rate of unemployment.

Recently interest in this area has grown as a result of the analysis of the consequences of both technical and organisational change. Most of this has focussed upon the effects of microelectronic technology. The central argument is that this form of technological change not only alters the material means of production, it also affects the social relations of production by causing a shift in relative bargaining power towards employers. Partly this is the result of the greater control of production speeds that microelectronic (especially robotics) technology gives to management. It is however also the result of a process of destruction and reconstruction of traditional occupational structures which weakens the power of workers and their trades unions.

In conventional analytical terms this argument implies that the adoption of microelectronic technology provides management with the opportunity to increase the rate of labour saving disembodied technical change, by changes in work organisation, production speeds and so on. This is in addition to any labour saving embodied in the new technology. In order to clarify this distinction we can think of the savings resulting from the embodied component as largely in the form of reduced manning levels. The gain in the disembodied component arises from the more intensive use of both capital and labour inputs. In order to realise these gains, however, employers have to make changes in work organisation. However, it is important to understand that this form of technical change is disembodied not in the sense that it falls like 'manna from heaven' but in the sense that it is conditional upon the introduction of microelectronic technology. In that sense it is embodied but since it is not an <u>inevitable</u> accompaniment, strictly it is not. Hence it is more appropriate to regard it as a form of disembodied technical progress.

These effects can be analysed with the aid of

the conventional production isoquant depicted in
Figure 8.3. Y_1' is the isoquant prevailing before the
introduction of the new technology that we assume is
wholly or partly a process innovation. We assume
there is no effect on the capital input so the
embodied component of labour saving technical change
will reduce manning levels to E_2 and the new isoquant
will be Y'_1. In this sense the introduction of
microelectronic technology is no different from any
other labour saving technical change. We make this
assumption because there seems little evidence that
the scale of labour saving is any greater for each
unit of this type of investment compared with any
other. The real difference is in the opportunity for
disembodied technical change. Increases in work
effort and labour productivity per unit of time will
reduce the desired employment of persons even further
so that the isoquant shifts to Y_1'' and employment to
E_3.

The argument can now be summarised. Any labour
saving technical change will reduce desired
employment for a given level of output. This raises
hiring standards lowering the offer probability for
searching workers. Microelectronic technology,
because of the enhanced opportunities it provides
management for further labour saving, has
potentially an even greater effect on U_t^*.

Before we consider the empirical evidence there
are two further issues that require attention.
Firstly, the analysis so far ignores the qualitative
effects of technical change in general and of
microelectronics in particular. It is not simply the
number of persons required that is altered but also
the character of jobs. Over the whole post-war period
there has been a transformation of the job structure
in Britain. Some indication of the changes that have
taken place is shown in Table 8.1. This shows the
significant growth in technical and scientific
employment. Over the time period 1951-80 the growth
(rows, 8, 9) in this type of employment greatly
exceeds the average. The general growth in non-manual
employment contrasts with the overall fall in manual
employment. We can also see from 1961 in particular,
the decline in skilled as well as in non-skilled
manual workers. Despite this de-skilling in
traditional occupations it seems clear that
technical change, especially since 1961, has led to
growing importance of types of labour for which there
is a higher degree of training and hence, higher
fixed (training) costs. As a result, hiring standards
will rise and the probability of a job offer will

decline for searching workers. Whether it also
creates a pool of workers who, given the nature of
vacancies, are 'mismatched' is something we will
examine later in this chapter.

Table 8.1: Changes in Occupational Employment 1951-
1980

Occupation	1951-61	1961-71	1971-80
1. All	7.9	0.2	2.6
2. All Manual	0.5	-8.5	-6.3
3. All Non-Manual	23.7	15.3	15.1
4. Managers and administration	21.3	17.0	11.8
5. Education profession	21.8	32.0	30.7
6. Health professions	23.5	27.1	28.6
7. Other professions	35.0	24.9	21.9
8. Engineers and Scientists	66.0	44.9	14.6
9. Technicians, draughtsmen	65.5	30.4	17.3
10. Skilled Operatives	20.3	-6.1	-16.8
11. Other Operatives	-0.7	-12.8	-5.0

Source: Institute of Employment Research, <u>Review of
the Economy and Employment</u>, 1983.

Secondly, we have given no attention so far to
the dynamic effects of technical change and the
adoption of microelectronic technology. These are of
considerable importance in assessing the employment
effects and are of several types. Firstly, since the
introduction of microelectronic technologies requires gross investment there will be an offsetting again
in employment in industries producing the new
technologies. Of course, the magnitude of these
offsetting employment effects depends on the rate of
diffusion of the microelectronic technology and the
extent to which it is domestically produced. Slow
diffusion or high importers' shares would both reduce
the degree of employment compensation from this
source.
    A further dynamic effect concerns the impact of
microelectronic technology on the level of output of
the good affected by the process innovation and of
other goods in the economy. Increases in output of
the directly affected good would shift the isoquant
outwards and offset in full or part the fall in

303

Figure 8.3

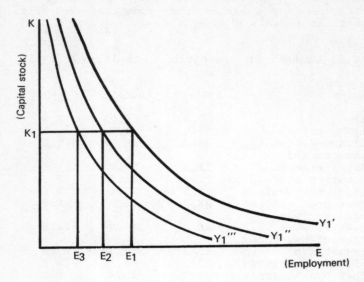

desired employment shown in Figure 8.3. When there is
a consequential increase in output and employment
elsewhere in the economy the reduction in desired
employment in one sector will be offset leading to a
smaller or even a zero fall in aggregate desired
employment, so, overall, hiring standards and the
average offer probability are unaffected. What
determines the scale of this effect? Clearly it
depends to a significant extent upon the post-
innovation movements of product demand. Critical to
this will be the adjustment of wages, prices and
profits. If we suppose markets clear and are
characterised by complete price flexibility then no
long run fall in desired employment results. The
reasoning underlying this is simple and is shown in
Figure 8.4, which depicts the familiar extended IS/LM
model of the macroeconomy. Initially the economy has
output of Y_1, employment of E_1 and a real wage W/P_1.
The process innovation has two direct effects on this
position. It shifts the employment function
downwards in frame b and the notional labour demand
schedule upwards (to D_E^2 in frame c). Note that it is
the notional demand curve that has shifted. Some of
the effects we have already considered suggest the
effective demand curve for labour will also shift but
downwards to $E_2 D_E^2$ with a horizontal (broken line)

section in frame 'c'. If this happens initially there is excess supply of labour of E_1-E_2. If money wages then fall and there is also a fall in product prices as the market clearing view suggests the economy will be restored to a new equilibrium level of employment of E_3. Note that not only has equilibrium employment not fallen it has actually risen and U_t^* has therefore fallen. The shifts in the IS/LM curves that are required for this to happen occur because of the asset and money supply effects on the fall in the price level. This will be reinforced if the innovation leads to an increase in autonomous spending. In an open economy the fall in product price boosts exports and import substitution. This helps to shift the IS curve upwards. Finally, in frame 'c' we can see that despite the fall in money wages and prices the real wage has risen to W/P_2 (prices fall by more). This is because the technical change has, in the long run, increased labour productivity and aggregate demand so that the effective demand curve is $E_3 D_E^2$. Employment is therefore on the notional demand curve with firms paying their employees a real wage of W/P_2.

Figure 8.4

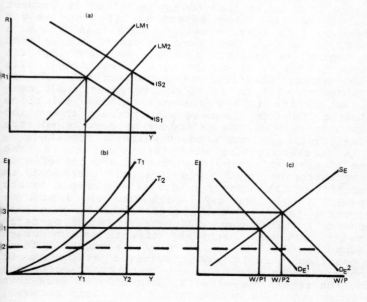

In the light of this analysis it is perhaps no surprise that those who support the market clearing paradigm also believe the effects of microelectronic technology will be unambiguously good. Technical change will reduce, <u>not</u> increase U^*_t. However, as we saw in Chapter 6, there are good theoretical and empirical grounds for rejecting the market clearing view even in the long run. The requirement that prices fall by more than wages is particularly stringent in this respect. If wage and price rigidities exist the consequences of process innovation will be rather different and rather clearer. The result as Stoneman (1983) shows will generally be a lower level of employment and every prospect of a fall in desired employment actually taking place. This will unambiguously drive up hiring standards in the economy. This happens because there is no mechanism to shift the IS and LM curves in the direction of higher product demand. As a result the economy is left on the effective demand curve $E_2 D_E^2$.

If we consider a product innovation the outcome is less clear cut. In this case the non-price characteristics of the single good produced in the economy change. If these changes boost the international non-price competitiveness in the economy the IS curve will move upwards as we require. <u>A priori</u> this could lead to any level of employment in excess of E_2 but we cannot say if the eventual outcome will be less, equal, or more than E_3. As a result we cannot be sure whether non-natural unemployment is negative $(E > E_3)$ positive $(E < E_3)$ or zero $(E = E_3)$. We can be sure, however that like in the market clearing case, the natural rate of unemployment will have fallen. Moreover employment will be greater in the presence of wage and price rigidities than is the case with process innovation which only changes the method of production not the characteristics of the product which is produced.

A further problem with this analysis is that since it assumes a single good economy, the effects of the introduction of microelectronic technology in one sector of the economy cannot affect output levels elsewhere in the economy. Apart from the impact on the output levels of the microelectronic technology producing industries any increase in income or falls in prices may have secondary effects on any other products in the multi-good economy. These compensation effects are considered at length in Stoneman (1983) from which it is clear that the net reduction in employment will invariably be less than the gross reduction once they are taken into account.

Theory, therefore, pinpoints the various employment effects that result from technical change in general and from microelectronic technology in particular. The effects are, however, ambiguous. In the market clearing world technical change increases the arrival rate of job offers and lowers the natural rate of unemployment. Only if the employment inducing effects are offset by changes in the persons/hours/ effort mix is the overall outward shift in the demand for labour services (persons x hours x effort per hour) offset by an inward shift in the demand for persons. In this case the size of opposing effects will determine the outcome for hiring standards and the value of U_t^*. In the non-market clearing world the effect on the natural rate is equally uncertain but also, not surprisingly, non-natural unemployment can also arise because of technical change. Product innovation makes this less likely. In view of the fact that unambiguous conclusions from theory about the effect of technical change on unemployment are not possible we need (more urgently than usual) to consider empirical work to help resolve the matter.

In the empirical work considerable use has been made of neoclassical production theory to assess both the scale of technical change, the extent to which it is labour saving and hence has the employment effects we have considered. Solow (1956) is the seminal work in this area. Using a variety of neoclassical production functions Solow estimates technical change in the US for the period 1909–1949. Typical of the results is that using the Cobb Douglas function. In this case (with no time subscripts)

8.2 $\quad Y = Ae^{gt} \, EH^{\alpha}K^{\beta}$

where

H = hours of work
E = persons
K = capital stock

and hence

8.3 $\quad \dfrac{\dot{Y}}{Y} = g + \alpha\left(\dfrac{\dot{EH}}{EH}\right) + \beta\left(\dfrac{\dot{K}}{K}\right)$

In equation 8.3. g represents the rate of technical change. Solow finds this to be significant and the cause of an inward shift of the production isoquant at a rate that doubled in the second half of his period of analysis. In fact, 87% of the doubling of output per man hour over the whole period is attributed by Solow to the effects of technical change. There is now an extensive literature in this area which has been critically surveyed by Kennedy and Thirlwall (1972) and Stoneman (1983).

A similar approach for Britain which focusses on the employment effects of technical change uses the employment function approach. The starting point is the model proposed by Ball and St. Cyr (1965) and outlined in Chapter 1. Equation (8.2) is inverted to form the desired employment function (see Chapter 1) with time subscripts in this case.

8.4 $\quad E_t^* = e^{-gt/\alpha} \cdot Y_t^{1/\alpha} \Big/ A^{1/\alpha} \cdot H_t$

Assuming a simple adjustment process (see Chapter 1)

8.5 $\quad \dfrac{E_t}{E_{t-1}} = \left[\dfrac{E_t^*}{E_{t-1}} \right]^{\lambda}$

from which the conventional estimating equation can be derived (in logs)

8.6 $\quad \log E_t = \gamma + (1-\lambda) \log E_{t-1} + \dfrac{\lambda}{\alpha} \log Y_t$

$\qquad - \dfrac{\lambda}{\alpha} g \, t$

where

γ = constant
t = time trend

The term 'g' again contains the employment effects of technical progress and is easy to calculate once we have estimated λ and α. Estimates vary according to the time period selected, the types of workers examined, and so on. Typical are the results of Deaton (1983) who finds a long run rate of job reduction (with output and real wages constant) in British manufacturing that lies between $2\frac{1}{2}\%$ and $3\frac{1}{2}\%$ per annum. There is also no evidence from Deaton's estimates that the employment loss that results from technical change has accelerated and that microelectronic technology is having a particularly severe effect on desired employment levels.

The problems with these estimates are, however,

308

considerable. As we have seen this type of employment function has several drawbacks. Of particular concern here is that the Ball and St. Cyr function assumes a constant capital stock so the coefficient on the time trend picks up the effect both of capital accumulation and of changes in capital intensity as well as technical progress. One solution to this problem is to employ the function proposed by Nadiri and Rosen (1969). Estimation of a model of this kind has been undertaken by Briscoe and Peel (1974) and this reveals a secular reduction in employment in manufacturing of a rather smaller magnitude (1.9% per annum) but which might reasonably be a closer approximation to the effects of technical change. However, several further problems arise even with estimates of this kind. Particularly serious are the problems associated with the measurement of inputs especially of capital and capital services. If, as some economists argue the measurement of capital is bedevilled by fundamental theoretical and empirical difficulties then these calculations are clearly of less value. Bias may also arise from the failure to consider imported raw material and energy inputs in the demand for labour. Similar problems may arise if (as we saw in Chapter 6) the level of output is assumed to be exogenous. Nickell (1984) has made a recent attempt to deal with these problems in a labour demand model and Layard and Nickell (1985) within a structural model of the labour market. These moves to greater realism in modelling labour demand significantly reduce the effect of technical progress on employment and on unemployment. Layard and Nickell, for example, conclude that although technical progress is labour saving the impact on employment with a given capital stock is 'negligible' (3).

Freeman, Clark and Soete (1982) consider the very long run relationship of employment and technical change. They argue that during the diffusion process of new technologies there is a significant reduction in the employment generated by each unit of investment. The dynamic effects that offset this initial loss of employment operate only imperfectly and with long delays so unemployment will rise and later fall. However the evidence advanced to support the view that currently high levels of unemployment can be explained by new technology is circumstantial and their view remains speculative.

More direct evidence comes from the work of Stoneman (1975), who considers the job losses and gains resulting from growing computer use in Britain.

By making assumptions about the gestation period for computer installation and the life of the computer and using information about the diffusion process between 1952-1970 Stoneman is able to consider the employment effects of computer use assuming the economy's output was not affected by that use. His findings show that the reduction in employment resulting from computer usage was offset by the additional labour required for computer construction. However, towards the end of the period considered by Stoneman the labour saving effects began to dominate implying an overall net reduction in jobs at the beginning of the 1970s. Stoneman also presents data on the qualitative effects of computer usage. This shows a marked change in the skill mix of the directly affected working population. There is a notable increase in the proportion of jobs requiring numerate and technical skills. These results suggest that the net effect of computer usage has been to raise hiring standards in employment by net cuts in desired employment and by significant changes in the skills required for potential employees.

Whitley and Wilson (1983) have recently considered the impact of microelectronic technology on a wider basis in the economy. In their model technical progress initially reduces desired employment. However it leads to cost and price reduction and this leads to offsetting effects on demand and employment. Whitley and Wilson argue that these are only the first round effects and that further boosts to demand come from the extra investment demand for the new technology, changes in intermediate demands and the stimulation to overseas trade performance given by the new technology. For the economy as a whole they perform a simulation of the effects of microelectronics on employment in Britain until 1990. These show the initial job loss of 342 thousand is offset by a first round compensation of 144,000 and a second round of 160,000.

The empirical work on the effect of technical change on desired employment confirms that the net effect of new technologies is significantly less than the gross effect. Estimates vary in their magnitude but at most it seems clear that only modest net job loss has taken place in Britain as a result of technical change. Despite the accompanying changes in the skill mix of the working population, it is likely that technical change has made only a very small contribution to the upward trend of hiring standards and unemployment in Britain.

Output, Investment, Employment and the Natural Rate

So far we have assumed that falls in output (expected or actual) or in output growth cause only non-natural unemployment. This is in contrast to the effects of increases in real wage levels which can cause extra equilibrium as well as disequilibrium unemployment. In this section we will consider the possible effect of <u>sustained</u> long run falls in the growth of output on the natural rate of unemployment.

The assumption used in Chapters 4-6 was that the offer probability (κ_t) was unaffected by a fall in output so all unemployment caused by such a fall was in excess of the natural rate. However, it is possible that a <u>sustained</u> fall in the level or rate of growth of aggregate output will affect κ_t and hence the natural rate. In order to see this possibility, consider the following rearrangement of equation 8.3.

8.7 $\quad \dfrac{\dot{E}H}{EH} = \dfrac{1}{\alpha} \left(\dfrac{\dot{Y}}{Y} - \beta \dfrac{\dot{K}}{K} - g \right)$

We have already seen the effects of an increase in the rate of labour saving technical progress on the labour requirement and, given a fixed relationship between E and H, upon employment. With a constant capital output ratio ($\dot{Y}/Y = \dot{K}/K$) a fall in the rate of growth of output would induce a fall in the $\dot{E}H/EH$ of $1-\beta/\alpha$. If, as most empirical work finds the coefficient β is less than unity this expression is positive. A fall in the rate of output and capital stock growth will reduce the growth in person hours (EH) and in general, in employment (E). If the capital output ratio rises as data for Britain suggests is the case in the 1970s (4) there will be an additional fall in $\dot{E}H/EH$ of β/α ($\dot{K}/K - \dot{Y}/Y$). In other words with a given rate of technical progress and a given capital output ratio, a fall in the long run rate of growth of output will, <u>ceteris paribus</u>, reduce the growth in desired employment. If the reduction takes output growth below the trend growth in labour productivity, as has happened in Britain, employment growth will be negative. The relevant data for the whole economy and the production sector is shown in Table 8.2.

The secular decline in the post-war rate of employment growth in Britain shown in Table 8.2 will have obvious effects on hiring standards (and hence on the average offer probability) in the economy. Consider Figure 8.5 which reproduces the diagram of Mortensen (1970). Initially the hiring standards in

Table 8.2: Employment, output and labour productivity growth in Britain 1954-85 (% per decade)

	Whole Economy			Production Industries		
	Employment	Output	Product-ivity	Employment	Output	Product-ivity
1954-64	4.4	36.9	26.4	0.6	31.8	2.9
1964-75	-0.8	25.4	26.0	-10.9	23.2	33.8
1974-84	-5.3	11.7	16.1	-26.6	3.4	39.9

Source: Historical Abstract of Labour Statistics, National Institute Economic Reviews (various issues)

an average firm is ρ_1^* with a relative wage of W_1. If for convenience we assume a constant pattern of relative wages across the economy, the effect of a general and secular fall in the rate of employment growth will be a general rise in hiring standards to ρ_4 ($\Delta E = \Delta E_4$). Since the diagram depicts the behaviour of an individual firm we are effectively assuming that in these circumstances no firm lowers its relative wage because it reckons all other competing (for labour) firms will do the same. In search theory terms the reduction in the rate of output growth reduces the marginal costs of not filling a job vacancy so employer search proceeds with a high target level of 'worker quality'. Since there occurs a secular increase in the hiring standard, the offer probability will fall and this will have a sustained effect on the natural rate of unemployment.

Figure 8.5

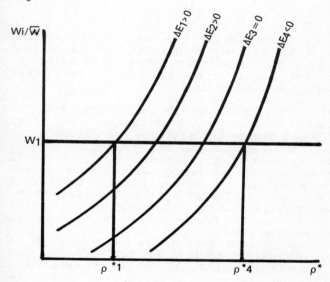

Note the difference between this and the conventional analysis of economic growth, which employs a simple stock definition of unemployment which is exogenously determined. In this case changes in output growth have no effect on the natural rate of unemployment since the warranted and natural rates of growth are independent. The analysis employed here is not unlike that of Rowthorn (1980) who argues that if unemployment (of the Keynesian type) in excess of natural rate exists, it is converted into structural unemployment and so it becomes part of the natural rate itself. Rowthorn suggests that this is the result of employers reorganising their production methods, scrapping equipment and eliminating excess capacity, so that increases in g are not offset by falls in $\dot{K}/K$. This involves a different mechanism from that emphasised here but the effect is the same. If output growth falls and this leads to persistent falls in desired employment then U_t^* will eventually rise.

Similar ideas have been advanced by Hargreaves-Heap (1980) who argues that the natural rate of unemployment in the current time period (U_t^*) is described by the following difference equation:

$$8.8 \quad U_t^* = U_{t-1}^* + \delta (U_{t-1} + U_{t-1}^*)$$

If the actual unemployment rate exceeds the natural rate ($U_{t-1} > U_{t-1}^*$) then the natural rate rises (and vice versa). The reason for this is similar to Rowthorn. If U_{t-1} exceeds U_{t-1}^* structural unemployment appears because

> those who are involuntarily unemployed in such a situation suffer a deterioration in their skills and become increasingly unemployable.

This occurs because of the dependence of individual re-employment probabilities on unemployment duration. If unemployment in excess of the natural rate persists and leads to longer spells of unemployment, an increasing proportion of the unemployed will have almost no chance of re-employment and are structurally unemployed.

A decline in the secular rates of growth of output (or employment) could arise for any number of reasons. Clearly it could be the consequence of a secular fall in the rate of growth of aggregate demand for goods. This gives rise to Keynesian unemployment in an economy characterised by non-market clearing. This we have depicted as non-natural unemployment. The argument of this section is that if the fall in the rate of growth of aggregate demand is sustained over a longer period, non-natural unemployment can be converted into structural natural unemployment. As we saw in Chapter 5 this could, of course, also occur as a consequence of increasing real wage levels. We would observe the long run equivalent of classical unemployment. In this case the effect of output growth on unemployment would be magnified if real wage increases were the cause of the increasing capital output ratio we have observed in Britain. As we have seen the ensuing fall in employment growth is even bigger when output growth declines. Direct evidence on these questions is scanty, but indirect evidence is available and that is considered next.

Structural Unemployment and the Natural Rate

The empirical work on the effects of a secular decline in output growth on the natural rate of unemployment has, in fact, concentrated on the production sector rather than on the British economy as a whole. The reasons are not hard to find. Table 8.2 shows that the secular decline in output and employment growth is a good deal more dramatic in the production sector. Indeed the decline in employment has been so substantial that the rate of productivity increase in the production industries has actually trended upwards. (5) The effects on unemployment of this decline in production sector jobs has been considered in a number of studies. Nickell (1982) finds that the decline in production industry jobs has had a significant effect on reducing the aggregate unemployment outflow probability. This raised the equilibrium rate of unemployment by 1.4 percentage points over the period 1969-77. This is just over one third of the total increase calculated by Nickell. Junankar and Price (1983) confirm this substantial effect on unemployment outflows while Junankar (1981), Andrews and Nickell (1982) and Layard and Nickell (1985) find a significant effect on unemployment stocks although in the latter case the global effect is not quite as marked. In the most recent of these studies Layard and Nickell calculate that the decline of production industry employment has added .78 of a percentage point to the natural unemployment rate between the mid 1960s and 1983 (just under 10% of their estimated increase in NAIRU). It would seem, therefore, that declining output and employment growth and the consequential increase in hiring standards in the production sector of the economy have had notable effects not only within the sector but on the natural rate of unemployment in the economy as a whole.

Nickell (1982) also presents evidence on the extent of structural unemployment in Britain by calculating indices of regional, industrial and occupational mismatching, which show to upward trend. He measures the degree of mismatching by

$$8.9 \quad M = \sum_i (V_i U_i)^{\frac{1}{2}}$$

where $V_i = V_i/V$ and $U_i = U_i/U$. Since V_i and U_i are defined as the share of each region, industry or occupation in the total then if $V_i = U_i = 1$ then there is 'perfect' matching. In other words vacancies and unemployment occur in the same proportion in each region, industry or occupation.

Although structural unemployment caused by industrial, occupational or regional decline remains a component of the natural rate of unemployment, Nickell's results suggest it is not an important feature of its rise in Britain. This view is confirmed by comparing current unemployment with the recession of the 1930s. Industrial and regional patterns of unemployment are much less concentrated now. In 1932 two thirds of the unemployed worked in production industries compared with 43% in 1982. The regional differences shown in Chapter 2 were also much more marked in the 1930s. The differential then led to unemployment rates three times as high in the North, compared with the South in Britain. Only the decline in manufacturing in the West Midlands has added greatly to structural unemployment of the traditional type and this appears, according the lack of a trend in Nickell's data, to have been offset elsewhere (especially in Scotland).

Some writers like Bonsanquet (1978) have suggested that age is now a more important source of mismatching and structural unemployment than location or industry. Unfortunately Nickell presents no matching indices by age or previous unemployment experience or by spell duration. Obviously this is because of inadequate data on the vacancy side. However, we have already seen in Chapter 2 that over the period of Nickell's analysis there has been a significant deterioration in the relative unemployment position of older and young workers and this may result from increased structural unemployment amongst these groups. Clearly the construction of a matching index by age would help to resolve the issue but the absence of data makes this impossible. However there is some evidence from the age composition of vacancies that employers discriminate in favour of prime age workers. Since both the unemployed flow and stock shows a heavy concentration of younger and older workers there is good reason to believe that mismatching by age has become a more serious problem. This may be related to the decline of the production industries in Britain since redundancies have been concentrated on older workers. Cuts in hiring have been similarly concentrated on the young. This kind of structural unemployment in which workers with low (or zero) offer probabilities become a larger proportion of the total stock leads to a decline in the economy wide average offer probability and hence a rise in U^*. This however is not shown up by Nickell's data which only considers regional, occupational and industrial mismatching.

A further source of the same kind of increasing structural unemployment and of a general fall in the offer probability may arise from the changing duration composition of the unemployed stock. We saw in Chapter 2 that the offer and re-employment probability decline dramatically with the duration of the current spell of unemployment. Although the evidence is not at all conclusive, it would seem (at least in Britain) that workers may be scarred by long unemployment. In some cases this may reflect the effect of long unemployment on skills, attitudes to work and so on. In addition employers may respond to this by assessing the training costs of employing a long term unemployed person as being higher than for someone currently or recently in employment. In this case the firm will raise its hiring standard, further lowering the offer probability for the long duration unemployed. There may also be a further significant aspect to this behaviour. If employers regard (rightly or wrongly) the long term unemployed as workers who have failed to get a job because they are of a low standard he will not make offers to them at all. Since there has been a general rise in the mean (completed and uncompleted) unemployment spell length in Britain, this could lead to a fall in the average offer probability and hence to an increase in the value of U^*. Again, the confirming statistic would be the mismatching index used by Nickell (1982). The relevant proportions to use in its construction would be each current uncompleted spell length as a proportion of the total and the share of vacancies open to workers of differing unemployment durations. This type of mismatching would occur when a rising share of the unemployed are experiencing long durations since they will also be eligible for a small share of total recorded vacancies. Such data on vacancies does not exist, so the matter is difficult to resolve.

Nonetheless, it may be that the major secular decline in employment (especially in production industries) in Britain has had a major effect in increasing the value of the natural rate of unemployment. Partly, this is because of the general effect on the mean offer probability in the labour market as employers raise their hiring standards and release redundant labour. However, because of its effect on the age and duration composition of the unemployed stock it is not unreasonable to depict this at least in part as a form of structural unemployment. Only further research can resolve these matters.

What is clear from Nickell's results is that it is not their location, their occupation or their industrial experience that is the problem for unemployed workers. If anything it is the age of the unemployed, and the debilitating effects of long periods of unemployment on skills, aptitude, motivation and acceptability for work that causes their structural long-term unemployment. Unfortunately the evidence does not exist to make possible a definite conclusion on the significance of these factors which could be substantial.

We have mainly concentrated the empirical analysis of structural unemployment in this section on the effects of a declining rate of output growth in the production sector of the British economy. What is the effect of the comparable decline in the non-production sector which is shown up by the data in Table 8.2.? Junankar and Price (1983) provide some evidence using bankruptcy data for the whole (England and Wales) economy. They find a significant positive association between the incidence of bankruptcy and the size of the inflow and the stock of unemployment. This result is consistent with the results of Wadhwani (1984) who considers the effects of bankruptcy on labour demand. Wadhwani (6) also emphasises the role that high nominal interest rates play in causing the kind of liquidity problems that lead to bankruptcy. Clearly the demise of firms is likely to have a real as well as a financial dimension. Secular stagnation in output growth in the macroeconomy is also bound therefore to lead to the demise of firms throughout the economy. Insofar as the resulting loss of jobs and the increased unemployment inflow affects the determinants of the natural rate $(\beta_t, \alpha_t, \kappa_t, V_t)$ this will reinforce the demand side impetus to higher levels of U_t^*.

We have so far concentrated on structural unemployment that can arise from stagnation caused by sectoral or general <u>decline</u> in existing areas of employment in the economy. It is also important to note that the same phenomenon can arise or be exacerbated because new areas of employment fail to appear. The mismatching index used by Nickell (1982) is not much help here. If new jobs to replace old fail to appear they clearly won't show up in the vacancy statistics. The fact that many of the existing unemployed are not suitable for 'new' jobs will not be revealed by a statistic that necessarily does not even include them. Only by constructing the vacancy composition we might expect to observe in the absence of this failure to generate new jobs and recalculate the mismatching index of equation 8.9 could we accurately estimate the extent of the rise in the natural rate arising from this cause. Clearly this is a difficult, if not an impossible task. Some clue might be obtained by examining the vacancy composition of more successful (lower unemployment) economies. However, inter-country differences in traditional specialisation and job structure would confuse the results.

One way to consider this issue is to examine historical evidence. Particularly illuminating is to contrast Britain in the 1980s with the 1930s when unemployment was at a comparable level. One of the striking features of the 1930s is that although unemployment was high, there was a dramatic increase in the number of new jobs in the economy. Between 1932 and 1936 there was a 14.1% increase in employment in all industries. The largest increase was in the construction industries (37%) but there were significant increases in manufacturing (23%) and services (9%). The jobs were available for all occupational groups including manual workers. Compare this with the data in Table 8.2 which shows a steady decline in total employment since the mid 1960s. The expansion of employment in services and public administration has been more than offset by the loss of jobs elsewhere. The reversal of the growth in public employment in the recent past has clearly worsened the overall trend, although Layard and Nickell (1985) report no clear results on the effect of this on the natural rate (NAIRU) of unemployment. There is some evidence of a recent recovery of employment with the total number growing by 0.7% between 1983 and 1984 (7). This, however, unlike the 1930s has been far too modest to make any impression on measured unemployment. Since much of the employment growth is in part-time work for women it may however have reduced the true (corrected for registration bias) rate.

Housebuilding and the emergence of new manufacturing industries, was a significant feature of the 1930s. New industries, especially those connected with services, electrical goods and electricity supply grew rapidly creating substantial new sources of employment. No comparable job creation has taken place in the last decade. This structural failure to create new jobs on the required scale leaves the unemployed with a lower job offer arrival rate and raises the natural rate of unemployment. Inevitably to put together precise econometric evidence on the effects of what has not happened is difficult. As a result any conclusion on these matters is inevitably tentative.

We have considered the possibility that left untreated in a stagnant economy non-natural unemployment can be converted into structural unemployment that raises the natural rate. The evidence is not clear cut but indicates that this is now a real possibility in Britain. The argument, of course, rests upon the view that the aggregate labour market clears very slowly or not at all and non-natural unemployment persists for a long time. Even if real wages were eventually to fall this may not induce employers to hire workers, who, because of age, infirmity or long periods of idleness are regarded as having a low or even zero marginal product in their firm. Even the efficient operation of the labour market's price signal will not reverse the increase in unemployment that has taken place. Market clearing is only then achieved through an eventual increase in the equilibrium market clearing rate of unemployment.

In the absence of a clear policy to deal with this form of structural unemployment only death or retirement will reduce it. From a policy point of view this issue is clearly important. If the adverse effects of high and prolonged unemployment on the employability of workers is significant, attempts to stimulate labour demand to arrest the long run decline of jobs and reduce unemployment by demand expansion, real wage cuts or any other policies will have a significantly smaller effect. Some of these policy issues are considered in Chapter 9.

Relative Wages, Unions and Employment

We have already seen how changes in desired employment and fixed labour costs affect hiring standards and the job offer arrival rate element of the natural rate of unemployment. In this section, we will consider the impact of any changes in relative wages on hiring standards that do occur. Firstly recall the basic ideas. A firm with a constant desired labour force faces normal labour turnover and so in every time period hires are positive. Firms can opt for a low hiring standard and a low relative wage but by employing 'low quality' workers incur heavier training costs. They fix a higher hiring standard to minimise the training and other hiring costs. However to do this requires that the firms attract 'better' workers by paying more. This, of course, assumes that the relative wage paid by a firm is endogenous. In fact, of course, the relative wage of a firm is to a significant degree exogenously determined by other firms in the market and, by the institutions of collective bargaining. At the firm level, therefore, the degree of control over the relative wage may be limited so that the firm takes the relative wage as given and determines its hiring standard accordingly. We have assumed this to be the case in the analysis of Figures 8.5 so that secular variables affect the hiring standard only.

However, exogenous changes in the structure of relative wages do occur and are likely to affect the hiring standards of individual firms. The effect on the aggregate hiring standard will clearly depend on the employment size distribution among firms and of the size of firms affected by relative wage changes. To see this, consider the effect of a particular settlement which increases the relative wage of a firm or a set of firms all party to the same collective agreement. For that firm (or firms) there is a desired flow of labour necessary for a constant labour force. This is reinforced by the desire to offset the increase in direct wage costs by a reduction in training costs. However, other firms not party to the agreement will experience a reduction in their relative wage and will need to cut their hiring standards to maintain a constant labour force. If firms with a higher relative wage are large employers compared to those with a worsened position, there will be a net increase in hiring standards and a fall in the aggregate offer probability. Workers looking for a job will find it takes them longer to get one.

The impact of trade union behaviour is important in this process. If unions impose a wage premium or increase the existing premium as the evidence suggests, (8) has happened in Britain, this affects the wage structure. If the newly or currently unionised firms are large then unions could, through the demand side repercussions, decrease the aggregate offer probability and increase U^*_t. There is evidence in Britain that in fact both union membership and activity are positively correlated with firm size. Bain and Elias (1981), for example, show the former relationship while a great deal of evidence including that of Smith et al (1978) exists to show that strike activity is concentrated in large firms and plants in Britain. Brown (1981) and Marginson (1984) also find that other aspects of union activity and presence are positively correlated with firm and plant size. These include the incidence of meetings between recognised shop stewards and management and of collective action other than strikes. In order words, there is, in principle, reason to believe that the observed effects of union behaviour on the wage structure may have increased hiring standards in large firms and hence in the economy as a whole. (9) This will affect the natural rate of unemployment via this demand side route.

In the last chapter we examined evidence that shows that measures of union activity and presence are positively related to the natural rate of unemployment. (10) However, this evidence is somewhat ambiguous if we take account of the demand side effects. We cannot be sure whether the positive effect of unions on unemployment is through the supply or the demand side of the economy. It could arise through the positive impact of unions on the labour supply curve, reservation wages and hence on real wage levels in the economy, or via the impact on hiring standards and on the demand for employees. As we also saw in the last Chapter disentangling the various ways in which unions affect unemployment may also become more complicated once we allow for the direct impact on labour productivity and on the demand curve. Necessarily, therefore, it should be re-emphasised that the relevant evidence should be interpreted with considerable caution.

Other changes in the pattern of relative wages could have had similar effects. One possibility is that the increasing monopolisation of British industry (11) has had a significant impact on relative wages and on hiring standards in the macroeconomy. There is considerable evidence (12) that wage levels are higher in firms which operate in

imperfectly competitive product markets. The
changing market structure is correlated with the
growth in firm size. Both of these trends will
accelerate the development of structured internal
labour markets characterised by long job tenure for
employees. It will also lead to a general rise in
hiring standards. Imperfectly competitive firms pay
more but hope to recoup this by hiring higher quality
workers. (13) Unfortunately, there is no clearcut
empirical evidence on this, so again we must regard
the effects of monopolisation on unemployment as a
matter for conjecture rather than one for which firm
conclusions can be drawn.

Conclusion

In this chapter we have outlined demand side
influences on the natural rate of unemployment. From
a theoretical point of view these are obviously of
considerable importance. The empirical evidence is
in several respects by no means conclusive, but it
does suggest that, in practice, demand side effects
are important in the determination of the natural
rate and of changes in the values that have taken
place in Britain. Of particular importance are the
effects of reductions in the long run rate of growth
of output and employment which convert non-natural to
long term structural and hence to natural rate
unemployment. Various changes that have raised the
fixed cost of employing workers have also had
significant effects. Although in principle
acceleration in technical progress and capital
shortage could have caused a rise on U_t^* there is
little convincing evidence to persuade us this has
been an important feature of this rise. Similarly
although the decline in production industry
employment as a whole has had important effects,
contraction in specific industries which causes
heavily localised structural unemployment has not
been as important in Britain as in the 1930s with the
possible exception of the West Midlands.

In this and the previous chapter we have seen
the extent to which changes in the natural rate of
unemployment are in theory and practice the outcome
of a wide variety of factors. There is no single,
simple explanation for rising unemployment. In the
next chapter we will see there is, as a result, no
single, simple remedy for the large scale
unemployment of Britain and of the industrial
economies as a whole.

Notes

1.   The Survey of Labour Costs is a useful source of data on this matter. It shows that as a proportion of total labour costs, fixed labour costs have doubled since 1963. For an extension of the theory and evidence in the text see Hart (1984).

2.   The reason is that the effect of labour taxes is picked up through the unemployment not the misspecified real wage equation used by Minford.

3.   Other economists have tried to endogenise technical progress itself. Schott (1984) is an example. In her model the employment function is shifted downwards as a result of the contribution of research and development to technical knowledge. Her results also show technical knowledge is a negative function of its user cost. More confusingly it is also a function of the same variables (expected output and real wages in particular) that are generally assumed to be direct determinants of employment. Conventional estimates of the impact of technical change may be biased downwards as a result because some of, say, the output effect, arises from the indirect effect of expected output changes on R & D activity in the economy.

4.   Blue Book data shows the average capital output ratio grew from 3.8 in 1963 to 4.7 in 1973 and 5.5 in 1983.

5.   Mendis and Muellbauer (1983) and Wren-Lewis (1984) obtain results which imply that this is principally the result of increased labour utilisation. Reduction of manning levels by plant closure and rationalisation has led to a series of 'shakeouts' of labour. There is little or no evidence that the upward trend of the growth in labour productivity, especially over the last decade, is the outcome of more rapid capital accumulation or accelerated technical progress in the production (especially manufacturing) industries.

6.   Wren-Lewis (1984) also finds that a variable, reflecting company liquidity, has a significant positive effect on employment in manufacturing. One difficulty with this variable and that used by Wadhwani is that it suffers from the problem discussed in Chapters 6 and 7 that it contains both short run and secular effects so the effect is likely to be felt on both the natural rate and non-natural unemployment.

7.   Recent revisions to the official series show larger overall increases than this. They also reveal that employment amongst males continues to fall.

8.   The differential is clearly positive as the survey of results by Blanchflower (1984) shows, and has increased in Britain as Metcalf and Nickell (1985) show (p.14).

9.   There is evidence that unionised employers raise hiring standards and only employ higher quality workers. This is one of the reasons for the finding of Brown and Medoff (1979) that labour productivity is higher in unionised firms in the US.

10.   Recall also that some of this measured effect may actually be on the excess of unemployment over the natural rate.

11.   These trends are documented in, for example, Mueller (1981).

12.   There is abundant evidence for this in both Britain and the US. For a recent examination of the issue see Geroski, Hamlin and Knight (1982).

13.   The seminal paper by Weiss (1966) for example, which explores the link between wages and market concentration demonstrates this.

Chapter Nine

UNEMPLOYMENT - POLICY AND PROSPECTS

In previous chapters we have considered the many
alternative explanations of high unemployment. An
important distinction has been made between the
natural rate of unemployment and unemployment in
excess of that rate. It should now be clear that
there is no single explanation of high unemployment.
Rather it is the outcome of a multiplicity of
factors. Consequently there is no single, simple
solution and a successful policy to reduce the
current high levels of unemployment will obviously
have to take that into account. This is rather a
different viewpoint from that which prevailed twenty
years ago. Then, most economists viewed unemployment
as principally the outcome of controllable
fluctuations in aggregate demand. Keynesian demand
management policies should be sufficient to
eliminate the problem. Of course, policies like
special regional measures designed to affect the
composition of unemployment were also adopted but the
main emphasis was placed on the management of
aggregate demand, particularly through the use of
fiscal policy.
Some of the deficiencies of this approach are
evident from the previous chapters. Even if we accept
that a significant component of current unemployment
is of a non-natural disequilibrium character it is
not at all clear that it can be solved simply by an
expansion of aggregate demand. The rapid increase in
money wages and the failure of real wages to respond
rapidly to supply side shocks (especially in the
1970's) has, as we have seen, revived the notion of
classical unemployment to which the application of
expansionary demand management is futile and also
potentially damaging. Real wage cuts may be necessary
to deal with this as well as some of the potent
causes of increases in the natural rate of

nemployment.

The experience of the 1970's has led many
conomists who accept the need for a demand expansion
o reduce unemployment to argue also for the use of
ncomes policy to supplement this kind of demand
anagement. Similarly, a case has been made for
ugmenting demand management by trade creating and
iverting instruments like import controls or
urrency depreciation because of the persistent
ifficulty in achieving both internal and external
alance in Britain. Events in the world economy as a
hole (like oil price increases) have also raised
oubts about the efficacy of nationally based
conomic policies. This has led to growing support
or a coordinated demand expansion in the industrial
conomies as a whole with Britain taking the lead in
alling for it.

In fact, as we have also seen there is a sound
heoretical and empirical case for believing that the
ncrease in unemployment in Britain is only partly
on-natural in character. The longer run observed
ise in the natural rate will not be reversed by the
doption of a simple reflationary policy even if the
ontraction in the growth of demand is partly the
ause. Specific policies need to be designed to do
his.

At the moment in Britain (and in many other
ndustrial economies) recognition of the inadequac-
es of the simple Keynesian approach has led to
adical changes in economic policy. In this chapter
e will consider current economic policy and the
uture prospects if this policy remains unchanged. We
ill also consider alternative policies,
articularly those designed to deal with some of the
imitations of demand management. Most of the
iscussion will concentrate on Britain but, where
ppropriate, reference will also be made to the
xperience of other countries.

urrent Policy in Britain and the Eclipse of Demand anagement

n the last ten years there has been a remarkable
urnabout in policies to deal with unemployment.
uring the Conservative government of Edward Heath in
he early seventies the then high levels of
nemployment of 1971 and 1972 were substantially
educed in 1973 by a major expansion in the aggregate
emand for goods. Taxes were cut, public investment
as increased and there was a large expansion in the
oney supply. These were the instrument of the so

327

called 'Barber boom' which assumed that sinc
unemployment was largely Keynesian such an expansio
was all that was necessary. The only significan
ingredient of policy that departed from thi
diagnosis was the emphasis placed on regiona
incentives to reduce 'structural' unemployment i
certain areas of Britain.

Since then much has changed, not only in Britai
but in many other industrial economies. Partly thi
is the result of the rise to power of politicians o
the right who have some ideological sympathy with th
prescriptions of modern classical economics
However, even governments of the non-right have bee
influenced by the re-emergence of classical economi
ideas. During the Callaghan government of the lat
seventies, for example, the need to control the PSB
and the money supply became an important objective o
economic policy.

However, it is the Thatcher government which ha
become particularly identified with this re
emergence of conservative macroeconomics in Britain
Cuts in public investment and public spendin
programmes have reduced the PSBR as a share of GDP t
one of the lowest in the industrial world and th
most recent (1985) restatement of the government'
medium term financial strategy projects a furthe
fall throughout the 1980's. In part this very tigh
fiscal stance has been justified by the government'
desire to control the growth in the money supply. I
this respect the policy has been less than successfu
with the actual growth (except for 1982-3) generall
in excess of the target. (1) However, there are othe
reasons for its adoption which reflect the sceptica
view of fiscal policy itself taken by the Thatche
government. In general it has rejected the notio
that a reflation of demand via increases in curren
public spending or public investment is a viabl
solution to high unemployment. A recent statement o
the government's position can be found in Employment
The Challenge for the Nation: (Cmnd 9474) (1985)
Keynesian unemployment caused by a lack of demand i
specifically rejected by the words 'The one thin
clearly not responsible for unemployment is lack o
demand' and its solution by a boost, for example, t
public investment projects 'rates poorly as a direc
means of creating jobs. Besides being slow to pla
and execute ... they push up borrowing and interes
rates'. This clear statement of the classical belie
in 'crowding out' as a result of which any increase
in public spending simply supplant private spendin
is further justification for Thatcherite fisca

policy. However, although · this adherence to the irrelevance of Keynesian notions of the causes and cures of non-natural unemployment is the norm in government statements since 1979 there has been one period in which in practice this was not the case. In the run up to the general election of 1983 real public spending rose by 2.4% and public investment by 13.5% per annum. Despite the possibility that this contributed to the renewed growth in output and employment in Britain in the period 1983-85 the most recent formal statement (in Cmnd 9474) of the government's view signals a return to the classical orthodoxy. In one important respect however this is not the case. A central component of the government's present strategy for reducing unemployment is cuts in taxes, especially direct taxes. Clearly despite the high import content of the expenditure induced by tax cuts there is bound to be a positive impact of these tax cuts on both aggregate demand and on any non-natural Keynesian unemployment that exists. However, the government's case for tax cuts does not rest simply on these aggregate demand effects and is not justifiable solely in terms of a view of unemployment that the government appears to reject.

It seems clear from 'Employment: the Challenge for the Nation' and other sources that the Thatcher government regards too high a level of real wages as a major cause of (natural and non-natural) unemployment. It states (2):

> The higher the real cost of labour the lower employment will be, both because employers will be forced to economise on labour, and because higher labour costs mean lower profits and competitiveness, less investment and less business. ... The biggest factor in our increasing labour costs is the growth in earnings.

In a similar vein the Chancellor of the Exchequer stated (Hansard, 30 October 1984):

> Over the past two years average earnings in Britain have increased by 3 per cent more than prices ... if, instead average earnings had merely kept pace with prices the number of extra jobs created would have been about 500,000 a year.

Clearly the Thatcher government believes that most of any non-natural unemployment in Britain is classical in character and can be remedied by real labour cost reductions. Tax cuts can, according to the government, play an important role here. Particularly important is the effect of direct tax cuts on the rate of increase of earnings. If direct employee taxes are cut workers should demand lower increases in average earnings to achieve a target level of real post-tax wages. Tax cuts should, therefore, help to restrain the growth or even reduce the level of pre-tax real labour costs thus boosting employment. In addition post-tax wages can actually rise which has the additional alleged benefit of increasing the incentive to work. Since the government believes this effect is large and the response of employment to this fall in pre-tax real wages is also large it follows that large cuts in unemployment are expected from a policy of this kind.

Tax cuts also have supply and demand side effects on the natural rate of unemployment as we have seen in Chapters 7 and 8. Recent changes in national insurance contributions have this in mind. The government believes that these changes:

> sharply reduce the amounts both employees and employers have to contribute at lower pay levels and will make a substantial difference to job prospects, especially for the young and unskilled (3)

This is not the only way the government aims to reduce the 'disincentive to work' which it believes to be an important feature of current unemployment. Raising employee tax thresholds (reducing the number of workers liable for taxes) reducing real unemployment benefit (especially through the abolition of the earnings related supplement) are also intended to reduce equilibrium real wages, lower the value of U_t^* and hence reduce unemployment overall.

On the demand side the removal of Wage Councils protection that lays down minimum pay rates for young workers and reducing the scope of the employment protection legislation are expected to have the same effect. Systematic attempts by legislation and other methods to reduce trade union power and influence can also be viewed as part and parcel of a strategy to increase employment through both supply and demand side effects on both natural and non-natural unemployment. Note however the emphasis on the inverse (positive) association of the natural rate of employment (unemployment) and pre-tax real wages at underlies these proposals. Real wages need to all if equilibrium employment is to be increased. heoretically this is not an obvious requirement ince, for example, a positive labour demand shock ould increase both employment and real wages. We eturn to this question later in this chapter.

Other aspects of current government policy in ritain confirms this broadly classical perspective f unemployment. The emphasis on the quality of the abour force, particularly as far as education and raining are concerned, and the extent to which this etermines the speed with which workers and employees dapt to (Cmnd 2474) (4): 'new products and processes nd new competitive pressures which offer new hallenges and opportunities' indicates this.

The Thatcher government believes that this daptability has not been characteristic of the ritish labour market and this has lowered the atural rates of output and employment. The White aper 'Better Schools' (Cmnd 9469) places emphasis on ork-related education and training. The Manpower ervice Commission Technical and Vocational ducation Initiative (TVEI) is motivated by the same bjective. The government also sees the Youth raining Scheme and other forms of training for dults as improving the quality of the labour force. his, it believes, will reduce the natural rate of utput and employment by making the labour force both re skilful and more flexible. Other special easures like the Community Programme are seen in the ame light as a way of reducing structural nemployment especially among the long term nemployed.

Hence, with its emphasis on policies to reduce he natural rate and its assertion that too high a evel of real wages rather than a shortage of ggregate demand is the primary cause of non-natural nemployment the Thatcher government has clearly dentified itself with a classical view of nemployment. With this in mind we next examine overnment policy in more detail and then consider in he remainder of this chapter the main ingredients of arious alternative proposals to reduce unemployment nd the prospects for success of each. Firstly, owever and by way of background we will consider uture prospects for jobs in Britain in the 1980s.

ob Prospects in the 1980s

t is possible to calculate the number of new jobs equired to reduce unemployment significantly in

331

Britain. This has been done, for example, by Metcal
(1984) who calculates the jobs needed to reduc
unemployment to 2 million by 1989. The total numbe
to absorb the growth in the labour force and t
reduce registered unemployment is 2.122 million o
1163 jobs per day between 1984 and 1989. Som
economists would argue Metcalf's estimate of the job
needed is on the low side because he hasn't take
full account of the effects of job creation o
unregistered unemployment. If (like in 1984) th
growth in jobs is concentrated on this group o
unemployed workers the number of jobs necessary t
reduce registered unemployment (especially) fo
males is even greater than he calculates. Other
would object that Metcalf's objective of 2 million i
too high and in particular higher than ful
employment when it is defined as the level o
employment when nobody is <u>involuntarily</u> unemployed.

Notwithstanding these objections, Metcalf'
calculation clearly indicate the enormous scale o
the problem facing Britain and to a less sever
extent much of the rest of Western Europe. What ar
the prospects for attaining the 2 million targe
level of unemployment by 1989? Metcalf shows th
required growth rate in jobs is far in excess of th
post war average. In the halcyon days of 1959-64, fo
example, the growth in jobs was only 730,000. Only i
the 1930s has job growth (1.290 million in 1932-37
been on the scale required now. Is it likely the sam
expansion will occur in the 1980s? There has been a
increase in jobs in 1983/5 which for the year endir
in September 1984 the government estimated to b
340,000. (5) Even if we accept the validity (6) o
this estimate it is still below the level required b
Metcalf's estimates. Moreover, much of this growt
has been in part-time jobs for married women, who, a
we have seen, are much more likely to be amongst th
unregistered unemployed. In fact the number of full
time jobs for men actually fell in 1984. The resul
is that registered unemployment has not falle
significantly. The growth in jobs is apparently onl
sufficient to absorb the growth in the labour suppl
and exerts its greatest impact on the unregistere
component of total unemployment. Clearly Britain i
<u>not</u> on target significantly to reduce registere
unemployment in this decade. This is no surprise t
those who forecast future trends in the labou
market. A recent survey (7) of the 23 short ter
forecasts for Britain finds only 3 who expec
unemployment to fall by 1987. Longer term forecast
which assume no major change of direction i

government policy confirm this pessimistic story. Forecasts prepared by the Institute of Employment Research at Warwick (1985) for example, predict an increase in jobs of only 145,000 between 1984-90 which is not enough to prevent a rise in unemployment, particularly at the end of the 1980s. There is also a marked divergence between the sexes in the forecast of unemployment. Amongst women the unemployment rate is expected to fall but the male rate is forecast to rise from 15% in 1984 to 18% in 1990. Because of the pessimism of the forecast in respect to output trends in the production sector of the economy all of the net increase in jobs is expected to occur in private service industries to which the government in Britain attaches great importance. In fact, even if sizeable growth in output in production industries did take place it is unlikely to generate jobs on the scale required. Technical change may not have been a potent cause of rising unemployment but its depressing effect on the output elasticity of employment especially in manufacturing, make its cure more difficult. The IER's forecast predicts that labour productivity increases in the manufacturing sector of the British economy will greatly exceed the average for the economy as a whole (3.7% per annum compared with 2.2% per annum between 1984 and 1990) and for private services (0.8% per annum). Even if the structural decline of the manufacturing sector which, as we have seen, has contributed to rising unemployment were totally reversed it is unlikely in the light of these figures that its direct counter-effect on reducing the stock of unemployment will be equivalently substantial.

Prospects for a major fall in unemployment in Britain (and in the rest of Europe) seem, therefore, bleak unless government policies change or have an unexpectedly large effect on jobs, especially in the non-production sector. Of course this does not mean current policy has been a failure. It could be that unemployment would have been even higher without the package of policies adopted by the Thatcher government. In the next section we will evaluate in the light of the analysis of the previous chapters the policy of the current government and its predecessors. Then we will move on to consider alternative and additional policies which might make an impact in the next decade.

Unemployment Policy Evaluation

We have already outlined the Thatcher government's policy for unemployment in Britain. If we consider it in the light of the empirical evidence reviewed in the previous chapters it is difficult to avoid the conclusion that the government has consistently backed the wrong horse. That is not to say that the policy has not had some degree of success but in general much less success than the alternatives available. The Thatcher government has chosen to pursue policies which, in general, the empirical evidence tells us will have a positive but modest effect on reducing unemployment and has also eschewed alternatives which again on the basis of the available evidence should produce better results.

First, consider the government's 'normal' (excluding 1982/3) stance on fiscal policy and demand management. As we have seen the government has been broadly sympathetic to the classical view of the neutrality of demand management. However, as we saw in Chapter 6, the evidence in support of this view is sketchy, especially in Britain. Indeed the evidence suggests that not only is demand management <u>not</u> neutral but that its non-neutrality is confirmed by government policy since 1979 which has contributed significantly to the major rise in unemployment experienced in Britain. Recall the evidence of Layard and Nickell (1985) which shows that, unlike the decade before (with both Labour and Conservative governments), lack of demand contributed substantially to the rise of unemployment over this period. The government's fiscal stance and the high exchange rate consequences of their monetary policy had a profound effect on the level of unemployment in Britain. A cautious estimate would be that about a quarter of current unemployment and just under a half of the increase since 1979 is the direct outcome of government demand management policy, particularly in the period up to 1982. Since that time and until 1985 there has been no evident positive effect on reducing unemployment but fiscal expansion especially in 1982/3 has at least contributed to the stabilisation of the unemployment rate in Britain. The 1984/5 return of the Thatcher government to 'normal' will, if it is sustained (about this there must be some doubt) have further positive effects on unemployment unless it is offset in some way.

In fact the impact of other aspects of policy has clearly offset the demand management effect since 1979. The reduction in the inflation rate in which government policy has played a part (but does not wholly explain) is an example. Not only does this help trade competitiveness, it also encourages private consumption, which has risen by around 3% per annum since 1982 and some of this additional demand offsets fiscal stringency. The stimulation to private consumption comes from the reduced rate of erosion of the real value of private sector assets that occurs when the inflation rate slows down.

A recent study by Kennally (1985) suggests this boost to private consumption would not have come about had consumer credit not become more readily available. If this is the case then the relaxation by the government of the stringency of credit control in 1982 is more important as a complementary factor than the direct effect of the reduction in the inflation rate between 1980 and 1982 (which is likely to be quite small). (8) Whatever its cause both this boost to private consumption and that to trading competitiveness partially offsets the reduction in aggregate demand occurring through previous fiscal stringency and will have had a positive effect on the unemployment rate especially in 1983/4. This boost to trade competitiveness was re-inforced by the depreciation of the pound in that period. As a result export volumes rose significantly (by 6.6%) in 1984 which increased both output (especially in manufacturing) and employment. (9)

Tax cuts may also have stimulated aggregate demand especially since 1982. During this period sustained increases in real terms in tax allowances will have had demand side effects that reinforce the 1982/84 relaxation on the expenditure side. However these tax cuts are thought by the government also to have supply side effects that reduce the natural rate of unemployment. As we saw in Chapter 7 there is little 'hard' evidence to support this view. More favourable is the effect of reductions in employer taxes and especially the gradual abolition of the national insurance surcharge. We saw in Chapter 8 the evidence that suggests the rising fixed cost of employing workers has been a non-trivial cause of increases in the natural rate of unemployment in Britain. Reductions (10) in this component of labour cost borne by employers has clearly had a favourable impact on unemployment since 1982 though it is by no means clear that the effect is so far sufficiently substantial to offset the rise in unemployment caused by increases over the last two decades.

As we have seen the government has also placed some emphasis on tax cuts as a means of restraining exogenously caused growth in real wages which its

335

classical viewpoint implies is a critical cause of rising unemployment. Again as we say in Chapter 6, 7 and 8 there is little evidence to support this view of the causes of rising unemployment in the 1980s though it clearly has a greater degree of substance in the 1970s. In fact there is little evidence that this aspect of policy has actually succeeded so far. According to the government's own figure (11), after an initial drop average real wages (12) have actually risen by 10% since 1979 and by 3% in 1984. Given these facts reductions in unemployment or increases in employment caused by real wage falls cannot have occurred. Since, however, reductions in the growth of real labour costs remains a critical part of the government's current strategy for reducing unemployment in the future we will consider this question in more detail later in this chapter.

Other policy measures have been adopted in an attempt to restrain the growth in real wages. Public sector pay restraint plus institutional and legal changes that weaken the bargaining power of British trades unions can be viewed in this light. These policies have certainly reduced some aspects of collective union activity. Strike frequency, for example, has fallen dramatically. However, we have also seen an increased scale in public sector disputes (like those with the miners and teachers). There is no evidence, however, that any of these changes has had any impact on reducing unemployment. Layard and Nickell (1985) in fact find a small positive effect of union behaviour on unemployment for the 1979-83 period. Similarly Metcalf and Nickell (1985) produce evidence that shows no tendency for the differential of union over non-union members to fall. In fact after a rise in 1979 it remains level until at least 1983. Of course, most of the evidence we surveyed in Chapters 7 and 8 tells us that even had government policy severely weakened unions and significantly reduced the union/non-union different-ial unemployment would still have fallen only by a modest amount. In fact, this aspect of policy appears not to have had even this effect.

Other policies to reduce the natural rate of unemployment which are given such strong emphasis in the classical view of unemployment also appear to have had a modest effect. Certainly no evidence exists to demonstrate any other conclusion. The abolition of the earnings related supplement is a good example. In this case there should be no surprise. Our survey of the evidence in Chapter 7 suggested the effect of cutting unemployment benefit was likely to be modest given the small scale of the response of unemployment to the introduction of the ERS in the 1960s. If a government adopts a policy of this kind and expects to observe a <u>large</u> fall in unemployment it is likely to be disappointed. The evidence tells us it is 'backing the wrong horse'.

The Thatcher government also sees its industrial policy as a way of generating equilibrium employment. This according to <u>Employment: The Challenge for the Nation</u> has five crucial elements (13):

(i) giving help and incentives to enterprise, especially in small firms;

(ii) supporting innovation and the exploitation of new technology;

(iii) easing the burden of regulation and simplifying the planning system;

(iv) breaking up monopolies and fostering competition;

(v) releasing as much business as possible out of public sector constraints into the challenge and opportunity of a free commercial setting.

There is no clearcut evidence that these policies have so far had a profound effect on the rate at which new jobs for the registered unemployed (especially males) are created. The government points to the accelerated rate of labour productivity growth in manufacturing which helps international competitiveness in that sector. In fact, since 1984 this growth has started to decelerate although it remains high compared with other sectors. This deceleration is consistent with the work by Muellbauer and Mendis (1982) and Wren-Lewis (1984) referred to in earlier chapters which suggests no acceleration to the <u>secular</u> rate of labour productivity, which would increase equilibrium employment and reduce U_t^*, appears to have taken place. Rather, British industry has experienced a major but once for all shakeout of low productivity plant, factories and firms that has actually caused a major <u>reduction</u> in equilibrium employment and increased U_t^*. Some of the evidence for this view was outlined in previous chapters especially in Chapter 8.

It would appear, therefore, that under the Thatcher government the rise in unemployment in Britain that goes back to the 1960s has accelerated, especially in the year 1979-82. In part this is the direct consequence of the macroeconomic policies which were adopted. Since that time, policies to reduce natural and non-natural unemployment have been successful only to the extent that the dramatic increase in unemployment has stopped. In general, government policy has (unlike the US in the post-1982 period) failed to bring unemployment down.

One major aspect of government policy has been ignored so far and that is the use of special measures to reduce unemployment and to assist the unemployed. Certain types of unemployment and certain groups of unemployed people have been particularly selected for attention. In this respect the Thatcher government is continuing (and has expanded) policies adopted by previous governments, especially the preceding 1974-79 Labour administration. In the remainder of this section we will examine in some detail the use of special measures in Britain and evaluate their success.

The extensive scope of special measures (excluding regional policy and adult training measures) to reduce unemployment since 1975 is shown in Tables 9.1 and 9.2. This indicates total expenditure up until 1985 in excess of £10 billion. It also shows real expenditure has doubled and the total number of participants has greatly increased as a result of the policy initiatives of the Thatcher government. Alongside this heavy expenditure there have been significant discontinuities in policy. As Tables 9.1 and 9.2 show there have been 18 different (often short lasting) initiatives over the last decade. The measures adopted can be put into four different categories.

(a)   wage subsidies
(b)   training programmes
(c)   worksharing measures
(d)   public employment programmes

Wage subsidies have generally been abandoned by the Thatcher government. In contrast, the preceding Labour government made more extensive use of this type of measure especially through the Temporary Employment and Small Firms Employment Subsidy which, partly as a response to pressure from the EEC, were withdrawn in 1980. The only remaining measure with a subsidy component is the Young Workers Scheme. This was started in 1982 but closed for application in March 1986. Under it employers could claim £15 per week for young workers (under 18) who earned less than £50 a week during the first year of their employment. This was really a recruitment subsidy that affected the employment of about a third of the relevant age group.

Training programmes are important especially for young workers. Although they are clearly intended as a means of reducing <u>current</u> unemployment greater emphasis has been placed on the pure training component of the policy. The intention here frequently justified by comparing Britain with Germany is to provide better training and hence a better qualified work force. In the long run by affecting overall economic performance, including the level of labour productivity, this should reduce the natural rate of unemployment in Britain.

The Youth Opportunity Programme introduced in 1978 followed a series of <u>ad hoc</u> initiatives by the Manpower Services Commission beginning in 1975. It was clearly aimed only at the short run reduction in unemployment amongst young workers. It provided little real training for young workers and, in general, made available only dead-end jobs that did nothing to enhance the employment prospects of those on the scheme. As a result it made little contribution to the long run objectives of a better trained, higher quality labour force. It was replaced in 1983 by the Youth Training Scheme (YTS). This is currently the most extensive of the special measures and in 1985 the government announced a further extention of its scope. YTS is intended to provide school leavers with an integrated year long programme of training and work experience and hence to have both short run and long run effects on unemployment. Most young people take up places offered by mainly private sector employers on 'Mode A' schemes. Firms participating in YTS got £2050 per annum in 1985. The firm does not pay the youngster a wage. Instead Trainees receive a weekly allowance (currently £25) paid by the government. A minority (14) of young workers (about one quarter) take up places on 'Mode B' schemes in which they train at Information Technology Centres (ITECS), Training Workshops, Community Projects or other community based schemes and receive, where possible, some on-the-job training at employer premises. The recently announced extension of the scheme will provide a second year of training for 16 year old school leavers. This will require 130,000 extra year-long places from 1986.

As far as adults are concerned the government spent £265 million in 1985-86. By 1986-87 the government plans to train a quarter of a million adults, half of whom will be unemployed. Part of this is the provision of 'enterprise training' which helps unemployed people to start up their own businesses.

Table 9.1: Gross Expenditure on Special Employment Measures, 1975/76 to 1984/85, £m 1985-86 Prices

Measure	1975/6	1976/7	1977/8	1978/9	1979/80	1980/1	1981/2	1982/3	1983/4	1984/5
Adults: Demand Side										
Jobs Creation Programme	3	83	153	147	8	1	neg	neg	-	-
Special Temporary Employment Programme	-	-	-	18	85	64	-	-	-	-
Community Enterprise Programme	-	-	-	-	-	-	107	178	443	562
Community Programme	-	-	-	-	-	-	-	-	-	-
Adult Employment Subsidy	-	-	-	neg	1	neg	-	-	-	-
Temporary Employment Subsidy	7	223	367	254	68	1	-	-	-	-
Small Firms Employment Subsidy	-	-	4	226	75	15	neg	neg	-	-
Enterprise Allowance Scheme	-	-	-	-	-	-	-	3	26	80
Adults: Supply Side										
Job Release Scheme	-	3	32	42	142	189	166	224	284	260
Short Time Working Compensation Scheme	-	-	-	2	-	-	-	-	-	-
Temporary Short Term Working Compensation Scheme	-	-	-	-	41	507	322	83	30	-
Job Splitting Scheme	-	-	-	-	-	-	-	neg	neg	1

Measure	1975/6	1976/7	1977/8	1978/9	1979/80	1980/1	1981/2	1982/3	1983/4	1984/5
Youths										
Community Industry	9	14	19	22	28	26	26	27	26	19
Work Experience Programme	-	2	27	-	-	-	-	-	-	-
Youth Opportunity Programme	-	-	-	109	192	298	492	600	349	-
Youth Training Scheme	-	-	-	-	-	-	-	-	414	790
Recruitment Subsidy to School Leavers	2	5	neg	-	-	-	-	-	-	-
Youth Employment Subsidy	-	1	11	7	neg	-	-	-	-	-
Young Workers	-	-	-	-	-	-	-	47	64	40
Total	22	331	613	827	639	1102	1007	1181	1636	1752

Notes: Expenditure figures from Hansard, 15 January 1985, col 74. That source gives expenditure in outturn prices, which is put into constant 1985-86 prices using the GDP deflator at market prices. Figures may not add to totals owing to rounding. The symbol 'neg' indicates figures less than £1m. 1984/85 figures are estimated.

Source: Metcalf (1982) and Davies and Metcalf (1985).

341

Table 9.2: Participants in Special Employment Measures, 1975/76 to 1984/85 – Thousands

Measure	1975/6	1976/7	1977/8	1978/9	1979/80	1980/1	1981/2	1982/3	1983/4	1984/5
Adults: Demand Side										
JCP (entrants)	14.1	79.3	106.1	–	–	–	–	–	–	–
STEP (entrants)	–	–	–	19.7	22.4	18.4	–	–	–	–
CEP (entrants)	–	–	–	–	–	–	27.6	39.5	–	–
CP (entrants)	–	–	–	–	–	–	–	12.1	134.4	131.0
AES (entrants)	–	–	–	–	1.4	–	–	–	–	–
TES (entrants)	11.3	161.0	197.7	129.1	–	–	–	–	–	–
SFES (entrants)	–	–	3.1	82.2	99.0	–	–	–	–	–
EAS (entrants)	–	–	–	–	–	–	–	2.1	26.9	39.0
Adults: Supply Side										
JRS (entrants)	–	10.0	14.5	25.6	68.2	24.2	38.7	46.1	44.8	75.0
STWCS (jobs saved)	–	–	–	15.0	–	–	–	–	–	–
TSTWCS (jobs saved)	–	–	–	–	92.9	635.1	166.7	101.4	29.6	–
JSS (jobs split)	–	–	–	–	–	–	–	0.2	0.7	1.0
Youths										
CI (filled places)	1.8	3.2	4.3	4.9	5.8	6.2	6.9	7.0	7.0	8.0
WEP (entrants)	–	7.6	54.0	–	–	–	–	–	–	–
YOP (entrants)	–	–	–	162.2	216.4	360.0	553.0	543.0	27.0	–
YTS (entrants)	–	–	–	–	–	–	–	–	354.0	332.0
RSSL (entrants)	30.2	–	–	–	–	–	–	–	–	–
YES (entrants)	–	14.8	–	32.6	–	–	–	–	–	–
YWS (subsidies commenced)	–	–	–	–	–	–	–	174.3	129.5	61.0

Notes: Hansard, 15 January 1985, col. 74. Note that a figure for total coverage cannot be given because some schemes are measured in terms of entrants, others in terms of filled places.

In 1984-85 6000 people will be trained in this way and the government plans an increase to 15000 in 1985-86. Allied to this is the Enterprise Allowance Scheme which was introduced in 1982. This aims to help unemployed people who want to start their own business. Entrants must have £1000 to invest in the business and they are paid a flat rate weekly allowance (currently £40) for a year. The government also intends to increase its expenditure on this scheme in 1985-86 to benefit 52,000 unemployed in that year. This is a significant increase over 1983-84 as Table 9.2 shows.

Spending on adult training for unemployed workers is not new. Since 1972 the Training Opportunities Scheme (TOPS) has provided courses mostly for the unemployed. Courses typically last a few months and have been generally provided at publicly owned skill centres and colleges. Recently, however, several skill centres have been closed. The 1984 White Paper, <u>Training for Jobs</u> (Cmnd 1984), reveals an intention to provide less training for the adult unemployed and more for those currently or about to be employed. It also seems intent on providing a greater number of significantly shorter courses than in the past. It also proposes a loan scheme for adult trainees. Current policy on adult training for the unemployed appears to involve some retrenchment and that it is in notable contrast with the great expansion in the provision for the young. (15)

Work sharing schemes are rather less important. The most important is the long running Job Release Scheme. This scheme encourages men aged 64 and over and women 59 and over to give up work and release their jobs to unemployed people. If the individual's employer agrees to replace the retiring worker by an unemployed worker he or she is paid a weekly allowance until the date at which the statutory retirement age is reached. The numbers involved are still quite small (see Table 9.2) but have increased significantly since its introduction in 1976. The only other work sharing scheme is the Job Splitting Scheme introduced in 1983. A grant is paid to an employer who splits an existing job into two part-time jobs, one of which must be filled by a person who would otherwise be employed. So far the take-up of their scheme is tiny and expenditure has, therefore, been trivial (see Table 9.1).

The final type of scheme used in Britain is that which provides public employment for the unemployed. The longest running of these schemes is Community

Industry which is a charitable company formed in 1972 and which provides temporary work for disadvantaged youngsters who undertake a variety of projects for the community. More recent and more significant is the Community Programme started in 1983 as a successor to a variety of similar schemes (JCP, STEP, CEP in Table 9.2) and involving a substantial and increasing expenditure in 1984/85. This scheme provides temporary work for 130,000 long term unemployed adults. The government has announced an expansion of the Programme to 230,000 places by 1987. Participants are paid the hourly rate for the job, most of which are unskilled and part-time so weekly earnings are not high (16). Projects undertaken under CP include a large proportion of public sector environmental schemes, like landscaping, gardening, the provision of tourist facilities and so on (17).

One element of government policy not covered in Table 9.1 and 9.2 is regional policy which has since the 1930s been a feature of British policy to reduce unemployment. During the 1960s and early 1970s there was a considerable expansion of both policy instruments and overall expenditure on this aspect of policy (18). Empirical work by Moore and Rhodes (1973, 1976) and others indicated a significant effect of these policy initiatives on employment and unemployment by region at that time. Since then there has been significant retrenchment in this area, partly through the intervention of the EEC which led, for example, to the abolition of the Regional Employment Premium (a wage subsidy paid to employees in unemployment black spots) but largely as a result of the deliberate policy decisions of British governments. Since 1979 there have been significant changes which have severely weakened the strength of regional policy. Of particular importance is that Industrial Development Certificates are no longer required for industrial expansion schemes. Moore and Rhodes (1976) found the use of the IDC was the most potent instrument of policy in the 1960s and 1970s. There have also been reductions in regional investment incentives. On the positive side the government has established 25 special enterprise zones in which new businesses are able to locate with a variety of concessions including exemption from local authority rates. Six experimental freeports have also been designated to encourage employment. On balance, however, these have not enough to prevent a significant weakening of policy designed to reduce unemployment in high unemployment areas of Britain. These various special measures and the changes

participate in special measures programmes would
otherwise have been employed or in the case of young
workers been in full time education. Similarly, the
existence of special measures may displace currently
non-participating workers from employment or even
currently employed workers. (19) Since, for example,
the relative cost of employing young workers falls
because of special measures, we can expect in
principle some substitution of these workers for
others. Empirical work on the demand for youth labour
which we considered in Chapter 6 clearly indicates
this will happen. The story is, however, rather more
complicated. Consider Figure 9.1 which depicts a
conventional isoquant for two kinds of labour
services (adults and youths). The substitution
effect will shift employment along the Y_1 isoquant to
E_2^Y and E_2^A from E_1^Y and E_1^A. Overall unemployment could
fall but it could also stay the same. The outcome
will depend on the relative marginal products of the
two groups of workers (the slope of the isoquant).
The fall in adult employment could equal the rise in
youth employment. This, however, is unlikely.

Figure 9.1

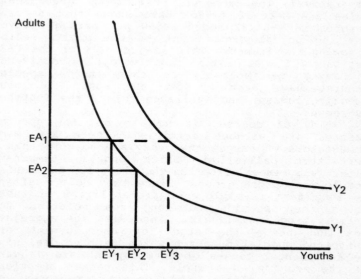

Any positive effect of experience on productivity
means that in practice the extra jobs created for

less productive youths will exceed the job loss for more productive adults.

The view that the net increase in employment (unemployment) is positive (negative) is strengthened when we also take account of scale effects. The impact of special measures is to reduce marginal costs and prices and this stimulates demand at the firm level. This shifts the isoquant upwards. In principle it could shift to Y_2 which implies no adult job losses at all. In practice, especially at the aggregate level in an economy characterised by substantial market imperfections this is unlikely to happen. The most likely outcome, therefore, is that some net displacement will occur but the impact of special measures on jobs overall is still positive. This is the view of the Department of Employment. It calculates the claimant count was reduced by these special measures below the level that would otherwise be the case by 440,000 in 1984 and 465,000 in 1985 <u>after</u> the displacement affect is allowed for. (20) As a result it is not unreasonable to conclude that this aspect of policy has since 1979 had a greater positive impact on restraining and stabilising the growth in registered (claimant) unemployment than any other. This has also been achieved at a comparatively low Exchequer cost to the government. Davies and Metcalf (1985) have shown that special measures in 1984/85 added £2050 per person removed from the unemployment count to the public sector borrowing requirement. This is just 20% of the PSBR cost of the lowest cost alternative option considered by Davies and Metcalf. In these terms special measures have been by far the most PSBR cost effective chosen (and available to) by the Thatcher government.

This, of course, is not to say the special measures are without criticism. There are many commentators who argue that they are no more than a short term palliative, which provide temporary relief (via removal from the register) for particular unemployment prone groups. Since they do not affect the long term re-employment probabilities of these groups they provide no long run solution for participating individuals. Since also the aggregate flow and hence the stock of unemployment are unaffected special measures which fail to deal with the fundamental causes of unemployment are no cure for the economy as a whole. This rather sceptical view of the effects of special measures on unemployment in the long run is compounded if the displacement effects of special measures are greater

than the rather cautious estimates of the Department
of Employment and if those (like the 58% on YTS in
1983-84) who get jobs afterwards would have done so
anyway. If this is the case the true Exchequer costs
of special measures will be a good deal higher than
that calculated by Davies and Metcalf (1985).

Unfortunately and surprisingly little convincing research has been done on the unemployment
effects of special measures that would help to
resolve this matter. Empirical work on the effects of
the wage subsidies adopted in the 1970s and largely
abandoned by the Thatcher government is an exception.
(21) Deakin and Pratten (1982), for example,
calculate a strongly beneficial effect of the
Temporary Employment Subsidy (TES) at least in the
short term. TES was paid for one year to firms that
deferred redundancies that would affect 10 or more
workers. The effect of this is calculated by Deakin
and Pratten to be a net job preservation rate of 39
jobs for every 100 subsidised. The details are shown
in Table 9.3.

Table 9.3: Effects of TES per 100 jobs subsidised

(1)	Jobs Lost	11
(2)	Jobs which would have continued without the subsidy (dead weight loss)	29
(3)	Job displacement in firms as a result of payment of TES	21
(4)	Net job saving	39

Source: Deakin and Pratten (1982)

There is a clear positive effect which reduces the
net exchequer cost of the subsidy to 60% of the gross
cost. However, the effect on jobs is likely to be
transitory and to be highly concentrated. Labour
intensive and significantly female employing sectors
like textiles, leather and clothing accounted for 43%
of the jobs covered by TES. There is no evidence that
confirms that the payment of TES had significant long
run effects on unemployment in Britain. Similar
conclusions have been arrived at by a Department of
Employment study (22) of the Temporary Short Time
Working Compensation Scheme (TSTWCS)which followed
TES and ran until 1984. The DE Study suggests that
TSTWCS postponed redundancies but it did not stop
them in the long run. This fact, of course, weakens
the argument that special measures actually inhibit

the kind of long run structural change that many commentators regard as essential for a permanent reduction in (especially natural rate) unemployment.

Some evidence is also available on specific special measures that have been used. A recent study by Turner (1985) of the Community Programme confirms the view that special measures have their greatest effect in the short run but may also be by no means ineffective in the longer term. The vast majority (65%) of long term unemployed workers who participated in the Community Programme and included in Turner's survey subsequently re-enter the unemployed stock. However an encouraging 23% went straight into jobs of whom 19% worked full time. This proportion moreover increased as time elapsed after leaving the programme, the average length of which was 7.7 months. The proportion in the sample in jobs was then 32%, with the 21-24 age group the most successful (37%) at finding jobs and women (41%) more successful than men (29%). This seems to suggest that the Community Programme has also had an effect in increasing the medium term job prospects of the long term unemployed. The evidence is, however, by no means totally conclusive. The survey was done in 1984 when employment was growing rapidly and unless a follow-up survey is conducted in 1985 and 1986 we cannot safely conclude the employment prospects of the long term unemployed have been permanently and significantly improved. In addition there is no indication of displacement effects or of the employment of workers not on the programme. Nonetheless Turner's results are encouraging and suggest that although the main effect of CP is transitory some longer run effects on employment do occur.

More surprisingly, given the scale of the expenditure there have been few satisfactory formal tests of other special measures. Little attempt has been made in the time series modelling of the youth labour market to estimate the impact of the special measures targetted at young workers. Junankar and Neale (1985) do make a rather crude attempt but by their own admission the results are curious and unsatisfactory. Clearly YTS, and its predecessors YOP and the Young Workers Scheme do reduce the count of unemployed young people in the short run but in the longer run the evidence is less clear cut. O'Connor (1982) conducted a follow-up survey of entrants to schemes under YOP. In particular he estimated the probabilities of employment of those on the relevent schemes. Unfortunately, little conclusion is obtained from his study about the effects of special measures since he does not consider a comparable group of workers who did not participate in YOP schemes. There is also some evidence from O'Connor's study that no significant difference exists between individuals with different periods of unemployment and who participated in YOP. If long unemployment scars an individual, YOP schemes seem to have reduced this problem. On the other hand duration dependence (scarring) may simply not be a feature of the experience of young workers as some but not all of the evidence surveyed in Chapter 2 suggests. In this case O'Connor's result is no surprise.

O'Connor also finds that the employment probability declines the longer an individual is on a YOP Scheme which again is hardly evidence for significant long run effects on job prospects. A study by Banks, Mullings and Jackson (1983) also provides evidence of the effects of YOP on a cohort of 1979 school leavers in Leeds. A quarter of the cohort went on YOP schemes and these were generally those with poor educational qualifications. Many were black. There is some evidence that job prospects for YOP participants were improved by this scheme, but not sufficiently to make them comparable to non-YOP participants.

To some extent this lack of conclusive evidence reflects the uncertainty about the success attained by the YOP (and now YTS) in meeting the twin objectives of reducing unemployment and of providing training. It is the latter which principally improves the long run job prospects of the young. For the economy as a whole it also assists towards economic regeneration. Most commentators (23) regard YOP as successful only in attaining the first objective. Raffe (1984a), for example, reports widespread criticism of YOP and substantial disillusion among participants who regarded it as a scheme to provide employers with cheap labour and as a way of keeping 'headline' unemployment down. There is no overwhelmingly clearcut objective evidence that challenges this view and perhaps this reflects the failure of YOP to provide satisfactory training for youngsters as well as a failure by government agencies thoroughly to appraise the schemes.

Doubts about the ability of YOP to achieve anything significant other than a short run reduction in the unemployment count led to the introduction of YTS. Although a move in the direction necessary for a permanent effect to occur there exists no unambiguous

evidence that it has been a significant improvement
so far. Raffe (1984b) reports that female school
leavers regarded YTS in the same light as YOP.
Amongst males attitudes are more equivocal.
Nonetheless Raffe concludes on the basic of his
survey of the experience of Scottish school leavers.
'YTS has functioned mainly as an unemployment-based
scheme. Any improvement on YOP in this respect has
been modest'. However this conclusion relates only to
the first year of YTS when school leavers attitudes
and expectations were based still on the experience
of YOP and clearly tells us nothing objective about
the actual effects of the scheme in the longer term.

Although the evidence is rather inconclusive it
does not seem that, with some exceptions, special
measures have so far done anything more than provide
a short term palliative for unemployment. Further
criticisms have also been made of special measures in
Britain. Some economists have argued that the
deadweight loss of special measures is unacceptably
high. The deadweight loss is the result of payments
or expenditure to bring about an increase in jobs or
prevent a reduction that would have happened anyway.
Table 3.3 contains some calculations in respect of
the Temporary Employment Subsidy that clearly reduce
the gross benefit of the scheme but not to a
significant extent. Unfortunately comparable calculations for other schemes have not been so carefully
done. However deadweight loss does seem to be an
important feature of the Young Workers Scheme (most
participants would have had the job anyway) and this
is one reason for its withdrawal. On the whole,
however, there is little evidence to justify the view
that this deadweight loss is large enough to justify
the withdrawal of most special measures.

A further problem with special measures is the
valuation of the output produced. In no sense have
the projects undertaken been evaluated to optimise
the allocation of public sector resources. Projects
are set up on an ad hoc basis with no apparent
overall strategy. It is far from clear from the
evidence that a conventional expansion of government
expenditure, though more exchequer costly per job, is
not superior on allocative grounds. A similar problem
concerns the optimal scale of special measures. If as
some economists assert the marginal costs of special
measures are rising then this is an issue that
deserves attention.

Despite these criticisms and the uncertainty
that surrounds the effect of special measures it
would appear that SEM's in general have been

successful in securing short run reductions in the level of unemployment in Britain. Given the costs especially of long term unemployment (see the discussion in Chapter 1) this may be sufficient. However the design of these policy initiatives may be improved to secure a more permanent and long run impact on unemployment and this would greatly increase their effectiveness. Whether this is possible without a complementary demand management strategy is something we consider in the next section.

It would seem from the analysis of this section that government policy over the last decade has had its greatest impact on reducing unemployment through the use of special measures. In general, macroeconomic, industrial and regional policy has done no better than stabilise the growth of unemployment. At worst it has also at times (especially in 1980-2) made the problem a good deal more severe by contributing to the rise in non-natural unemployment. In the next sections we consider alternative policy initiatives that have been or might be taken to improve job prospects in the 1980s and which might make attainable the modest target of 2 million out of work at the end of 1989.

Alternative Economic Policies for Non-natural Unemployment

In previous chapters we have emphasised the distinction between equilibrium natural rate unemployment and the disequilibrium non-natural equivalent. We have also emphasised the diversity of cause and the consequent complexity of cure. In this and the next section we will consider the prospects of success for a wide range of alternative policy initiatives that have recently been announced or might be adopted to reduce mass unemployment. As we have seen, policy in Britain has achieved little so far in meeting this objective. The evidence we have reviewed in earlier chapters broadly favours the adoption of a non-market clearing framework and hence non-natural unemployment can exist and persist. In principle it can arise, however, both because of a too high level of real wages as well as a reduction in the level of aggregate demand for goods. In fact the empirical evidence suggests the former cause is more important in the 1970s while the latter is dominant in the 1980s. Notwithstanding this evidence the Thatcher government is, as we have seen, seeking cuts in real wage growth in the rest of the 1980s.

Of course such a policy does not necessarily rely on disequilibrium arguments. From a classical equilibrium perspective real wage cuts are also necessary to ensure a reduction in the natural rate of unemployment but in this case it is important to specify carefully the means by which this is achieved. It is not entirely clear which theoretical viewpoint lies at the basis of this policy but recent simulations by the Treasury (HM Treasury 1985) imply a non-market clearing view and we deal with it here. In this Treasury paper although it is argued 'firms face no long run quantity constraints in the market for goods' this team of Treasury economists also say that their work does not depend upon market clearing. Indeed they note with approval the evidence (reviewed in Chapter 6) from recent <u>single</u> equation studies of labour demand which show significant negative real wage elasticities. With excess supply a feature of the aggregate labour market in the 1980s they argue 'the assumption that employment can be explained solely in terms of factors determining labour demand has become increasingly valid'. These arguments only make sense if one believes there is substantial non-natural Classical Unemployment. Consider Figure 9.2. If the effective demand curve is $E_1 D_E$ there is no quantity constraint from the goods market preventing labour market equilibrium so output and hence employment can be readily increased if is below E_1. In this case only if the real wage exceeds W/P* (at W/P for example) can there be any disequilibrium excess supply (c-a in Figure 9.2). This is the conventional notion of Classical unemployment described in greater detail in Chapter 5 and which is also characterised by the presence of excess demand in the goods market.

There are other ways we can interpret the statements in H.M. Treasury (1985). An increase in real wages (to, say, W/P_1) also could shift the effective demand curve down to $E_2 D_E$. In this case there is no excess demand for goods because its effective aggregate level is inversely related to the level of real wages. This is not, of course, the usual argument which emphasises the <u>increases</u> in the personal sector demand for goods which accompany an exogenous increase in real wages. It is this which leads to excess demand in the goods market. As a result it is important to consider the causes for an opposite set of events occurring. The Treasury team outline a number of reasons. Firstly, a rise in real wages squeezes company sector real income with consequent effects on investment demand. Secondly, there is likely to be a loss of international competitiveness so net export demand falls. Thirdly, since real wage increases in Britain have generally been accompanied by increases in prices there are demand reducing wealth effects on the household sector's propensity to consume. Given this type of analysis it follows that real wage cuts alone can reduce non-natural unemployment. This is because real wage cuts induce a movement up the demand curve from a to b <u>and</u> a shift of the effective demand curve to $E_1 D_E$. In other words real wage cuts actually prevent from binding any quantity constraints that do exist and moreover reduce them. In one other respect the Treasury analysis differs from the conventional analysis of classical unemployment and that is in the emphasis on factor substitution as a prime mover in the generation of new jobs from real pay cuts. Since firms have actually to substitute labour for other inputs the adjustment process is bound to be rather slow.

Figure 9.2

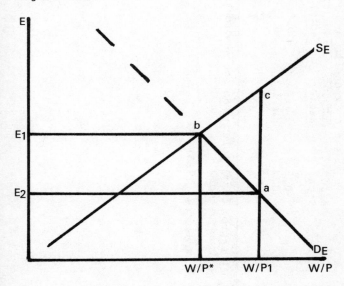

Notwithstanding these minor differences from the analysis of Chapter 5 it is clear the Treasury economists effectively <u>assume</u> there is non-natural unemployment and it is caused by too high a level of real wages. Not surprisingly (like their political

Table 9.4: The effects of a 2% cut in real wages on expenditure and output

| | Domestic Expenditure | | | External Trade | | Output |
	Personal Sector	Company Sector	Public Sector	Exports	Imports	GDP (1)
Year 1	-0.2	0.2	0.0	0.1	-0.1	0.3
Year 2	0.7	1.1	0.0	0.6	0.4	1.8
Year 3	1.3	0.9	0.1	0.6	0.7	2.0
Year 4	1.4	0.8	0.1	0.6	0.5	2.0

Notes: (1) At factor cost; columns do not sum to total because of rounding and changes to factor cost adjustment.

Source: H.M. Treasury (1985)

masters and mistresses) they also believe real wage cuts (or cuts in the rate of growth in a real world in which both labour supply and demand curves are shifted by secular factors) will bring about major reductions in unemployment. The empirical support for this view relies upon simulations performed with the aid of the Treasury model of the British economy. These simulations assess the effect of a 2% reduction in real wages which results from a greater percentage <u>reduction</u> in money wages than in prices. How and why this happens is not considered - it is simply imposed on the model.

The precise effect of this reduction depends critically upon the assumptions made about the stance of fiscal and monetary policy. The largest effects are obtained if the PSBR/GDP ratio and the money supply are assumed constant. In this case employment rises by 1½% (about 300,000) of which only a quarter is accounted for by factor substitution (a to b in Figure 9.2). The majority of the effect comes about via the boost to demand and output which induces an upward shift in the horizontal section of the effective demand curve in Figure 9.2. How does this come about? It turns out that much of this output effect occurs because of the stimulation to aggregate demand results from the totally arbitrary assumption in these simulations that prices <u>fall</u> when real wages fall. Although the fall in real wages boosts company sector real income and expenditure it is the fall in prices that stimulates the eventual increase in personal sector and foreign sector expenditure shown in Table 9.4. This is central to the results of the simulation.

In the first year reductions in personal sector income and expenditure are offset by the boost to company spending and net exports. Subsequently there is a notable recovery of personal sector expenditure growth. Why? The answer is the assumed fall in prices. Apart from the wealth effects that stimulate private consumption, the assumption of a fixed PSBR/GDP and money supply means falls in direct taxes and interest rates take place and these stimulate spending. In fact the fall in direct taxes also mean that post-tax real wages hardly fall at all in this simulation.

These experiments provide some support for a policy of cutting real wages but as they stand they are hardly overwhelmingly persuasive. To generate the 2.122 million extra jobs required for a level of unemployment of 2 million in 1989 requires real wage levels to be something like 15% below what they

otherwise would have been. It also depends on the
reduction in real pay being accompanied by a
significant <u>reduction</u> in the price <u>level</u>. Without
this the employment effect in the Treasury simulation
would be small. It is difficult to believe such a
reduction is possible. Simulations based on this
remote possibility seem rather fanciful and hardly
the basis for sound economic policy. Doubts about the
credibility of this policy option are heightened if
we also consider the effects on company spending of a
cut in real wages. It is difficult to believe on the
basis of the evidence from investment functions that
the large effect (especially in year 1) shown in
Table 9.4 will actually materialise.

A recent study by Andrews, Bell, Fisher, Wallis
and Whitley (1985) also casts considerable doubt upon
the usefulness of these Treasury simulations. Of
particular importance is the arbitrary way in which
real wages are cut in the Treasury model. What is the
mechanism through which this change is brought about?
In fact the Treasury economists suggest no mechanism
and Andrews et al conclude: 'In the absence of a
credible policy scenario the predictions themselves
are not credible'.

Classical economic analysis has always
emphasised the role of the market forces in attaining
full employment through real wage cuts. However, the
extensive body of evidence we have reviewed suggests
that the market mechanism alone is unlikely to bring
about the adjustment of real wages needed to secure
full employment. Indeed there are good reasons for
believing this mechanism has grown weaker through
this century. (24) Principally this is due to the
reduced disciplinary effect of high unemployment on
employed workers. Consider events since 1979. As we
have seen, real wages haven't generally fallen
despite the high unemployment of the Thatcher
government and any 'classical' component of the
current level has therefore been left largely
untouched by Thatcher's policies.

How might this be changed and what kinds of
policy initiatives could bring about cuts in real
wages? The Thatcher government places considerable
emphasis on direct tax cuts to achieve this
objective. As we have seen the basic idea is that
direct tax cuts lead to lower increases in average
gross earnings because workers bargain for real post-
tax wages. With a given rate of price inflation (it
needs to be negative for the Treasury simulation to
hold) this should mean cuts in gross real wages occur
which could be augmented by further cuts in employer

(especially national insurance) taxes. In fact, Wallis (1984) shows the Treasury model of the economy has an extremely large direct tax cut effect of this kind built in. This contrasts with the consensus view on this matter which regards the effects to be more modest. As a result Davies and Metcalf (1985) observe:

> The Treasury model therefore appears to be out on a limb on this crucial variable and this is disturbing because the Warwick team (Wallis (1984)) suggest that the coefficients on the Treasury equation may have been largely imposed on judgemental grounds rather than freely estimated from empirical data.

On this basis it would seem there are few grounds for optimism that the real wage/direct tax cut strategy will generate a significant number of additional jobs in Britain. It is partly for this reason that Davies and Metcalf calculate the PSBR (Exchequer) cost per person removed through direct tax cuts as very high at £47,000 at 1984/5 prices. Although this is lower than other kinds of tax cuts (see Table 9.5) it is significantly higher than alternative instruments available to the government.

Suspicion that the H.M. Treasury (1985) simulation may be a 'pie in the sky' projection is further confirmed by the study of Andrews et al (1985). Using the same policy assumption that generates the largest effect in the Treasury simulations (constant PSBR/GDP and money supply) they find an effect which is only just a half (55%) of that claimed by the Treasury simulations. Andrews et al also perform their calculations using not one but five macroeconometric models of the British economy.

On the basis of this evidence real wage cuts will clearly reduce unemployment but only to a modest extent. Although some unemployment is Classical and non-natural in character the real wage reduction needed to remove it may be very large indeed - much larger in fact than either the market mechanism or direct tax cuts are likely to achieve. Are there any other policy changes which might have a significant effect on real wage levels and hence on Classical unemployment? One obvious candidate is a statutory or voluntary prices <u>and</u> incomes policy which seeks to influence real wages via institutional instruments which control money wages and prices separately. The Thatcher government through the control over public sector pay has an incomes policy but not of this kind. Historical experience (25), however, has shown it to be very difficult to achieve. Although some incomes policy experiments have reduced the level of money (and real) wages the effect has generally been transitory and largely via money wages rather than through price control. A sustained effect on the level of real wages has proved difficult to achieve. This is unlikely to alter in the future and the practical problems involved are also likely to prove formidable. It is unlikely that a successful policy will occur without some effective control over prices and without major institutional changes in the pattern of bargaining and industrial relations in Britain. Metcalf and Nickell (1985), for example, argue that a move towards a more centralised corporatist bargaining system (like Sweden, Norway and Austria) is necessary for 'some form of seriously worked out incomes policy'. In support of this argument Metcalf and Nickell cite the recent work of Bruno and Sachs (1983) which finds that among those countries which have a high degree of responsiveness of money wages to price changes those with centralised and corporate wage bargaining institutions generally recovered better (in terms of unemployment and inflation) from the oil price shocks of the 1970s. However to believe that these institutional changes can be successfully implemented in the current situation without other accompanying changes in the way we organise and structure production is rather naive. Achieving the appropriate institutional structure is a good deal more difficult that Metcalf and Nickell concede but it is clearly a desirable objective to which we return later.

Real wage reductions significantly to reduce Classical unemployment have, therefore, to be large, are likely to be costly (to the government if it uses tax cuts) and difficult to achieve. What are the alternatives? Clearly the most obvious candidate is to use demand management instruments to reduce Keynesian non-natural unemployment. We have already shown the considerable body of evidence that suggests reductions in aggregate demand are the most potent cause of the rise in unemployment since 1979. This means that in Figure 9.2 the effective demand curve is at E_2D_E. The evidence suggests firms <u>are</u> constrained by a lack of demand and that <u>currently</u> there is consequent substantial non-natural Keynesian unemployment although the Thatcher government is reluctant to agree. If this is the case a major demand expansion is required and this could reduce total unemployment significantly. Which instruments are available to the government? Tax cuts, increases in public investment or current expenditure and a relaxation of monetary controls are the principal alternatives. Direct tax cuts designed to boost consumer spending are an obvious candidate. This was clearly a feature of the pre-election expansion of 1982/3. The problem is the relatively small impact direct tax cuts have on unemployment. This is shown in Wallis (1984) using several models of the British economy. In one case, somewhat bizarrely (26) unemployment actually increases following a 2% cut in the basic rate of income tax. In only one model is the effect on the unemployment count of this cut (in the long run (after 5 years), in excess of 150,000. The result of these small effects is the very high PSBR cost of direct tax cuts shown in Table 9.5.

Table 9.5: Exchequer Costs of Various Measures to Reduce Unemployment. (PSBR cost per person removed £ per annum at 1984/5 prices)

1.	Tax Cuts		
	(a)	Income Tax	47,000
	(b)	VAT	58,800
	(c)	Employers' National Insurance Contributions	59,200
2.	Public Investment		26,200
3.	Current Public Expenditure		15,300
4.	Special Employment Measures		2,050

Source: Davies and Metcalf (1985).

Why are direct tax cuts so relatively impotent in their <u>direct</u> effects on aggregate demand? (27) Although they increase saving as well as consumption the most important reason is the large import content of consumer's expenditure. The average propensity to import out of consumer's expenditure was 21.2% in 1979. (28) There are, however, good reasons for believing the marginal propensity is a good deal higher. Following the tax cuts (and the relaxation of credit controls) in 1982/83 real consumer's expenditure rose by 3.7%. Expenditure on consumer durables was the principal reason for this increase

359

(it went up to 16.6%). The import content of consumer durable expenditure is higher than for consumer expenditure as a whole. As a result, imported finished manufactures as a whole went up by 11.5% and motor vehicle imports alone by 16.9% in 1982/83. It is these large import (and saving) leakages that mean direct tax cuts are a comparatively impotent mechanism for increasing aggregate demand and reducing unemployment by this route. Similar objections can be made to measures like the relaxation of hire purchase controls which ease consumer credit in the economy.

The obvious alternatives are either to increase public investment or current expenditure. Table 9.5 shows that both are considerably less costly in Exchequer terms than any form of tax cut. There are exceptions. Because of technical complexity and capital intensity increases in capital investment in the Health Service and in current expenditure on defence are just as costly. (29) In general, however, this is not the case and increases in current expenditure on health and education have particularly low PSBR costs per person employed. Why? Simulations reported in Wallis (1984) and Andrews et al (1985) show relatively substantial (largely public) employment effects from an expansion in current government expenditure costing the Exchequer the same as a cut of 2% in the basic rate of income tax. These employment effects are significantly larger than those resulting from tax cuts. The reason is obvious. Most current government expenditure is labour intensive. Increases, therefore, have an immediate and substantial effect on unemployment. Import and savings leakages may reduce secondary spending increases but have no effect early on in the first round of the process. Although more costly, increases in public investment are also more effective in reducing unemployment than tax cuts. A recent analysis (Huhne (1984)) by three modelling teams confirms this. The reason is not hard to find. Although the import content of investment as a whole is high (29.9%) this is not generally true of public investment. A substantial proportion of total public investment is domestically produced. Given the reliance of public investments projects on the construction industry this is not surprising. In that industry the import content in 1979 was only 14% of output.

In terms of their direct employment effects current public expenditure increases are the most effective in increasing jobs. This is shown by Neale and Wilson (1984) who show the jobs content of current expenditure is 70% higher than capital expenditure. Of course this is not the only consideration in choosing between current and capital public expenditure. The latter has a much greater impact on private sector employment. There are also other allocative aspects of the decision which require consideration. However, both instruments are generally more effective than tax cuts as a way of stimulating demand to reduce non-natural unemployment caused by deficient demand for goods in the economy.

However, there are problems involved in any demand expansion. The most frequently emphasised in the worsening of the balance of payments. Despite the presence of North Sea Oil, the loss of competitiveness by the manufacturing sector of the British economy has severely worsened this problem. Advocates of demand expansion usually argue for demand side expenditure switching policies like currency depreciation or import controls to deal with this. Some also argue for supply side industrial policies to generate net exports. These, however, are of more relevance to the long term. Others (Dornbusch (1985)) argue that higher interest rates to attract a capital account inflow to offset any current account deterioration are necessary. This is the solution adopted by the Reagan administration in the U.S. The problem with this is that high interest rates may crowd out some private sector spending reducing the impact of the demand expansion. This could arise because of the direct effects of higher interest charges (on mortgages, for example) and the indirect effects on inflation, the exchange rate and on domestic and foreign spending. There is not a lot of evidence, however, that these effects are so substantial as to make significant inroads into the unemployment reducing effect of a demand expansion.

Nonetheless, there is a need to adopt one or all of these policies to ease the adverse effect on the balance of external payments that will result from a demand expansion. This problem is, of course, a good deal more severe when the demand expansion is a unilateral one. If other countries are not simultaneously adopting expansionist policies domestic imports rise much faster than exports. The consequent deterioration in the external payments position could be dramatic and result in very high levels of the domestic interest rate to induce a compensating capital account inflow. To some extent this has been a problem confronted both by the

Socialist government in France and the Reagan administration in the U.S.

Given the problems that result from a unilateral demand expansion there is obviously a strong case for an internationally coordinated programme. Many economists urge the use of a variety of existing international economic institutions (like the EEC) to achieve this. However, there are clear difficulties of which the most profound is the generally classical orientation of current policy in the advanced industrial economies. As long as governments remain sceptical about the benefits of demand expansion in their own economy they are less likely to see its merits on an international basis. Clearly, however, if an increase in aggregate demand is thought necessary to reduce non-natural unemployment in Britain its probability of success will be greatly enhanced if other industrial economies pursue the same kind of policy in a co-operative manner.

A further and associated problem is the impact of demand expansion on inflation. Clearly this has loomed large in the thinking of the Thatcher government. Despite the rather weak evidence it believes high inflation dampens to a substantial extent both domestic and foreign demand for goods. The unemployment reducing effects of a demand expansion could be completely offset by this rise in inflation. Of course, this is what classical analysis (which assumes market clearing) tells us. However, once we accept that unemployment exceeds the natural rate because the labour market fails to clear (as the Treasury economists' (H.M. Treasury (1985) do) this is by no means evident.

However, even if the labour market is not in equilibrium some offsetting reduction in employment from a demand expansion can be expected because of the potential effects on the rate of inflation. In this respect, at least, direct tax cuts do have an advantage. This is because of the effect on money wage increases which we have already identified. Although not large (except in the Treasury model) direct employee tax cuts give lower inflation and less demand dampening through this source as a result. The evidence from simulations contained in Wallis (1984) suggests, however, the effect is small and not significant enough to undermine the overall advantage of reducing unemployment by public spending (current or capital) increases.

In conclusion, real wage cuts and demand expansion can both, in principle reduce non-natural unemployment. The impact of the former is small in comparison with the latter, with tax cuts being the least effective and with the highest Exchequer costs of the demand instruments available. The evidence we have surveyed in Chapter 6 also suggests that the need for demand expansion is <u>relatively</u> greater since demand deficiency is a <u>relatively</u> more important cause of the increase in non-natural unemployment in the 1980s. This kind of macroeconomic policy is however likely to require augmentation by policies to deal with the balance of payments, exchange rate and inflation side effects. Of particular importance here is the role of a policy for incomes <u>and</u> prices that may also have a direct and indirect impact on all (including Classical) types of unemployment in excess of the natural rate.

Although policies to reduce disequilibrium non-natural unemployment are essential it is clear from the analysis of Chapters 7 and 8 that a substantial amount of natural rate (equilibrium) unemployment would remain. It is also evident that a significant component of this unemployment is involuntary in the sense that it is the outcome of demand side decisions by employers (see Chapter 8). In the next section we will consider policy instruments specifically targetted at equilibrium unemployment though spillover effects on non-natural unemployment may also occur.

Alternative Policies for Unemployment – The Natural Rate

Policies to reduce the <u>equilibrium</u> natural rate of unemployment are also necessary to reduce unemployment to the levels experienced in the early post-war period. The instruments of such a policy can be analysed from either a stock or a flow point of view. Consider Figure 9.3, details for which can be found in the discussion of Figure 4.3 in Chapter 4.

The labour market is (in frame 'a') in equilibrium at W/P* with a natural rate of employment of E_1^* and unemployment (in frame 'b') of U_1^*. In order, with a given labour force, to reduce this to U_2^* equilibrium employment must rise to E_2^*. In frame 'a' this can happen either through a supply side shift to S_2 or a demand side shift to D_E. Note the different effect on real wage levels. A supply side shift <u>reduces</u> the real wage and to that extent is analogous to the real wage cut policy we considered in the previous section. On the other hand in the demand side case real wages <u>rise</u>.

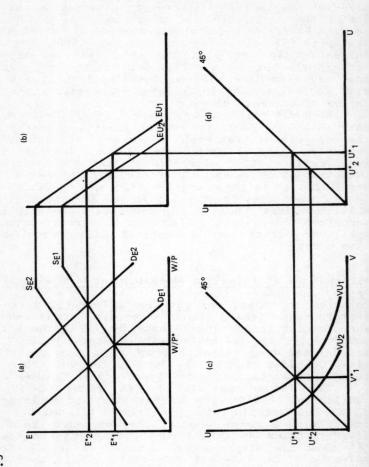

Figure 9.3

364

Unemployment - Policy and Prospects

We can also analyse the policy from a flow point of view using the perspective adopted in Chapter 3. A reduction in U* to U*₂ also requires a downwards shift in the VU curve to VU₂ in frame 'c'. This can occur (see equation 3 in Chapter 3) via a reduction in the inflow probability (α_t) or an increase in the outflow probability which, with a given level of vacancies, can arise through a general fall in reservation wages and an increase in the acceptance probability (β_t) or an increase in the offer probability (κ_t). Changes in κ_t reflect changes in the flow demand for labour and are analogous to shifts in the stock demand curve (D_E) while changes in β_t are similarly analogous to shifts in the S_E curve. A reduction in α_t can reflect both supply side (quits) and demand side (layoffs) forces. In practice we have seen this to be a less important source of increase in U* in Britain so we will conduct the analysis via the outflow probability effects of different policy initiatives.

On the supply side the most commonly advocated policies in Britain are cuts in unemployment benefit, further reduction in trades union power and influence, and direct tax cuts. All of these will in principle shift the supply curve to S_E and will lower reservation wages thus increasing β_t (the acceptance probability) and shifting the VU curve to VU₂. The evidence we have surveyed in Chapters 7 and 8 suggest that reports that imply these supply side forces have been a major cause of rising natural rate unemployment are much exaggerated. Consequently there is little convincing evidence that leads us to believe that any of these supply side policies will have anything other than a modest effect on jobs and unemployment. To implement policies of this kind appear, therefore, to be more of an act of faith than a carefully thought out strategy for the large scale reduction of mass unemployment.

Much more persuasive are proposals greatly to enhance the scope of the programme of special measures. The Thatcher government has announced its intention to double the number of places on the Community Programme to 250,000 and to make 2 year YTS places available to 16 year olds in 1986. Cynical observers have also noted that the changes announced in the 1985 Budget will have their peak impact in 1986/87 during the run-up to the next general election in Britain. In addition many economists regard these changes as too modest. Layard (1985) and Davies and Metcalf (1985) for example have urged a much more dramatic increase to the point at which the number of places on the Community Programme would provide a job guarantee for the long term unemployed. The great advantage of these proposals greatly to extend the scope of special measures provision is that in Exchequer cost terms they are cheap and that they can have an immediate impact on the unemployment count.

How do these policies fit into the framework shown in Figure 9.3? Work creation measures like CP shift the labour demand curve towards D_E^2 and increases the offer probability (κ_t) by increasing the economy wide demand for employees. Recall most of the long term unemployed who have close to zero re-employment probabilities are part of the natural unemployment rate stock. Hence measures like CP that reduce this stock are reducing equilibrium unemployment. Of course there may be some spillover into non-natural unemployment but the principal effect is to reduce unemployment among those who have become structurally unemployed because of their long term experience in that state.

In principle real wages rise as a consequence of this change and this may have additional demand side effects. In practice this may not happen to any significant extent because workers on CP on the scheme or out of work will have little impact on real pay in the rest of the economy. In addition, a ceiling has been imposed on the earnings of CP participants. In fact, the demand side effects of any increase in real wages may actually be beneficial by stimulating private spending. Only if one wholly accepts the claims of H.M. Treasury (1985) is the increase in real wages a significantly unfavourable side effect.

In general there seem to be good grounds for a major expansion of CP to provide far more places for longer periods than the government envisages and to provide a job offer for all long term unemployed workers. Some major improvements could also be made in the scheme. The earnings ceiling could be removed to make CP more attractive to married workers. This would also make more full-time places available and provide long term unemployed workers with a form of job experience that could further enhance their long term employment prospects. Note, however, that the success of CP or any other scheme of this type is dependent on the existence of demand expansion in the economy as a whole. The favourable result for CP reported by Turner (1985) depends to a significant extent on the time period chosen. O'Connor (1982) also demonstrates this clearly. He calculates the probability of employment for young workers on a work experience programme between 1978 and 1981 and shows a clear inverse association with the degree of recession in the economy as a whole. It is clear that without a matching demand expansion to provide post-scheme jobs the most that an expanded CP programme would achieve is a transitory reduction in the 'headline' unemployment count.

If CP were expanded some strategic attention would also need to be given to the kind of jobs offered and to the provision of relevant adult training on the scheme. It seems curious that the YTS programme is not matched by equivalent provision for long term unemployed adults. It is clear that there is enormous scope for places in the social services, for example, many of which require (medical orderlies, for example) some degree of training. A planned expansion of current government spending in sectors where CP places are increased makes some sense and would turn CP into a training and work experience programme for adults for whom the current job prospects are nil. It would also mean that a demand expansion in the current provision of public services would not run into bottlenecks due to a shortage of suitably trained and experienced workers. CP could provide a transition between long term unemployment and long term employment but, of course, this requires a different view of public employment than currently prevails.

Although an expansion in public employment by this route is desirable because of the large employment effects and because of the greater ease with which training provision can be monitored within the public sector an expanded CP would also generate jobs in the private sector. Particularly important here is the construction industry. CP programmes could provide, for example, on-the-job training in basic building skills that could then be used on construction projects. Clearly this is much more likely if CP programmes are tied into public investment projects like housebuilding that are generally undertaken by private sector firms. If this were the case any outward shift in the D_E curve in Figure 9.3 could then become permanent.

In generating jobs within the private sector the provision of suitable training places is of fundamental importance. In this regard the proposed extension of YTS has been widely welcomed. Greater provision of more lengthy (3 year) universal training, as exists in West Germany, is clearly desirable in principle. Apart from its obvious short run effects on labour demand and offer probabilities for new entrants to the labour market (which lower U_t^*) there is also potentially a longer run impact of the scheme. This is because of the impact of training on labour productivity and on the long run performance of the economy as a whole (which affects U_t^* as we saw in Chapter 8). The importance of training has been emphasised by recent empirical work that shows differences in economic performance between Britain and West Germany may be related to differences in the quality and quantity of training in the two countries. (30)

Although the Thatcher government has introduced and expanded YTS there remain significant doubts about the effectiveness of the policy, especially in generating permanent jobs. The principle of universal training embodied in YTS is not much good unless participants can expect to get a job at its conclusion. Unless there is some expansion of labour demand this will not be true so the future success of YTS requires a complementary programme of demand expansion especially for young workers. If this does not happen attitudes of workers on YTS will be adversely affected and any skills acquired on the scheme will depreciate with non-use. The growth in demand for young workers requires a general expansion of aggregate demand but also other measures (like an expanded Job Release Scheme) which we will consider later.

A further problem with YTS is that unless there is sound monitoring and control the quality of training provided may be no better than under YOP. Ryan (1984) reports some misgivings on this score and notes YTS in practice has not always attained the quality initially proposed and the MSC has few sanctions to prevent this slippage occurring. He observes:

> The prospect that YTS will provide high training quality relies heavily upon the goodwill of employers. Many firms will undoubtedly provide quality training out of a sense of social duty but they are likely to be in a minority.

The success of universal training in West Germany relies on the control exercised by the government by incentives and threats. Unless the effectiveness of monitoring on YTS is improved it is unlikely to meet the long run employment and unemployment targets it could. An associated problem is the failure of YTS to deal with the long standing problem of high quality training for key skills. Previous training policy has failed to prevent a chronic drop in apprenticeship training in Britain for the basic reason that public subsidy covered only about one quarter of the total cost to employers. Not surprisingly, in recession firms made major cut backs in apprenticeship provision. YTS has done nothing to deal with this problem of lack of training in depth in Britain which is particularly acute in areas affected by microelectronic technology. (31) The solution to this problem requires YTS to be viewed as an entry route to apprenticeship and for public subsidy to be provided at a significantly higher level for all apprenticeship schemes in both the private and public sectors.

A further curious feature of YTS is its emphasis on training in the private sector. Ryan (1984) argues that this emphasis has meant that the drive for a large number of places only succeeded at the expense of training quality. Clearly, youth training can and should take place in the public sector (including public services) on a much grander scale than at present. Good training is necessary for effective public sector performance but this policy makes sense from other points of view. As we have seen, public sector employment is labour intensive and hence with steady expansion highly job creative. Again this would require a reversal of current policy with a planned expansion of public sector employment. Such a policy would need to deal with the allocative question of the desirable size of the public sector and of the sub-sectors within it so that training provision could be geared to the generation of jobs (like CP).

So far we have concentrated the discussion on the crucial area of training policy for the young receiving their initial training. Adult training is also important in providing both short run and long run reductions in long term natural rate unemployment. Although the government claims its adult training strategy makes 'training more widespread, more flexible and more relevant to modern needs' this seems to be achieved at the expense of in-depth training. This seems particularly true in the case of training for unemployed adults. Just as there are good grounds for increasing the training content of CP in what are largely public sector jobs so is there a case for increasing private sector 'on the job' experience for adult workers who are trained by government agencies. The 1984 White Paper 'Training for Jobs' falls far short of universal training for unemployed adults and this is an area where they seem good grounds for expansion rather for retrenchment.

We have emphasised the importance of training in securing a permanent increase in labour demand and job offer probabilities for unemployed (especially long term) workers. Training is also important to prevent a general expansion in demand leading rapidly to severe excess demand in certain segments of the labour market. Planning a programme of training in tandem with a programme of planned (by sector) demand expansion is likely to prove essential for a sustained cut in unemployed. However it is also evident that long run success for this kind of special measure (including public employment programmes) requires such a complementary expansion in job opportunities in both the public and private sector.

Other kinds of special measures may also help in this respect and may not be so dependent on demand expansion for success. Firstly, we will consider the case for further employment subsidies including changes in the labour taxes paid by employers. Secondly, we will examine a wide range of work sharing measures that have or might be adopted.

We have already reviewed in Chapter 8 the effects of rising employer taxes (especially national insurance contributions) and other fixed components of total labour cost on employment. Basically these shift the demand curve for employees down and reduce offer probabilities for unemployed workers. Since they encourage employers to substitute hours for workers they increase unemployment. Empirical evidence confirms these ideas. What then would be the effect of reductions in employer taxes and fixed labour costs? Simulations reported by Huhne (1983) show the desired effect. Cuts in employer taxes (and in fixed labour costs associated with employer protection legislation) will shift the demand curve and the offer probabilities in the direction necessary for a reduction in U_t^*. However, Huhne's simulations also show that the effect is rather small and the PSBR cost per job created by a cut in employer's national insurance contributions is extremely large at £59,200 (see Table 9.5 for relevant comparisons).

This result has led to the view that cuts in employer taxes or the introduction of further employment subsidies have to be targetted more precisely at the employment of the unemployed. There are grounds for believing this is desirable. The

significant effect on jobs of previous studies like
the Regional Employment Premium and Temporary
Employment Subsidy results in part from the
concentration of these measures on a clearly and
narrowly defined group of workers.

The most significant reason for the small effect
on jobs and unemployment of reductions in national
insurance contributions is that it applies to all
workers, not simply to the marginal workers who are
about to be laid off (like TES) or who could be
employed. This had led to many economists arguing for
the introduction of a <u>marginal</u> employment subsidy
which is paid to firms for additional workers who are
hired. This increases the offer probability and
lowers natural rate unemployment and has a
particularly pronounced effect in the private
sector, especially in the services component where
employment growth is most rapid. Layard and Nickell
(1980) suggest a lump sum subsidy (£80 per week at
1984/85 prices) for all increases in employment over
some defined benchmark for each employer. Clearly,
such increases in employment would need to be
calculated on a full-time equivalent basis.
Otherwise firms would have a substantial incentive to
take on only part-timers. A marginal employment
subsidy gives an obvious incentive to firms to
substitute additional employees for hours worked by
existing employees which gives the required shift in
Figure 9.3. It also reduces labour costs which boosts
international competitiveness and ultimately aggregate demand. Layard and Nickell's simulations of the
effects of introducing a marginal employment subsidy
imply a significant effect on unemployment. This
also implies a low Exchequer cost per job created.
There is, however, some considerable doubt about the
scale of these effects. Whitley and Wilson (1983)
consider Layard and Nickell's scheme and predict much
smaller employment effects. As a result, Exchequer
costs are little different from an across-the-board
reduction in employers' national insurance
contributions. Perhaps the most persuasive piece of
evidence in support of marginal employment subsidies
is that of an OECD study (1982) of the schemes
adopted by various industrial economies. This
concludes:

> employment subsidies which are carefully
> targetted on problem groups in the labour market
> do stimulate employment increases at budget
> costs below those of general macroeconomic
> demand management policies

371

This conclusion provides general support for a marginal employment subsidy that relates the scale of the subsidy to the period of time an individual has been unemployed. A larger subsidy would be paid for the employment of long term unemployed people. Similarly large subsidies could also be paid for the full-time employment of recent graduates of Community Programme, Adult Training (like TOPS) or Youth Training Schemes. To be really effective and permit a major reduction in natural rate unemployment there is good reason for targetting a marginal employment subsidy in this way. Cuts in employers' national insurance could be targetted in a similar way. The changes announced in the 1985 Budget decrease the employers' contribution for low paid workers. This might encourage the employment of lower paid employees but since it also raises the contribution for higher paid workers may be offset by displacement of higher paid workers. Layard (1985) proposes that employers who take on long term (more than a year) unemployed workers should be relieved of national insurance contributions for these workers for a period of two years. This is a watered down version of the marginal employment subsidy proposal but it is clearly simpler from an administrative point of view and has much to recommend it.

Work sharing measures are an alternative way of reducing natural rate unemployment which have not been widely adopted in Britain though in Europe they have been more widely used. Some of the proposed measures involve cuts in the labour force and others would lead to a substitution of more employees for shorter hours of work. The former type of increase shifts inwards the EU curve in frame 'b' of Figure 9.3 to EU_2. With a given value of $E*$ (like E_1^*) this lowers $U*$ (to U_1^*). An equivalent shift also takes place in the VU curve (to VU_2) because of the favourable changes in the inflow probability (down) and the offer probability (up) that result from this type of change. The most important type of measure that brings about this shift is that which encourages earlier retirement. The Job Release Scheme is an example of this type of measure but as we have seen its scope has been rather limited even though it has appeared to be rather successful. A survey by Robertson (1982) found clear evidence that at least 60% of those retiring early under JRS were definitely replaced by an unemployed worker. Assessment of the remaining cases led to an estimate of the overall success rate of 85%.

One obvious change would be to reduce the age of

eligibility of men to 60 or even 55. This would put able bodied men in the same position as the disabled for whom the eligible age could also be reduced to 55. There has been between 1983 and 1985 a part-time JRS which allowed men aged 62 and over to shift to part-time work but the take-up was trivial so concentration on full-time jobs seems more promising. Apart from a major reduction of eligibility and improved monitoring to increase the overall success rate the attractiveness of the scheme could be increased by additions to the current weekly tax free allowance and by financial incentives to firms to encourage the take-up of JRS. A major extension of JRS has considerable advantages over alternative ways of increasing the rate of early retirement. It is voluntary and does not enforce earlier retirement in the way a reduction in the statutory retirement age would. In budgetary terms the scheme is cheap because of the savings in benefit paid to previously unemployed people. Davies and Metcalf (1985) calculate the PSBR cost of removing one person from the unemployment count by JRS to be only £1,650 at 1984/85 prices. A general reduction in the statutory retirement age will be considerably more costly to the government. The Department of Employment (1978) calculate the net cost will be three times that of JRS. There are other disadvantages attached to a general reduction in a retiring age compared with JRS. The effect of unemployment is more uncertain and it may create labour shortages in certain occupations or industries. In the case of JRS this is less likely. A further problem is that a reduction in the statutory retirement age would put pressure on occupational pension schemes to move into line. The Department of Employment (1978) calculates this would increase employers' fixed labour costs by over 2% for the average scheme. Since this would have an adverse effect on labour demand and the average offer probability in the economy the favourable impact of reducing the retirement age on the natural rate could be a good deal reduced.

These considerations favour a much expanded JRS scheme but clearly there is some danger that labour productivity and output will fall as a result. Since new workers are likely to be less productive and may require some training or incur other induction costs to their employers there is a case for paying firms a lump sum to compensate for these effects and to offset any adverse long run effects on the economy as a whole. In tandem with the kind of concession on national insurance contributions proposed by Layard (1985) an expanded JRS could also do much to encourage the employment, especially of the long term unemployed.

The case for extending JRS is very strong but there are other policy options which would have similar effects. Measures to reduce women's labour force participation have been proposed but have been rejected on many grounds most notably that any such measures would be discriminatory. More serious attention has been given to the introduction of a statutory right to one year's sabbatical leave during which workers would undergo an approved course of training (or retraining) and education. Apart from the direct effect on jobs this would generate a major job creating expansion in education and training services. Since it would also improve the 'quality' of the labour force which, as we have seen, has been recently emphasised as a crucial determinant of macroeconomic performance it will also have a further indirect effect on jobs. Unfortunately, no precise simulation of the effects of a policy of this kind have been done. It is likely to prove expensive in PSBR terms but we have no idea of its cost effectiveness. Clearly this is an area where more research is required.

Some work sharing measures also aim to substitute more employees for shorter hours of work. This has the effect of increasing the demand for employees and increasing the offer probability for unemployed workers. The labour demand curve (for employees) shifts to D_{E2} and the VU curve to VU_2 in Figure 9.3. If work sharing succeeds natural rate unemployment falls. This is the idea underlying proposals for a significant reduction in the working week. The TUC in Britain and trades unions in much of the EEC are committed to major reductions in the working week (without reductions in normal weekly pay) in order to boost employment. The crudest kind of justification for the adoption of a policy of this kind assumes constant output and a constant labour requirement. This necessarily means that a cut in normal hours will shift the demand curve in Figure 9.3 in the required direction.

A more subtle version emphasises the substitution of employees for hours by altering the relative cost of both types of labour input. This is illustrated in Figure 9.4 which reproduces Figure 8.2. EH indicates the total labour requirement for the production of a given level of output. Initially assume average hours are H_1, and employment is E_1.

374

Cuts in the standard working week increase the number of hours payable at an overtime premium rate. There is an incentive for firms to shift to a less hours intensive mix of the labour input (to H_2E_2 for example) because of this change in the relative cost structure. (32)

Figure 9.4

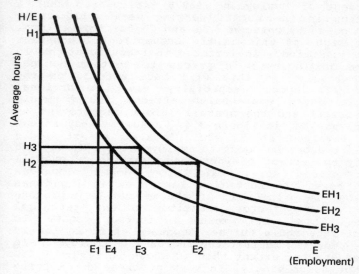

However, the increase in employment through a cut in the standard working week could be a good deal less than this. The reduction in actual hours may be less than H_1-H_2. Since actual hours fall less than normal hours overtime increases. The Department of Employment (1978) has calculated that the fall in the normal week from 44 hours to 40 in the years 1964 to 1966 actually led to an increase in overtime that halved the potential increase in employment. This increase in overtime could occur because overtime hours are more productive as empirical work by Feldstein (1967) and Craine (1973) suggests. This would raise the overall productivity of man hours and shift (for a given output) the labour requirements curve to EH_2. With hours at H_3, for example, this means an increase in employment of significantly less (E_3-E_1 rather than E_2-E_1). It may also occur because employed workers resist cuts in the working week either to prevent a cut in their gross weekly earnings or to secure an actual increase. This might

375

be conceded by employers who pass on the effects to consumers by raising prices.

With a fixed output, work sharing schemes involve sharing income and this can only be achieved by reductions in profit or in the income of those currently employed. Working extra overtime shifts the burden of work sharing away from currently employed workers but this raises labour costs. The Department of Employment (1978) calculates that a reduction in the normal working week would raise labour costs by between 6.1% and 7% for this reason. In the light of this is the assumption of constant output justified? An increase in labour costs would provoke an increase in prices to restore nominal profit levels and this will have effects on the demand for goods (especially via international competitiveness and wealth effects) which would cause output and the overall labour requirement to fall to say EH_3 in Figure 9.4. Assuming that actual hours remained at H_3 this 'scale' effect would further reduce the boost to employment (to E_4-E_1) and magnify the effect of increased overtime on overall labour productivity. The story doesn't however finish here. The fact that labour as an input has increased in price will in the medium term provoke labour saving factor substitution and technical change. This will mean a further boost to productivity and a further downward shift in the EH curve, reducing further the increase in employment to an even greater extent than is shown in Figure 9.4.

Not surprisingly, in view of these conflicting effects there is great variation in the estimates of the effects on employment of cutting the working week to 35 hours. The Department of Employment estimates a maximum effect of 480,000 and a minimum of 100,000. TUC estimates are a little larger (between 150,000 and 750,000). (33) They also depend on the effects on overtime and productivity of such a reduction. The evidence clearly indicates some gain in employment will be made from cuts in the working week. Brechling's (1965) paper which we considered in Chapter 8, for example, shows the reduction in the normal week in the 1950s and 1960s raised employment above the level that otherwise would have prevailed. However, the effect is rather small though in the current high unemployment period this may not be totally reliable evidence from a quantitative point of view.

It looks as if some reduction in natural rate unemployment could result from cutting the normal working week to 35 hours but the effect could be quite modest. An alternative proposal would be for an across the board increase in the overtime premium paid in Britain. This works directly on overtime hours and induces firms to move to a position like H_2E_2 in Figure 9.4. Of course there could be offsetting output and factor substitution effects which would mean the EH curve shifts downwards but not the overtime effects which offsets much of the benefits of a cut in the normal working week. Ehrenberg (1971) and Ehrenberg and Schumann (1982) undertake some tests for the U.S. that suggests the employment effects of increasing the overtime premium are quite large. There is, however, a great deal of uncertainty about the estimates. Clearly this is another area in which more research is required. Other ways of increasing employment at the expense of hours of work include increasing the holiday entitlement of workers in Britain and job splitting which would generate extra part-time jobs. The low take-up of the part-time variant of the Job Release Scheme suggests little scope for job splitting as a means of reducing natural rate male unemployment. However, at the moment no clear cut evidence exists to permit any unambiguous conclusion to be drawn although there are some interesting developments in the rest of Europe from which something might be learnt. In Holland, which is Europe's trailblazer in work sharing, some companies have introduced a shorter working week by allowing employees to take more half day holidays in the year. It is too early to say what the effect of these changes on unemployment has been in Holland but clearly the analysis of the experience of other countries may be fruitful and shed more light on the effects of work sharing than can be obtained from the results of uncertain simulations in the British economy.

Metcalf (1985) describes work sharing and reduction in the labour force as a 'counsel of despair in the face of high unemployment'. It is not at all clear that this is the case and although caution is clearly advisable these measures can bring about a reduction in equilibrium unemployment. The strongest arguments are for a major expansion of the Job Release Scheme but other changes need also to be considered and subject to more rigorous investigation than hitherto.

The analysis of alternative measures to reduce the natural rate of unemployment has concentrated so far on the labour market. In the remainder of this section we will turn our attention to the goods market and in particular on the role of industrial policy. Industrial policy is aimed at regenerating existing products and processes and generating new ones. It operates at the microeconomic level of the industry and the firm. Its effect on reducing unemployment in the long term can be profound. Insofar as it helps to generate additional aggregate demand in an economy where firms are constrained it reduces non-natural unemployment. If it assists in making domestic industry more internationally competitive it also does this and in addition relaxes any balance of payments constraints on a government induced demand expansion. It also has long run structural effects on equilibrium employment and unemployment. If it succeeds, industrial policy increases the pace of technical change, raises labour productivity and the natural level of output. In the long run these induce outward shifts in the labour demand curve and also increase job opportunities which raise the offer probability for unemployed workers (especially if combined with a training strategy). The intention is clearly to reverse the effects of a decline in the long run rate of growth of output and employment which has had severe effects on the value of U_t^* in Britain as we saw in Chapter 8. To some extent also industrial policy has direct demand inducing effects which the Thatcher government with its emphasis on the importance of the supply side of the economy believes to be sufficiently strong for a complementary general expansion in aggregate demand to be unnecessary.

In general, proposals for extending the scope of industrial policy initiatives are targetted at the production industries in Britain. This reflects the effects on overall unemployment of the structural decline of these industries. It also reflects the view that although the direct job creation effects of improved production industry performance may be small the indirect effects could be large. Often the basis for this view is that labour demand expansion in non-production industries is constrained by British trade performance. If the number of jobs rose outside of the production industries this will cause an unacceptable deterioration of the balance of payments. Insofar as industrial policy is targetted at the trading intensive production sector it can, if successful, reduce the severity of this problem. The attainable level of non-production employment is increased by the relaxation of the external constraint. As a result the economy wide demand curve for employees shifts out and equilibrium employment rises. The average offer probability also goes up, shifting the VU curve favourably downwards and all of this will reduce U*.

We have already outlined the essential ingredients of the industrial policy of the Thatcher government. A great deal of emphasis has been placed on the efficacy of the market mechanism. As a result deregulation and privatisation are central to the strategy. The Employment White Paper (Cmnd 9474) says: 'Government cannot do what the nation will not. It cannot on its own create jobs ...'. The view that a '<u>laissez faire</u>' industrial policy will reduce natural rate unemployment underlies this statement. Left to itself the private sector could and should make the changes in both products and processes that will increase the natural rates of output and employment. The government has merely to give them the freedom to act. This is clearly stated in the recent (1985) White Paper 'Lifting the Burden' (Cmnd 9571) the objectives of which are:

First, freeing markets and increasing opportunities for competition and Second, lifting administrative and legislative burdens which take time, energy, and resources from fundamental business activity.

The hotch-potch of 80 proposals in this White Paper include the relaxation of planning controls in so-called 'Simplified Planning Zones' and reducing the health and safety requirements for small business. There is no clear evidence that this policy will succeed. Steps taken so far in the direction of 'freeing markets' and 'lifting administrative and legislative burdens' have had no clear demonstrable impact on unemployment. It is equally unclear what the future impact will be of this kind of industrial policy which aims to deregulate and privatise.

What are the alternatives? Many proposals have been made but at the basis of almost all of them is a more active and interventionist view of industrial policy. Many of these ideas are justified by reference to the experience of other countries in the world but on the basis of clear cut British evidence are almost as speculative in terms of their impact on unemployment as those of the Thatcher government. A general and powerful argument in their favour is that they do not presume the efficiency of markets (labour, product or financial) and indeed assert the inevitability of failure for policies that do. In the face of this inability of market forces to generate the kind of change in the natural rate the Thatcher government envisages these alternative proposals favour an interventionist industrial policy to achieve the same end. In a sense the dispute about the appropriate form of industrial policy mirrors the market clearing versus non-market clearing debate that characterises opposing approaches to unemployment as a whole. Since, as we have seen, the evidence strongly favours the adoption of a non-market clearing perspective of unemployment there is a general presumption in favour of industrial policies that also reject the classical view of the capacity of market forces spontaneously to bring about the kind of structural change (the development of new products and processes) that is required to achieve a permanent reduction in equilibrium unemployment in Britain.

There are a great variety of extant detailed proposals for an active industrial policy but there are certain common themes that characterise most of them. One central theme is the need for a conscious and planned strategy to encourage product and process innovation. As we have seen the need for this is given particular emphasis in the internationally trading production sector which has fared so badly since the early 1960s but is also recognised in other sectors like agriculture and services (public and private). In this regard a policy for greatly increased levels of fixed investment is generally thought important. Most interventionists favour the adoption of more generous (if selective) public support for fixed investment and reject the general weakening of policy in this area especially in the 1984 Budget. In addition, there is a wide support for the creation of new institutions to provide investment finance. Often this is justified by reference to the failure of existing financial institutions like banks and pension funds (particularly in the absence of exchange controls) to finance the investment needed on the scale required at an acceptable price and on acceptable terms (on payback periods, for example). Proposals of this kind are frequently justified by reference to other economies (like West Germany and France) where public sector banking institutions have played a more prominent role than in Britain. Reference is also made to the favourable experience of agencies like the National Enterprise Board in the 1970s and similar local bodies that have been established in some areas (like London and the West Midlands) of this country.

Most interventionist policy packages also

accept that higher levels of fixed investment are a necessary but <u>not</u> sufficient component of a successful industrial policy. Considerable emphasis is therefore placed on the encouragement of research and development and the role of the government in this regard. To some extent this requires a degree of economic planning which has not been characteristic of Britain. Strategic planning, according to interventionists, should specify the sectors to which special support for the research, development and fixed investment is given. Motor cars (of the more traditional industries) and information technology and biotechnology (of the so called 'sunrise' industries) are often singled out. In general, however, most interventionists now not only presume the weaknesses of market forces but also acknowledge the limitations of centralised state activity. Strategic planning is therefore rarely conceived of in detailed and comprehensive central planning terms, but rather as the process of setting a general context in which detailed allocative decisions are taken at the microeconomic level. In fact, some of the institutions capable of performing this role already exist in Britain. However, most interventionists believe a significant expansion of the scope and scale of the activities of NEDO and its range of industry level, little "NEDDIES" is necessary.

Most interventionist industrial policies also involve the introduction of some degree of industrial democracy which extends the control of industry to workers and in some cases consumers. Although there is no agreement in detail the objective of this type of policy is twofold. Firstly, it assists in the development of a decentralised planning system which involves workers, managers and even consumers at all levels by strengthening the commitment to collective economic objectives. Secondly, it improves the pattern of industrial relations at the work place and assists in the development of more cooperative patterns of industrial behaviour. Of course, many interventionists would argue that this cannot be achieved without fundamental change in the pattern of ownership and in the distribution of power in British industry. Others (like the Alliance parties) take a less extreme view but the common ingredient is the recognition that some institutional change is a necessary component of any successful unemployment reducing industrial policy. To some extent the form of institutional change that is favoured also reflects the extent to which it is believed greater

381

control and influence by the state and employees needs to be exercised over business decisions currently made in the private sector, especially those made by multinational corporations. More radical views of the form and extent of institutional change are generally taken by those interventionists who doubt the capacity of the currently organised private sector to make the appropriate (for industrial policy) decisions.

Whatever view is taken, industrial (supply side of the goods market) policy is of considerable importance (particularly via the demand side of the labour market) in permanently reducing unemployment, especially of the equilibrium natural rate kind. We have outlined (not blue printed) the broad alternative strategies currently being pursued and proposed in Britain. The choices cannot be made solely by careful appraisal of the evidence since it does not exist in any clearcut form. Much is speculative. However an interventionist policy that does not presume the efficiency of market forces in providing a solution looks in general the better bet and is more in keeping with the evidence we have surveyed in this book.

Conclusion

There is no single solution to unemployment because there is no single cause. If we regard the failure of the labour market to clear as a fundamental feature of the economy, a demand expansion which is preferably internationally coordinated is a crucial ingredient of a policy to reduce unemployment in Britain and in Europe as a whole. However, there is also good reason to believe it needs complementary action. Policies to regulate the movements of real incomes have a role to play in reducing both non-natural (disequilibrium) and natural (equilibrium) unemployment. However policies with a clear microeconomic focus are perhaps more important especially in the latter respect. Policies to encourage work sharing, special measures especially those which have a strong, well structured training content and industrial policies that encourage the development of new products and processes hold the key to a permanent reduction in natural rate unemployment as well as having some potential impact on non-natural unemployment. The complex bundle of policies needed to reduce unemployment in Britain and elsewhere requires, however a coordinated and coherent approach which recognises the complementarity of policy instruments each of which is designed to deal with the different causes of high unemployment we have considered in the preceding chapters.

Notes

1. A critique of the use of monetary targets in Britain can be found in Savage (1984).
2. Page 12.
3. Cmnd 9474, page 20.
4. Page 14.
5. This is the number cited in Cmnd 7474, page 11.
6. A number of objections have been made to these figures in addition to those made in the text. Partly, this is to do with the revision to the estimates which appear to increase the growth in employment. These revisions involve the use of the Labour Force Survey. This appears to have a profound effect. On the previously used basis statistics in the Department of Employment Gazette, March 1985 show the growth in employment is only 226,000 in the year preceding September 1984. Apart from the growth in part-time jobs the most important source of the increase in 1983/84 and of the difference in estimates is in self employment. There are some problems with interpreting these changes which are discussed by David Lipsey Sunday Times, 13th April 1985.
7. By the Financial Times and published on 23rd June 1985.
8. An excellent review of the impact of inflation on consumption and of wealth effects in general is to be found in Grice (1981). The empirical estimate presented in the paper show, however, that wealth effects on aggregate consumption are indeed rather small.
9. In 1983/84 there was also the rapid growth in the U.S. economy which further stimulated demand for British exports.
10. Through the gradual abolition of the National Insurance Surcharge and the changes in employers' contributions announced in the 1985 Budget.
11. Cmnd 9474, Page 19.
12. There is a wide variety of experience concealed by these aggregate figures. The increase in real wages is greatest for white collar and least for manual workers. Similarly, public sector workers have, in general, done worse. According to data in

Trinder and Biswas (1985) local authority manuals have suffered a 7.2% cut in their real pay since 1980. In fact as the pattern of unemployment shown in Chapter 2 reveals, these workers are now <u>more</u> not <u>less</u> likely to be unemployed. This evidence is equally unfavourable to the notion described in the text that by selective real wage cuts the government has increased employment and reduced unemployment. The causation appears to be the reverse to that required (from employment to real wages rather than vice versa.)

13. A complete check list of government policy initiatives in this area can be found in the White Paper (Cmnd 9474), pages 28/9.

14. In fact one third of the 1983 target places were for 'Mode B' schemes. There was a large short fall (about 25,000) on these schemes because of this apparent over provision.

15. More details as well as a critical review of these developments can be found in Ryan (1984).

16. £63 per week in 1985.

17. Further details of the types of job done under CP can be found in Turner (1985).

18. An account of the history of this period can be found in Armstrong and Taylor (1978), Appendix C.

19. Many trades unions which have a large proportion of low paid members like NUPE and USDAW argue that the displacement of otherwise employed workers is an important effect of special measures, especially those designed like YOP and YTS to benefit the young.

20. This is calculated by the Department of Employment and is obtained from Davies and Metcalf (1985).

21. There is little recent published evidence on the effects of either regional or industrial policy. In the latter case this is surprising since substantial grants have been paid under section 7 of the Industry Act 1972. A recent unpublished attempt to fill this gap is by Richards (1985).

22. This study is cited by Davies and Metcalf (1985), page 21.

23. Fuller reviews of youth training measures in this country can be found in Ryan (1984) and Dutton (1984).

24. A greatly extended version of this argument can be found in Knight (1983). Part of the reason for the insensitivity of wages to excess supply is the major increase in duration that has taken place. This creates a pool of labour who

constitute no threat to those employed. This has been recently confirmed by Layard and Nickell (1985) and Layard (1985) who find a large, long term unemployment stock exerts no influence on the rate of increase of <u>money</u> wages in Britain.

25. A number of studies have considered the impact of incomes policies in Britain. Lipsey and Parkin (1970), Henry and Ormerod (1978) and Whitley (1983) are examples. There are also several collections of useful papers that do the same. A good example here is Fallick and Elliott (1981).

26. This is the result obtained from the use of Minford's Liverpool model. It results from the fact that in this model the PSBR/GDP ratio is fixed so if taxes are cut so is public expenditure. The expected qualitative result from the balanced budget theorem is, therefore, obtained and the result is less bizarre than it initially seems.

27. Note only the direct effects are considered here. The indirect effects on the rate of price inflation and hence on demand considered earlier in this section of Chapter 9 are ignored at this point.

28. These data are obtained from CSO: <u>Input-Output Tables for the U.K</u>. (1983).

29. Davies and Metcalf (1985) show the PSBR cost per person removed from the unemployment count at 1984/5 prices is £51,000 for public investment in health and £45,200 for current spending on defence.

30. The NIESR has played a significant role in this research. A number of articles have appeared to illustrate this point including Prais and Wagner (1983) and a collection of papers in Worswick (1984b).

31. The value of grants available from training boards has generally covered only about a quarter of the cost (to employers) of training. YTS provides no more in the first year and nothing in subsequent years. The issue is discussed further in Ryan (1984).

32. The relevant theory is laid out in greater detail in Hart (1984), especially Chapter 5.

33. Leslie and Wise (1980) examine the productivity of hours in British production industries and obtain estimates that suggest the shift in the EH curve would not be substantial so that a cut in the working week would have effects closer to the TUC than the Department of Employment estimates and greater than implied in the text.

BIBLIOGRAPHY

Ackley, G., (1961), <u>Macroeconomic Theory</u>, Macmillan.

Akerlof, G., (1982), 'Labour contracts as partial gift exchange', <u>Quarterly Journal of Economics</u>

Alchian, A., (1970), 'Information costs, pricing and resource unemployment' in E. Phelps (ed.) <u>Microeconomic Foundations of Employment and Inflation Theory</u>, Macmillan

Alden, J., (1977), 'The extent and nature of double jobholding in Great Britain', <u>Industrial Relations Journal</u>

Allen, S.G. (1984), 'Unionized construction workers are more productive', <u>Quarterly Journal of Economics</u>

Alogoskoufis, G.A. and Pissarides, C., (1983), 'A test of price sluggishness in the simple rational expectations model: UK 1950-1980', <u>Economic Journal</u>

Altonji, J., (1982), 'The intertemporal substitution model of labour market fluctuations: an empirical analysis', <u>Review of Economic Studies</u>

Altonji, J. and Ashenfelter, O., (1980), 'Wage movements and the labour market equilibrium hypothesis', <u>Economica</u>

Anderson, L.C. and Jordan, J.L., (1968), 'Monetary and fiscal actions: a test of their relative importance in economic stabilisation', <u>Federal Reserve Bank of St Louis Review</u>

Andrews, M., (1983), 'The aggregate labour market - an empirical investigation into market clearing', Centre of Labour Economics, L.S.E. Discussion Paper No. 154

Andrews, M., (1984), 'The aggregate labour market: an empirical investigation into market clearing', University of Warwick, mimeo

Andrews, M., (1985), 'Empirical models of the UK aggregate labour market: a partial survey',

Economic Perspectives
Andrews, M. and Nickell, S., (1982), 'Unemployment in the United Kingdom since the war', Review of Economic Studies
Andrews, M. and Nickell, S. (1984), 'A disaggregated disequilibrium model of the labour market', London School of Economics Centre for Labour Economics, Working Paper 669
Andrews, M., Bell, D., Fisher, P., Wallis, K., and Whitley, J., (1985), 'Models of the UK economy and the real wage-employment debate', National Institute Economic Review
Armstrong, H. and Taylor, J., (1978), Regional Economic Policy, Phillip Allan
Armstrong, H. and Taylor, J., (1981), 'The measurement of different types of unemployment' in J. Creedy (ed.), The Economics of Unemployment in Britain, Butterworth
Arrow, K.J., (1959), 'Towards a theory of price adjustment in M. Abramovitz et al, 'The Allocation of Economic Resources', Stanford
Artis, M.J. and Nobay, A.R., (1969), 'Two aspects of the monetary debate', National Institute Economic Review
Ashenfelter, O., (1980), 'Unemployment as disequilibrium in a model of aggregate labour supply', Econometrica
Ashenfelter, O. and Card, D., (1982), 'Time series representation of economic variables and alternative models of the labour market', Review of Economic Studies
Atkinson, A.B., Gomulka, J., Micklewright, J., and Rau, N., (1984), 'Unemployment benefit, duration and incentives in Britain', Journal of Public Economics
Attfield, C., Demery, D. and Duck, N., (1981a), 'Unanticipated monetary growth, output and the price level in the UK 1946-1977', European Economic Review
Attfield, C., Demery, D. and Duck, N., (1981b), 'A quarterly model of unanticipated monetary growth, output and the price level in the UK 1963-1978', Journal of Monetary Economics
Azariadis, C., (1975), 'Implicit contracts and underemployment equilibria', Journal of Political Economy
Azariadis, C., (1981), 'Implicit Contracts and Related Topics. A Survey' in Z. Hornstein, J. Grice and A. Webb (eds.), The Economics of the Labour Market, HMSO
Baily, M.N., (1974), 'Wages and employment under

uncertain demand', <u>Review of Economic Studies</u>

Bain, G. and el Sheikh, F., (1976), <u>Union Growth and the Business Cycle</u>, Basil Blackwell

Ball, R.J. and St.Cyr, E., (1966), 'Short term employment functions, in British manufacturing industry', <u>Review of Economic Studies</u>

Ball, R.J., Burns, T. and Laury, J.S.E. (1977), 'The role of exchange rate changes in balance of payment adjustment. The United Kingdom case', <u>Economic Journal</u>

Ballard, B., (1984), 'Women part-time workers. Evidence from the 1980 Women and Employment Survey', <u>Department of Employment Gazette</u>

Banks, M., Mullings, C. and Jackson, E.I., (1983), 'A bench-mark for youth opportunities', <u>Department of Employment Gazette</u>

Barber, A., (1980), 'Ethnic origin and the labour force'. <u>Department of Employment Gazette</u>

Barnes, W.F., (1975), 'Job search models, the duration of unemployment and the asking price of labour', <u>Journal of Human Resources</u>

Barro, R., (1976), 'Rational expectations and the role of monetary policy', <u>Journal of Monetary Economics</u>

Barro, R.J., (1977), 'Unanticipated money growth and unemployment in the United States', <u>American Economic Review</u>

Barro, R.J., (1978), 'Unanticipated money, output and the price level in the United States', <u>Journal of Political Economy</u>

Barro, R.J. and Grossman, H., (1976), <u>Money, Employment and Inflation</u>, Cambridge University Press

Barro, R.J. and Rush, M., (1980), 'Unanticipated money and economic activity', in S. Fischer (ed.) <u>Rational Expectations and Economic Policy</u>, University of Chicago Press

Barron, J. and McCafferty, S., (1977), 'Job search, labour supply and the quit decision: theory and evidence', <u>American Economic Review</u>

Batchelor, R.A., (1982), 'Expectations, output and inflation. The European experience', <u>European Economic Review</u>

Batchelor, R.A. and Sheriff, T.D., (1980), 'Unemployment and unanticipated inflation in Britain, <u>Economica</u>

Bean, C., (1984), 'A little bit more evidence on the natural rate hypothesis from the UK', <u>European Economic Review</u>

Beenstock, M. and Warburton, P., (1982), 'An aggregative model of the UK labour market',

Oxford Economic Papers

Begg, D.K.H., (1982a), The Rational expectations Revolution in Macroeconomics: Theory and Evidence, Phillip Allan

Begg, D.K.H., (1982b), 'Rational expectations, wage rigidity and involuntary unemployment', Oxford Economic Papers

Bell, D., (1981), 'Regional output, employment and unemployment fluctuations', Oxford Economic Papers

Bell, D. and Hart, R., (1980), 'The regional demand for labour services', Scottish Journal of Political Economy

Benjamin, D.K. and Kochin, L.A., (1979), 'Searching for an explanation of unemployment in interwar Britain', Journal of Political Economy

Berndt, E.R. and Wood, D.O., (1975), 'Technology, prices and the desired demand for energy', Review of Economics and Statistics

Blinder, A.S., (1982), 'Inventories and sticky prices: More on the micro-foundations of macroeconomics', American Economic Review

Bornstein, M., (1978), 'Unemployment in capitalist regulated market economies and centrally planned socialist economies', American Economic Association Papers and Proceedings

Bosanquet, N., (1978), 'Structuralism and 'structural unemployment'', British Journal of Industrial Relations

Bowden, R.J., (1980), 'On the existence and secular stability of u-v loci', Economica

Bowers, J., Cheshire, P., Webb, A., and Weeden, R., (1972), 'Some aspects of unemployment and the labour market 1966-71', National Institute Economic Review

Bowers, J. and Deaton, D., (1980), 'Employment functions and the measurement of labour hoarding', Manchester School

Bowers, J., Deaton, D. and Turk, J., (1982), Labour Hoarding in British Industries, Basil Blackwell

Bowers, J. and Harkess, D., (1979), 'Duration of unemployment by age and sex', Economica

Bowles, S., (1981), 'Competitive wage determination and involuntary unemployment: a conflict model', mimeo, University of Massachusetts

Branson, W., (1979), Macroeconomic Theory and Policy, Harper and Row

Brechling, F., (1965), 'The relationship between output and employment in British manufacturing industries', Review of Economic Studies

Brenner, M.H., (1979), 'Mortality and the national

economy: a review and the experience of England and Wales 1936-76', The Lancet.

Briscoe, G. and Peel, D., (1975), 'The specification of the short run employment function. An empirical investigation of the demand for labour in the UK manufacturing sector 1954-72', Bulletin of the Oxford University Institute of Statistics and Economics

Briscoe, G. and Roberts, C., (1977), 'Structural breaks in employment functions', Manchester School of Economic and Social Studies

Broadberry, S., (1983), 'Unemployment in inter-war Britain: a disequilibrium approach', Oxford Economic Papers

Brown, C., (1984), Black and White in Britain, Heinemann

Brown, C. and Medoff, J., (1979), 'Trade unions in the production process', Journal of Political Economy

Brown, C.V., (1980), Taxation and the Incentive to work, Oxford University Press

Brown, W., (1981), The Changing Contours of British Industrial Relations, Basil Blackwell

Bruno, M., (1980), 'Import prices and stagflation in the industrial countries: a cross-section analysis', Economic Journal

Bruno, M. and Sachs, J., (1983), 'Labour markets and comparative macroeconomic performance', mimeo, Harvard University

Buiter, W., (1981), 'The role of economic policy after the new macroeconomics', in D. Currie, A.R. Nobay and D. Peel (eds.), Macroeconomic Analysis, Croom Helm

Cable, J.R., (1982), 'Industry', in A.R. Prest and D. J. Coppock, The UK Economy, 9th edition, Weidenfeld and Nicholson

Cagan, P., (1956), 'The monetary dynamics of hyperinflation' in M. Friedman (ed), Studies in the Quantity Theory of Money, University of Chicago Press

Carby, H., (1982), 'Schooling in Babylon', in The Empire Strikes Back, Centre for Contemporary Cultural Studies

Carlson, J.A. and Parkin, M. (1975), 'Inflation expectations', Economica

Carmichael, H.L. (1981), 'Firm specific human capital and seniority rules', NBER working paper No. 101

Carr-Hill, R.A. and Stern, N.H., (1983), Crime, The Police and Criminal Statistics, Academic Press

Cartter, A., (1959), Theory of wages and employment,

Irwin

Casson, M., (1979), <u>Youth Unemployment</u>, Macmillan.

Chalkley, M., (1982), 'Models of search in the labour market', <u>Warwick Economic Research Paper No. 206</u>

Cheshire, P.C., (1973), 'Regional unemployment differences in Great Britain', <u>NIESR Regional Papers II</u>

Clark, K., (1980), 'Unionization and productivity: some micro-econometric evidence', <u>Quarterly Journal of Economics</u>

Clark, K., (1984), 'Unionization and firm performance: the impact on profits, growth and productivity', <u>American Economic Review</u>

Clark, K., and Freeman, R., (1979), 'How elastic is the demand for labor?', <u>NBER Working Paper No. 309</u>

Clark, K. and Summers, L., (1979), 'Labor market dynamics and unemployment: a reconsideration', <u>Brookings Paper on Economic Activity</u>

Clower, R., (1965), 'The Keynesian counter-revolution: a theoretical appraisal in F.H. Hahn and F.P.R. Brechling (eds.), <u>The Theory of Interest Rates</u>, Macmillan

Coard, B., (1981), 'What the British school system does to the black child', in A. James and R. Jeffcoate (eds.), <u>The School in the Multicultural Society</u>, Harper and Row

Craine, R., (1973), 'On the service flow from labour', <u>Review of Economic Studies</u>

Creedy, J. and Disney, R., (1981), 'Changes in labour market states in Great Britain', <u>Scottish Journal of Political Economy</u>

Cubbin, J. and Foley, K., (1977), 'The extent of benefit-induced unemployment in Great Britain: some new evidence', <u>Oxford Economic Papers</u>

Daniel, W.W. and Millward, N., (1983), <u>Workplace Industrial Relations in Britain</u>, Heinemann

Davies, G. and Metcalf, D., (1985), 'Generating jobs: The cost effectiveness of tax cuts, public expenditure and special employment measures in cutting unemployment', Simon and Coates

Deakin, B. and Pratten, C., (1982), <u>Effect of the Temporary Employment Subsidy</u>, Cambridge University Press

Deaton, D., (1982), 'Employers' demand for labour', in J. Creedy and R.B. Thomas (eds.), <u>The Economics of Labour</u>, Butterworth

Demery, D., (1984), 'Aggregate demand, rational expectations and real output: some new evidence for the UK 1963-1983', <u>Economic Journal</u>

Bibliography

Department of Employment Gazette, (1978), 'Measures
    to alleviate unemployment in the medium term:
    work sharing'
Department of Employment Gazette, (1978), 'Age and
    redundancy'
Department of Employment Gazette, (1978), 'The young
    and out of work'
Department of Employment Gazette, (1983), 'The
    unemployed: survey estimates for 1981 compared
    with the monthly count'
Department of Employment Gazette, (1983), 'Ethnic
    Origin and economic status'
Department of Employment Gazette, (1984), 'The
    unemployed: survey estimates for 1983 compared
    with the monthly count'
Dex, S. and Perry, S., (1984), 'Women's employment in
    the 1970's, Department of Employment Gazette
Dilnot, A.W. and Morris, C.N., (1983), 'Private costs
    and benefits of unemployment: measuring
    replacement rates', Oxford Economic Papers
Dimsdale, N., (1984), 'Employment and real wages in
    the inter-war period', National Institute
    Economic Review
Disney, R., (1979), 'Recurrent spells and the
    concentration of unemployment in Great
    Britain', Economic Journal
Disney, R., (1981), 'Unemployment insurance in
    Britain', in J. Creedy, The Economics of
    Unemployment in Britain, Butterworth
Dixon, R. and Thirlwall, A., (1976), Regional growth
    and unemployment in the United Kingdom,
    Macmillan
Doeringer, P., and Piore, M., (1971), Internal Labor
    Markets and Manpower Analysis, Heath & Co
Domberger, S., (1979), 'Price adjustment and market
    structure', Economic Journal
Dornbusch, R., (1985), 'Sound currency and full
    employment', Employment Institute
Dow, J.C.R. and Dick-Mireaux, L., (1956), 'The excess
    demand for labour: a study of conditions in
    Great Britain, 1946-56', Oxford Economic Papers
Dutton, P., (1984), 'YTS - Training for the future',
    Public Administration
Ehrenberg, R.G., (1971), Fringe Benefits and
    Overtime Behaviour, Heath & Co
Ehrenberg, R.G. and Schumann, P.L., (1982), 'Longer
    hours or more jobs', Cornell Studies in
    Industrial and Labor Relations, No. 22
Encaoua, D. and Geroski, P., (1984), 'Price dynamics
    and competition in five countries', University
    of Southampton Discussion Paper in Economics

and Econometrics, No. 8414

Evans, A., (1977), 'Notes on the changing relationship between registered unemployment and notified vacancies: 1961-71', Economica

Fallick, J.I. and Elliott, R.F., (1981), Income Policies, Inflation and Relative Pay, George Allen and Unwin

Feldstein, M., (1967), 'Specification of the labour input in the aggregate production function', Review of Economic Studies

Feldstein, M., (1976), 'Temporary layoffs in the theory of unemployment, Journal of Political Economy

Fellner, W., (1951), 'Competition among the Few' Alfred A. Knopf Inc.

Figlewski, S. and Wachtel, P., (1981), 'The formation of inflationary expectations', Review of Economics and Statistics

Fisher, I., (1930), 'The Theory of Interest', Macmillan

Fischer, S., (1977), 'Long term contracts, rational expectations and the optimal money supply rule', Journal of Political Economy

Flanagan, R.J., (1984), 'Implicit contracts, explicit contracts and wages', American Economic Association Papers and Proceedings

Fleming, J.M., (1962), 'Domestic financial policies under fixed and floating exchange rates', IMF Staff Papers

Flinn, C. and Heckman, J., (1982), 'Models for the analysis of labor force dynamics' in Advances in Econometrics, JAI Press

Foster, J.I., (1974), 'The behaviour of unemployment and unfilled vacancies: a comment', Economic Journal

Freeman, C., Clark, J. and Soete, L., (1982), Unemployment and Technical Innovation, Frances Pinter

Freeman, R., (1976), 'Individual mobility and union voice in the labour market', American Economic Association Papers and Proceedings

Freeman, R., (1980), 'The effect of unionism on worker attachment to firms', Journal of Labor Research

Freeman, R. and Medoff, J., (1984), What do Unions do? Basic Books

Friedman, M., (1956), A Theory of the Consumption Function, Princeton University Press

Friedman, M., (1968), 'The role of monetary policy', American Economic Review

Geary, P.T. and Kennan, J., (1982), 'The employment-real wage relationship: an international study', Journal of Political Economy

George K. and Ward, T., (1975), The Structure of Industry in the EEC, Cambridge University Press

Geroski, P.A., Hamlin, A. and Knight, K.G., (1982), 'Wages, Strikes and Market Structure', Oxford Economic Papers

Geroski, P.A. and Knight, K.G., (1983), 'Wages, strikes and market structure: Some further evidence', Oxford Economic Papers

Geroski, P.A. and Knight, K.G., (1984), 'Corporate merger and collective bargaining in the UK', Industrial Relations Journal

Geroski, P.A. and Stewart, M.B., (1985), 'Specification induced uncertainty in the estimation of trade union wage differentials from industry level data', Economica

Glyn, A. and Sutcliffe, B., (1972), British Capitalism, Workers and the Profits Squeeze, Penguin

Goodhart C.A.E. and Crockett, A.D. (1970), 'The importance of money', Bank of England Quarterly Bulletin

Gordon, D.F., (1974), 'A neoclassical theory of Keynesian unemployment', Economic Inquiry

Gordon, R.J. (1982), 'Price inertia and policy ineffectiveness in the US 1890-1980', Journal of Political Economy

Gordon, R.J., (1982), 'Why US wage and employment behaviour differs from that in Britain and Japan', Economic Journal

Granger, C., (1969), 'Investigating causal relations by econometric models and cross spectral methods', Econometrica

Gravelle, H.S., Hutchinson, G. and Stern, J., (1981), 'Mortality and unemployment: a critique of Brenner's time series analysis', The Lancet

Gray, J., (1978), 'On indexation and contract length', Journal of Political Economy

Greenhalgh, C., (1977), 'A labour supply function for married women in Great Britain', Economica

Greenhalgh, C., (1980), 'Participation and hours of work for married women in Great Britain', Oxford Economic Papers

Greenhalgh, C. and Mayhew, K., (1981), 'Labour supply in Britain: theory and evidence', in Z. Hornstein, J. Grice and A. Webb (eds.), The Economics of the Labour Market, HMSO

Grice, J., (1981), 'Wealth effects and expenditure functions: a survey of the evidence', in M. Artis and M. Miller (eds.), Essays in Fiscal and

<u>Monetary Policy</u>, Oxford University Press

Gronau, R., (1971), 'Information and frictional unemployment', <u>American Economic Review</u>

Grubb, D., Jackman, R. and Layard, R., (1982), 'Causes of the current stagflation', <u>Review of Economic Studies</u>

Grubb, D., Jackman, R. and Layard, R., (1983), 'Wage rigidity and unemployment in OECD countries', <u>European Economic Review</u>.

Grubb, D., Layard, R. and Symons, J., (1983), 'Wages, unemployment and incomes policy', London School of Economics Centre for Labour Economics, Discussion Paper No. 168

Gujarati, D., (1972), 'The behaviour of unemployment and unfilled vacancies', <u>Economic Journal</u>

Gylfason, T. and Lindbeck, A., (1984), 'Union rivalry and wages: an oligopolistic approach', <u>Economica</u>

Hahn, F.H., (1980), 'Unemployment from a theoretical viewpoint', <u>Economica</u>

Hahn, F.H., (1982), 'Reflections on the invisible hand', <u>Lloyds Bank Review</u>

Hakim C., (1978), 'Sexual divisions within the labour force: occupational segregation', <u>Department of Employment Gazette</u>

Hall, R., (1972), 'Turnover in the labour force', <u>Brookings Paper on Economic Activity</u>

Hall, R., (1975), 'The rigidity of wages and the persistence of unemployment', <u>Brookings Paper on Economic Activity</u>

Hall, R., (1980), 'Employment fluctuations and wage rigidity', <u>Brookings Paper on Economic Activity</u>

Hammermesh, D., (1977), 'A note on income and substitution effects in search unemployment', <u>Economic Journal</u>

Hammermesh, D. and Rees, A., (1984), <u>Economics of Work and Pay</u>, Harper and Row

Hannah, S.P., (1983), 'Unemployment and real wage speculations: Empirical tests for Great Britain 1967-1980', <u>Scottish Journal of Political Economy</u>

Hannah, S.P., (1984), 'Cyclical and structural determinants of the UV relation', <u>Applied Economics</u>

Hansen, B., (1970), 'Excess demand, unemployment, vacancies and wages', <u>Quarterly Journal of Economics</u>

Harris, C.P. and Thirlwall, A., (1968), 'Inter-regional variations in cyclical sensitivity to unemployment in the UK 1949-66', <u>Oxford University Institute of Statistics and</u>

Economics Bulletin

Hart, R., (1984), The Economics of Non-Wage Labour Costs, George Allen and Unwin

Hart, R. and Sharot, T., (1978), 'The short-run demand for workers and hours: a recursive model', Review of Economic Studies

Hatton, T., (1983), 'Unemployment benefits and the macroeconomics of the inter-war labour market', Oxford Economic Papers

Hazledine, T., (1981), 'Employment functions and the demand for labour in the short run', in Z. Hornstein, J. Grice and A. Webb (eds.), The Economics of the Labour Market, HMSO.

Heckman, J. and Borjas, G., (1980), 'Does unemployment cause future unemployment? Definitions, questions and answers from a continuous time model of heterogeneity and state dependence', Economica

Heckman, J. and Macurdy, T.M. (1980), 'A life cycle model of female labour supply', Review of Economic Studies

Henry, S.G.B. and Ormerod, P., (1978), 'Incomes policy and wage inflation: empirical evidence for the UK 1961-1977', National Institute Economic Review

Henry, S.G.B., Payne, J.M. and Trinder, C., (1985), 'Unemployment and real wages: the role of unemployment, social security benefits and unionisation', Oxford Economic Papers

Henry, S.G.B., Sawyer, M. and Smith, P., (1976), 'Models of Inflation in the United Kingdom', National Institute Economic Review

Hines, A.G., (1968), 'Unemployment and the rate of change of money wage rates in the United Kingdom 1862-1963: a reappraisal', Review of Economics and Statistics

H.M. Treasury, (1985), 'The relationship between wages and employment'

House of Lords Select Committee on Unemployment, (1982), HMSO

Huhne, C., (1984), 'Tax cuts are no help to the jobless', The Guardian

Hutchinson, G., Barr, N. and Drobny, A., (1984), 'The employment of young males in a segmented labour market: the case of Great Britain', Applied Economics

Institute of Employment Research, (1985), 'Review of the Economy and Employment 1985 - Vol. I'

Jackman, R., Layard, R. and Pissarides, C., (1984), 'On vacancies', London School of Economics Centre for Labour Economics. Discussion Paper

No. 165 (revised)

Joll, C., McKenna, C., McNabb, R. and Shorey, J., (1983), Developments in Labour Market Analysis, George Allen and Unwin

Jolly, J., Mingay, A. and Creigh, S.W., (1978), 'Age qualifications in job vacancies', Department of Employment Gazette

Joshi, H., Layard, R. and Owen, S., (1985), 'Why are more women working in Britain,' Journal of Labour Economics

Junankar, P., (1981), 'An econometric analysis of unemployment in Great Britain 1952-75', Oxford Economic Papers

Junankar, P., (1984), 'Youth unemployment and youth crime: a preliminary analysis', mimeo, Australian National University

Junankar, P. and Neale, A., (1985), 'Relative wages in the youth labour market', Institute for Employment Research, Discussion Paper No. 29

Junankar, P. and Price, S., (1983), 'The dynamics of unemployment: structural change and unemployment', Economic Journal

Kahn, L.M. and Low, S.A., (1982), 'The relative effects of employed and unemployed job search', Review of Economic and Statistics

Kaldor, N. and Trevithick, J., (1981), 'A Keynesian perspective on money', Lloyds Bank Review

Kasper, H., (1967), 'The asking price of labour and the duration of unemployment', Review of Economics and Statistics

Kennally, G., (1985), 'Committed and discretionary saving of households', National Institute Economic Review

Kennedy, C. and Thirlwall, A.P., (1972), 'Technical Progress: A Survey', Economic Journal

Keynes, J.M., (1936), General Theory of Employment, Interest and Money, Macmillan

Kiefer, N.M. and Neumann, G.R., (1979), 'An empirical job-search model with a test of the constant reservation wage hypothesis', Journal of Political Economy

Killingsworth, M., (1971), 'A critical survey of neoclassical models of labour', Bulletin of the Oxford University Institute of Statistics and Economics

Knight, K.G., (1981), 'The composition of unemployment', in Socialist Economic Review, edited by D. Currie and R. Smith

Knight, K.G., (1984), 'Investment, profits and employment: the prospects for economic recovery', in Out of Work by K Cowling et al,

University of Warwick, Department of Economics

Knight, K.G. and Stewart, M.B. (1982), 'The age structure of unemployment', Warwick Economic Research Paper No. 215

Knight, K.G. and Wilson, R.A., (1974), 'Labour hoarding, employment and unemployment in British manufacturing industry', Applied Economics

Kohn, M.L., (1976), 'Occupational structure and alienation', American Journal of Sociology

Lancaster, T., (1979), 'Econometric methods for the duration of unemployment', Econometrica

Lancaster, T. and Nickell, S., (1980), 'The analysis of re-employment probabilities of the unemployed', Journal of the Royal Statistical Society.

Layard, R., (1981), 'Measuring the duration of unemployment', Scottish Journal of Political Economy

Layard, R., (1982), 'Youth unemployment in Britain and the US compared', in R.B. Freeman and D.A. Wise (eds.), 'The Youth Labour Market Problem', University of Chicago Press

Layard, R., (1983), More Jobs, Less Inflation, Grant McIntyre

Layard, R., (1985), 'How to reduce unemployment by changing national insurance and providing a job-guarantee', London School of Economics. Centre for Labour Economics, Discussion Paper No. 218

Layard, R., Basevi, G., Blanchard, O., Buiter, W. and Dornbusch, R., (1984), 'Europe: the case for unsustainable growth', Centre for European Policy Studies, Paper No. 819

Layard R. and Nickell, S., (1980), 'The case for subsidising extra jobs', Economic Journal

Layard, R. and Nickell, S., (1985), 'The causes of British unemployment', National Institute for Economic Review

Layard, R. and Symons, J., (1984), 'Do higher real wages reduce employment?' Economic Review

Lazear, E., (1981), 'Agency, earnings profiles, productivity and hours restriction', American Economic Review

Leibenstein, H., (1966), 'Allocative efficiency vs. 'X-efficiency'', American Economic Review

Leijonhufvud, A., (1968), On Keynesian Economics and the Economics of Keynes, Oxford University Press

Leslie, D. and Wise, J., (1980), 'The productivity of hours in UK manufacturing and production industries', <u>Economic Journal</u>

Levacic, R. and Rebmann, A., (1982), <u>Macroeconomics: An Introduction to Keynesian-Neoclassical Controversies</u>, Macmillan

Lewis, H.G., (1983), 'Union relative wage effects: a survey of macro estimates', <u>Journal of Labour Economics</u>

Lindley, R. (ed.), (1980), <u>Britain's Medium Term Prospects</u>, Macmillan

Lippman, S. and McCall, J., (1976), 'The economics of job search', <u>Economic Inquiry</u>

Lipsey, R.G., (1965), 'Structural and deficient-demand unemployment reconsidered' in A.M. Ross (ed.), <u>Employment policy and the Labour Market</u>, University of California Press

Lipsey, R. and Parkin, M., (1970), 'Incomes Policy: a Reappraisal', <u>Economica</u>

Lucas, R., (1973), 'Some international evidence on output-inflation trade-offs', <u>American Economic Review</u>

Lucas, R. (1981), '<u>Studies in Business-Cycle Theory</u>', Basil Blackwell

Lucas, R. and Rapping, L., (1970), 'Real wages, output and inflation', in E. Phelps (ed.), <u>Microeconomic Foundations of Employment and Inflation Theory</u>, Macmillan

Lucas, R. and Sargent, T.J., (1979), 'After Keynesian Macroeconomics', <u>Federal Reserve Bank of Minneapolis Quarterly Review</u>

Lucas, R. and Sargent, T., (1981), <u>Rational expectations and Econometric Practice</u>, Allen and Unwin

Lynch, L., (1983), 'Job search and youth unemployment', <u>Oxford Economic Papers</u>

Lynch, L., (1984), 'State dependency in youth unemployment: a lost generation?' Centre for Labour Economics, London School of Economics Discussion Paper No. 184

McCall, J.J., (1970), 'Economics of information and job search', <u>Quarterly Journal of Economics</u>

McCallum, J., (1983), 'Inflation and social consensus in the seventies', <u>Economic Journal</u>

McCrone, G., (1969), <u>Regional Policy in Britain</u>, Unwin University Books

McDonald, I.M. and Solow, R., (1981), 'Wage bargaining and employment', <u>American Economic Review</u>

McGregor, A., (1980), 'Employment instability and unemployment', <u>Manchester School</u>

Mackay, D.I., Boddy, D., Brack, J., Diack, J.A., and Jones, N., (1981), <u>Labour Markets under</u>

Different Employment Conditions, George Allen
and Unwin

Mackay, D.I., (1972), 'After the 'shake-out'',
Oxford Economic Papers

Mackay, D.I. and Reid, G.L., (1972), 'Redundancy,
unemployment and manpower policy', Economics
Journal

McKendrick, S., (1975), 'An inter-industry analysis
of labour hoarding in Britain', Applied
Economics

McNabb, R., (1979), 'A socio-economic model of
migration', Regional Studies

Main, B., (1981), 'The length of employment and
unemployment in Great Britain', Scottish
Journal of Political Economy

Maki, D. and Spindler, Z., (1975), 'The effect of
unemployment compensation on the rate of
unemployment in Great Britain', Oxford Economic
Papers

Malcomson, J., (1981), 'Unemployment and the
efficiency wage hypothesis', Economic Journal

Malinvaud, E., (1980), Theory of Unemployment
Reconsidered, Basil Blackwell

Malinvaud, E., (1982), 'Wages and unemployment',
Economic Journal

Marginson, P., (1984), 'The distinctive effects of
plant and company size on workplace industrial
relations', British Journal of Industrial
Relations

Martin, J. and Roberts, C., (1984), 'Women's
employment in the 1980s', Department of
Employment Gazette

Mattila, J.P., (1974), 'Job quitting and frictional
unemployment', American Economic Review

Mayhew, K. and Rosewell, B., (1979), 'Labour market
segmentation in Britain', Oxford Bulletin of
Economics and Statistics

Means, G.C., (1972), 'The administered price thesis
reconfirmed', American Economic Review

Medoff, J.L., (1979), 'Layoffs and alternatives
under trade unions in US manufacturing',
American Economic Review

Mendis, L. and Muellbauer, J., (1983), 'Has there
been a British productivity break-through?'
London School of Economics, Centre for Labour
Economics, Discussion Paper No. 170

Metcalf, D., (1975), 'Urban unemployment in
England', Economic Journal

Metcalf, D., (1984), 'On the measurement of
employment and unemployment', National Institute Economic Review, August 1984

Metcalf, D., (1985), 'Shrinking work time and
    unemployment', London School of Economics,
    Centre for Labour Economics, Working Paper No.
    708
Metcalf, D. and Nickell, S., (1985), 'Pay and jobs',
    Midland Bank Review
Micklewright, J., (1985), 'On earnings related
    unemployment benefits and their relation to
    earnings', Economic Journal
Miller, R.L., (1971), 'The reserve labour
    hypothesis: some tests of its implications',
    Economic Journal
Mills, T. and Wood, G., (1978), 'Money-income
    relationships and the exchange rate regime',
    Federal Reserve Bank of St Louis Review
Minford, P., (1981), 'Labour market equilibrium in an
    open economy', mimeo, University of Liverpool
Minford, P., (1983), 'Labour market equilibrium in an
    open economy', Oxford Economic Papers
Minford, P. and Peel, D., (1980), 'The natural rate
    hypothesis and rational expectations: a
    critique of some recent developments', Oxford
    Economic Papers
Minford, P. and Peel, D., (1982), 'Is the
    government's economic strategy on course?',
    Lloyds Bank Review
Mishkin, F.S., (1982), 'Does anticipated monetary
    policy matter? An econometric investigation',
    Journal of Political Economy
Moore, B. and Rhodes, J., (1973), 'Evaluating the
    effects of British regional economic policy',
    Economic Journal
Moore, B. and Rhodes, J., (1976), 'Regional economic
    policy and the movement of manufacturing
    firms', Economica
Morgan, P., (1979), 'Employment functions in
    manufacturing industry', Government Economic
    Service, Working Paper No. 24
Mortensen, D., (1970), 'Job search, the duration of
    unemployment and the Phillips curve', American
    Economic Review
Moy, J. and Sorrentino, C., (1981), 'Unemployment,
    labor force trends and layoff practices in 10
    countries', Monthly Labor Review
Moylan, S. and Davies, B., (1980), 'The disadvantages
    of the unemployed', Department of Employment
    Gazette
Mueller, D., (ed.), (1981), The Determinants and
    Effects of Merger
Mundell, R., (1962), 'The appropriate use of monetary
    and fiscal policy for internal and external

stability', IMF Staff Papers

Nadiri, M.I. and Rosen, S., (1969), 'Inter-related factor demand functions', American Economic Review

Narendranathan, W., Nickell, S. and Stern, J., (1985), 'Unemployment Benefits Revisited', Economic Journal

Neal, A.G. and Grout, H.T., (1970), 'Alienation correlates of Catholic fertility', American Journal of Sociology

Neale, A. and Wilson, R.A., (1984), 'Employment' in P. Cockle (editor), Public Expenditure Policy 1984-85

Nickell, S., (1979a), 'The effect of unemployment and related benefits on the duration of unemployment', Economic Journal

Nickell, S., (1979b), 'Estimating the probability of leaving unemployment', Econometrica

Nickell, S., (1980), 'A picture of male unemployment in Britain', Economic Journal

Nickell, S., (1982), 'The determinants of equilibrium unemployment in Britain', Economic Journal

Nickell, S., (1984a), 'The modelling of wages and employment in D.F. Hendry and K.F. Wallis (editors), Econometrics and Quantitative Economics, Basil Blackwell

Nickell, S., (1984b), Review of 'Unemployment: Cause and Cure' by P. Minford et al, Economic Journal

Nickell, S., (1984c), 'An investigation of the determinants of manufacturing employment in the United Kingdom', Review of Economic Studies

Nickell, S. and Andrews, M., (1983), 'Trade unions, real wages and employment in Britain 1957-79', Oxford Economic Papers

O'Connor, D., (1982), 'Probabilities of employment after work experience', Department of Employment Gazette

OECD, (1982), Marginal Employment Subsidies.

Oi, W., (1962), 'Labor as a quasi-fixed factor', Journal of Political Economy

Okun, A., (1981), Prices and Quantities. A Macroeconomic Analysis, Basil Blackwell

Ormerod, P., (1982), 'Rational and non-rational expectations of inflation in wage equations for the United Kingdom', Economica

Oswald, A.J., (1982a), 'The microeconomic theory of the trade union', Economic Journal

Oswald, A.J., (1982b), 'Wages, trade unions and unemployment. What can simple models tell us?' Oxford Economic Papers

Parikh, A. and Allen, F., (1982), 'Relationship between unemployment and vacancies in the United Kingdom: a mimic approach', Oxford Economic Papers

Parkin M. and Bade, R., (1982), Modern Macro-Macroeconomics, Phillip Allan

Pesaran, M.H., (1982), 'A critique of the proposed tests of the natural rate-rational expectations hypothesis', Economic Journal

Perry, G.L., (1972), 'Unemployment flows in the US labor market', Brookings Papers on Economic Activity

Petersen, R.L., (1971), 'Economics of information and job search: another view', Quarterly Journal of Economics

Phelps, E.S., (1970), 'Money wage dynamics and labor market equilibrium', in E. Phelps (ed.), Microeconomic Foundations of Employment and Inflation Theory, Macmillan

Pierson, G., (1968), 'Union strength and the U.S. 'Phillips Curve'', American Economic Review

Pike, M., (1984), 'Female discrimination in the labour market', Economic Review

Prais, S. and Wagner, K., (1983), 'Some practical aspects of human capital investments: training standards in five occupations in Britain and Germany', National Institute Economic Review

Raffe, D., (1984a), 'The transition from school to work and the recession 1977-83: evidence from the Scottish school leavers survey', British Journal of Sociology of Education

Raffe, D., (1984b), 'Small expectations: The first year of YTS', paper presented at Conference of the Young Persons Labour Market, Warwick, November 1984

Rice, P.G., (1984), 'Juvenile unemployment, relative wages and social security in Britain', University of Sussex (mimeo)

Richards, J., (1985), 'The allocation and effects of special employment measures: the case of the temporary employment subsidy and schemes operated by the Department of Industry', Ph.D. Thesis, University of Kent

Robertson, J.A.S., (1982), 'Does job release reduce unemployment?', Department of Employment Gazette

Robinson, O. and Wallace, J., (1984), 'Growth and utilisation of part-time labour in Great Britain', Department of Employment Gazette

Roethlisberger, T.A. and Dickson, W.J., (1939), Management and the Worker, Harvard University

Press

Romer, D., (1981), 'Rosen and Quandt's disequilibrium model of the labor market', Review c Economics and Statistics

Rosen, H. and Quandt, R., (1978), 'Estimation of a disequilibrium aggregate labour market', Revie of Economics and Statistics

Ross, A., (1948), Trade Union Wage Policy, Californi University Press

Rowthorn, R., (1980), 'Conflict, inflation and money' in Rowthorn, R. Capitalism, Conflict ar Inflation, Lawrence and Wishart

Rowthorn, R. and Ward, T., (1979), 'How to run a company and run down an economy: the effects c closing down steel making in Corby', Cambridc Journal of Economics

Ryan, P., (1984), 'The New Training Initiative afte two years', Lloyds Bank Review

Sachs, J., (1979), 'Wages, profits and macroeconomi adjustment: a comparative study', Brookinc Paper on Economic Activity

Sachs, J., (1980), 'The changing cyclical behaviour of wages and prices: 1890-1976', America Economic Review

Salop, S., (1973), 'Systematic job search and unemployment', Review of Economic Studies

Sargent, T.J., (1973), 'Rational expectations, the real rate of interest and the natural rate c unemployment', Brookings Paper on Economi Activity

Sargent, T.J., (1976), 'A classical macroeconometri model of the United States', Journal c Political Economy

Sargent, T.J., (1978), 'Estimation of dynamic labo demand schedules under rational expectations' Journal of Political Economy

Sargent, T.J., and Wallace, N., (1976), 'Rational expectations and the theory of economi policy', Journal of Monetary Policy

Savage, D., (1978), 'The channels of monetary influence: a survey of the empirical evidence' National Institute Economic Review

Savage, D., (1984), 'Monetary targets - a short history', Economic Review

Sawyer, M., (1979), 'The effects of unemployment compensation on the rate of unemployment i Great Britain: A comment', Oxford Economi Papers

Shapiro, C. and Stiglitz, J., (1984), 'Equilibrium unemployment as a worker discipline device' American Economic Review

Sherer, F., (1973), <u>Industrial Market Structure and Economic Performance</u>, Rand, McNally and Co

Shorey, J., (1976), 'An inter-industry analysis of strike frequency', <u>Economica</u>

Shorey, J., (1980), 'An analysis of quits using industry turnover data', <u>Economic Journal</u>

Smith, C., Clifton, R., Makeham, P., Creigh, S. and Burn, R., (1978), <u>Strikes in Britain</u>, HMSO

Smith, D., (1977), <u>Racial Disadvantage in Britain</u>, Penguin

Smith R., (1981), 'Crisis in world capitalism' in S. Aaronovitch, R. Smith, J. Gardiner and R. Moore <u>The Political Economy of British Capitalism</u>, McGraw-Hill

Smyth, D.J., (1983), 'The British labour market in disequilibrium: did the dole reduce unemployment in inter-war Britain?', <u>Journal of Macroeconomics</u>

Solow, R., (1957), 'Technical change and the aggregate production function', <u>Review of Economics and Statistics</u>

Solow, R., (1980), 'On theories of unemployment', <u>American Economic Review</u>

Spence, M., (1973), 'Job market signaling', <u>Quarterly Journal of Economics</u>

Stern, J., (1979), 'Who bears the burden of unemployment?' in W. Beckerman, <u>Slow Growth in Britain</u>, Oxford University Press

Stern, J., (1982), 'Unemployment inflow rates for Autumn 1978', London School of Economics, Centre for Labour Economics, Discussion Paper No. 129

Stern, J., (1983), 'Who becomes unemployed? Unemployment inflow rates in Great Britain for 1978', <u>Department of Employment Gazette</u>

Stern, J., (1984), 'Repeat unemployment spells: the effect of unemployment benefit on unemployment entry', London School of Economics. Centre for Labour Economics, Discussion Paper No. 192

Stewart, M.B., (1983a), 'Relative earnings and individual union membership in the UK', <u>Economica</u>

Stewart, M.B., (1983b), 'Racial discrimination and occupational attainment in Britain', <u>Economic Journal</u>

Stewart, M.B. and Greenhalgh, C., (1984), 'Work history patterns and the occupational attainment of women', <u>Economic Journal</u>

Stigler, G., (1962), 'Information in the labor market', <u>Journal of Political Economy</u>

Stiglitz, J., (1984), 'Theories of wage rigidity',

paper presented at conference on Keynes Economic Legacy 1984

Stoneman, P.L., (1975), 'The effects of computers on the demand for labour in the United Kingdom', Economic Journal

Stoneman, P.L., (1979), 'A simple diagrammatic apparatus for the investigation of a macroeconomic model of temporary equilibria', Economica

Stoneman, P.L., (1983), The Economic Analysis of Technological Change, Oxford University Press

Sumner, M.T., (1978), 'Wage determination', in M. Parkin and M.T. Sumner (editors), Inflation in the United Kingdom

Symons, J., (1985), 'Relative prices and the demand for labour in British manufacturing', Economica

Symons, J. and Layard, R., (1984), 'Neo-classical demand for labour functions for six major economies', Economic Journal

Taylor, J., (1972), 'The behaviour of unemployment and unfilled vacancies: an alternative view', Economic Journal

Taylor, J., (1977), 'A note on the comparative behaviour of male and female unemployment rates in the United Kingdom 1953-73', Discussion Paper. University of Lancaster

Taylor, J.B., (1979), 'Staggered wage setting in a macro model', American Economic Association Papers and Proceedings

Thirlwall, A.P., (1966), 'Regional unemployment as a cyclical phenomenon', Scottish Journal of Political Economy

Trinder, C. and Biswas, R., (1985), 'Public services pay in the 1980s, National Institute Economic Review

Turner, P., (1985), 'After the Community Programme – Results of the first follow-up survey', Department of Employment Gazette

Wachter, M.L., (1975), 'Primary and secondary labor markets: a critique of the dual approach', Brookings Paper on Economic Activity

Wadhwani, S., (1985), 'The effects of aggregate demand, inflation, real wage and uncertainty on manufacturing employment', London School of Economics, Centre for Labour Economics, Discussion Paper No. 210

Wallis, K., (ed.) Andrews, M., Bell, D., Fisher, P. and Whitley, J.D., (1984), Models of UK economy, Oxford University Press

Ward, T., (1981), 'The case for an import control strategy in the UK' in D. Currie and R. Smith (editor), Socialist Economic Review

Warren, R.S., (1978), 'The behaviour of unemployment and unfilled vacancies in Great Britain: a search-turnover view', Applied Economics

Weiss, A., (1980), 'Job queues and layoffs in labor markets with flexible wages', Journal of Political Economy

Weiss, L., (1966), 'Concentration and labor earnings', American Economic Review

Weitzmann, M.L., (1982), 'Increasing returns and the foundations of unemployment theory', Economic Journal

Wells, W., (1983), 'The relative pay and employment of young people', Department of Employment, Research Paper No. 42

White, M., (1983), 'Long term unemployment - labour market aspects', Department of Employment Gazette

Whitley, J.D., (1983), 'Causes of wage inflation - a sceptical view', Review of the Economy and Employment, Institute for Employment Research, University of Warwick

Whitley J.D., and Wilson, R.A. (1982), 'The effects of new technology on jobs' in Institute of Employment Research, Review of the Economy and Employment

Whitley, J. D. and Wilson, R.A., (1983), 'The macroeconomic merits of a marginal employment subsidy', Economic Journal

Williamson, O.E., (1964), The Economics of Discretionary Behaviour: Managerial Objectives in a Theory of the Firm, Prentice Hall

Williamson, O.E., Wachter, M.L. and Harris, J.E., (1975), 'Understanding the employment relation: the analysis of idiosyncratic exchange', Bell Journal of Economics

Worswick, G.D.N., (1984a), 'The sources of recovery in the 1930s', National Institute Economic Review

Worswick, G.D.N., (1984b), Education and Economic Performance, Gower

Wren-Lewis, S., (1984), 'The roles of output expectations and liquidity in explaining recent productivity movements', National Institute Economic Review

Yatchew, A.J., (1981), 'Further evidence on 'estimations of a disequilibrium aggregate labor market'', Review of Economics and Statistics

Yellen, J., (1984), 'Efficiency wage models of unemployment', American Economic Association

381

Papers and Proceedings

INDEX

acceptance probability 77-83, 87, 101, 104, 259-64, 271-3, 363-5

acceptance wage 19, 84

adaptive expectations 119-22

adult training 339-40, 369-70

asymmetric information and wage rigidity 157

classical unemployment 178-84, 191-2, 193-6, 238-52, 329-30, 352-5, 357-9

community measures 343-4, 348, 365-7

company liquidity and employment 318-19

contract models of wage rigidity 157-62, 187-91

costs of unemployment 17-21

crowding out 108, 132, 328

discouraged workers 3, 4, 270

DHSS Cohort Study 43, 274-5

duration dependence 67-70

educational and economic performance 331, 367-70

efficiency wages 164-7

efficient bargain models 174-6

employer search 83-8

employment functions 9, 10, 26, 61, 63, 105-6, 145-6, 193, 239-47, 308-9

Exchequer costs
of unemployment 22
of policy measures 359

errors in expectations
effects on unemployment 114-17, 121, 123, 125-6, 130-1, 207-9, 234

fiscal policy 108-10, 125-33, 134-9, 151-4, 190-1, 204-5, 327-30, 334-5

fixed labour costs 14-16, 295-300, 330, 335, 370-7

frictional unemployment 93, 99, 112, 259-60

hiring standards 86, 96, 97, 260-4, 294-310, 313, 315

hiring strategy 260-4

historical comparisons 7, 59-67, 248-9, 268, 269-70, 274, 276, 302-3, 311-12, 316, 319-20, 327-30, 332

hours of work and employment 295-300, 374-7

increasing returns 173

industrial policy 337, 377-82

imported input prices 192-6, 239-42, 244

inflow probability 32-4, 38, 43, 44, 46, 47, 50, 51, 54, 57, 59-62, 64, 67, 89-92, 95-6, 259-64, 270, 272-3, 299-300, 365

inter-country comparisons 7-9, 13, 270

involuntary unemployment 94, 106-8, 332